*The Cambridge Introduction to*
## Modernism

More than a century after its beginnings, modernism still has the power
to shock, alienate or challenge readers. Modernist art and literature
remain thought of as complex and difficult. This *Introduction* explains in
a readable, lively style how modernism emerged, how it is defined, and
how it developed in different forms and genres. Pericles Lewis offers
students a survey of literature and art in England, Ireland, and Europe at
the beginning of the twentieth century. He also provides an overview of
critical thought on modernism and its continuing influence on the arts
today, reflecting the interests of current scholarship in the social and
cultural contexts of modernism. The comparative perspective on
Anglo-American and European modernism shows how European
movements have influenced the development of English-language
modernism. Illustrated with works of art and featuring suggestions for
further study, this is the ideal introduction to understanding and
enjoying modernist literature and art.

PERICLES LEWIS is Associate Professor of English and Comparative
Literature at Yale University. He is the author of *Modernism, Nationalism
and the Novel* (Cambridge University Press, 2000).

# Cambridge Introductions to Literature

This series is designed to introduce students to key topics and authors. Accessible and lively, these introductions will also appeal to readers who want to broaden their understanding of the books and authors they enjoy.

- Ideal for students, teachers, and lecturers
- Concise, yet packed with essential information
- Key suggestions for further reading

Titles in this series:

# The Cambridge Introduction to
# Modernism

PERICLES LEWIS

CAMBRIDGE
UNIVERSITY PRESS

# CAMBRIDGE
## UNIVERSITY PRESS

University Printing House, Cambridge CB2 8BS, United Kingdom

Published in the United States of America by Cambridge University Press, New York

Cambridge University Press is part of the University of Cambridge.

It furthers the University's mission by disseminating knowledge in the pursuit of education, learning and research at the highest international levels of excellence.

www.cambridge.org
Information on this title: www.cambridge.org/9780521535274

© Pericles Lewis 2007

First published 2007
7th printing 2013

Printed in the United Kingdom by the CPI Group Ltd, Croydon CR0 4YY

*A catalogue record for this publication is available from the British Library*

*Library of Congress Cataloguing in Publication data*
Lewis, Pericles.
The Cambridge introduction to modernism / Pericles Lewis.
  p.   cm. – (Cambridge introductions to literature)
Includes bibliographical references and index.
ISBN-13: 978-0-521-82809-3 (hardback : alk. paper)
ISBN-10: 0-521-82809-0 (hardback : alk. paper)
ISBN-13: 978-0-521-53527-4 (pbk. : alk. paper)
ISBN-10: 0-521-53527-1 (pbk. : alk. paper)
1. Modernism (Literature).   2. Literature, Modern – 20th century – History and criticism.
3. Literature, Modern – 19th century – History and criticism.   I. Title.   II. Series.
PN56.M54L49   2007
809′.911 – dc22

ISBN   978-0-521-82809-3 Hardback
ISBN   978-0-521-53527-4 Paperback

# Contents

**Conclusion: after modernism?**     237

## Illustrations

# Tables

## Abbreviations and editions used

| | |
|---|---|
| *Auden Generation* | Samuel Hynes, *The Auden Generation: Literature and Politics in England in the 1930s.* New York: Viking, 1977. |
| *Brecht on Theatre* | Bertolt Brecht, *Brecht on Theatre*, ed. and trans. John Willett. New York: Hill and Wang, 1964. |
| *Century of Innovation* | Oscar G. Brockett and Robert R. Findlay, *Century of Innovation: A History of European and American Theatre and Drama Since 1870.* Englewood Cliffs, NJ: Prentice-Hall, 1973. |
| *Critical Tradition* | David Richter, ed. *The Critical Tradition: Classic Texts and Contemporary Trends.* 3rd edn. Boston: Bedford/St. Martin's, 2007. |
| *Edwardian Turn* | Samuel Hynes, *The Edwardian Turn of Mind.* Princeton: Princeton University Press, 1968. |
| *Eliot Selected Prose* | T. S. Eliot, *Selected Prose of T. S. Eliot*, ed. Frank Kermode. New York: Farrar, Straus, and Giroux, 1975. |
| *Futurist Moment* | Marjorie Perloff, *The Futurist Moment: Avant-Garde, Avant Guerre, and the Language of Rupture.* Chicago: University of Chicago Press, 1986. |
| *Illuminations* | Walter Benjamin, *Illuminations: Essays and Reflections*, ed. Hannah Arendt, trans. Harry Zohn. New York: Schocken, 1969. |

| | |
|---|---|
| *James Joyce* | Richard Ellmann, *James Joyce*, rev. edn. Oxford: Oxford University Press, 1983. |
| *Mimesis* | Erich Auerbach, *Mimesis: The Representation of Reality in Western Literature*, trans. Willard R. Trask. Princeton: Princeton University Press, 1953. |
| *Modernism 1890–1930* | Malcolm Bradbury and James McFarlane, eds. *Modernism: A Guide to European Literature, 1890–1930*. London: Penguin, 1976. |
| *Modernism Anthology* | Vassiliki Kolocotroni, Jane Goldman, and Olga Taxidoe, eds. *Modernism: An Anthology of Sources and Documents*. Edinburgh: Edinburgh University Press, 1998. |
| *Let's Murder the Moonshine* | F. T. Marinetti, *Let's Murder the Moonshine: Selected Writings*, ed. and trans. R. W. Flint. Los Angeles: Sun & Moon, 1991. |
| *Pound Era* | Hugh Kenner, *The Pound Era*. Berkeley and Los Angeles: University of California Press, 1971. |
| *Strindberg: Five Plays* | August Strindberg, *Strindberg: Five Plays*, trans. Harry G. Carlson. Berkeley and Los Angeles: University of California Press, 1983. |
| *Theories of Modern Art* | Hershel B. Chipp, ed. *Theories of Modern Art: A Source Book by Artists and Critics*. Berkeley and Los Angeles: University of California Press, 1984. |
| *War Imagined* | Samuel Hynes, *A War Imagined: The First World War and English Culture*. New York: Atheneum, 1991. |

For literary works that are available in various editions, I have not given citations. Where I refer frequently to a particular edition or translation, however, I have included publication information in the suggestions for further reading at the end of each chapter. For the texts of many of the English-language poems I quote, see the *Norton Anthology of Modern and Contemporary Poetry*, 2 vols., 3rd edn, ed. Jahan Ramazani, Richard Ellmann, and Robert O'Clair (New York: Norton, 2003). In all cases I have tried to refer to readily available editions. In quoting from authors' critical writings, I have made use of the excellent volume *Modernism: An Anthology of Sources and Documents* (*Modernism Anthology*).

## Acknowledgments

Like most teachers, I have learned much from my students. I am indebted to the undergraduates and graduate teaching assistants at Yale University, particularly those in the "Modern British Novel" and "Major English Poets" courses, to whom I presented this material in its rawest form. Their responses to my lectures and seminars helped me to gauge how an introduction to modernism should work. A number of professionals at Yale assisted me with the design of the "Modern British Novel" course, on which about half of this book is based: Tim Young of the Beinecke Rare Book and Manuscript Library, Pam Franks and Aja Armey of the Yale University Art Gallery, Michael Hatt and Gillian Forrester of the Yale Center for British Art, Ken Crilly and Karl Schrom of the Irving S. Gilmore Music Library, Danuta Nitecki and Ernie Marinko of the Yale University Library, and Ed Kairiss and Pam Patterson of Instructional Technology Services. Support from the Davis Educational Foundation made the design of the course possible, and support from the A. Whitney Griswold and Frederick B. Hilles funds at Yale subsidized the research and illustrations for the book. I thank Grolier, Inc. for permission to reprint a brief excerpt that appeared originally in the *Encyclopedia Americana*.

Modernism has fascinated me ever since high school, and I am grateful to those who first taught me about it: Norah Maier at the University of Toronto Schools; Mary Davison at McGill University; and Hans Ulrich Gumbrecht, Marjorie Perloff, Jeffrey Schnapp, Michael Tratner, and the late Ian Watt at Stanford University. Colleagues in the American Comparative Literature Association and the Modernist Studies Association have also taught me a great deal, and Daniel Albright and Helen Vendler of Harvard University offered helpful advice on framing this project in the early stages. At Yale, Nigel Alderman, Elinor Fuchs, David Krasner, James Leverett, Joseph Roach, Marc Robinson, and Robert Slifkin kindly advised me on bibliography, while Jessica Brantley, William Deresiewicz, Elizabeth Dillon, Langdon Hammer, Catherine Labio, Barry McCrea, Haun Saussy, and Elliott Visconsi generously read and commented on drafts of various chapters. My colleague Amy Hungerford read the entire manuscript and provided much useful advice. I am also grateful to

Eric Hayot of the University of Arizona and Michael Walsh of Eastern Mediterranean University for their comments on portions of the manuscript. Jesse Matz, of Kenyon College, advised me on the project at various stages of completion and offered especially helpful guidance on the final draft, which he read with his usual perspicacity.

I am particularly indebted to five research assistants who drew on their own considerable expertise to aid me in putting together this study: Megan Quigley helped me to develop the framework for the book; Maria Fackler advised me on gender and literary theory and arranged permissions; Matthew Mutter patiently contributed to my understanding of modern poetry and intellectual history; John Muse tactfully guided my reading and interpretation of modern drama; Anna Lewis helped to amass the Chronology and Notes. All five offered substantive advice on various drafts. Of course, any errors of fact or judgment that remain are my own.

The staff at Cambridge University Press, particularly Elizabeth Davey and Maartje Scheltens, have been very helpful. My editor at Cambridge, Ray Ryan, showed an interest in this project from the start, and I am grateful to him and to the readers he assembled for their stimulating responses to an early draft. I have relied on the love and support of my family, including my parents, sisters, and in-laws. My wife, Sheila Hayre, has encouraged me in this and all my other projects. I dedicate the book to our children, Siddhartha and Maya; I hope that one day soon they will read it with pleasure.

                                        Pericles Lewis
                                        New Haven, Connecticut
                                        July, 2006

## Preface

The term *modernism*, in its literary sense, became current in English shortly after the First World War to describe new experimental literature, notably works by T. S. Eliot, James Joyce, Ezra Pound, and Virginia Woolf. Since then, it has continually expanded in scope. The expression now encompasses a wide variety of movements in modern art and literature, including, in some definitions, naturalism, symbolism, impressionism, post-impressionism, cubism, futurism, imagism, vorticism, dada, and surrealism, as well as a number of writers and artists not associated with any one of these movements. In its broadest sense, modernism has become the label for an entire tendency in literature and the arts, sometimes indeed for a whole period in cultural history, stretching as far back as the middle of the nineteenth century and continuing at least until the middle of the twentieth. Modernism has thus become a term of very wide application. While it does not have quite the expansiveness of names for earlier periods in cultural history, such as the Renaissance or the Enlightenment (whose solidity is demonstrated by the use of the definite article), it approaches the breadth of romanticism, a term that also embraces various sometimes opposed cultural phenomena and that can likewise be used to name either an international movement or an entire historical period. Despite the danger that such a term will become so vague in its reference as to be rendered meaningless, I believe that the word modernism designates a central phenomenon in cultural history. The task of this book is to introduce that phenomenon to nonspecialists and to describe it in as much concrete detail as possible, assuming no prior knowledge of the subject on the part of the reader.

What, then, is modernism? In English the word refers primarily to the tendency of experimental literature of the early twentieth century to break away from traditional verse forms, narrative techniques, and generic conventions in order to seek new methods of representation appropriate to life in an urban, industrial, mass-oriented age. Other terms have been used for related phenomena: "modernity" in philosophy, "modernization" in sociology, "modern music," "modern art," and "modern history." Literary modernism is intimately bound up with these other phenomena, and these links will be explored in detail in this book. In particular, modernism in literature went hand in hand with modern art, and I shall include modern art under the rubric of modernism, while sometimes calling attention to the differences between literature and the other arts. The focus, however, remains on literary modernism. Other European languages use other terms for the same general tendency in literature: *avant-garde* in French, *Expressionismus* in German, *decadentismo* in Italian. In Chinese the expression *modeng*, a transliteration of the European "modern," used widely in 1930s Shanghai, came to be replaced by the less foreign-sounding *xiandai zhuyi*, as the concept of modernism became naturalized. In Spanish *modernismo* referred as early as 1888 to a movement closely allied with symbolism and led by the Nicaraguan poet Rubén Darío. What links all these movements is the shared apprehension of a crisis in the ability of art and literature to represent reality.

Modernism offered an artistic and literary response to a widespread sense that the ways of knowing and representing the world developed in the Renaissance, but going back in many ways to the ancient Greeks, distorted the actual experience of reality, of art, and of literature. The crisis involved both the content and the form of representation. That is to say, it concerned the appropriate subject matter for literature and the appropriate techniques and styles by which literature could represent that subject matter. Some modernists went so far as to argue that literature should not represent any subject matter at all – it should represent only itself; they emphasized the sounds of words or their appearance on the page, rather than their referential function. My working definition of modernism will be: the literature that acknowledged and attempted to respond to a crisis of representation beginning in the mid-nineteenth century. The earlier roots of this crisis and the varied nature of the modernists' responses to it will be explored in the Introduction below. The emphasis in some recent scholarly work on "modernisms," the multiple, competing movements of the modernist period, does fruitfully address the complexity of the concept modernism. However, I have maintained the singular formulation because I believe that it helpfully draws attention to the underlying unity of the literary and artistic problem facing writers in the late nineteenth and early twentieth centuries: how to respond to the crisis of representation.

Before proceeding, however, it is necessary to consider another term that remains current and suggests the end-point of the modernism that this study takes as its central object. For more than a generation, artists, writers, and critics have frequently claimed to be beyond modernism, in an era of "postmodernism." Although early literary uses of the term postmodernism emphasized continuity with modernism, this literary usage was soon eclipsed by a broader philosophical or sociological analysis of the "postmodern condition," a condition contrasted with that of philosophical modernity, a category that goes back at least to the Enlightenment or even to the Renaissance (relabeled "the early modern period"), and whose central figures were the seventeenth-century philosopher René Descartes and the eighteenth-century philosopher Immanuel Kant. In the broadest terms, philosophical postmodernism criticizes the Enlightenment faith, prevalent from Descartes to Kant, in sovereign human reason. The philosophical debate over modernity *vs.* postmodernity, notably in the works of the philosophers Jürgen Habermas and Jean-François Lyotard, came also to dominate discussion of literary modernism and postmodernism. The noted critic Fredric Jameson acknowledged the origins of the postmodern "crisis of representation" in literary modernism in his influential foreword to Lyotard's *The Postmodern Condition* (1984). The geographer David Harvey took up the phrase in his *Condition of Postmodernity* (1990), once again tracing the crisis to literary experiments beginning in the mid-nineteenth century. Thus the philosophical attempt to define an age after modernity acknowledged its origins in the literary work of modernism, with its critique of traditional modes of representation.

In some later works on postmodernism, however, a false analogy presented literary modernism as the literary defense of philosophical modernity or even of sociological modernization. In fact, literary modernists, though often celebrating the dawning of the modern age in a general historical sense, were themselves engaged in a critique of some of the assumptions underlying philosophical modernity. Notably, the nineteenth-century philosopher Friedrich Nietzsche, himself a relentless critic of Enlightenment conceptions of reason, inspired both the literary modernists and the philosophical postmodernists. The historian J. W. Burrow has described the late nineteenth century as the era of the "crisis of reason," and the effects of this crisis, the philosophical counterpart of the literary "crisis of representation," are still with us in our own time, whether we label it modern, postmodern, or simply contemporary. Recognizing the continuity of our cultural situation with that of the modernists, literary critics and art historians have been paying renewed attention to modernism over the past generation. In the 1980s some of the champions of postmodernism rejected modernism as the product of an arrogant elite. More recent scholarly work has embraced a broader conception of the movement, both historically and culturally. Scholars have traced the roots of modernism back into the nineteenth century, found modernist currents outside the European mainstream, and explored the interaction among the various modern arts. They have also manifested a growing interest in the relationship between the arts and social and cultural history: gender, sexuality, technology, science, politics, empire, cross-cultural encounters, and the publishing industry. *The Cambridge*

*Introduction to Modernism* offers a synthesis of this new, historical understanding of modernism. Instead of isolating the "great works" of modernism, this book emphasizes the immersion of modernist literature in a culture of experiment. Rather than understand the modernists as elitists, hermetically sealed off from the broader culture, I explore their engagements with that culture and the distinctively literary solutions that they found for the central problems of their time.

In deciding how to present modernism to those who may be encountering it for the first time, I have faced several challenges. A study of this length cannot offer a comprehensive history of all the forms of modernism. Instead, I explore certain concepts that remained central to modernism across art forms and national boundaries, while emphasizing the multiple shapes that these concepts took in particular cultures. Previous surveys of modernism have tended to fall into two groups. There are those European-oriented studies that focus on the avant-garde movements (what Peter Nicholls, in the title of his 1995 "literary guide," aptly called *Modernisms*) and others that focus more narrowly on English literature from the imagists to W. H. Auden (as for example in Michael Levenson's edited collection of 1999, *The Cambridge Companion to Modernism*). Both approaches are valid, but each tends to present a rather one-sided view of modernism. Those who emphasize the European avant-gardes generally treat the most cosmopolitan of writers in English, such as Pound, Eliot, and Joyce, in detail, but they tend to neglect major figures in English-language modernism, such as Auden, Samuel Beckett, Joseph Conrad, D. H. Lawrence, Woolf, and W. B. Yeats, who had little involvement with any particular "-ism" and varying degrees of interest in Europe. Conversely, those who treat the major English writers in isolation lose the sense of modernism as an international phenomenon and thus offer a relatively homogeneous picture of what was really, despite its underlying unity of purpose, a heterogeneous set of movements. This study attempts to steer between these two extremes by situating the major works of English modernism that students or general readers are most likely to encounter in relation to developments in non-English-speaking countries. In this context, I am unable to treat non-Western literature in depth, but I do address the shaping of modernism by the Western powers' conquests and losses in the colonized world. When treating European matters, I have emphasized those that had a direct impact on English literature. In the chapter on modern drama, the most international of literary forms, I have paid special attention to European developments. Where relevant, I have discussed developments in the United States, but most of the Americans who play a major role in my story pursued their careers in England or France. The exception is the chapter on modern poetry, an area in which Americans had a disproportionate influence.

This comparative emphasis also applies to the genres of modernism. Major early studies of modernism, such as Hugh Kenner's magisterial *The Pound Era* (1971), tended to follow Pound and Eliot in treating poetry as the prime modernist genre. In the past generation, however, interest has shifted to the prose fiction and drama of modernism. This study gives equal attention to all three genres and recognizes that, while perhaps less abrupt than the transformations of poetry, the changes undergone by the novel and the theater in the modernist period contributed their share to the rethinking of representation. By treating all three genres extensively, I hope also to correct the impression of modernism as elitist that drove many postmodernist critiques. This study discusses acknowledged leaders of the avant-garde movements as well as a number of writers whose work, while attuned to the crisis of representation, remained relatively accessible to a broad audience. It is my intention to show that modernism, the reconfiguration of literary forms and genres for the modern age, went far beyond the coterie audiences of the avant-gardes. I thus replace earlier accounts of modernism as the invention of a few visionary geniuses with a more expansive understanding of the transformations of art and literature in the early twentieth century.

A survey of this breadth must necessarily be a work of synthesis, and I have relied in forming my own judgments on the expertise of earlier critics. These are acknowledged in the suggestions for further reading which appear at the end of each chapter, and in the Notes at the end of the book. However, I would like to call attention in particular to the fine overview of European trends in Malcolm Bradbury and James McFarlane's edited collection, *Modernism: A Guide to European Literature, 1890–1930*, first published in 1976, and the masterful trilogy on English literature and politics written by Samuel Hynes, *The Edwardian Turn of Mind* (1968), *The Auden Generation* (1977), and *A War Imagined* (1991). I have drawn heavily on these four works, updating them where necessary, but not hoping to surpass them. I recommend them as the best starting point for the reader who would like to explore the themes of this book further. Recognizing that British and European history are less familiar to some readers than they were a generation ago, I have discussed at some length the historical events most relevant to the development of modernism, notably the early feminist movement, the clashes over empire, the First World War, the Russian Revolution, and the rise of fascism and Nazism.

An introductory chapter surveys the intellectual history of the crisis of representation, as well as its more immediate roots in the newly industrialized and democratized culture of the late nineteenth century. The first section of the book (Chapters One to Three) addresses the "Origins" of modernism in a roughly chronological fashion. Rather than stick strictly to chronology, however, I have organized each chapter around a major theme of modernism, such as the problem of the artist in modernity, the modernists' interest in "primitive" cultures and modern technology, and the workings of avant-garde movements. A central section, "Genres," treats the major types of modernist literature: poetry, prose fiction, and drama. This section is more analytical than historical, offering explanations of the main features of modernist literature along with explorations of salient examples. A final chapter and a conclusion address the "Fate" of modernism, including the relationship between literature and politics in the 1930s, the question of how postmodernism differs from or continues modernist practice, and the legacy of modernism for the late twentieth and early twenty-first centuries.

Both the postmodernists of the 1980s and more recent "historicist" literary critics have been suspicious of modernist claims for art's autonomy and of related celebrations of "art for art's sake." Historically minded critics, at least since Karl Marx, tend to believe that art serves particular ideological purposes and may even have political effects, though most would agree that these effects are seldom foreseen by the artist. Without prejudging the question of the autonomy of the work of art, I have attempted both to describe the development of modernist literary forms and to place the new and unusual qualities of modernist art and literature in the context of a rapidly changing society. While tracing ongoing crises in the means of representation and in the content of modernist representations, I do not try to determine the primacy of one over the other. This study, then, describes the development of literary and artistic works in their historical, cultural context, without claiming either that the context fully explains the works or that the works finally transcend the history of their production and reception. When asked about the impact of the French Revolution of 1789, Zhou Enlai, prime minister of communist China, is said to have replied "Too soon to tell." We are the heirs of the modernists – both of their literary and artistic achievements and of their historical situation – and it is perhaps too soon to say what are the ultimate consequences of the crisis of representation that they first explored.

# Introduction

In the late nineteenth century, writers and artists perceived a crisis in their fields of endeavor. The symbolist poet Stéphane Mallarmé wrote of a "crisis in verse," the naturalist playwright August Strindberg of a "theatrical crisis."[1] Over the following generation, this crisis would manifest itself in questions about a central feature of literature and art: their ability to represent reality. At least since Plato and Aristotle, the arts had been associated with *mimesis,* the imitation or representation of reality. Although other features of art, notably its rhetorical effects on its audience and its ability to express the emotions or thoughts of the artist, had been prized by various periods or movements, these had never been entirely detached from art's power of representation.[2] By the early twentieth century, however, some artists began to pursue an art that no longer claimed to represent reality. The symbolist painter Maurice Denis observed in 1890, "It is well to remember that a picture – before being a battle horse, a nude woman, or some anecdote – is essentially a flat surface covered with colors assembled in a certain order."[3] Twenty years later, painters were arranging colors on flat surfaces – or even pasting objects onto flat surfaces – in order to create abstract designs, with no battle horse, nude woman, or other anecdote whatsoever.

Abstract, or "nonrepresentational," or "nonobjective," art has often been taken as the epitome of modern art. As a result, the history of modern art has been understood in terms of an almost scientific set of experiments leading up to the ultimate discovery, abstraction. Parallels have been found in modern literature – free verse, the "stream of consciousness," the breaking down of the fourth wall in the theater. Such formal innovations may appear in the history of artistic forms as discoveries, akin to Isaac Newton's formulation of the law of gravity, Charles Darwin's theory of evolution, or Albert Einstein's relativity theorem, apparently a discovery of a truth that preceded the scientist's or artist's inquiry. However, like those scientific discoveries, formal developments in art and literature take place in a historical context, and since art has traditionally aimed to represent reality, innovations in the means of representation cannot be entirely extricated from the problem of the new realities that the artist feels no longer able to represent by the old means. The modernist crisis of representation was two-fold: a crisis in what could be represented and a crisis in how it should be represented, or in other words a crisis in both the content and the form of artistic representation. One especially influential strand of modernism, often taken as emblematic of the movement as a whole, rejected representation altogether. In part because the early theorists of modernism were particularly concerned with the formal characteristics of the work of art or literature, the history of modernism has largely been written in terms of formal developments. Equally, however, modernism resulted from the challenge of representing new content, the historical experiences of the modern world, in the context of changing social norms about the status of art and literature themselves.

Historians of modernism have frequently concerned themselves with the relationship between content and form in the crisis of representation. In the 1930s the German-Jewish Marxist critic Walter Benjamin identified a "crisis of artistic reproduction" that corresponded to a "crisis of perception itself" and had begun with Charles Baudelaire in the mid-nineteenth century.[4] Leftist English writers of Benjamin's generation, such as John Cornford, Cecil Day-Lewis, Michael Roberts, and Alick West, used the term "crisis" to explore the relationship between the radical innovations in the arts of the previous decade or two and the social, economic, and political catastrophes of their own time.[5] Most of these writers were convinced that modernism reflected a crisis in capitalism. Later critics inspired by Marxism, including Fredric Jameson, traced the historical roots of the "crisis of representation" to literary modernism, but saw its effects as continuing into their own "postmodern" era.[6] In this book I trace the unfolding of the crisis of representation in English and European literature and in the arts. While I share with Benjamin, Jameson, and others a sense that the revolution in the arts now called "modernism" stems from social and political transformations that began in the mid-nineteenth century, I do not believe that a simple causal relationship can be discerned between a crisis in capitalism and a crisis in the arts. Rather, I believe that multiple causes, some internal to the arts and others deriving from broader historical forces, interacted in the development of modernism. I hope to show how developments in literary form emerge out of a background of social, political, intellectual, and existential ferment. The relationship between literary or artistic innovations and changing historical circumstances is complex, and it is mediated by the history of ideas. The nineteenth century experienced simultaneous crises that contributed in a variety of ways to the development of modernism in the early twentieth century. These transformations can be grouped into three major categories: the literary and artistic (crisis of representation); the socio-political (crisis of liberalism); and the philosophical and scientific (crisis of reason). The following discussion of these three crises surveys each in a roughly chronological fashion. To balance the emphasis in later chapters on the social and political context of modernism, this Introduction focuses on its roots in intellectual and literary history.

## Crisis of representation

Modern art and literature are known for their rejection of traditional conventions for representing the world and constructing works of art. An all-white canvas by Kasimir Malevich, or a mass-produced snow shovel exhibited by Marcel Duchamp as *In Advance of the Broken Arm* (1915), challenge museum-goers to question the definition of art, the expertise of curators, and their own status as connoisseurs. In general, work that is considered "modern" is experimental, rather than traditional, though many of these experiments draw on and develop techniques inherent in more traditional art. The modernists consciously sought to make art that was radically different from the art of earlier periods. To do so, they experimented with new styles and techniques as well as subject matter that had not been treated seriously by artists and writers in previous generations. Four technical innovations can illustrate the formal aspect of the crisis of representation. Nonobjective (or, loosely, "abstract") painting presented patterns of lines and colors on a canvas with no ostensible "subject." Free verse abandoned traditional versification methods including meter, rhyme, and stanza forms; it often also violated standard syntax. In narrative, the stream of consciousness purported to represent the thoughts of an individual character without any intervention of a narrator figure. And in theater playwrights broke down the "fourth wall" that separates the stage from the audience and allowed their characters to discuss their own status as characters in a play. These innovations, drawn from different media and genres, indicate the range of the crisis of representation and also how various its effects could be in diverse contexts. Certain shared concerns defined all these experiments as modernist. In each case modernism called attention to the medium of the literary or artistic work, defined itself in contrast to convention, and radically altered the means of representation.

Modern painting demonstrates most dramatically the break with earlier modes. Beginning with Paul Cézanne and Edouard Manet, painters challenged the Renaissance system of perspective that created an illusion of three-dimensional depth on a flat, two-dimensional canvas. The cubism of Georges Braque and Pablo Picasso, and the subsequent turn to purely nonrepresentational or abstract art by Wassily Kandinsky, Malevich, Piet Mondrian, and others, abandoned all effort at illusionism and instead celebrated the flat plane of the canvas, representing nothing but itself. In literature, too, the early twentieth century witnessed attempts to escape from mimesis: the Russian futurists invented *zaum*, a poetic language made up entirely of nonsense words; in their *Stationendramen* German expressionist playwrights replaced lifelike characters with abstractions representing states of mind or the different parts of a protagonist's soul; the novelist James Joyce wrote his last novel, *Finnegans Wake* (1939), in a multilingual jargon meant to represent the logic of dreams. In all these cases the modernists turned away from the ideal of a language that would offer a transparent window onto reality; they favored instead a complex language that drew attention to its own texture. The poet Archibald MacLeish wrote, in his "Ars Poetica" (1926), that "A poem should not mean / But be."

Despite the more radical experiments of the literary avant-garde, however, literature in general clung stubbornly to reality. Although writers might stress the importance of the sounds of words or the visual organization of words on the page, words tended, except in extreme cases, to maintain their referential function; in addition to being, they meant. Literature therefore continued to represent reality, sometimes in distorted forms or in nightmarish parody, sometimes in comic detail or with multiple layers of symbolic intention, but usually with some implicit ideal of mimesis underlying all the literary experiments. Modernist literature seldom went as far as modern art in the direction of pure abstraction, and therefore parallels with the arts present a challenge: it would be unwise to suggest that modern art had "succeeded" in escaping from representation where modernist literature had "failed." Furthermore, some art historians have challenged the version of the history of modern art that makes the rejection of mimesis the sole truly modern characteristic. Such a history privileges cubism and abstract art over other movements, such as expressionism, dada, or surrealism. It obviously fails to account for the career of a major modern artist such as Henri Matisse, whose art never really approached pure abstraction; more surprisingly, it also fails to account for the works of Picasso after his cubist period, when, having introduced the technical innovations that would lead to abstract art, he returned to mimesis.

In literature a purely formal account of modernism distorts the record even further. The mimetic intention underlies much apparently nonmimetic art.

The victory of free verse over traditional meters, decisively won in English by Ezra Pound and his friends, was actually undertaken in the name of mimesis. Pound emphasized that poetry should imitate spoken language rather than conventional meters. It should contain "nothing, *nothing*, that you couldn't, in some circumstance, in the stress of some emotion, *actually say*."[7] The stream of consciousness, while breaking from the "realist" convention of the omniscient narrator, in fact corresponded to another form of realism, what Ian Watt has called the "realism of presentation," which attempts to present reality as it is experienced by the individual character, rather than from the viewpoint of an omniscient narrator.[8] The modern theater broke not so much with the representation of reality as with the illusionism that claimed that a stage set could represent reality. Ever since the seventeenth century, plays had been presented on a stage framed by a proscenium arch, as if the audience were looking in on a scene painted according to the rules of perspective developed in the Renaissance. A number of modern playwrights destroyed this illusion, allowing their characters to acknowledge their fictive status, while modern producers and directors experimented with other methods of staging plays, abolishing the proscenium arch. In all the literary cases just mentioned, conventional representations were replaced not with nonrepresentations, but with new systems of representation that acknowledged the limitations of the old conventions.

Recognizing this fact about modernist literature, which may indeed distinguish it from modern art, illuminates a central problem about the originality of modernism. The defenders and interpreters of modernism have oscillated between two related views: on the one hand, that modernism means an end to all conventional forms of representation, and on the other hand that modernism means the creation of new conventions of representation, more appropriate than the old ones to the modern age. The foregoing analysis suggests that modernism represents not the rejection of conventions altogether but simply a new, more authentic set of conventions. However, the originality of modernism consists, perhaps, not in its introduction of just one more set of conventions (the Renaissance and romanticism had each introduced new conventions in the past). Rather, its specificity lies in the recognition that the conventions of art needed constant renewal, a sort of permanent revolution, to borrow a phrase from the political world. Modernism insisted that each artist or writer must create anew the appropriate conventions for representing reality as he or she experienced it. Indeed, for the greatest modernists, like Picasso or Joyce, the task was to create these conventions anew for each subsequent phase of the artist's career. Modernism put an intense emphasis on originality, famously formulated by Baudelaire: "Modernity is the transitory, the fugitive, the contingent; it is one half of art, the other being the eternal and immutable . . . nearly all our originality comes from the stamp that time impresses upon our sensibility."[9] Originality lay not in discovering timeless truths but in embracing the transitory nature of modernity itself. Since the modernists had to invent brand-new means of representation for the modern world, they could not assume that an audience would understand their innovations. The famous hostility of audiences to the productions of modern art and literature results from the internal imperative of modernism always to reinvent the means of representation. The crisis of representation becomes permanent, but this does not mean, in most cases, that representation itself is abandoned. The modernists were not necessarily seeking an art without any conventions, but rather an art that examined its own conventionality, that put the conventions of art on display, an art that put art itself in question.

In the history of philosophy, the crisis of representation can be traced to the writings of the eighteenth-century philosopher Immanuel Kant. Kant formulated some of the crucial philosophical problems of modernity, and he is as central a figure in the crises of liberalism and of reason as in the crisis of representation. A crucial difficulty in the traditional conception of art as representation is the dualism that distinguishes the image or representation of a thing from the thing represented. One influential view, going back to Plato, holds that art can never be true because it is never more than an imitation of the appearances of reality, rather than (like philosophy) an analysis of their underlying forms or ideas. Art is therefore twice removed from the ultimate reality, the reality of forms. This dualism came under attack in the work of Kant, who argued that we can never have direct, unmediated access to reality. Since all our perceptions come to us through our senses and our thoughts, we can never directly know the "thing in itself," the underlying form at which Plato aimed, but only its appearances, what Kant called "phenomena." The strict dualism between reality and the representation of reality therefore breaks down: the only reality that humans can perceive is appearance. Art, or philosophy, can give a more or less adequate representation of these appearances, but neither has direct access to an ultimate reality behind appearances. Later philosophers thought that art might in some respects offer a better account of the world of appearances than philosophy could and that reality could never be disentangled from our representations of it.[10]

The philosophy of Friedrich Nietzsche, Edmund Husserl, and Martin Heidegger showed the errors into which the opposition of reality and representation had led Western thought. Nietzsche challenged the Platonic preference for reality over representation, depth over surface (his philosophy is discussed in the section on "Hermeneutics of suspicion" below). Husserl, a contemporary of the modernists, created a system, phenomenology, meant to avoid the dualism between reality and representation. Since we as perceivers have access only to phenomena, appearances, he "bracketed" or refused to answer the question of correspondence – whether those phenomena correspond to an actually existing reality "out there."[11] This "phenomenological reduction" shares much with modernist literature and art, which attempt a rigorous analysis of the phenomena of perception, often without claiming the ability to represent any reality external to the perceiving subject. Cubism can be understood as a phenomenology of vision, an attempt to render what the eye sees before the mind has processed it. The stream-of-consciousness novel offers a phenomenology of mind, an account of the contents, in Virginia Woolf's phrase, of "an ordinary mind on an ordinary day," without any filtering devices. Modernist writers, in particular, emphasized the attempt to capture immediate experience, "to record the atoms as they fall upon the mind," independent of all philosophical categories or ideas, experience as it is actually lived.[12] They found inspiration for this effort in the philosophies of Henri Bergson, F. H. Bradley, and especially William James, who introduced the dominant metaphor of a "stream of consciousness."[13]

The modernist effort to record the phenomena of perception differed from the traditional understanding that art represented a reality outside the mind. When modern artists and writers turned away from the mimetic or representational function of art, they had two obvious alternatives: the rhetorical and the expressive functions. The rhetorical function, art's ability to move or convince an audience, was a traditional justification of art, most famously summarized by the Latin poet Horace, who wrote that the purpose of art was "to instruct and to delight." Rhetoric held a certain primacy in classicism, a view of art dominant in the eighteenth century. The expressive function, the ability of art or literature to express the thoughts or feelings of the artist, had become central to justifications of art in the romantic period, beginning in the late eighteenth century. The romantics prefigured many aspects of modernism: the emphasis on the lone genius who follows his (or occasionally her) own inspiration and disregards the tenets and rules of art; a faith in the spiritual qualities of art understood as independent of organized religion; the basic hostility of the artist to society and convention; and the effort to create an art that speaks the language of the common people.

The philosopher Charles Taylor has summarized a fundamentally modern attitude of "romantic expressivism," and has argued that this expressivism had a profound influence on modernism. The romantics sought in art a way to combat the tendency of modernity to "fragment human life: dividing it into disconnected departments, like reason and feeling; dividing us from nature; dividing us from each other."[14] They sought to reintegrate the human personality through art. This impulse remains strong in modernism, too, for example in the work of D. H. Lawrence. However, most modernists were more likely than the romantics to accept the fragmentation of human life, nature, and society as inevitable, and to expect that art and literature would reflect the fragmentary nature of the modern experience in their own forms. In some cases this fragmentation seems to have been aimed at achieving a higher reintegration, symbolized for example by Molly Bloom's "yes" at the end of Joyce's *Ulysses* (1922) or the Sanskrit words "Shantih shantih shantih" at the end of T. S. Eliot's *The Waste Land* (1922), which Eliot glossed with the biblical phrase "The Peace which passeth understanding." Often, however, the modernists were willing to accept that no reintegration of human life through art was possible and therefore to leave their works with the appearance of being unfinished or incomplete; the same rejection of the integrating force of art also accounts for the modernist fascination with the ugly (see Chapter One). For the romantics, the world was full of a hidden meaning which the artist had to discover. The modernists generally saw the world as devoid of inherent significance. For them, the task of the artist was not to discover a preexistent meaning, but to create a new meaning out of the chaos and anarchy of actual modern life. If anything, this gave art an even higher value than it had for romanticism. As Taylor puts it, "Art becomes one of the, if not the, paradigm medium in which we express, hence define, hence realize ourselves."[15] This high status of the work of art was contested in modernism. Where some, such as Heidegger, saw art and poetry as a special mode of human activity that could disclose truths unavailable through other modes, others, like the dadaists, mocked the very idea of art or claimed to break down the distance between the "high" art of the museums and the reality of modern, especially urban, life.

Some critics (including M. H. Abrams, Paul de Man, and Taylor) have treated modernism essentially as a late form of romanticism.[16] Yet, in addition to the general differences of attitude just outlined, which may be seen as an intensification of tendencies already inherent in romanticism, modernism differs from the earlier movement in its emphasis on the need continually to reinvent the means of representation. Modernism involves a much more wholesale challenge than romanticism to such systems of representation as pictorial perspective and to the ideal of transparent or mimetic language. The transition from romanticism to modernism can be understood in part as resulting from a new justification of the work of art. Historically, art had been understood in terms of its mimetic function (as a representation of reality, ever since the Greeks), its rhetorical function (its effect on the audience, emphasized by Horace and later neoclassical theorists), or its expressive function (as the expression of the artist's genius, emphasized by the romantics). In modernism art came to be justified for no function at all, or rather for its artistic function, for its status as a work of art independent of its relations to reality, an audience, or an artist. This justification of art, like the crisis of representation itself, goes back to Kant, and Kant offered a term for it: the autonomy, or self-regulation, of art. Those who defend art's autonomy generally emphasize its formal features, the way that the work of art itself creates the rules by which it can be interpreted and understood. In this sense, what the modernist work of art expresses is not "ourselves" but itself. It becomes an almost hieratic object, containing a meaning that transcends not only its status as representation and the understanding of its audience but even the intentions of its creator. For some modernists, art approaches a sacred function, no longer (as in the Middle Ages) subservient to the rituals of the Church, but understood as itself a site of sacred power.

In Kant's view, the work of art, in so far as it is art, serves no purpose outside itself. Although obviously created by actual people in the course of their lives in history, the work of art does not exist to serve their interests or further their ideological beliefs or any ideological beliefs at all. The market value of a work of art, and its propaganda value, may be of interest to the artist, the dealer or publisher, or to a political movement, but they are irrelevant (perhaps even deleterious) to its quality as art. Kant defended the work of art against earlier attacks by claiming that it has no direct effect on the world, or more precisely that it serves no particular interests: you cannot eat it; it does not (or should not) promote any particular ideology; it does not give you any sexual pleasure; it has no real purpose; it serves no end other than itself. The mystery for Kant was that, despite its lack of an end outside itself, the work of art is purposive, it has shape and form, it seems the product of someone's intention. This "purposiveness without a purpose" is what makes art an end in itself.[17] According to Kant, we go to the work of art not to learn something about the outside world, not to fulfill our own desires, not to have our minds changed about a matter of politics, but for the sake of the work of art itself. In this sense, a work of art is an expression of our highest humanity, for Kant saw the difference between humans and animals as consisting in the fact that we can be disinterested, we can do something for its own sake.[18]

Kant emphasized the autonomy of the work of art and developed a formalist aesthetics. In late nineteenth-century England, a literary movement known as aestheticism married formalist aesthetics to a worldview that cultivated the autonomy of art as the ultimate expression of human values (see Chapter One). Despite his formalism, Kant tended to understand the work of art as serving very general moral ends – in particular, the development of human disinterestedness. The aestheticists elevated art above other moral ends. Walter Pater praised the "love of art for its own sake," while, more aggressively, Oscar Wilde wrote with approval that "all art is quite useless."[19] This element of aestheticism had a great influence on modernism, and even so political a poet as W. H. Auden eventually came around to the view that "poetry makes nothing happen."[20] Those who share the aestheticist sensibility tend also to emphasize the formal qualities of the literary work, as opposed to its thematic content, and therefore the privileging of the history of formal innovation in accounts of modernism reflects the modernists' own concern with form as the distinguishing characteristic of the work of art, independent of author, audience, or reality.

The crisis of representation, though most easily illustrated by the visual arts, was exacerbated in literature by the very medium out of which literature is created: language. In the early twentieth century, several linguists and philosophers, most influentially Ferdinand de Saussure and Ludwig Wittgenstein, analyzed the way that language functions as a system of representation. Saussure emphasized the arbitrariness of the relationship between what he called "the signifier" and "the signified," that is, between the words dog, *chien*, *Hund*, *perro*, or *cane*, and the concept of a dog.[21] Wittgenstein studied how the rules of language make up a sort of "language game," and suggested that the rules of the game, rather than the reality it is meant to describe, govern how language is used. On the eve of the Russian Revolution, the Russian formalists created the first modern school of literary theory, emphasizing the primacy of the self-referential "literary" function of language over its mimetic function. These conceptions of language drew attention to the fact, familiar to the opponents of poetry ever since Plato proposed the banishment of poets from the ideal republic, that language represents reality in an especially unreliable manner. Many modernists embraced the idea of the literary work as a particularly sophisticated sort of language game, in which the relations among words were more important than the relations of words to nonlinguistic reality. They broke up syntax, created linguistic puzzles, and made use of quotation, allusion, and parody, all to challenge the conception of language as straightforwardly mimetic. Thus, while language did stubbornly maintain its tendency to refer to outside reality, the modernists often thwarted this inherent tendency toward representation by organizing their literary works according to the nonreferential functions of language. The development of modernist literary technique is largely the story of writers' attempts to wrest their own styles from the maelstrom created by the constant interplay between the referential and the nonreferential forces of language.

## Modern times

The modernists' sense of the inadequacy of earlier means of representation resulted in part from their attempts to represent a new reality. Modernist writers and artists were often keenly aware of living in a world that was utterly different from that of their parents, whether because of new religious and scientific beliefs, of industrialization, of changing attitudes to sex and gender, or of transformative political events. Many modernists produced their works in an effort to display what was distinctively modern about the times in which they were living. Because of the difficulty and self-referentiality of their works, the modernists have sometimes been seen as isolated from the historical currents of their time. However, many were actively involved in political debates, and even those who disdained formal politics were shaped by the broad social changes of their era.

Crucial to the social and political background of modernism was a crisis of political liberalism that had its roots in the radically transformed nature of social relations in the nineteenth century. The Industrial Revolution, which began in Britain in the eighteenth century and spread throughout Western Europe and North America in the nineteenth, brought about a profound transformation in human modes of life. For the first time in history, large numbers of people were separated from the diurnal and seasonal cycles of life on the land and went to work in factories and live in cities, where they became part of the urban proletariat or the crowd or mass, a social phenomenon that fascinated the modernists and that was analyzed at the end of the nineteenth century by the French theorist Gustave Le Bon. The impersonal nature of urban existence, which could be both exciting and threatening, became a major theme of modernist literature.

Earlier technological innovations, notably the steam engine, the cotton gin, and the railroad, enabled this revolution. In the later nineteenth century, a new set of technologies transformed people's experience of time and space and of the possibilities of art: they included electric light, the telegraph, the telephone, the portable camera, the cinema, the bicycle, the automobile, the airplane, and the machine gun.[22] While allowing people to bridge great distances and to represent the visible or audible world in new forms, these inventions also quickened the pace of life and transformed the experience of time. World Standard Time was established in 1884 partly in order to facilitate the coordination of railroad timetables; it replaced a patchwork system in which, for example, the United States had more than eighty time zones. Standardization sharpened the sense of a division between the time of private experience and the time of public life. Public time sped up in other ways, too. Industrial capitalism promoted constant change in people's working lives and patterns of consumption, as new technologies and products were continually being introduced. Some modernists, like F. T. Marinetti's futurists, embraced the inventiveness of industrial capitalism and sought to create a faster, more industrial type of art. Others, such as the members of the Bloomsbury Group affiliated with Roger Fry's Omega Workshops, conceived of the work of art as an alternative to the products of mass industry. Such champions of hand craftsmanship drew inspiration from the Arts and Crafts movement of the nineteenth-century socialist William Morris. Still other modernists turned their back on industrial society and Western civilization and sought closer contact with the "primitive," whether embodied in colonized peoples or in the ancient past of Europe itself. These divergent attitudes to the historical present are the subject of Chapter Two, "Primitivists and modernizers."

The American Revolution of 1776 and the French Revolution of 1789 had ushered in the modern political era, in which the principles of universal human rights and democratic self-government challenged all forms of hereditary privilege. Although the old order was restored in Europe by the Congress of Vienna in 1815, the history of the nineteenth century would be shaped by the struggle for liberal and democratic government, which was in part a struggle between the entrenched monarchy and aristocracy and the rising middle and working classes. Industrial capitalism transformed not only people's experiences of the world but also their relations with one another. Vast new accumulations of capital gave increased power to the bourgeoisie, the property-owning middle classes. Whether through gradual electoral reform, as in Britain, or through revolution, as in France, the middle classes came to dominate political life. The power of capital supplanted the landed wealth of the aristocracy. The political philosophy most attuned to the middle classes, liberalism, inspired revolutions throughout Europe in 1848, as the supporters of liberal republican government attempted to overthrow absolute monarchies. Although these were mostly put down, liberal systems of government gradually came to power, often in the form of constitutional monarchies.

"Liberalism" at this time referred to a political order that allowed basic freedoms, such as freedom of religion, speech, and assembly, and above all to parliamentary politics, in which competing parties represented various interests but in which the middle and upper classes held most of the power, usually through restriction of the right to vote. This system achieved a certain hegemony in the later nineteenth century, and became part of what the modernists would later rebel against. In economics liberals favored free trade and the unfettered development of capitalism, symbolized by the repeal of the Corn Laws (tariffs on grain) in Britain in 1846. In philosophical terms, liberalism championed the individual over the collective, reason over prejudice, and progress over reaction. Individualism, reason, and progress would all be questioned by the modernists and their contemporaries in the early twentieth century. Although most modernists came from the middle classes, their experiments occurred at the fringes of the literary and artistic world. Those involved in such experiments were frequently hostile to middle-class life and to the political liberalism of the nineteenth century. They sought, in words often attributed to Charles Baudelaire, to "shock the middle classes" ("*épater les bourgeois*"). Many modernists achieved their initial successes because of the scandalous nature of their work, and so Baudelaire's attitude could be profitable; the middle classes often enjoyed being shocked.

Liberalism could be grounded philosophically either in Immanuel Kant's notion of autonomy – here the autonomy or self-governance of the rational individual – or in the utilitarian ideal, proposed by Jeremy Bentham and later elaborated by John Stuart Mill, of the greatest good for the greatest number. In either case, it challenged established authorities, such as monarchy and aristocracy, and favored the deliberative decision-making of those judged capable of self-government. Liberalism had its limits, however. Mill argued for female suffrage, but most nineteenth-century liberals assumed that women, children, the poor, and nonwhites were incapable of self-government. Liberalism therefore expressed a point of view in keeping with the interests of middle-class men, and it remained generally unresponsive to the problems of the working classes and women, and internally divided over the question of empire. These three problems led to an ongoing crisis in liberalism, which manifested itself at distinct historical moments: after the betrayal of the 1848 revolution in France (see Chapter One), after the fall of Charles Stewart Parnell in Ireland, and on the eve of the First World War in England (see Chapter Two). Each of these moments was crucial to the history of modernism, as artists and writers who had shared some liberal ideals – Baudelaire and Gustave Flaubert in France, James Joyce and W. B. Yeats in Ireland, E. M. Forster and Virginia Woolf in England – became disillusioned with liberalism and sought either more radical political solutions or (as in the case of these six writers) an entirely different type of solution in the realm of art. The most devastating crisis of liberalism took place between the two world wars with the rise of communism in Russia and fascism in Italy and Germany (see Chapter Seven). Modernism never recovered from this final crisis.

The modernists hoped to shock the middle classes out of their complacency, but the bourgeoisie faced a more formidable challenge to its power from the

working classes, who began to organize into labor unions and to demand political representation and laws regulating working conditions. These included, for
example, a maximum workday for women and children of ten hours Monday
to Friday (plus eight on Saturdays), enacted into British law in 1847, despite the
protests of the liberals, who believed firmly in totally unregulated (*laissez-faire*)
economics. In France a workers' revolution in June 1848 was put down by the
republican government that had come to power after the liberal revolution four
months earlier. Communist and socialist parties, often with direct links to the
trades unions, eventually achieved representation in most national parliaments
near the end of the nineteenth century, by which time the franchise had been
extended to at least a significant minority of working-class men throughout
Europe, except in Russia. Many liberals welcomed the growing democracy as
an extension of liberal principles, but others expressed the fear that it would
naturally lead to socialism or communism. The Russian Revolution of 1917
seemed to its participants to herald the worldwide revolution promised by Karl
Marx. In the event, the Russian communists, facing economic pressures and the
united opposition of the West, had to make do with "socialism in one country."
Western capitalism adopted some elements of the socialist program by regulating working conditions, providing free public education, and introducing
social insurance and state pensions. The result was the modern welfare state.
Many modernists made common cause with the working classes; others identified with the fading aristocracy; still others simply reveled in the perceived
immolation of the bourgeois order.

   At the turn of the century, a new set of demands for expansion of the franchise
dominated political debate in the United Kingdom and the United States, as
women insisted on the right to vote. The women's suffrage movement reflected
changing social attitudes to gender, as the rise of the "New Woman," who was
relatively independent of her male relatives and might even pursue her own
career, challenged Victorian notions of relations between the sexes. Changing
attitudes to sex and sexuality had a particularly important impact on modern
art and literature. In place of elegant classical nudes, Pablo Picasso and others painted women with distorted features. The free-form, evocative dances of
Isadora Duncan heralded modern dance. A particularly large number of women
writers were involved in modernism, notably H. D. (Hilda Doolittle), Mina Loy,
Katherine Mansfield, Marianne Moore, Dorothy Richardson, Gertrude Stein,
and Woolf. The modern period also witnessed the beginnings of a new attitude toward sexuality. In the wake of Oscar Wilde's conviction and imprisonment for sodomy in 1895, a new consciousness of homosexuality emerged (see
Chapter One). Despite continued legal persecution, homosexuals in artistic
circles were more open than they had previously been about their orientation.

Among the many important modernists who either openly or clandestinely flouted what has been called "compulsory heterosexuality" were Djuna Barnes, Sergei Diaghilev, Forster, André Gide, Vaslav Nijinsky, Marcel Proust, Stein, Lytton Strachey, and Woolf.[23] These transformations of English culture in the years just before the First World War contributed to the sense of a rapid demise of the liberal consensus, what George Dangerfield would later describe as "the strange death of Liberal England."[24]

Writers and artists explored the changing status of women and the working classes. Many also concerned themselves with another crucial failing of the liberal system, its inability to resolve problems of nationhood and empire. The revolutions of 1848 had combined liberalism with nationalism, and the two were seen as compatible: nationalists championed the self-determination of peoples just as liberals heralded individual self-determination. Later in the century, liberalism was often subordinated to nationalism. After the Indian Mutiny of 1857, the British government assumed direct control over India, which had previously been ruled by the British East India Company. Imperialism, still a new word in the 1870s, became an official part of British policy when Queen Victoria was named Empress of India in 1876. The Liberal Party split over the question of Home Rule for Ireland, assuring domination of late nineteenth-century politics by the Conservative Party and the pro-empire Liberal Unionists. The international liberal political consensus was threatened by the excesses of the European powers' imperialist policies, which reached a crescendo in the scramble for control of Africa in the last decades of the nineteenth century, resulting for Britain in the Boer War (1899–1902), in which the British army was barely able to defeat the small Afrikaner population, descended from Dutch settlers. As a result of the Spanish-American War, the United States for the first time acquired an overseas empire, in Cuba, Guam, the Philippines, and Puerto Rico. The British imperialist poet Rudyard Kipling celebrated the occasion in a poem urging the Americans to "take up the white man's burden." Even Kipling foresaw the decline of empire, however, and the treatment of imperialism in the works of modernist authors, notably Joseph Conrad and Forster, reflected a growing unease at the barbarity of the colonizers' behavior toward colonized peoples. A related problem, anti-Semitism, led to the Dreyfus Affair, a major political crisis in France in the last decade of the nineteenth century (see Chapter One). It also became widespread in Germany and Austria in the wake of the westward migration of many Eastern European Jews, fleeing the pogroms in Russia.[25]

Later, the philosopher Hannah Arendt would locate the origins of twentieth-century totalitarianism in nineteenth-century imperialism and anti-Semitism.[26] These blind spots of political liberalism eventually led to its undoing. Both Germany and Italy, though ancient nations or peoples, were new nation-states at the end of the nineteenth century. They had been divided among small states and foreign powers for centuries and, despite the liberal nationalist revolutions of 1848, finally achieved unity only as monarchies after the Franco-Prussian War in 1871. The new nation-states developed relatively fragile liberal political systems, in which concerns for national unity often over-rode political freedoms. Among the reasons for the later success of fascism in these two countries were the absence of well-established liberal-democratic political systems, the economic crises of the postwar years, the electorate's fear of socialism and communism, and the sense of national humiliation that both felt (for different reasons) after the First World War.

From 1914 to 1918 that conflict appeared to confirm the bankruptcy of the nineteenth-century liberal political system. The war involved virtually all of Europe and troops from around the world, and killed about ten million people – more than any previous war. The use of modern technologies such as the machine gun made it particularly murderous. The war seemed to spell the end of an era of consensus in which the dominance of the middle classes was unques-tioned. The various movements and experiments chronicled in Chapters One and Two culminated in the invention of a distinctive English modernism dur-ing and immediately after the war (see Chapter Three). Contemporaries saw the postwar period as one of increased "collectivism," state action, and class-consciousness, motivated partly by the Russian Revolution of 1917, but also by the general sense of disillusionment with the governments that had run the war. T. S. Eliot's *The Waste Land* (1922) expressed a widespread feeling of exhaustion and cultural crisis in the aftermath of the war. In the United States the demobilization of African-American soldiers coincided with an era of race riots, the refounding of the Ku Klux Klan, and African-American attempts to forge a new image of the race as the "New Negro" in the Harlem Renaissance.[27] The Russian Revolution and the rise of fascism and Nazism radically trans-formed life in most of Europe and threatened the capitalist democracies of the United Kingdom and the United States. All these social and political upheavals contributed in one way or another to the rise of modernism. Modernists dif-fered widely in their politics, but most were conscious of living in what the historian Eric Hobsbawm would later call an "age of extremes," and frequently they were drawn to extreme political ideologies.[28] A significant number of modernist writers thought that their work could serve as a sort of prophecy that might guide their own nations or all of Western civilization through this period of conflict. In the years between the two world wars, the question of art's relationship to politics became central to the modernists' conception of their movement. It is the focus of Chapter Seven, "Literature and politics."

In a sense, the crisis of liberalism was itself a crisis of representation, that is of political representation or "representative government," as nineteenth-century liberals called their political system.[29] One of the defining questions of nineteenth-century politics was who merited representation in the parliaments of the liberal powers and what the relationship should be between parliament and the heads of state and government (monarch, president, prime minister, or chancellor). As the principle of universal male (and eventually universal adult) suffrage became established, the debate over political representation came to focus on how effectively parliaments could in fact represent their constituents. The new dictators of the 1920s and 1930s justified themselves as representatives, or simply leaders, of the entire people, and denigrated parliaments as ineffectual debating societies, made up of representatives not of the people but of special interests. The futurist Marinetti allied himself with the fascist Benito Mussolini and hoped to "free Italy from the Papacy, the Monarchy, the Senate, marriage, Parliament," all associated with the outmoded nineteenth century.[30] Adolf Hitler assumed extraordinary powers in February 1933 after a fire burned down the Reichstag, the German parliament. Although some historians have considered the Reichstag fire the result of a Nazi plot, most believe that it was indeed the act of the Dutch communist van der Lubbe, whom the Nazis executed for the crime. However, the Reichstag fire served Hitler's interests, as it allowed him to substitute his own dictatorial powers for those of parliament. In this sense, the burning of the German parliament symbolized the ultimate consequence of the crisis of nineteenth-century liberalism – its overthrow by totalitarianism, and the replacement of representative government with dictatorship.

## Hermeneutics of suspicion

There were many direct links between the political realm of debates over suffrage, parliament, and empire and the aesthetic realm where new modes of representation were being formed. Some of these are explored in the chapters that follow. The aesthetic and political crises examined so far cannot, however, be disentangled from a broader intellectual phenomenon, the crisis of reason. This phenomenon, too, has deep roots. Like the crisis of representation, the crisis of reason was first analyzed by philosophers of the modernist generation (José Ortega y Gasset and Edmund Husserl, though neither used the precise phrase), but it has also been a central concern of postmodern philosophers, notably Jacques Derrida.[31] In terms of its implications for modernist literature, one of the distinctive characteristics of the late nineteenth-century crisis of reason was the development of a new attitude toward interpretation, what the philosopher Paul Ricoeur has called a "hermeneutics of suspicion," in which the apparent, or manifest, meaning of an idea or a text is thought to need decoding in order to discover another hidden, or latent, meaning, generally unknown to the original thinker or author.[32] The hermeneutics of suspicion involved an attack on all the forms of Kantian autonomy: individuals, subject to unconscious forces, no longer regulated their own actions; liberal politics, based on the autonomous individual, had to give way to collective approaches; and the work of art reflected the unrecognized prejudices or class interests of its creator. This approach, which insists on interpreting statements and texts "against the grain," eventually came to dominate literary study. It also affected the way that authors saw their own characters' mental lives – the stream of consciousness, while purporting to represent the surface activity of consciousness, seems to invite a "suspicious" reading that can uncover the hidden, unconscious mental processes inaccessible to the consciousness of the fictional character. Faced with a hermeneutics of suspicion, authors often became more indirect, hiding their meanings so as to force the interpreter to work harder. James Joyce boasted of *Ulysses* (1922), "I've put in so many enigmas and puzzles that it will keep the professors busy for centuries arguing over what I meant, and that's the only way of insuring one's immortality."[33]

Hermeneutics itself originated in the interpretation of sacred texts, and, in a sense, the hermeneutics of suspicion originated in the attempt to read the Bible critically. Reason and faith are often seen as existing in tension with one another, but the crisis of reason in the mid-nineteenth century resulted in part from an antecedent crisis of faith. In the early nineteenth century, a series of scientific discoveries began to undermine belief in the literal truth of the Bible. As early as the 1830s, Sir Charles Lyell found geological and fossil evidence that contradicted the timespan of the biblical creation narrative. David Friedrich Strauss's *The Life of Jesus* (1835) marked a more direct assault on the historicity of the gospels. Strauss inspired generations of scholars who sought to explain biblical events through the techniques of modern scholarship and employed textual criticism to challenge traditional accounts of the authorship of the Bible. For example, the Pentateuch (the first five books of the Bible), which had been attributed to Moses, was found to have multiple authors, as were the book of Isaiah and the letters of St. Paul. Especially in Britain, the challenge to biblical literalism had a political element. The universities of Oxford and Cambridge were open only to members of the Church of England, and liberals fought for the admission of non-Anglicans to the academy, to parliament, and to other professions.

The crises of faith of such Victorians as George Eliot, Thomas Hardy, John Ruskin and Leslie Stephen (father of Virginia Woolf) did not depend on the discoveries of Charles Darwin. However, Darwin's theory of evolution provided the most intellectually coherent alternative to the biblical account of creation. Although it was a great achievement of human intellect, Darwinism also provided a challenge to the supremacy of reason. Darwinian evolution initially seemed to offer scientific evidence for the optimistic liberal idea of social progress. Science promised an alternative to religion, or the basis for a new "religion of humanity," such as that promoted by Auguste Comte. Many hoped that a new science of culture could be modeled on evolution, showing the inevitable progress of human civilization toward greater complexity and individual freedom. The leading exponents of such a science of culture, known as "positivism," were Comte in France and Herbert Spencer in England.

By the last quarter of the century, however, the bleaker implications of Darwin's theory became more apparent. Unlike earlier theorists of evolutionary progress, including J. B. Lamarck, Darwin divorced evolution from teleology: within species, variations were inherited randomly, and, although the variations best adapted to a particular environment tended to survive, there was no ultimate goal toward which nature or culture necessarily developed. Darwin's natural selection, rechristened "survival of the fittest" by Spencer, implied that blind chance ruled the development of species, including the human species. While Spencer might celebrate the evolution of human beings as a story of increasing rationalization and specialization, others highlighted the implication that human reason was no more than a tool for survival, and that humans were not so easily distinguished from other animals as the eighteenth-century proponents of the Enlightenment had assumed. The theorists whom historians have labeled "social Darwinists" generally emphasized pessimistic inferences from Darwin's theory: they viewed nations, races, and classes as competing, like species, for limited resources. They sometimes sought to improve their own side's chances through programs encouraging the breeding of the "fittest" and even the sterilization of those deemed unfit. Such programs drew on the widespread fear that evolution might lead not only to progress but also to "degeneration."[34]

The implications of the essential animality of human nature were the shared concern of three more distinguished critics of reason who were to shape twentieth-century thought, Karl Marx, Friedrich Nietzsche, and Sigmund Freud. All three emphasized the idea that humans are primarily biological beings and are not fully aware of all the motives behind their own actions. Ricoeur described these three thinkers as the "masters of suspicion," and as such they established key problems not only for twentieth-century philosophy but also for modernist literature.[35] Marx's formulation of his views preceded Darwin's discoveries, but Marx shared with later Darwinists a materialist conception of history. He emphasized the need for sustenance, which humans share with all other animals. Religion, reason, ideas, beliefs, art – all of consciousness – resulted, in his view, from the need to sustain life in a material sense: the need for food and shelter. In 1845 he wrote, with Friedrich Engels, *The German Ideology*, which remained unpublished until 1932. In it they argued that "Life is not determined by consciousness, but consciousness by life" and that "Consciousness is . . . from the very beginning a social product." In any given period society has a dominant set of values, and "the ideas of the ruling class are in every epoch the ruling ideas": Greek democracy, feudalism, absolute monarchy, modern liberalism. Each develops, according to Marx, not out of pure abstract thought, but in response to the development of the means of production, that is, out of the economic organization by which society fulfills the material needs of its members. Marx interpreted the whole of human history in terms of a class struggle between those who control the means of production and those who do not, beginning with the first division of labor between men and women "in the sexual act," a sort of original sin for Marx. The modern urban proletariat, completely without property, would bring an end to the cycle of class conflict, since the inevitable proletarian revolution would usher in a classless society and abolish private property.

   The 1848 revolutions across Europe seemed at first to promise this long-awaited transformation of history, and it was on the eve of these revolutions that Marx and Engels published their *Communist Manifesto*, urging, "Working men of all countries, unite!" and proclaiming that "The proletarians have nothing to lose but their chains. They have a world to win." When the revolutions failed, however, Marx, like others, became more pessimistic, emphasizing in his account of the 1848 revolution in France that "Men make their own history, but they do not make it just as they please; they do not make it under circumstances chosen by themselves, but under circumstances directly found, given and transmitted from the past. The tradition of all the dead generations weighs like a nightmare on the brain of the living." Marx's strong sense of the weight of tradition shares something with the later modernists, and is distantly echoed in Joyce's *Ulysses*, when Stephen Dedalus declares that "History is a nightmare from which I am trying to awake." Marx's views became increasingly deterministic, and the whole field of consciousness came to be defined as "superstructure," which merely reflected the development of the economic "base." The implications of Marx's views for the arts are complex. He himself favored realism, in his day the most "modern" of literary forms, because it seemed to him to represent the class struggle clearly (Marx was thinking of the realism of Honoré de Balzac, not that of Gustave Flaubert; on realism, see Chapter One). His twentieth-century followers, especially in the Soviet Union, generally maintained this preference for realism, but Western European Marxists of the 1920s and 1930s defended modernism as breaking with bourgeois conventions of representation and allowing the fractured nature of the social totality to be expressed in literary form.[36]

A more direct inspiration to the modernists was Nietzsche, in whose work the crisis of faith and the crisis of reason come together. Nietzsche is perhaps best known today for his proclamation (placed in the mouth of a madman) that "God is dead." Nietzsche did not, however, see the death of God as leading to the triumph of human reason. The ideal of Greek rationality, inherited by the Enlightenment, is expressed in the motto inscribed on the temple to Apollo at Delphi, "know thyself," but Nietzsche criticized this ideal, which he associated both with Plato and with Immanuel Kant:

> What, indeed, does man know of himself! Can he even once perceive himself completely, laid out as if in an illuminated glass case? Does not nature keep much the most from him, even about his body, to spellbind and confine him in a proud, deceptive consciousness, far from the coils of the intestines, the quick current of the blood stream, and the involved tremors of the fibers? '

The biological basis of our behavior seemed, for Nietzsche, to undermine the idea that humans are ultimately rational creatures. Along with reason, Nietzsche criticized the ideal of truth, anticipating Ferdinand de Saussure by calling attention to the conventionality of language: "And moreover what about these conventions of language? Are they really the products of knowledge, of the sense of truth? Do the designations and the things coincide? Is language the adequate expression of all realities?" Nietzsche's critique of language formed part of his broader critique of morality and society, and it prefigured modernist experiments with language. All language, Nietzsche suggested, starts out as metaphor. That is, we use something (a word) to mean something else (a thing). Truth, Nietzsche claimed, is no more than

> [a] mobile army of metaphors, metonyms, and anthropomorphisms – in short, a sum of human relations, which have been enhanced, transposed, and embellished poetically and rhetorically, and which after long use seem firm, canonical, and obligatory to a people: truths are illusions about which one has forgotten that this is what they are; metaphors which are worn out and without sensuous power; coins which have lost their pictures and now matter only as metal, no longer as coins.

Nietzsche celebrated the liar, the one person who might be able to transform the outmoded conventions of language, and by implication, the poet, whom he understood as a sort of elevated liar, capable of reviving the dead metaphors on which what society accepts as truth is based.[37]

Nietzsche was, in a sense, the most radical of Ricoeur's "masters of suspicion." Rather than claim simply that there is a latent truth underlying all appearances, he questioned the very existence of truth and suggested that no "reality" out there precedes all our perceptions of it. Nietzsche's view of the constructed nature of truth came to be labeled "perspectivism," calling attention to the fact that reality looks different when seen from different perspectives, and indeed questioning whether there was any absolute perspective from which reality could be viewed objectively. His views anticipate those of twentieth-century phenomenologists like Husserl and existentialists like Martin Heidegger and Jean-Paul Sartre. The concern with perspectivism inspired many philosophers and social scientists at the turn of the century, including William James and Max Weber, and also crucially influenced the development of modernism, which so often concerned itself with the problem of reconciling, or refusing to reconcile, multiple perspectives on events. More broadly, Nietzsche also contributed to the modernist fascination with myth, through his myth of the *Übermensch*, or superman, and to the critique of conventional morality, which he regarded as the product of the Christian "herd mentality," to be overcome by the superman who sets his own moral standards. Nietzsche celebrated as the "will to power" the instinctual drives – including sexual and aggressive drives – that conventional morality tried to control. To this end, he proposed a "transvaluation of values," a quest for an entirely new ethical system. Many modernists regarded Nietzsche as a prophet of liberation; they emulated his attacks on Christianity, morality, truth, and reason and saw their own literary and artistic work as participating in the transvaluation of values.

Nietzsche, like some other German philosophers of the nineteenth century, including Arthur Schopenhauer and Eduard von Hartmann, emphasized the unconscious motives that contribute to our moral view of the world. The founder of psychoanalysis, Freud, tried to erect a science on the notion of the unconscious. Freudian concepts such as the unconscious, repression, the Oedipus complex, neurosis, infantile sexuality, anal retentiveness, penis envy, parapraxis ("the Freudian slip"), and the talking-cure all had a deep influence on twentieth-century culture, as did Freud's emphasis on generational conflict, a theme which motivated so many writers of modernist manifestos. His own theories about literary creation as an analogue to daydreaming do not in fact tell us much about literature, but his use of literature and myth – especially Sophocles' *Oedipus the King* and Shakespeare's *Hamlet* – influenced later writers by suggesting that literary works contain deep insights into psychological conflicts that remain hidden in everyday life. Freud often used evidence from poets and playwrights because he thought that they had paid a type of attention to unconscious desires, and particularly to conflicting desires, that psychologists, philosophers, and others had not. D. H. Lawrence and Woolf both read Freud, and Woolf's publishing house, the Hogarth Press, published the first English translations of his works. Freud's emphasis on the role that sexual instincts play in unconscious life inspired some forms of modernist primitivism (see Chapter Two), which claimed that it drew on sexual and other impulses normally repressed in civilized society.

Freud also had a great, but indirect, impact on the interpretation of literature, by way of his method of interpreting dreams. He called dreams "the royal road to the unconscious," and claimed that all dreams fulfilled the dreamer's wishes. (One of his favorite examples of wish-fulfillment was a little girl's dream that she was eating strawberries.) According to Freud, apparently anxious or bad dreams fulfill wishes about which the dreamer feels conflicted – for example, the wish that one's father might die. In such cases the unconscious engages in a form of self-censorship, hiding the troublesome wish through the processes of displacement and condensation, which later critics were to compare to the rhetorical devices metonymy and metaphor. In order to reveal the latent "dream content," the psychoanalyst had to decode dreams, reversing the process of dream censorship by which the conscious self hides its unavowed desires from itself. Freud's technique of interpreting dreams, by having patients "free associate," that is, relate their associations with a particular word or image in an uncensored fashion, seemed to offer a glimpse into the processes of the unconscious mind. Forms of free association were taken up by many modernists, notably the surrealists. Even more influentially, however, Freud's insistence that the manifest meaning of a dream needed to be decoded by the psychoanalyst provided a model for the interpretation of literary texts. Perhaps they, too, hid latent meanings, unconsciously placed there by the author. Some authors tried to preempt such interpretation by consciously including in their narratives the unconscious motives of their characters.

Freud's theory appealed to writers in part because of the tremendous emphasis it placed on the power of language. As Freud put it in his *Introductory Lectures on Psychoanalysis* (1916–17), "Words were originally magic and to this day words have retained much of their ancient magical power."[38] Freud thought that words themselves were invested with much of the unconscious desire that runs through each one of us. In Freud's view, our use of language is charged with unconscious meanings. He was particularly interested in mistaken uses of words, riddles, and other examples where language seems to have more than one meaning – the very province of literature. Although Freud was optimistic about the possibility of curing neuroses through psychoanalysis, he was pessimistic about the future of civilization as a whole. For Freud, repression itself was necessary to civilization, because if the members of society always immediately fulfilled their desires, no work would get done. In fact, the greatest work, according to Freud, is often a product of displaced sexual desires, so that civilization in some sense stands in for, replaces, sexual drives, at the same time as it competes with them. As a result, however, civilization exacts a considerable psychic toll on individuals. At the end of his life, Freud thought that he saw in the rise of Nazism a "return of the repressed," and a reversion to barbarism.

The masters of suspicion taught the twentieth century to look for hidden meanings behind the apparent surface of a text, especially a literary text; the great scientific revolution of the early twentieth century taught people to be suspicious of the appearances of the physical world. Albert Einstein introduced his special theory of relativity in 1905 and his general theory in 1916. Experiments conducted in the years just before and after the First World War demonstrated the truth of Einstein's theories. If Marx, Nietzsche, and Freud challenged Kant's sovereign human reason, Einstein challenged the distinction between two categories through which Kant thought that we necessarily perceive the world: time and space. Kant lived in a Newtonian universe in which time and space were absolute and could be measured in the same way for everyone, with space plotted out on three-dimensional coordinates known as Cartesian (because they had been invented by that other great Enlightenment philosopher, Descartes). In Newtonian science time and space are qualitatively distinct systems of measurement, and for Kant they were the two organizing principles of all perception.

Einstein's discoveries warped the Newtonian notions of time and space. Einstein showed that when objects move at speeds approaching that of light, they appear to have their own system of time quite different from that of another object that is at rest. As Einstein explained, "every reference body has its own particular time," and we should imagine that the various gravitational fields of the universe consist of "as many clocks as we like." For the modernists, Einstein's key discovery was that a sequence of events might appear to take place in a different temporal order if viewed from two separate observation points that were moving in different directions or at different speeds. This implied the possibility that two different narrative orderings of the same sequence of events could both be true. Although Einstein's theory may not have directly influenced the many experiments with narrative time in his generation, it gave an air of scientific legitimacy to those experiments. The result was that, while Greenwich Mean Time, the telegraph, and other technological innovations seemed to place the whole world on one measurement of time, theoretical physics revealed that time is in fact different for every system of reference.

Similarly, by showing that space was a phenomenon of measurement, Einstein demonstrated that standardized measures of space were just as dependent on the frame of reference as measurements of time. He summarized his findings thus: "There is an infinite number of spaces, which are in motion with respect to each other." Space, rather than being rectilinear as in the Cartesian and Newtonian system, is curved, and time and space, rather than being qualitatively distinct, belong on the same continuum. As Einstein put it, "It appears therefore more natural to think of physical reality as a four-dimensional existence, instead of, as hitherto, the *evolution* of a three-dimensional existence." Thus time no longer appeared to progress forward in a homogeneous fashion, and the theory of relativity seemed to discredit nineteenth-century notions of progress as well as Enlightenment conceptions of time and space. As the historian Stephen Kern has shown, modernist experiments with organizing time in narrative and space on the canvas exploited the new imaginative possibilities opened up by the demise of the Newtonian system.[39]

The social and intellectual world of the early twentieth century differed immensely from that of fifty years earlier. Democracy, socialism, and communism challenged the established liberal political systems and the dominance of the upper and middle classes. Women challenged their subordinate social status and lack of political rights. The European powers, having rapidly expanded their empires, faced the limits of overseas expansion and the contradictions of liberal ideology made evident by continued domination of the non-Western world. Nineteenth-century ideals, such as individualism and progress, were contradicted by new forms of collective action and a growing pessimism about historical change. Most of all, the supremacy of reason, self-evident to Descartes, Kant, and nineteenth-century liberals such as John Stuart Mill and Spencer, was being questioned, undermined in particular by the recognition of humans' animal nature.

The masters of suspicion preached the death of God and the limitations of human self-understanding. The desire for economic dominance, the will to power, and the preeminence of the sexual instinct all seemed to conflict with the self-assurance of the Enlightenment and of liberalism. Science showed that humans had evolved from apes rather than being created intact by God and that no absolute measure of time or space was possible. Literature and the arts responded, already in the nineteenth century, to the changed place of the human intellect in the universe. The rejection of conventional techniques for representation of the visual world, experiments with free verse, new means of representing consciousness, and challenges to the norms of the theater were partly independent developments, but the practitioners of the new modernism were often also actively engaged in the other social and intellectual transformations of the period. As the playwright August Strindberg put it, "New forms have not been found for the new contents, so that the new wine has burst the old bottles."[40] The new social and intellectual content demanded new literary and artistic forms, and the modernists were ready to supply them.

## Making it new

The poet Ezra Pound expressed the aspirations of modernism in the slogan "Make it New." He wanted his poetry to show new sides of reality to people who had become accustomed to seeing only one side. The Russian literary theorist Viktor Shklovsky, a contemporary of the Russian cubo-futurists, wrote that art's distinctive contribution is defamiliarization. By this he meant that most people see the world through inherited conventions, what Nietzsche had called "metaphors which are worn out and have lost their sensuous power." Shklovsky argued that art makes those conventions come alive again by making them seem new or strange. Like many modernists, he emphasized that this shock effect manifested itself in new forms of art (new techniques or styles) rather than just in new subject matter: "The technique of art is to make objects 'unfamiliar,' to make forms difficult . . . *Art is a way of experiencing the artfulness of an object; the object is not important.*"[41] The playwright Bertolt Brecht, possibly influenced by Shklovsky, sought an estrangement or alienation effect ("*Verfremdungseffekt*") that would shock audiences out of their complacency and make them more critical of capitalism.[42] His theater departed radically from the nineteenth-century tradition, which emphasized sympathetic identification between the audience and the actors. If modernists were aware of the novelty of their age and its demand for new art forms, however, they were equally conscious of the weight and significance of tradition. Pound noted that the slogan "Make it New," which he first offered as advice to translators of poetry, was itself a translation of a phrase that, according to the ancient Chinese philosopher Confucius, was inscribed on the bathtub of an old king. The desire for the new is a very old one. This attempt to make it new entailed a rethinking of literary and artistic tradition and resulted in works that seemed particularly difficult to their first readers and viewers – and that remain difficult even a century later. To some, modernism seemed merely obscene. After briefly surveying these controversies, this chapter concludes with an evaluation of three major categories of human experience that were reimagined in modernist literature and art: gender, space, and time.

Modernist experiments seldom simply destroyed or rejected traditional methods of representation or traditional literary forms. Rather, the modernists sought to enter into a sort of conversation with the art of the past, sometimes reverently, sometimes mockingly. The poet and critic T. S. Eliot expressed a typically ambivalent view of the past when he wrote in his essay "Tradition and the Individual Talent" (1919):

> No poet, no artist of any art, has his complete meaning alone. His sig-
> nificance, his appreciation is the appreciation of his relation to the dead
> poets and artists. . . . The existing monuments [of art] form an ideal order
> among themselves, which is modified by the introduction of the new (the
> really new) work of art among them. The existing order is complete before
> the new work arrives; for order to persist after the supervention of nov-
> elty, the whole existing order must be, if ever so slightly, altered . . . the
> past [is] altered by the present as much as the present is directed by the
> past.[43]

Eliot emphasizes both the way that tradition shapes the modern artist and the way that a "really new" work of art makes us see that tradition anew. Much less reverent than Eliot, the dadaists were equally aware of the importance of art as tradition. In the same year that Eliot wrote "Tradition and the Individual Talent," the dadaist Marcel Duchamp exhibited one of his "assisted ready-mades," which consisted of a reproduction of Leonardo da Vinci's *Mona Lisa*, on which Duchamp drew a moustache and scrawled five letters that alluded to a French obscenity: "L. H. O. O. Q." (Duchamp's polite translation of the phrase was "There is fire down below.") This act seems to mock one of the most famous of Renaissance masterpieces, but Duchamp's own artistic product (the "assisted ready-made") has an artistic meaning of its own only because we as viewers recognize the status of Leonardo's painting as an icon of high art.

Because modern art and literature were so new and sometimes so shocking in their techniques and subject matter, they frequently faced opposition both from audiences and from political authorities. A major reason for the hostility of many critics and much of the public to modernism was the fact that modern literature and art were often difficult to understand. This difficulty resulted from the attempt to reconfigure language and art in ways that would challenge existing assumptions. Eliot argued that modern poetry had to be difficult in order to respond adequately to the complexity of the modern world:

> We can only say that it appears likely that poets in our civilization, as
> it exists at present, must be *difficult*. Our civilization comprehends great
> variety and complexity, and this variety and complexity, playing upon a
> refined sensibility, must produce various and complex results. The poet
> must become more and more comprehensive, more allusive, more indi-
> rect, in order to force, to dislocate if necessary, language to his meaning.[44]

Eliot's notion of "dislocating" language emphasizes that the work of the modern writer entails transforming language, the basic medium of literature, by finding in it possibilities that we overlook in our everyday use of clichés and formulas. The philosopher Theodor Adorno argued that art that is familiar or easy can be too easily consumed. Great art, on the other hand, shows how reality itself is full of complexity and contradictions. Adorno wrote that the essence of great works of art "consists in giving form to the crucial contradictions in real existence."[45] Great art, thinkers like Eliot and Adorno claimed, makes us uncomfortable.

For both Eliot and Adorno, the formal difficulty of modern art relates closely to the other aspect of the crisis of representation: the problem of content. Apart from that small number who actively pursued a totally nonrepresentational literature, the modernists for the most part sought new means of representation. Their methods helped them to account for the historically new types of experience surveyed in this chapter: modern technology and mass culture; a new scale of warfare; changing gender roles and attitudes to sexuality; the questioning of empire. This new content found its way into poems, plays, and novels that abandoned many of the earlier conventions of literary representation, in particular conventions about heroism. The modernists wrote about new types of hero and heroine: the ragpicker, the advertising canvasser, the middle-aged woman, the adulteress. Such figures were often "antiheroes," who might be the object of their authors' irony or even disdain but who also seemed to embody what Baudelaire called the "heroism of modern life."[46] Such heroism, like that of the soldiers in the trenches of the First World War, often had as much to do with passive suffering of the changing circumstances of history as with transcendent bravery or accomplishment. This absence of conventional heroes contributed to the feeling that modernist literature was difficult.

The most evident transformation of literature and the arts in the period, however, and the one that brought about the most direct conflict, was the modernists' attention to previously taboo subject matters, such as masturbation, sodomy and other sexual acts, homosexuality, menstruation, and digestion. The modernists often encountered censorship, and it is sometimes difficult to say whether this censorship resulted from the content of modernist representations or from their form and especially their apparent moral ambiguity (see Chapter One). Modern writers frequently present works in which conventional morality is challenged, often without specifically telling readers whether or not they should approve of the behavior of the characters in the books. However, much of the motive for censorship can be traced simply to the taboo subject matter of portions of these authors' works: adultery (described somewhat sympathetically in Gustave Flaubert's *Madame Bovary* [1856]), defecation and masturbation (James Joyce's *Ulysses* [1922]), lesbianism (Radclyffe Hall's *The*

*Well of Loneliness* [1928]), explicit sexuality (D. H. Lawrence's *Lady Chatter-ley's Lover* [1928]), pedophilia (Vladimir Nabokov's *Lolita* [1955]), and male homosexuality (James Baldwin's *Giovanni's Room* [1956]). Those artists who broke the conventions of traditional art were often also interested in breaking the conventions of traditional morality.

One source for the changing standards of representation was the broad mass culture, ushered in by new technologies like the phonograph and the cinema, to which modernists reacted in a variety of ways. Some historians of modernism have emphasized the "elitist" character of modernist experimentation, which was often understood or appreciated only by a small coterie, and have seen in this alleged elitism an attempt to escape from the modern world of mass culture. However, many modernists not only appreciated the new forms of culture but also incorporated them into their own art works, as Joyce did in his frequent borrowings from advertising, popular music, and "women's" maga-zines. It is partly in retrospect that modernism has come to be seen primarily in opposition to this mass culture, on which it drew far more extensively than any earlier literary movement had done. In fact, mass culture arguably served as an inspiration for the modernists in something like the way that folk ballads and popular culture had for the romantics. At the same time, mass culture was often understood as specifically associated with women, in their role as con-sumers of fashion, and some modernist ambivalence toward mass culture is entangled with anxieties about changing gender roles.[47] Nonetheless, because of the difficulty of their works and the effects of censorship, the modernists did not immediately reach as broad an audience as their predecessors. In the United States, where thousands of fans of Charles Dickens's *The Old Curiosity Shop* (1840–1) had stood in line at the New York docks to learn the fate of Little Nell in the next edition of *Household Words*, shipments of the first edition of Joyce's *Ulysses* were met only by Post Office censors, who burned them.

Modernist experiments in the area of gender reflect a wholesale revision of relations between the sexes in the early twentieth century. The accounts of the suffrage movement and psychoanalysis above have outlined the changes in these fields during the modernist period. In addition to the central shared goal of women's right to vote, feminists began to explore a number of concerns that still shape feminist thought. Virginia Woolf's feminist writing can be taken as representative. Woolf wrote extensively on the problem of women's access to the learned professions, such as academia, the church, the law, and medicine, a problem that was exacerbated by women's exclusion from the Universities of Oxford and Cambridge. Woolf herself never went to university, and she resented the fact that her brothers had had an opportunity that was denied to her. Even in the realm of literature, Woolf found, women in literary families like her own were expected to write memoirs of their fathers or to edit their correspondence. Woolf did in fact write a memoir of her father, Leslie Stephen, after his death, but she later wrote that if he had not died when she was relatively young (twenty-two), she never would have become a writer. Woolf also concerned herself with the question of women's equality with men in marriage, and she brilliantly evoked the inequality of her parents' marriage in her novel *To the Lighthouse* (1927). Woolf's mother was always eager to fulfill the Victorian ideal that Woolf later described, in a figure borrowed from a pious Victorian poem, as that of the "Angel in the House." Woolf spoke of her partly successful attempts to kill off the "Angel in the House," and to describe the possibilities for emancipated women independently of her mother's sense of the proprieties.

Related to the unequal status of marriage was the sexual double standard which treated lack of chastity in a woman as a serious social offense whereas in men it attracted far less censure. Woolf herself was almost certainly the victim of some kind of sexual abuse at the hands of one of her half-brothers, and she had a difficult sex life. More broadly, she was highly conscious of the ways that men had access to and knowledge of sex, whereas women of the middle and upper classes were expected to remain ignorant of it. She often puzzled over the possibility of a literature that would treat sexuality, and especially the sexual life of women, frankly, but her own works discuss sex rather indirectly. One of her lighter but particularly enjoyable novels, *Orlando* (1928), is about a man who becomes a woman (and lives for more than three hundred years), thus updating the myth of Tiresias, the man who became a woman. Tiresias was a central figure in modernist attempts to explore sexual identity, playing a notable role in Eliot's *The Waste Land* (1922), Pound's *Cantos* (1919–70), and the first surrealist play, Guillaume Apollinaire's *The Breasts of Tiresias* (1917).

If much of Woolf's feminist writing concerns the problem of equality of access to goods that have traditionally been monopolized by men, her literary criticism prefigures two other concerns of later feminism: the reclaiming of a female tradition of writing and the deconstruction of gender difference. In *A Room of One's Own* (1929), Woolf imagines the fate of Shakespeare's equally brilliant sister Judith (in fact, his sister's name was Joan). Unable to gain access to the all-male stage of Elizabethan England, or to obtain any formal education, Judith would have been forced to marry and abandon her literary gifts or, if she had chosen to run away from home, would have been driven to prostitution. Woolf traces the rise of women writers, emphasizing in particular Jane Austen, the Brontës, and George Eliot, but alluding, too, to Sappho, one of the first lyric poets. Faced with the question of whether women's writing is specifically feminine, she concludes that the great female authors "wrote as women write, not as men write." She thus raises the possibility of a specifically feminine style, but at the same time she emphasizes (citing the authority of Samuel Taylor Coleridge) that the greatest writers, among whom she includes Shakespeare, Austen, and Marcel Proust, are androgynous, able to see the world equally from a man's and a woman's perspective.

Sex and gender profoundly affect all human relations; space and time organize all of human perception. In the modernist period these two organizing systems were reconceived as perceptual constructs, dependent on the perceptions of the observer.[48] Albert Einstein's theory of relativity reshaped scientific conceptions of space and time, but independent developments in the arts suggest that Einstein's theory formed part of a broad cultural shift. Impressionists and post-impressionists, departing from the Renaissance system of perspective, saw the visual field as constructed by the mind from planes of color experienced by the eye. The most influential of the post-impressionists, Paul Cézanne, believed that all painting should be organized according to three shapes underlying the visible world: the cylinder, the sphere, and the cone. The cubists Pablo Picasso and Georges Braque divided the canvas into innumerable tiny planes, representing the various facets of an object perceived in space, but thereby calling attention to the representation of these planes on the canvas and away from the represented object. The role of perspective in our perception of the world is most apparent in the visual arts. In literature, too, novelists began to present a much wider range of perspectives on the events they narrated, while poets often seemed to present only cubist facets of experience. Both types of experiment deprived the reader of the familiar convention of an omniscient narrator or unified speaker who makes it easy for the reader to share the writer's vision.

The reorganization of space was undertaken primarily in the visual arts. Its counterpart, the transformation of time, was central to modernist narrative (see Chapter Five). Novelists departed from strict chronology, made extensive use of flashbacks and foreshadowing, and explored the disjuncture between private and public time. Joseph Conrad's *The Secret Agent* (1907) imagines an anarchist plot to blow up Greenwich Observatory, where standard time was measured, as a symbol of a more general attack on publicly shared standards. In Conrad's novel time itself is out of joint; after relating the explosion, the narrative flashes back without warning to an earlier timeframe, leaving the reader uncertain of the sequence of crucial events. Modernist awareness of the passage of time was inspired perhaps as much by the philosophy of Henri Bergson as by the newly propounded theory of relativity. A critic, like Edmund Husserl and Friedrich Nietzsche, of Cartesian dualism, Bergson sought access to the flux of immediate experience, prior to the imposition of human concepts on that experience. He believed that concepts artificially separated time into discrete units when in fact it should be experienced as a continuous duration (*durée*).[49]

Both Bergson and Einstein, with their emphasis on the subjective experience or measurement of time, probably reinforced the perceptions of individual artists at a more human level. Time seemed to move more quickly in the industrialized world of the twentieth century, and the rapid succession of world-changing historical events in the early decades of the century strengthened this sense of acceleration. Two famous modernist images emphasize the resulting fear that the individual human being had lost control of time. At the end of *The Great Gatsby* (1925), F. Scott Fitzgerald writes,

> Gatsby believed in the green light, the orgastic future that year by year recedes before us. It eluded us then, but that's no matter – tomorrow we will run faster, stretch out our arms further . . . And one fine morning – So we beat on, boats against the current, borne back ceaselessly into the past.

Here, the continual striving for a bright future of total happiness, typical of modern American life, is forever undercut by the force of tradition or history, represented here by the current, which continually turns our forward-looking present into an unalterable past. In a striking image the German-Jewish literary critic Walter Benjamin wrote, in his "Theses on the Philosophy of History" (1940), of Paul Klee's painting *Angelus Novus* (1920), interpreting its central figure as the angel of history, whose "face is turned toward the past":

> Where we perceive a chain of events, he sees one single catastrophe which keeps piling wreckage upon wreckage and hurls it in front of his feet. The angel would like to stay, awaken the dead, and make whole what has been smashed. But a storm is blowing from Paradise; it has got caught in his wings with such violence that the angel can no longer close them. This storm irresistibly propels him into the future to which his back is turned, while the pile of debris before him grows skyward. This storm is what we call progress.[50]

In Benjamin's interpretation of the painting, the angel is looking at us, the human beings who move through time. Just as Fitzgerald's modern Americans in their boats are ceaselessly borne into the past, Benjamin's angel of history is irresistibly propelled into the future. History would be the attempt to make sense of the continual passage of time, but history is defeated by the same force that makes it impossible to fulfill all our dreams of an orgastic future. Time, progress, history – all are forces that constantly transform our lives and that we cannot halt or even adequately represent. When we reach toward the future, we find ourselves already living in the past. When we turn back to try to make sense of the past, we are blown into the future. The modernist crisis of representation responded to this sense of a world moving too fast to be comprehended by traditional techniques. The history of modernist literature and art is the history of a century of crisis, from the revolutions of 1848 to the Second World War.

## Further reading

### General

Malcolm Bradbury and James McFarlane, eds. *Modernism: A Guide to European Literature, 1890–1930.* London: Penguin, 1976.
Vassiliki Kolocotroni, Jane Goldman, and Olga Taxidoe, eds. *Modernism: An Anthology of Sources and Documents.* Edinburgh: Edinburgh University Press, 1998.
Michael Levenson, ed., *The Cambridge Companion to Modernism.* Cambridge: Cambridge University Press, 1999.
Peter Nicholls, *Modernisms: A Literary Guide.* Berkeley and Los Angeles: University of California Press, 1995.

### Surveys of modern art

H. H. Arnason and Peter Kalb, *History of Modern Art*, 5th edn. Englewood Cliffs, NJ: Prentice-Hall, 2003.
Hershel B. Chipp, ed. *Theories of Modern Art: A Source Book by Artists and Critics.* Berkeley and Los Angeles: University of California Press, 1984.
Penelope J. E. Davies *et al.*, *Janson's History of Art: Western Tradition*, 7th edn. Englewood Cliffs, NJ: Prentice-Hall, 2006.
Robert Hughes, *The Shock of the New*, rev. edn. New York: Knopf, 1991.
Norbert Lynton, *The Story of Modern Art*, 2nd edn. London: Phaidon, 1989.

### Historical surveys

J. W. Burrow, *The Crisis of Reason: European Thought, 1848–1914.* New Haven: Yale University Press, 2000.
J. W. Burrow, *Evolution and Society: A Study in Victorian Social Theory.* Cambridge: Cambridge University Press, 1966.
E. J. Hobsbawm, *The Age of Revolution, 1789–1848.* New York: New American Library, 1962.
E. J. Hobsbawm, *The Age of Capital, 1848–1875.* New York: Scribner, 1975.

E. J. Hobsbawm, *The Age of Empire, 1875–1914*. New York: Vintage Books, 1989.
E. J. Hobsbawm, *The Age of Extremes: A History of the World, 1914–1991*. New York: Vintage Books, 1994.
Stephen Kern, *The Culture of Time and Space, 1880–1918*. Cambridge, MA: Harvard University Press, 1983.

## Philosophical and scientific works

Charles Darwin, *The Darwin Reader*, ed. Mark Ridley. New York: Norton, 1987.
Albert Einstein, *Relativity: The Special and the General Theory*, trans. Robert W. Lawson. London: Routledge, 2001.
Sigmund Freud, *The Freud Reader*, ed. Peter Gay. New York: Norton, 1995.
Karl Marx and Friedrich Engels, *The Marx-Engels Reader*, ed. Robert C. Tucker, 2nd edn. New York: Norton, 1978.
Friedrich Nietzsche, *The Portable Nietzsche*, ed. and trans. Walter Kaufmann. New York: Penguin, 1982.

# Part I

## *Origins*

*Chapter 1*

# Trials of modernity

In January 1857 French prosecutor Ernest Pinard accused Gustave Flaubert of an "offense to public and religious morality and to good morals" for publishing *Madame Bovary* (1856), the story of a bored housewife who has two extramarital affairs but finds adultery almost as disappointing as marriage.[1] Pinard failed to win a conviction, but the court reprimanded Flaubert for forgetting that art "must be chaste and pure not only in its form but in its expression."[2] In August of the same year, Pinard had greater success in prosecuting Charles Baudelaire for *The Flowers of Evil* (*Les Fleurs du Mal*) (1857). The court banned six of Baudelaire's erotic poems, two of them on lesbian themes and the other four heterosexual but mildly sadomasochistic. The ban was not officially lifted until 1949, by which time Baudelaire and Flaubert had achieved "classic" status as among the most important influences on modern literature in France and throughout Europe. The trials of the two writers mark a new form of tension between the arts and the established social order that helped to define the oppositional spirit of modernism. Like the later modernists, Baudelaire and Flaubert believed that the standards of the artist might conflict with those of society, and that beauty, truth, and justice might sometimes conflict with one another.

The two were among the first authors to register the crisis of representation that would lead to the development of literary modernism in the twentieth century. Their trials bespoke the broader trials, such as industrial revolution, changing attitudes to sex, and social transformation, through which French society was passing in the process of modernization. When a society passes judgment on artists and their works, it determines what can and cannot be said or represented. While such trials may have a chilling effect on the works of other artists who fear prosecution, they may also make the accused artists famous and help them to win a public or artistic following. The trials of 1857 established Baudelaire and Flaubert as leaders of the "realist" movement, the most modern form of literature in the middle of the nineteenth century. These proceedings offer a starting point for a history of modernism because they raise the problem of official and public incomprehension in the face of new literary techniques. The authors, while accused of "realism," went on to shape two other major currents in nineteenth-century French literature – naturalism and symbolism – both of which contributed to the development of English literary modernism. This chapter will explore the legacies of Baudelaire and Flaubert for six movements in the late nineteenth-century arts, which together demonstrate the variety of possible responses to the crisis of representation (see table 1.1). These movements would interact after the turn of the century in a distinctively modernist literature.

The two emblematic trials took place in Paris during the Second Empire, the reign of Napoleon III. After a brief experiment with republican government after the revolution of 1848, Napoleon III (nephew of the first Napoleon) had established himself as emperor in a *coup d'état*, later confirmed by popular plebiscite. Baudelaire and Flaubert, both twenty-seven in 1848, had been sympathetic observers of the revolution and had hoped for a more liberal form of government, including popular representation and freedom of assembly and the press. As J. W. Burrow has noted, the revolution involved an element of generational conflict.[3] Baudelaire had taken to the streets, chanting enthusiastically "General Aupick must be killed." Aupick, later a senator under Napoleon III, was Baudelaire's stepfather. Flaubert took a more detached view. In *Sentimental Education* (1869) he brilliantly described the revolution from the point of view of an unsuccessful would-be writer, who misses most of the political action because he is distracted by his pursuit of a love affair with an older, married woman. "Ah, they're killing off a few bourgeois," Frédéric Moreau comments nonchalantly, when he hears troops firing on some of the demonstrators. After Napoleon III reestablished the Empire and defeated the hopes of the 1848 revolutionaries, a mood of disillusionment with politics dominated intellectual and artistic life in the following decades; this was the first stage of the crisis of liberalism (see Introduction). This mood contributed to the alienation between artist and society that had already been implicit in early nineteenth-century romanticism. Baudelaire compared the poet to an albatross, "monarch of the clouds," who flew gracefully through the air of imagination but whose giant wings interfered with his ability to walk and made him "clumsy and full of shame" when brought down to earth by jeering sailors, Baudelaire's figure for an uncomprehending public.[4] Baudelaire and Flaubert felt compelled to resist the conservative, authoritarian culture of the Second Empire, but they resisted

Table 1.1. *Literary movements in the late nineteenth century*

**Realism**

Active from 1840s    Leading figures: Gustave Courbet, Gustave Flaubert    Manifesto: Courbet, "Realist Manifesto" (1855)
A reaction against idealism and romanticism; realism proposed to represent life as it really was, rather than ideal beauty.
"To be capable of depicting the manners, ideas, and appearance of my time as I see it, in short, to produce living art, that is my goal." (Courbet)[a]

**Naturalism**

Active from 1860s    Leading figures: August Strindberg, Emile Zola    Manifesto: Zola, *The Experimental Novel* (1880)
An extension of realism; naturalism intended to incorporate scientific principles, especially determinism.
"The novelist is but a recorder who is forbidden to judge and to conclude." (Zola)[b]

**Impressionism**

Active from 1870s    Leading figures: Claude Monet, Camille Pissarro    Manifesto: Jules Laforgue, "Impressionism" (1883)
Inspired in part by realism; impressionism sought to convey the impression of reality at a given moment, free from academic restrictions.
The impressionists rejected "the three supreme illusions by which technicians of painting have always lived – line, perspective, studio lighting." (Laforgue)[c]

**Decadence**

Active from 1880s    Leading figure: Joris-Karl Huysmans    Manifesto: Huysmans, *Against Nature* (1884)
A reaction against naturalism; decadence celebrated aesthetic experience and predicted the decline of Western civilization.
"To fix the last fine shade, the quintessence of things; to fix it fleetingly; to be disembodied voice, and yet the voice of a human soul: that is the ideal of Decadence." (Arthur Symons)[d]

(*cont.*)

Table 1.1. (Cont.)

## Symbolism

Active from 1880s    Leading figures: Stéphane Mallarmé, Arthur Rimbaud    Manifesto: Mallarmé, "The Crisis in Poetry" (1886)

A reaction against naturalism, closely allied to decadence; symbolism fragmented syntax and logic in the attempt to capture elusive, private meanings.

"To *name* the object is to destroy three quarters of the enjoyment of the poem, which comes from guessing at it bit by bit: to *suggest* the object, that is the dream. It is the perfect practice of this mystery which constitutes the symbol." (Mallarmé)[e]

## Aestheticism

Active from 1870s    Leading figures: Walter Pater, Oscar Wilde                Manifesto: Pater, *The Renaissance* (1873)

English movement celebrating art for art's sake. Corresponds roughly to French symbolism and decadence.

"For art comes to you proposing frankly to give nothing but the highest quality to your moments as they pass, and simply for those moments' sake." (Pater)[f]

[a] Gustave Courbet, "Realist Manifesto," in *Modernism Anthology*, p. 169.

[b] Emile Zola, "Naturalism on the Stage," in *Modernism Anthology*, p. 172.

[c] Jules Laforgue, "Impressionism," in Linda Nochlin, ed. *Impressionism and Post-Impressionism, 1874–1904: Sources and Documents* (Englewood Cliffs, NJ: Prentice-Hall, 1966), p. 15.

[d] Arthur Symons, "The Decadent Movement in Literature" (*Harper's Magazine*, November 1893).

[e] Stéphane Mallarmé, "Literary Evolution," quoted in Ian Watt, *Conrad in the Nineteenth Century* (Berkeley and Los Angeles: University of California Press, 1979), p. 186.

[f] Walter Pater, Conclusion to *The Renaissance*, in *Modernism Anthology*, p. 114.

it through literary experiment, rather than political action. Later modernist writers, especially those writing in the wake of failed liberal movements, often shared the two men's disillusionment with politics. Even under the empire, however, and with brief exceptions such as the prosecutions led by Pinard, France maintained a relatively liberal intellectual culture which permitted the expression of hostility to the ruling order and discussion of themes like adultery that would be prohibited elsewhere. This is one reason why the early movements that would inspire modernism took root first in France.

## Flaubert, realism, and naturalism

Charles Baudelaire and Gustave Flaubert shared an aesthetic sensibility in so far as both were interested in the banal, the ugly, the evil, and the stupid – everything detestable in modern life. Both *The Flowers of Evil* (1857) and *Madame Bovary* (1856) display the artist's disdain for bourgeois mores and for cliché. In a phrase quoted repeatedly at his trial, Flaubert refers to the "defilements of marriage and the disillusions of adultery," thus reversing the cliché that marriage may disappoint but only adultery can defile. In chastising Flaubert, the court noted that his work tended toward "a realism that would be the negation of the beautiful and the good."[5] By realism the judges seem to have meant an undue interest in those aspects of human behavior not discussed in polite society. Realism rejected the idealizing tendency of earlier classicism, which had sought to represent only the beautiful and the good. Like many other terms in the history of modern literature, "realism" was originally an insult. Also like later terms, it referred to the visual arts before it referred to literature. The term had been applied to the work of Gustave Courbet, a friend of Baudelaire, who was known for his left-wing politics and for his paintings of the everyday life of peasants and the middle classes, but whose legacy for modern painting had more to do with the rough paint textures of his canvases, which inspired the impressionists, than with his political program.

Realism subsequently became the name for a literary style that presents a wide range of social phenomena from an apparently objective point of view (the perspective of the "omniscient narrator," though in fact not all narrators in realist novels are strictly omniscient). In this broad sense, the major novelists of the last half of the nineteenth century, such as Fyodor Dostoevsky, George Eliot, Henry James, and Leo Tolstoy were all realists. The term was also applied retrospectively to novelists such as Honoré de Balzac and Charles Dickens. Modernism in the novel is often seen as a rebellion against realism because the modernists frequently reject such conventions as the omniscient narrator.

However, the development of realism in the late nineteenth century in fact paved the way for such modernist techniques as the "stream of consciousness." Realism tended over the course of the century to become increasingly psychological, concerned with the accurate representation of thoughts and emotions rather than of external things. Flaubert played an important role in this development.

Flaubert attempted to cure the banality of modern "received ideas" through the dispassionate and precise use of language. He wrote that "The artist in his work should be like God in the universe, present everywhere and visible nowhere."[6] His idea of the godlike artist did not involve meting out punishments or pronouncing moral judgments. Rather, his narrators were generally unobtrusive. His use of what literary critics call "free indirect discourse" (in French, "*style indirect libre*," "free indirect style") tended if anything to undermine the idea of the objective narrator, by making it difficult to distinguish between the perspective of the narrator and that of the character. The method transformed realism and even became an issue in the trial. In direct discourse the narrator quotes a character: "Madame Bovary said, 'I have a lover! a lover!'" In indirect discourse the narrator paraphrases a character's statement or thought: "Madame Bovary said that she had a lover." In free indirect discourse, however, the narrator paraphrases the thoughts of a character, sometimes at great length, without marking them off with a phrase like "Madame Bovary thought that . . ." In a well-known example, Emma Bovary looks forward to life as an adulteress while regarding herself in a mirror: "She repeated, 'I have a lover! a lover!' delighting at the idea as if a second puberty had come to her. So at last she was to know those joys of love, that fever of happiness of which she had despaired! She was entering upon a marvelous world where all would be passion, ecstasy, delirium." The last two quoted sentences appear in free indirect discourse. Flaubert seems to be summarizing Madame Bovary's thoughts, in her own language, but he does not explicitly state that these are her thoughts, rather than his own opinions as author or narrator. Indeed, the prosecutor Pinard quoted these two sentences at Flaubert's trial as if to suggest that they represented the view of adultery promoted by the novel.[7]

Although free indirect discourse belongs to the traditional methods of the novel, and was used extensively by Jane Austen, Flaubert's use of the technique took full advantage of its potential to create irony and ambiguity and thus prefigured such modern experiments as the stream of consciousness. What was remarkable about Flaubert's use of the style was that virtually every value judgment in the novel, indeed every descriptive statement, seemed to be made from the point of view of one of his characters. The impersonality of the author, for Flaubert, meant showing Emma Bovary's reality as it appeared to her and the other characters in the novel, rather than telling the reader what view of her situation was correct. The prosecutor Pinard even seems to have touched on the nature of free indirect discourse when he asked, "Who can condemn this woman in the book? Nobody. Such is the conclusion. There is not in the book a character who can condemn her . . . Would you condemn her in the name of the author's conscience? I do not know what the author's conscience thinks." Flaubert's refusal to render an explicit moral judgment on Emma Bovary challenged the prevailing conception of an author's duty. Pinard complained that "Art without rules is no longer art; it is like a woman who takes off all her clothes."[8] Flaubert's manipulation of the rules of art to create moral ambiguity and irony seems to have offended Pinard and the court more than the simple fact that he wrote a novel about an adulteress. This aspect of Flaubert's achievement appealed strongly to the modernists, who were to make ambiguity and irony central to their literary work.

The ideals of impersonality and objectivity also inspired naturalists like Emile Zola, who tended, however, to avoid Flaubertian ambiguity. Zola, a younger friend of Flaubert, believed that the artist could discover the laws governing society in something like the way the scientist discovers physical laws. Inspired by Darwinism, Zola was particularly concerned with deterministic accounts of human behavior and laws governing heredity, and wrote a series of novels, beginning with *Thérèse Raquin* (1867), about a family, the Rougon-Macquarts, afflicted with hereditary criminality. He also turned *Thérèse Raquin* into a play (1873), one of the first examples of dramatic naturalism. The naturalists formed the leading new movement in the novel and the theater toward the end of the nineteenth century. Naturalists often had left-wing political convictions, sympathized with socialism, and campaigned for reforms to antiquated laws. Like Flaubert, they challenged traditional assumptions about the family and gender roles. The German Theodor Fontane and the American Theodore Dreiser explored the implications of the double standard that made adultery a social crime for women but a pardonable offense for men. English divorce law, for example, allowed a man to divorce his wife for adultery, while a woman could divorce her husband only if his adultery was aggravated by such offenses as abuse, cruelty, desertion, or sodomy. Not all naturalists were feminist, however; the Swedish playwright August Strindberg used naturalist drama to show men's lives being destroyed by liberated women.[9]

The Norwegian playwright Henrik Ibsen, the most influential dramatist of the nineteenth century, explored the question of the status of women in the plays of his realist phase, sometimes also called naturalist, though Ibsen did not subscribe to all the tenets of naturalism. When produced in London in 1889, Ibsen's *A Doll's House* (1879) led to a debate about sexual roles and the theater. The play begins as melodrama, the popular dramatic form in which an innocent woman was often beset by a seducer or blackmailer. The unworldly wife Nora, constantly belittled by her husband Torvald Helmer as his "starling" and "squirrel," has forged her father's signature without realizing the significance of her crime. An unscrupulous banker blackmails her, but, after revealing the forgery to Torvald, the blackmailer undergoes a change of heart and releases her from her debt to him. Torvald is relieved to think that he can have his wife back, but Nora refuses to allow a conventional happy ending. At this point, melodrama gives way to naturalism. "Sit down, Torvald," Nora says, "we have a lot to talk over." Their debate about marriage dominates the final act. Nora complains that she has been a "doll-wife" to Torvald and declares that she will leave him:

> [TORVALD] HELMER: Oh, it's outrageous. So you'll run out like this on your most sacred vows [to your husband and children]? . . .
>
> NORA: I have other duties, equally sacred.
>
> HELMER: That isn't true. What duties are they?
>
> NORA: Duties to myself.
>
> HELMER: Before all else, you're a wife and a mother.
>
> NORA: I don't believe in that anymore. I believe that, before all else, I'm a human being. . . .

Nora abandons her husband and children. In order to have the play acted in Germany, Ibsen was forced to write an alternative ending in which Nora decides to stay with her family. He called the revised ending "a barbaric outrage" and later refused to have it performed.[10]

The controversy surrounding *A Doll's House* in England spawned a number of imitators, such as Henry Arthur Jones and Sir Arthur Wing Pinero, who wrote "problem plays" about marriage.[11] Most of these plays ended, however, like the German version of *A Doll's House*, with the wife submitting to her husband. The conservatism of the English stage resulted in part from the heavy hand of the Lord Chamberlain, the official censor of plays, who prevented the serious discussion of many controversial subjects, including religion, politics, and sex. Ibsen's *Ghosts* (1881), which portrays the incestuous longings of the son of a syphilitic philanderer for his illegitimate half-sister, was not licensed for public performance in England until 1914.[12] The Irish-born playwright and critic George Bernard Shaw, Ibsen's prime defender in England and a leader of the socialist Fabian Society, fought an ongoing battle with the Lord Chamberlain. Shaw wrote frankly and satirically on political and social topics such as class, war, feminism, and the Salvation Army, in plays such as *Arms and the Man* (1894), *Major Barbara* (1905), and *Pygmalion* (1913). His work introduced the theater of ideas to the English stage; where Ibsen turned melo-drama into naturalism, Shaw parodied melodrama in order to develop an intellectual comedy of manners. He became the leading playwright of modern Britain and won the Nobel Prize for Literature in 1925.

Scholars debate whether naturalism was the first modernist movement or the last movement before modernism. Many twentieth-century modernists thought of themselves as rebelling against the conventions of nineteenth-century naturalism, but the naturalists' interest in describing the objective world in detail, and their willingness to break taboos about subject matter, con-tributed importantly to the development of modernism. As reactions against melodrama, the realism and naturalism of Ibsen and Strindberg were particu-larly important to modern drama. Thus both realism and naturalism, claiming descent from Flaubert, helped to inspire modernist experiments. The antipathy of governmental authorities to naturalism resulted frequently from the explic-itly political concerns of the great naturalists. Zola was famous for his novels, which often described the lives of the lower classes or those without a social class (prostitutes, criminals, drunkards), but he became a hero to the left for his essay "J'accuse," in which he championed the cause of Alfred Dreyfus, a Jewish captain in the French army who had been falsely convicted of treason. French society had been sharply split between the conservative supporters of the army and liberals and radicals who believed in Dreyfus's innocence. In 1898, in a trial quite different from those of Baudelaire and Flaubert, Zola was convicted of libel for having accused the French authorities of a miscarriage of justice in the Dreyfus affair. Zola was exiled to London for a year, but Dreyfus's case was reopened and he was eventually exonerated. Zola's role in the affair confirmed the image of the artist as truth-speaking, left-wing intellectual, thus solidifying the antipathy between advanced literature and the state evidenced in the earlier trials of Baudelaire and Flaubert.[13]

## Baudelaire, decadence, symbolism, and impressionism

Like Gustave Flaubert, Charles Baudelaire was rebuked by the court for his "realism." The judges held that some of his poems "necessarily lead to the excitement of the senses by a crude realism offensive to public decency."[14] The poet had already distanced himself from Gustave Courbet's visual realism, and the court was using the term in a very general sense, but Baudelaire's fascination with the detritus of urban life did chime with realist concerns. His most infamous love poem, "A Carrion," describes in detail the rotting corpse of an animal, with its "legs flexed in the air like a courtesan." The poet reminds his beloved that after her death, "even you will come to this foul shame, / This ultimate infection," thus making disgustingly literal the traditional poetic theme of the fleetingness of earthly love. Baudelaire translated Edgar Allan Poe's detective stories into French and wrote several poems about Paris ("seething city, city full of dreams"), peopled with figures like the "red-haired beggar girl," the "hideous Jewess," the "consumptive negress," and the drunken ragpicker. Yet Baudelaire aimed not at a sociological analysis of the city but at a poetry that could express the new experience of the city-dweller, Poe's "man of the crowd." In his essay on the dandy, the idle man who strolls about town, Baudelaire celebrated the "cult of the ego" and typified the modern urban experience of viewing the world as if through the plate glass of a shop window.[15] The new economic relations that created vast urban areas and a consumer culture thus had a direct impact on the way poets perceived their surroundings. In "To a Passer-by" the poet laments that he will never again see a beautiful woman who has passed by him in the street: "We might have loved, and you knew this might be!" The literary critic Walter Benjamin later observed that, for Baudelaire, "The delight of the city-dweller is not so much love at first sight as love at last sight."[16] This is the city seen not from a God's-eye-view but from the streets, or the gutters.

Baudelaire presented his new subject matter in a defiant poetic idiom. The first poem of *The Flowers of Evil*, "To the Reader," invites the reader to identify with the poet and with the beggars and prostitutes he describes. We all take what clandestine pleasure we can, he writes, "Like an exhausted rake who mouths and chews / The martyrized breast of an old withered whore." If only we had more guts, he suggests, we would all be rapists, murderers, and arsonists. Our evil arises not so much from the enticements of Satan as from the most typical of modern vices, boredom ("l'Ennui"): "[Boredom] in his hookah-dreams, / Produces hangmen and real tears together, / How well you know this fastidious monster, reader, / – Hypocrite reader, you – my double! my brother!" Baudelaire here celebrates the evil lurking inside the average reader, in an attitude far removed from the social concerns typical of realism. T. S. Eliot would later quote the last line, in the original French, in his poem *The Waste Land* (1922), a defining work of English modernism: "You! hypocrite lecteur! – mon semblable, – mon frère!" Despite his earlier sympathy for the revolution, Baudelaire had none of the political ambitions of a naturalist like Emile Zola. Nor did he attempt the detachment typical of Flaubert. Rather, he wallows in evil in order to snatch away the veil of polite manners that turns too much poetry into cliché and high sentiment. This aspect of Baudelaire's work announces a new mood typical of some later nineteenth-century and modernist writing that Baudelaire himself celebrated as "decadence."[17]

Near the end of the century (often referred to by the French term *fin de siècle*), partly in response to the nightmare scenarios of social Darwinism, a number of artists and intellectuals were drawn to the idea that civilizations inevitably decline, and that European civilization would soon go the way of the late Roman Empire. For those who feared this decline, it was understood pathologically, as "degeneration." The physician and writer Max Nordau claimed in *Degeneration* (1895) that modern art and literature were symptoms of a "severe mental epidemic" gripping Europe.[18] Although Nordau and Zola lamented this supposed degeneration, many writers celebrated it as "decadence." The spirit of decadence achieved a brief flowering in the work of Joris-Karl Huysmans, who broke away from Zola's naturalism with his novel *Against Nature* (*À Rebours*, 1884). The novel describes the quest for experience of an effeminate aristocrat, Des Esseintes, the last of his line, who prefers not to leave his room, which he has turned into a museum, complete with a tortoise encrusted in jewels. Having collected all the colors, tastes, and smells of the world so that he can travel without ever going anywhere, he becomes increasingly debilitated and is forced to take his food through an enema. He celebrates this experience as a victory over nature, allowing him to eliminate from his life "the tiresome, vulgar chore of eating." Huysmans himself took an ambivalent attitude toward his protagonist's decadence, but the sickly Des Esseintes became a hero to a generation of minor poets and one major one, Stéphane Mallarmé, who wrote a poem in praise of him. Although it briefly gave its name to a movement, decadence is best understood as a predominant mood near the end of the nineteenth century and a shared theme of competing literary tendencies, such as naturalism and symbolism.

The naturalists traced their lineage back to Flaubert; the symbolists, the main rival literary movement of the period, owed a debt to Baudelaire. In "Correspondences" Baudelaire wrote of nature as containing "forests of symbols" through which man passes, "Where all things watch him with familiar eyes." Realism and naturalism, while fascinated with the objective world, tended to focus on what could be seen or described: the state of medical science in a given era, women's fashions, political events. Symbolism, by contrast, concerned itself with the invisible, and with those hermetic meanings available only to the poet or the skilled reader. For Baudelaire, who was both a late romantic and an early modernist, these meanings were inherent in nature: "All scents and sounds and colors meet as one." For the symbolists, however, these meanings might exist only in the mind of the poet. The symbol crystallizes a meaning not available to rational thought or expressible by prose paraphrase. Poetry, then, must be allusive, opaque, and difficult. The techniques of the French symbolists were decisive in Eliot's later formulation of English modernist poetics. The leading

1. Edouard Manet (1832–1883), *Le Déjeuner sur l'herbe* (*Luncheon on the Grass*), 1863. Oil on canvas, 208 × 264.5 cm. Photo: Hervé Lewandowski.
Photo Credit: Réunion des Musées Nationaux/Art Resource, NY.
Musée d'Orsay, Paris, France.

symbolist, Mallarmé, explained to the painter Edgar Degas, who said that he had plenty of ideas for poems, that "it is hardly with ideas, my dear Degas, that one makes poetry. It is with words."[19] In poems such as *The Afternoon of a Faun* (1876), Mallarmé compressed syntax and incorporated symbols with essentially private meanings, so that two readers of the poem might well disagree about what it meant. The symbolists also sought a mixing of the various senses – synesthesia – modeled on the aesthetic ideas of Baudelaire and of the composer Richard Wagner, theorist of the "*Gesamtkunstwerk*," the total work of art. Mallarmé's *The Afternoon of a Faun*, for example, would later inspire a modern ballet composed by Claude Debussy and danced by Sergei Diaghilev's and Vaslav Nijinsky's Ballets Russes.

Despite the novelty of Baudelaire's poetic concerns, diction, and subject matter, he had generally used the metrical and stanzaic forms typical of French poetry, such as the alexandrine (the twelve-syllable line used by such classical French dramatists as Racine) and the sonnet. In his criticism Mallarmé championed free verse, written with lines other than the alexandrine, and rare rhyme, in which (as in some limericks) the sound of a word is stretched in order to make it rhyme with another. In 1897 he published *A Throw of the Dice* (*Un coup de dés*), which used typography and the spacing of words on the page as elements in the structure of the poem and abandoned regular meter altogether. For most readers, the result verged on the incomprehensible.[20]

An inspiration to the symbolist poets, Baudelaire was also the defender of the early movements in modern painting that inspired the development of impressionism, and especially the work of his friend Edouard Manet. Baudelaire had called, as early as 1845, for a new style of painting that would show "how great and poetic we are in our neckties and patent-leather boots."[21] He tempered his celebration of the fleetingness of modernity with nostalgia for the past. In a poem about a swan trying to drink from a Paris ditch that no longer has any water in it, he wrote, "The old Paris is gone (the face of a town / Is more changeable than the heart of mortal man)." Nonetheless, he sought a modern art that would show what was particular about the time in which it was created, rather than aim at the eternal. For Baudelaire, modern art had to be original. These views seem so natural to the dominant conception of art in the twenty-first century that it is important to recall that Baudelaire was championing modernity against the still pervasive classical view that art should obey established conventions and seek to achieve timelessness.

Around the middle of the nineteenth century, several important painters, notably Manet and the impressionists, broke away from those earlier conventions. In 1863 Manet's painting *Luncheon on the Grass* (*Le Déjeuner sur l'herbe*, 1863; figure 1) was rejected by the salon that displayed painting approved by the official French academy. The rejection was occasioned not so much by the female nudes in Manet's painting, a classical subject, as by their presence in a modern setting, accompanied by clothed bourgeois men. The incongruity suggested that the women were not goddesses but models, or possibly prostitutes. Manet displayed the painting instead at the Salon des Refusés, an alternative salon established by those who had been refused entry to the official one. Like his friend Courbet, Manet influenced modern painting not only by his use of realistic subject matter but also by his challenge to the three-dimensional perspectivalism established in Renaissance painting. Manet painted figures with a flatness derived partly from Japanese art and resembling (as Courbet commented) the flatness of the king or queen on a playing card. The modernist reinvention of pictorial space had begun.

Following Courbet and Manet, the impressionists frequently painted urban scenes, country landscapes, or beach scenes crowded with holiday revelers, rather than historical or religious subjects. They attempted to catch the subjective impressions of reality experienced at a particular moment. Claude Monet said that "One does not paint a landscape, a seascape, a figure. One paints an impression of an hour of the day."[22] Human figures might appear in these paintings simply as small blobs of gray. The impressionists prepared the way for modernism in part through their interest in the ways the eye experiences color. Influenced by the studies of the chemist Eugène Chevreul, they juxtaposed bright, often complementary colors, which the viewer was expected to synthesize. Some of the impressionists were also influenced by early photography; they rejected the clear contours of classical painting in favor of blurred outlines and visible brushstrokes, and they allowed the borders of their canvas to break up the unity of their painted subjects, just as a snapshot does. Their emphasis lay on the experience of seeing the world, rather than on the particular object being seen or painted. This was an early example of the modernist fascination with experience unfiltered by active thought, described in the Introduction as a "phenomenology of vision." The impressionists also prefigured tendencies in modern art in other respects: they aroused the fury of an uncomprehending public and, in response, banded together in a movement. Rejected, like Manet, by the official salons, Paul Cézanne, Degas, Berthe Morisot, Camille Pissarro, Pierre Auguste Renoir, and thirty-three other artists set up their own exhibition in 1874. The name impressionism was given to the whole group by a hostile critic, Louis Leroy, in reference to one of Monet's paintings, *Impression: Sunrise* (1872). Critics responded with derision to the blurriness, bright colors, and everyday subject matters of these radical impressionist paintings, whose reproductions today adorn the walls of college rooms and department stores. Shortly afterwards, the American-born painter James Abbott McNeill Whistler, who had exhibited with Manet at the Salon des Refusés, sued the British art critic John Ruskin for libel. Ruskin had described one of Whistler's exhibitions as "flinging a pot of paint in the public's face." Whistler won his court case but was awarded damages of only a farthing (a few cents). He also won considerable notoriety.[23]

Impressionist experiments emphasized the extent to which the individual viewer mentally constructs the viewed object out of the primary data of colors, light, and darkness. While fidelity to visual experience was one aspect of the impressionists' work, another involved a movement analogous to that of symbolism in poetry, away from the represented world and toward a focus on how the work of art itself orders experience, toward form. Post-impressionist painters began at the end of the nineteenth century to move away from the notion that art had to represent reality at all. As noted in the Introduction, Mallarmé's friend Maurice Denis wrote that a painting is not primarily a representation, but "essentially a flat surface covered with colors assembled in a certain order."[24] The emphasis on the arrangement of the painting, and the possibility of breaking with the traditional illusion of three-dimensional space, pointed the way toward abstract art, just as Mallarmé's emphasis on a pure poetry pointed away from literature as representation of the objective world. Cézanne's painting offers an example of how the interplay of colors and planes on the surface of a canvas can take on greater importance than the ostensible "subject" of the painting. His ambition to "make out of Impressionism something solid and lasting like the art of the museums," led him to emphasize the design of a painting, as a pattern made up of simplified forms, often outlined with dark contours, and to break the rules of perspective in such still-lifes as *Apples and Oranges* (*ca.* 1895–1900; figure 2), in which the table and the two dishes of fruit look as if they have each been painted from a different perspective.[25] Vincent van Gogh's *Night Café* (*Le Café de nuit*, 1888; figure 3) also challenges perspectivalism and divides the space of the café into planes of bright color (the red wall, the green ceiling, the brown floor). Van Gogh said of the painting, "I have tried to express the terrible passions of humanity by means of red and green."[26] These innovations were to have a major impact on the development of cubism and modern art. The roots of modernism, then, can be found in the mid-nineteenth-century works charged with "realism," works by Baudelaire, Courbet, and Flaubert. Although their followers took the new spirit in art in various directions, those paths converged once again in the twentieth century. When the French court chastised those two writers in 1857, it was attacking tendencies that would dominate modern art and literature over the next century.

2. Paul Cézanne (1839–1906), *Still-Life with Apples and Oranges,*
*ca.* 1895–1900. Oil on canvas. Photo: Hervé Lewandowski.
Photo Credit: Réunion des Musées Nationaux/Art Resource, NY.
Musée d'Orsay, Paris, France.

3. Vincent van Gogh (1853–1890), *Night Café (Le café de nuit)*, 1888. Oil on canvas, 28½ × 36¼ in. (72.4 × 92.1 cm). Yale University Art Gallery. Bequest of Stephen Carlton Clark, BA, 1903.

## Wilde and aestheticism

Yet another set of trials dominated the literary and theatrical scene of London in the 1890s – the trials of Oscar Wilde. Wilde had carried on an affair with Lord Alfred Douglas ("Bosie"), an estranged younger son of the ninth Marquess of Queensberry, who lent his name to the rules that govern modern boxing. Early in 1895, the pugilistic marquess left a card at Wilde's club, inscribed "For Oscar Wilde, posing Somdomite [*sic*]." The accusation was serious, since sodomy (homosexual conduct) and even "posing" as a homosexual were crimes punishable by imprisonment, as well as social disgrace. Spurred on by Bosie, who hated his father, and ignoring the good advice of his friends and lawyers, Wilde sued Queensberry for libel. Queensberry's lawyer, Edward Carson, had been a childhood playmate of Wilde as well as his classmate at Trinity College, Dublin. In his "plea of justification," showing that the charge of posing as a sodomite was not libellous because it was true, Carson introduced evidence of Wilde's involvement with a number of boys and young men, mostly prostitutes. He also charged Wilde's novel *The Picture of Dorian Gray* (1891) with immorality, for its depiction of the struggle between an artist and an aristocrat for the love of a young man. Wilde himself was a famous wit, whose best plays, *An Ideal Husband* and *The Importance of Being Earnest* (both 1895), were drawing huge crowds in London's West End during the trial. He treated the trial as a piece of theater, too, and it received extensive press coverage. When asked by Carson whether he had ever "adored a young man madly," Wilde replied, "I have never given adoration to anybody except myself."[27] Carson's evidence of Wilde's activities, and the fact that Wilde had paid blackmail money to hush them up, forced Wilde to admit that Queensberry was in fact justified in calling him a sodomite.

Shortly after the libel trial ended, Wilde was arrested on a charge of "committing indecent acts." Now that he was on trial for a crime, Wilde became more cautious; he defended what his lover Bosie had famously called "The Love that dare not speak its name" as pure and perfect, "a deep, spiritual affection," where "the elder man has intellect, and the younger man has all the joy, hope and glamour of life before him." He cited David and Jonathan, Plato, Michelangelo, and Shakespeare as precursors. Still, he could not avoid making witty remarks. When asked by the prosecution, "Why did you take up with these youths?," Wilde responded, "I am a lover of youth," amusing the courtroom audience but damaging his defense. The first jury to hear the case could not reach a verdict, owing to the objections of a single juror, but the case was retried. Wilde did not take the opportunity to escape to France before the verdict was announced – "I decided that it was nobler and more beautiful to stay."[28] He was convicted and sentenced to two years' hard labor. After serving out the sentence at Reading gaol, he did leave England for France, where he died in 1900 at the age of forty-six.

Wilde's trials, like Emile Zola's three years later, had little explicit connection to literature. *Dorian Gray* bespoke the influence of French decadence – Dorian is corrupted in part by reading Joris-Karl Huysmans's *Against Nature*, which Wilde himself had read on his honeymoon. Yet while the novel was used against him in the libel trial, he was prosecuted for his sexual conduct, not his literary output. Nonetheless, the trials had an impact on British literary life, and especially on the theater. Wilde's own plays, while not touching on homosexuality, had dealt irreverently with the question of marriage. These were no longer produced, and even the fairly conservative "problem plays" of Henry Arthur Jones and Sir Arthur Wing Pinero gave way to less challenging or iconoclastic works. As the critic Samuel Hynes has observed, "It was as though the Victorian age, in its last years, had determined to be relentlessly Victorian while it could."[29]

Wilde's conviction also seemed to seal the fate of aestheticism, the specifically English movement most closely corresponding to decadence. Aestheticism found the ultimate purpose of life in art, and strove to make life itself into a work of art. The critic Walter Pater had written of art's role in the encounter between the "individual mind" and "experience." In the conclusion to his book *The Renaissance* (1873), Pater wrote of the responsibility of each individual to experience life in all its intensity, to "burn always with this hard, gem-like flame, to maintain this ecstasy." Pater's emphasis on individual experience chimed with the concerns of the modern European literary movements:

> Experience, already reduced to a group of impressions, is ringed round for each one of us by that thick wall of personality through which no real voice has ever pierced on its way to us, or from us to that which we can only conjecture to be without. Every one of those impressions is the impression of the individual in his isolation, each mind keeping as a solitary prisoner its own dream of a world.

The critic Ian Watt has suggested that the basic problem of the relationship between the outer world and interior consciousness underlies both impressionism and symbolism. Impressionism is concerned with the difficulty of recording the individual experience of the outer world, while symbolism addresses the problem of expressing to the outer world the most interior of experiences. Pater's emphasis on experiencing intensely the impressions of the passing moment led him to place a high value on art as the mode of human experience in which such impressions could be most fully savored. He wrote of the wisdom that could be gained by the "love of art for its own sake."[30] Aestheticism valued the uniqueness of individual experience; the chief sin for the aesthete was hypocrisy, the craven submission to the dominant values of a crass society dominated by money and outmoded notions of propriety. Wilde's preface to *Dorian Gray* echoed Pater's argument in favor of "art for art's sake," but in paradoxical language that emphasized the irrelevance of conventional morality to art: "There is no such thing as a moral or an immoral book. Books are well written, or badly written. That is all . . . No artist has ethical sympathies. An ethical sympathy in an artist is an unpardonable mannerism of style . . . All art is quite useless."[31] Wilde's downfall seemed to taint aestheticism with a flavor not just of uselessness, but of immorality. Aestheticism represented the extreme form of the view that the work of art is autonomous, an end in itself, first developed by Immanuel Kant. Detached from Kant's moral system, the claim for art's autonomy became a rallying cry in modernism's assault on socially imposed standards for art.

In fact, Wilde's works did contain moral messages. Dorian Gray himself serves as an example of the dangers of a life devoted solely to pleasure. In the novel the beautiful young man sees a portrait of himself painted by his friend Basil Hallward and wishes that the painting would age while he stays young. He gets his wish and sets out on a life of debauchery and crime, ultimately killing Basil. While Dorian retains his beauty, the portrait betrays his sins: "in the eyes there was a look of cunning and in the mouth the curved wrinkle of the hypocrite." At the end of the novel, Dorian tries to destroy the picture, attacking it with the same knife he used to kill Basil. By striking the picture he kills himself, and his beautiful body is transformed into a corpse, "withered, wrinkled, and loathsome of visage." The moral hardly suggests a worship of "art for art's sake": here, the confusion between life and art transforms a beautiful young man into a loathsome hypocrite. The mood and tone of the novel are high Victorian gothic melodrama, following many of the conventions that, on the stage, Wilde would parody and reject. Wilde's plays take up similar themes – dual identities, hidden desires, sincerity *vs.* artificiality – but are much funnier. In *The Importance of Being Earnest*, Cecily says to her reputedly wicked cousin Algernon, "I hope you have not been living a double life, pretending to be wicked and being really good all the time. That would be hypocrisy." Wilde was earnest enough in the disgust he felt for hypocrisy to allow himself to become the most famous martyr to Victorian morality.

## English literature at the turn of the twentieth century

The history of French literature in the nineteenth century demonstrates the increasing hostility between artists on the one hand and the public, the government, and official institutions of art on the other. Apart from the controversy over the Oscar Wilde trials, there was not such an extreme sense of discord in late nineteenth-century England. Rather, English writers and artists, with a few exceptions, seemed to share a broad consensus about what was appropriate in art, in terms both of what could be represented and of the conventions for representing it, until the first decade of the twentieth century. Thanks to national insularity, French and other European movements tended to reach England rather late, and when they did so they often arrived through the mediation of Irish Protestants, such as George Bernard Shaw, Wilde, and W. B. Yeats, or Americans such as Henry James and Abbott McNeill Whistler.

Many major English writers of the 1890s, though relatively untouched by continental trends, did express a fatalism akin to that of the naturalists and decadents, inspired by the sense that nature was an amoral system of laws tending to no particular purpose. Such pessimism infuses the work of Thomas Hardy, who gave up writing novels after *Tess of the D'Urbervilles* (1891) and *Jude the Obscure* (1896) were castigated by critics for their liberal treatment of adultery and their morbidity. Tess kills her lover and is hanged; Jude's family is impoverished, and his son hangs himself and two younger children, leaving a note, "Done because we are too menny." At the other end of the political spectrum, the imperialist Rudyard Kipling, the most popular serious writer of the era, continually expressed fatalism about England's prospects. In "Recessional," written for the diamond jubilee of Queen Victoria in 1897, he lamented that British power would go the way of ancient empires: "Lo, all our pomp of yesterday / Is one with Nineveh and Tyre." The general sense that civilization was headed for decline helped to inspire later modernist musings on the subject, notably T. S. Eliot's in *The Waste Land* (1922), which combines Kiplingesque dismay with Baudelairean surreality: "Falling towers / Jerusalem Athens Alexandria / Vienna London / Unreal." Several writers of the 1890s, such as Ernest Dowson, George Gissing, and George Moore, dwelt on the theme of decay, but their reputations did not long survive the turn of the century.

Three writers of the period who were all born outside England – the Irishman William Butler Yeats, the American Henry James, and the Polish-born Joseph Conrad – had reputations that would not only survive the year 1900 but also exert a determining influence on the twentieth century. These authors contributed to the fusion of the interrelated techniques of the late nineteenth century – especially impressionism and symbolism – into the broader synthesis that came to be known in English as "modernism." Among English-language poets, Yeats best illustrates the legacy of symbolism for modernism. The movement was influentially introduced to an English-speaking public by Arthur Symons, translator of Charles Baudelaire and the Italian decadent Gabriele d'Annunzio.

Symons wrote of symbolism as "an attempt to spiritualise literature" in his 1899 book *The Symbolist Movement in Literature*, which he dedicated to Yeats: "Description is banished that beautiful things may be evoked, magically; the regular beat of the verse is broken in order that words may fly, upon subtler wings."[32] Yeats developed his own conception of symbolism, however, from the visionary poems of the romantic William Blake and from his experiences of the occult, rather than from Baudelaire or Stéphane Mallarmé.[33] Like Walter Pater and Wilde, Yeats believed that the artist was capable of a finer and more complete perception than the ordinary person. This sense of the artist's elevation above and isolation from the public became a keynote of modernism.

Early in his career, Yeats fused images from Irish folklore and contemporary spiritualist movements like Theosophy in a somewhat vague symbolism. Some of his poetry contained fairly straightforward symbols, such as the rose that conventionally represents Ireland or what he later called the "allegorical dreams" of *The Wanderings of Oisin* (1889). Yeats aimed, however, not at the simple one-to-one correspondence that the symbolists dismissed as allegory, but at a more subtle symbolism, resistant to deciphering. In the short lyric "Who Goes With Fergus?" (1892), "love's bitter mystery" and the mysteries of poetry are symbolized by the various aspects of the natural world governed by the mythical Irish poet-king Fergus: "For Fergus rules the brazen cars, / And rules the shadows of the wood, / And the white breast of the dim sea, / And all dishevelled wandering stars." The poem's shadowy, liminal imagery suggests rather than describes the infinite vista of Fergus's kingdom, which is not of this world. In this symbolist phase Yeats's reliance on private meanings competed with his desire to create a public, national poetry for Ireland. Yeats played an important part in the Celtic Twilight movement of the 1890s (named after a book of Yeats's Irish peasant stories), which incorporated Irish folklore and fairy stories into a *fin-de-siècle* atmosphere. With Lady Augusta Gregory he established the national Abbey Theatre in Dublin in 1904. He found the business of managing a theater unbearable, though, not least because of his distaste for the straightforward nationalist propaganda favored by some others in the movement, notably his beloved but inaccessible muse, Maud Gonne, a revolutionary opponent of English rule in Ireland.

Yeats's symbolism grew ever more personal and idiosyncratic later in his career, even while his poetry addressed contemporary and political matters more explicitly. The combination resulted in such "masterful images" (as Yeats would describe them at the end of his life) as the "broken wall, the burning roof and tower" of Troy, "that dolphin-torn, that gong-tormented sea" of Byzantium, and most famously the "rough beast" that "slouches towards Bethlehem to be born" in "The Second Coming" (1920), all symbols of the ending of one age and the beginning of another, but also symbols of much else. In "The Circus Animals' Desertion" (1939), he represents the creation of images out of the residue of emotional life as a form of sublimation, symbolized by his crazy muse, now all desublimated, "that raving slut / Who keeps the till" in "the foul rag and bone shop of the heart."[34] Frank Kermode has shown how Yeats's great poem "Among School Children" (1928) embodies his conception of the almost magical powers of the image or symbol: "O chestnut tree, great rooted blossomer, / Are you the leaf, the blossom or the bole? / O body swayed to music, O brightening glance, / How can we know the dancer from the dance?" The symbol bridges the gap in modern life between mind and body; it is the embodiment of an idea, and more than that, of a spirit. Like the dancer, whose body is fully involved in the dance, a form of labor which appears effortless, or like the tree, organic unity of leaf, blossom, and bole, the symbol makes no distinction between body and mind; it fully embodies its meaning.

The novelist Joseph Conrad provided another crucial image for understanding the symbolism of modern literature in *Heart of Darkness* (1899), where his frame narrator writes of how the stories of Marlow, the narrator of most of the novella, differ from those of other sailors: "The yarns of seamen have a direct simplicity, the whole meaning of which lies within the shell of a cracked nut . . . [But to Marlow,] the meaning of an episode was not inside like a kernel but outside, enveloping the tale which brought it out only as a glow brings out a haze." *Heart of Darkness* does not reveal its meaning in digestible morsels, like the kernel of a nut. Rather, its meanings evade the interpreter; they are larger than the story itself. Conrad, a Pole who had worked as a sailor and then captain on French and British ships before becoming a naturalized British subject, admired Flaubert and knew French literature well. While not aligning himself specifically with French symbolism, he wrote that "a work of art is very seldom limited to one exclusive meaning and not necessarily tending to a definite conclusion. And this for the reason that the nearer it approaches art, the more it acquires a symbolic character."[35] One reason for the centrality of *Heart of Darkness* to the history of modernism is its openness to interpretation: Marlow's journey to Central Africa to confront the power-mad Kurtz can be interpreted as a political statement about imperialism and race, a critique of bureaucracy, a journey to the center of the self, a descent into hell, or a voyage up the birth canal. No single interpretation exhausts its meaning.

Conrad's use of polyvalent symbols such as the knitters of black wool, the grove of death, or Kurtz himself, suggests his connection to symbolist tendencies, but his famously hazy literary technique owed more to impressionism. As Conrad's interpreter, Ian Watt, has observed, "the abstract geometry of the

[nut] metaphor is symbolist because the meaning of the story, represented by the shell of a nut or the haze around the glow, is larger than its narrative vehicle, the kernel or the glow; but the sensory quality of the metaphor, the mist and haze, is essentially impressionist."[36] Most of the story is told from the perspective of Marlow, and much of the time he seems unsure what is happening to him. Through the narrative device that Watt has defined as "delayed decoding," Conrad records first the impressions that an event makes on Marlow and only later Marlow's arrival at an explanation of the event. Thus, when his boat is suddenly attacked by natives loyal to Kurtz, Marlow is unable to explain why his helmsman suddenly falls down:

> the end of what appeared a long cane clattered round and knocked over a little camp-stool. . . . my feet felt so warm and wet that I had to look down. The man had rolled on his back and stared straight up at me; both his hands clutched that cane. It was the shaft of a spear . . . my shoes were full; a pool of blood lay very still gleaming dark-red under the wheel.

The reader realizes only gradually what has happened and thus shares in the experience of Marlow's perplexity. A similar structure dominates the narrative on a larger scale, as Marlow continually jumps around in the telling of his story, layering impressions from various times in his attempt to make sense of his experience. This resulted in breaking up the temporal continuity associated with the nineteenth-century novel. Conrad's use of multiple narrators undermines the nineteenth-century convention of narrative omniscience. The literary critic F. R. Leavis complained that Conrad frequently seemed "intent on making a virtue out of not knowing what he means."[37] Yet this technique for forcing the reader to share the impressions of the characters became central to modernist fiction.

Conrad never called himself an impressionist. The term was applied retrospectively by his friend and collaborator Ford Madox Ford (then known as Ford Madox Hueffer; he changed his name because of anti-German feeling during the First World War). Ford, one of the leading proponents of European literary theories in early twentieth-century London, founded two important modernist journals, the *English Review* and the *Transatlantic Review*. He also included James, Conrad's "master," among the impressionists. In fact, all three of these men owed more to Gustave Flaubert than to Claude Monet or any other painter. The impact of one art form on another is seldom direct and often involves a time lag. Impressionist and post-impressionist painters served as prestigious models for writers in the first decades of the twentieth century and especially in 1913, when Ford wrote "On Impressionism." Ford admired the painters' success in challenging conventions of artistic representation and sought a literary equivalent to the new pictorial modes of representing the subjective awareness of reality in time and space. All three novelists lived to some extent in the shadow of painting and sought, like Horace, to "paint pictures with words." Ford was the grandson of the painter Ford Madox Brown, an associate of Dante Gabriel Rossetti's Pre-Raphaelite Brotherhood. Conrad wrote that the primary task of the novelist was "to make you see."[38]

James, whose older brother, the psychologist William James, was an accomplished painter, had earned a reputation as a paragon of realism for works such as "Daisy Miller: A Study" (1878) and *The Portrait of a Lady* (1881), both allied with painting by their titles. James inspired Conrad mainly through the play with perspective in his experimental fiction of the 1890s, including *What Maisie Knew* (1897), the story of a disintegrating marriage told in free indirect discourse from the perspective of a young child. The question implicit in the title, namely how much Maisie really understands about her parents' mistreatment of each other, offered James great scope for the exploration of the limits of knowledge and self-knowledge that Ford would label impressionism. James's persistent themes of the divided self, moral ambiguity, and unreliable narration made him a model for later modernists, too, including Eliot, Ezra Pound, and Virginia Woolf. His last three major novels, *The Wings of the Dove* (1902), *The Ambassadors* (1903), and *The Golden Bowl* (1904), combined his interest in the problem of recording the experiences of a central consciousness with a use of symbolism derived partly from the American tradition of Nathaniel Hawthorne and Herman Melville. The attempt to register the uncertainty and even haziness of the subjective experience of events remained a central concern of modernist fiction, influential throughout the history of modernism. Woolf, in many respects a descendant of the impressionists, later wrote that "Life is not a series of gig lamps symmetrically arranged; life is a luminous halo, a semi-transparent envelope surrounding us from the beginning of consciousness to the end."[39] The images of light, translucence, and haze indicate her impressionist heritage.

James, who would become a prophet to the later modernists, foresaw radical change when the nineteenth century ended for England, a year late, with the death of Queen Victoria in 1901: "One knew then that one had taken her for a kind of nursing mother of the land and of the empire, and by attaching to her duration an extraordinary idea of beneficence. This idea was just and her duration is over. It's a new era – and we don't know what it is." He feared for the future: "Her death, in short, will let loose incalculable forces for possible ill. I am very pessimistic." In fact, of course, the trials of the twentieth century – war, revolution, and genocide – would far exceed the worst imaginings even of Yeats, Conrad, or James. In its first decade, however, under the rule of Victoria's son Edward VII, whom James considered "an arch-vulgarian," the new century would do its best to continue the traditions of the old.[40]

## Further reading

### *Literary works*

Charles Baudelaire, *The Flowers of Evil*, ed. Marthiel and Jackson Mathews, rev. edn. New York: New Directions, 1989.
Joseph Conrad, *The Portable Conrad*, ed. Morton Dauwen Zabel. New York: Penguin, 1976.
Gustave Flaubert, *Madame Bovary*, ed. and trans. Paul de Man. New York: Norton, 1965.
Gustave Flaubert, *Sentimental Education*, trans. Robert Baldick. Harmondsworth: Penguin, 1964.
Joris-Karl Huysmans, *Against Nature*, trans. Margaret Mauldon. Oxford: Oxford University Press, 1998.
Henrik Ibsen, *Complete Major Prose Plays*, trans. and ed. Rolf Fjelde. New York: New American Library, 1978.
Henry James, *The Wings of the Dove*, *The Ambassadors*, and *The Golden Bowl* (various editions).
Enid Rhodes Peschel, trans. *Four French Symbolist Poets: Baudelaire, Rimbaud, Verlaine, Mallarmé: Translation and Introduction*. Athens, Ohio: Ohio State University Press, 1981.
William Rees, ed. and trans. *The Penguin Book of French Poetry, 1820–1950*. London: Penguin, 1992.
George Bernard Shaw, *Arms and the Man*, *Pygmalion*, and *Major Barbara* (various editions).
Oscar Wilde, *The Complete Works of Oscar Wilde*. New York: HarperCollins, 1989.
Emile Zola, *Nana*, trans. George Holden. London: Penguin, 1972.
Emile Zola, *Thérèse Raquin*, trans. Leonard Tancock. London: Penguin, 1962.

### *Contemporary critical statements*

Charles Baudelaire, "The Painter of Modern Life," in *Modernism Anthology*.
Joseph Conrad, Preface to *The Nigger of the "Narcissus,"* in *Modernism Anthology*.
Ford Madox Ford, "On Impressionism," in *Modernism Anthology*.
Stéphane Mallarmé, "Crisis in Poetry," in *Modernism Anthology*.
Linda Nochlin, ed. *Impressionism and Post-Impressionism, 1874–1904: Sources and Documents*. Englewood Cliffs, NJ: Prentice-Hall, 1966.
Max Nordau, *Degeneration*, ed. George L. Mosse. Lincoln: University of Nebraska Press, 1993.
Walter Pater, Conclusion to *The Renaissance*, in *Modernism Anthology*.

Arthur Symons, *The Symbolist Movement in Literature*, 1899. Rev. edn. rpt. New York: Dutton, 1958.

James Abbott McNeill Whistler, *The Gentle Art of Making Enemies*, 1890. Rpt. New York: Dover Publications, 1967.

Emile Zola, *The Experimental Novel, and Other Essays*. Trans. Belle M. Sherman. New York: Haskell House, 1964.

## Later criticism

Erich Auerbach, *Mimesis: The Representation of Reality in Western Literature*, trans. Willard R. Trask. Princeton: Princeton University Press, 1953.

Richard Ellmann, *Oscar Wilde*. New York: Knopf, 1988.

Richard Ellmann, *W. B. Yeats: The Man and the Masks*. New York: Macmillan, 1948.

Francis Frascina *et al.*, *Modernity and Modernism: French Painting in the Nineteenth Century*. New Haven: Yale University Press, 1993.

R. F. Foster, *W. B. Yeats: A Life*, 2 vols. Oxford: Oxford University Press, 1997–2003.

Frank Kermode, *The Romantic Image*, 1957. Rpt. London: Routledge, 2002.

Dominick LaCapra, *"Madame Bovary" on Trial*. Ithaca, NY: Cornell University Press, 1982.

Jesse Matz, *Literary Impressionism and Modernist Aesthetics*. Cambridge: Cambridge University Press, 2001.

Phoebe Pool, *Impressionism*. London: Thames and Hudson, 1967.

Ian Watt, *Conrad in the Nineteenth Century*. Berkeley and Los Angeles: University of California Press, 1979.

# Chapter 2

# Primitivists and modernizers

In 1924, during the heyday of literary modernism, Virginia Woolf tried to account for what was new about "modern" fiction. She wrote that while all fiction tried to express human character, modern fiction had to describe character in a new way because "on or about December, 1910, human character changed."[1] Her main example of this change in human character was the "character of one's cook." Whereas the "Victorian cook lived like a leviathan in the lower depths," modern cooks were forever coming out of the kitchen to borrow the *Daily Herald* and ask "advice about a hat." Woolf's choice of December 1910 as a watershed referred above all to the first post-impressionist exhibition, organized by her friend Roger Fry in collaboration with her brother-in-law Clive Bell. The exhibition ran from November 8, 1910, to January 15, 1911, and introduced the English public to developments in the visual arts that had already been taking place in France for a generation. More broadly, however, Woolf was alluding to social and political changes that overtook England soon after the death of Edward VII in May 1910, symbolized by the changing patterns of deference and class and gender relations implicit in the transformation of the Victorian cook. Henry James considered that the death of Edward's mother Victoria meant the end of one age; Edward's reign was short (1901–10), but to those who lived through it, it seemed to stand on the border between the old world and the new. The crisis of representation made itself felt rather belatedly in England, but when it arrived it combined with a series of social conflicts to announce a sudden transformation not only of art but of human character itself. The crises of liberalism and of representation occurred almost simultaneously in England on or about December 1910.

In order to define "modern fiction," Woolf began by explaining what it was not: Edwardian. She labeled three prominent novelists – Arnold Bennett, John

Galsworthy, and H. G. Wells – "the Edwardians," and complained that all three were "materialists," more interested in the external trappings of life than in the internal lives of their characters. Woolf wanted to represent the writing of modernists such as T. S. Eliot, James Joyce, D. H. Lawrence, and Lytton Strachey as a rebellion against the conservatism of English fiction during Edward's reign. She also championed the "spiritual" qualities of Russian literature, by which she meant primarily the novels of Fyodor Dostoevsky and the plays of Anton Chekhov; both authors became widely known in England shortly before the First World War. Like most writers of manifestoes, Woolf relies to some extent on caricature. The rejection of the Edwardians by the modernists has made the Edwardian period seem, in retrospect, one of simple intellectual and artistic conservatism, but the reality is more complex. An era highly conscious of the approach of radical social changes – in the British Empire, the status of women, and the relations among the classes – the Edwardian age hesitantly prepared the way for the transformations that would be celebrated by modernism. At the same time, the spread of new technologies heralded the arrival of the twentieth century.

Along with these social and political transformations came changes in the arts. In Britain these were gradual, and the main signs of the development of modernism were the novels of Joseph Conrad and Henry James and the founding of Ford Madox Ford's *English Review*. In continental Europe, however, the crucial developments that would define modern art and literature were well under way. The nineteenth century, the century of gradual progress, was over, and the future seemed to offer two alternatives: embrace technology, radical change, and the future; or return to a primitive past. Many writers and artists, notably the futurists, embraced the modern world, including its technology and its speed. They saw the automobile, the airplane, the X-ray, the gramophone, and even the machine gun as keys to the human future. Others sought instead to reconnect with the remote past, often labeled "primitive." Primitivists believed that in order to survive, people must stay connected to their bodily reality and flout the repression inherent in modern society. In the first decade of the twentieth century, whether rushing toward the future or turning toward the distant past, European artists rejected everything they associated with the bourgeois civilization of their immediate precursors in the nineteenth century.

In England the intellectual and political classes held on for a brief decade to the nineteenth-century liberal ideal of gradual progress. The Liberal Party, in power from 1906, embodied this cautious optimism. It stood for the middle classes, religious tolerance, and a cautious approach to democratization. Many leading Liberals, however, had difficulty adjusting to the rise of the organized working class, the women's suffrage movement, and the pressures that would lead to the outbreak of the First World War and the decline of the British Empire. Liberal optimism gradually gave way to nostalgia and pessimism as the war approached. Woolf's hostile depiction of the Edwardians needs to be tempered by a more nuanced account of the period and by attention to the rise of primitivism and the fascination with modernity throughout Europe during these same years. The Edwardians, primitivists, and futurists all prepared the way for the change in "human character" announced by Woolf. After reviewing the contributions of these three groups of writers and artists in the first decade of the twentieth century, this chapter will explore how that change made itself felt in England on or about December 1910.

## Edwardians

Virginia Woolf's main complaint about the Edwardians concerned their "materialism." By this she meant that they did not explore the spiritual or mental lives of their characters. Closely linked to this materialism, however, was the Edwardians' concern with political and social problems. Woolf's dislike of the Edwardians stemmed in part from her sense that they were more concerned with promoting worthy causes than with rethinking the uses of literature. Attempts to link political and artistic radicalism often failed in the modernist period. Although social conservatives did usually have conservative tastes in art, the most radical experimenters did not always hold the most radical political views; they were often highly individualistic or even antisocial. Woolf saw the Edwardians' political liberalism as tied to their artistic conservatism. She criticized Arnold Bennett, for example, for his realist attention to getting and spending, the economic side of life – train schedules, the cost of jewelry, real estate, "rents and freeholds and copyholds and fines." A follower of the realists and naturalists, Bennett was perhaps conservative in his literary practice but not in his political sympathies. He campaigned against censorship and in favor of a more liberal divorce law, admired Anton Chekhov and Fyodor Dostoevsky, lived in Paris for several years, joined the socialist Fabian Society, and wrote admiringly of French post-impressionism at a time when most writers in England were attacking it. Bennett's less accomplished contemporary, John Galsworthy, was a minor target for Woolf, who described him as "burning with indignation, stuffed with information, arraigning civilization." Like Bennett, he was involved in several public campaigns for reform of outdated practices, including solitary confinement of prisoners, the antiquated divorce laws, censorship of the theater, and especially mistreatment of animals. His novels offered satirical accounts of the passions and misdeeds of the upper-middle-class Forsyte family, while his plays treated social and political problems. Their combination of literary insignificance and moral righteousness won Galsworthy the Nobel Prize in 1932.

H. G. Wells, whom Woolf partially exempts from her critique of the Edwardians, seems to belong more firmly to the modern age than either Bennett or Galsworthy. His science fiction, while far removed from the literary experiments of the modernists, predicted many of the horrors of the twentieth century, including trench warfare, aerial bombardment, poison gas, the nuclear bomb, and world war. In *The War of the Worlds* (1898), his highly evolved Martians are inhuman in every sense, exterminating the inhabitants of earth as thoughtlessly as a human might destroy an anthill or as a colonizer might destroy the institutions of native culture. Wells's first novel, *The Time Machine* (1895), serves almost as an inverted allegory for the way the artists of his generation imagined the future, as either technological utopia or reversion to barbarism. Wells's novel contains both fates. Having traveled more than 800,000 years into the future, an inventor discovers that "Man had not remained one species, but had differentiated into two distinct animals." The graceful but effete Eloi rule the upper world by day, but underground lives an entirely different species, the Morlocks, apelike creatures with large eyes, who operate complex machinery and emerge from their lairs only at night. The time traveler discovers, to his disgust, that the beautiful but dim-witted Eloi are nothing but "fatted cattle," whom the Morlocks kidnap at night and then roast and eat in their underground chambers. Wells's science fiction speaks to the implications of the theories of evolution and degeneration for social development. Two imagined futures for the human race both come to pass: the rich evolve into delicate, beautiful creatures incapable of exertion, the extreme form of Joris-Karl Huysmans's Des Esseintes in *Against Nature* (1884), while the poor degenerate into savage but sharp-witted beasts. The masters, however, turn out to lose all practical knowledge, and thus are consumed by their own servants. It is a fate that neither a primitivist nor a futurist could celebrate.

Wells's political attitudes, though in some ways typical of his age, differed from the cautious reformism of Bennett, Galsworthy, and the Liberal Party. Wells joined the Fabian Society, a reformist socialist group that had been founded by George Bernard Shaw and Sydney and Beatrice Webb, but he rejected the Fabians' gradual approach to social problems. In particular, he encouraged the society to support a resolution rejecting the monogamous family, headed by a man, as a form of private property. Attacked by conservatives and by other socialists as a champion of "free love" and sexual anarchy, Wells failed in his attempts to take over the Fabian Society from Shaw and the Webbs, in part because of his personal reputation – he was known for his extramarital affairs with young women. One of these, Amber Reeves, the daughter of Fabian socialists, served as the model for his controversial novel *Ann Veronica* (1909), about a relationship between a liberated young woman and a married man. More a prophet than a politician, Wells seemed to foresee the radical changes in society that were finally unleashed by the First World War. He viewed literature, however, more as propaganda than as art, and on this point he quarreled with Henry James, whose ideas about fiction as art inspired later modernists like Woolf.[2] Wells soon began another affair with a young feminist writer, born Cicely Fairfield, who had taken the name of one of Henrik Ibsen's heroines, Rebecca West. West later wrote an early modernist novel about the traumatic effects of the First World War, *The Return of the Soldier* (1918). Her best-known works, however, were her nonfiction accounts of Yugoslavia on the eve of the Second World War and the Nuremberg trials of Nazi war criminals immediately after the war. Like Wells, she was a powerful analyst of the effect of mass warfare on European society.

In her catalogue of Edwardians and moderns, Woolf ambivalently placed her friend Edward Morgan Forster between the two groups, and complained that he had ruined his early work by "trying to compromise" with the methods of the Edwardians. For the most part, however, Forster's novels are quite critical of the society in which he lived. A homosexual, he recognized and condemned the sexual hypocrisy of Edwardian morality. A liberal, he also longed for a society less polarized by class. The major novel of Forster's early period, *Howards End* (1910), describes the encounter between the commercial Wilcox family and the intellectual Schlegels, representatives of the competing attitudes of the Edwardian upper classes toward modernity and social convention. The victims of their encounter, the impoverished Leonard and Jackie Bast, are both crushed under the wheel of the class system. The novel addresses the double standard for adultery, the vicious aspects of class privilege, and the limitations of the well-intentioned liberalism of the Schlegels. The novel's famous motto, "Only connect," spoke to high liberal and humanist ideals, but in the plot of the novel only the well-connected survive.

Forster's next novel, *Maurice*, written in 1913 but published only posthumously in 1971, tells the story of a homosexual love affair, again in the context of a society riven by class conflict. It ends with the title character escaping from civilization and going to live in the country with his working-class lover, the gamekeeper Alec. Similarly, the last novel that Forster wrote, *A Passage to India* (1924), ends with the question of whether two men can overcome social divisions, this time of race rather than class. Here, the hoped-for destruction of the barriers of prejudice is deferred. At the end of the novel, the Englishman Fielding and the Indian Dr. Aziz ride together through the Indian landscape, and, as they embrace, Fielding asks whether it is possible for the two men to be friends, despite the colonial relationship between England and India: "Why can't we be friends now? It's what I want. It's what you want." As their horses swerve in opposite directions, the landscape itself seems to answer Fielding's question: "No, not yet . . . No, not there." Forster began writing *A Passage to India* in 1913, after his first visit to India, but he did not complete it until after his second visit in 1921. By this time, modernist experiments with the form of novels had made his Edwardian works appear old-fashioned. *A Passage to India*, though in many respects a traditional English novel, contains one central plot device that links it to the sort of "modern fiction" that Woolf championed. On a trip to visit the Marabar caves, Miss Adela Quested hears a loud echo, which causes her such confusion that the innocent Dr. Aziz is arrested for assaulting her. Forster leaves the source of the echo unexplained, thus breaking with the realist conventions which would have accounted for its origins and embracing the ambiguity typical of modernist narrative. Forster wrote of the echo: "In the cave it is *either* a man, *or* the supernatural, *or* an illusion. If I say, it becomes whatever the answer a different book. And even if I know!"[3] Forster's disavowal of narratorial and even authorial omniscience bespoke the transition from the Edwardian to the modernist age.

Forster's decision not to publish *Maurice* suggests some of the constraints under which writers of the Edwardian period labored. Both playwrights and novelists faced a challenge in addressing sexual issues frankly, in particular because of the continuing power of censorship, one area in which the Edwardian period continued Victorian traditions. The actor, playwright, and director Harley Granville-Barker, who contributed much to modern staging as director of the Royal Court Theater, and performed in many of Shaw's plays, himself wrote a play, *Waste* (1907), whose female protagonist dies of a botched abortion. Denied a license by the Lord Chamberlain, Granville-Barker could only produce the play privately. Many of the leading writers of the day – Bennett, Joseph Conrad, Galsworthy, Thomas Hardy, Henry James, Shaw, Wells, and W. B. Yeats, along with J. M. Barrie, the author of *Peter Pan*, and Sir Arthur Conan Doyle, the creator of Sherlock Holmes – fought the continuing imposition of Victorian standards in the censorship of the theater. However, the Liberal government, preoccupied with the questions of Irish Home Rule, working-class agitations, and the suffrage movement, failed to amend the laws. The Lord Chamberlain imposed laughably rigid rules forbidding the discussion of sex, politics, or religion in serious theater, and went so far as to prevent the staging of Sophocles' *Oedipus the King* and (during the visit of a Japanese dignitary) Gilbert and Sullivan's *The Mikado* (1885). The effect on contemporary playwrights was chilling.[4]

While the censor of plays was a public official, novels underwent a more indirect form of censorship. The circulating libraries, which lent out books for a fee, dominated the book market. They had tremendous power to influence the decisions of publishers about which books to accept for publication. The libraries feared offending the conservative tastes of some of their patrons, particularly those who belonged to organized pressure groups like the National Purity League. In response to demands from such groups, the Circulating Libraries Association introduced a system of censorship designed to avoid the distribution of "objectionable" or "doubtful" books. The libraries refused, for example, to stock Wells's *Ann Veronica*, thus limiting its circulation and making it difficult to obtain. James Joyce's collection of short stories, *Dubliners*, though completed in 1905, could not be published for nine years. Joyce's stories contained nothing like the masturbation scene that would later cause his *Ulysses* (1922) to be judged obscene. The publishers and printer of *Dubliners* nonetheless feared being prosecuted for obscenity and libel for printing the word "bloody," the names of real companies in Dublin, and an unflattering reference to Edward VII. When the book finally came out (with the addition of Joyce's finest story, "The Dead") in 1914, Edward was dead and the word bloody had apparently become more acceptable. Neither printer nor publisher was prosecuted, but this would not be Joyce's last encounter with censorship.[5]

## Primitivists

While English writers were struggling to bring their literature into the new century, many European artists were searching for inspiration in the distant past. The African-American intellectual W. E. B. Du Bois argued in 1903 that "the problem of the Twentieth Century is the problem of the color line."[6] The world had been divided into the light-skinned colonizers and the dark-skinned colonized. The early European modernists raided the other side of the color line in search of inspiration. The desire of E. M. Forster's heroes, like Maurice and Fielding, to return to a simpler way of life, embodied in men of a different class or race, responded to a sense of the continual sacrifices and repression demanded of the individual by Western civilization. Nietzschean philosophy and Freudian psychoanalysis both inspired critics of society's repressive mechanisms. The more radical rejections of that civilization and its artistic techniques near the turn of the century came to be known as primitivism. Joseph Conrad feared that European civilization was on the verge of plunging into barbarism; in *Heart of Darkness* (1899), his Kurtz, intoxicated with power, turned himself into a god, to be worshiped by the Africans he ruled. Over the course of the century, this idea turned out to be terribly prophetic of modern savagery in the processes of colonization and decolonization, and in Europe itself. As the century began, however, the concept of a return to the primitive seemed liberating to many.

In the last decades of the nineteenth century, the European powers had explored Africa and carved it up among themselves so that there were no longer, as Conrad put it, any "blank spaces" on maps of the continent. Whites began to ask questions about their kinship with Africans, frequently belittling them as "primitive," but sometimes finding in their contacts with colonized peoples the occasion for rethinking the assumptions of European culture. Similar colonial expansion in such regions as the South Pacific, and the development of anthropology, brought tribal cultures and artworks to the attention of European artists, often through exhibitions of native artifacts from Africa, North America, and Oceania in such museums as the Dresden Ethnographical Museum and the Trocadéro in Paris. In response to the decadents' notion that European civilization would soon enter a period of decline, the primitivists sought an infusion of energy from primitive cultures, by which they referred not only to colonized peoples but also to medieval Europe and preclassical antiquity.

Primitivism in the visual arts expressed itself through a rejection of precisely delineated and drawn forms. Primitivists often used bright "nonnatural" colors, that is, colors that did not correspond to the natural colors of the subjects they portrayed. Welcoming the perennial complaint that their paintings looked as if a child could have done them, the primitivists emphasized the authenticity of their self-expression and the need to tap into the deepest sources of creative power in order to break away from the conventions of Western art since the Renaissance. While visiting an exhibition of drawings by children, Pablo Picasso told a friend, "When I was a child I drew like Raphael. I have been trying to draw like these children ever since."[7] Without becoming political activists, primitivists also sometimes saw their work as championing the cause of colonized people against the abuses of modern European imperialism. However, they frequently maintained colonialist attitudes of their own toward the native arts on which they drew.

Many artists saw in primitive cultures a more open, less hypocritical attitude to sexuality than the prevailing European one. The first modern primitivist, Paul Gauguin, found that rural Brittany did not sate his appetite for the "savage," and so went to live in colonial Tahiti. Gauguin's boldly colored representations of naked or partly clothed native women stood for primitive nature, uncorrupted by masculine civilization, but they also echoed Edouard Manet's paintings of European female nudes, such as *Olympia* (1863) and *Luncheon on the Grass* (1863), with their sometimes aggressive assertion of female sexuality.

4. Henri Matisse (1869–1954), *Le Bonheur de vivre* (*Joy of Life*), 1905–6. Oil on canvas, BF719 Photograph © Reproduced with the Permission of the Barnes Foundation™, All Rights Reserved. © 2006 Succession Henri Matisse, Paris/Artists Rights Society (ARS), New York.

Gauguin's female nudes combine the allure of whores with the innocence of virgins, and in fact prostitution and alcoholism were rampant in the Tahiti that Gauguin visited, which had had its Edenic past destroyed by more than a century of colonialism.[8] Yet Gauguin idealizes the women of a culture foreign to his own, who seemed to have a special access to religious experience. This ideal of the spiritual primitive woman gave ultramodern French painters the sensation of escaping from the dreariness of their civilization.

In the early twentieth century, partly in response to Gauguin, a number of painters sought out primitive subjects and techniques. A group of artists exhibiting in Paris in 1905, among them Henri Matisse, were labeled "*Fauves*," or wild beasts, for their use of vivid color contrasts, their foreshortening of perspective, and the unfinished appearance of their paintings. By this time, the rejection of one's work by the critics was a badge of true modernity, and Matisse and his colleagues celebrated and perhaps even exaggerated the critics' hostility to their work. Like the poet W. B. Yeats, Matisse found in dance and dancers a source of inspiration for his work, which sought to achieve rhythmic effects similar to those of the dance, as in *Joy of Life* (*Le Bonheur de vivre*, 1905–6; figure 4). Here, the joy of lovemaking, piping, and dancing infuses the colors and rhythmic shapes of the canvas. Matisse inspired the expressionist current in twentieth-century art, which celebrated the body. His friend Picasso, the other major figure in the history of modern art, took a more ascetic view of the human body, and Picasso's sense of art as a demanding form, expressing anguish rather than joy, had the greater influence on modernist aesthetics.

Matisse took Picasso to see the displays of African art at the Trocadéro. The use of geometric forms and planes in African masks helped to inspire the rise of cubism and abstract art, as seen most famously in Picasso's painting *The Young Ladies of Avignon* (*Les Demoiselles d'Avignon*) of 1907 (figure 5). Here, Picasso plays with the tradition that makes the female nude a symbol of natural purity; the subjects of his painting are prostitutes. The distorted shapes of the women's bodies, as also in Matisse's *Blue Nude* of the same year, challenge the expectation that paintings will offer idealized representations of female beauty. Like Charles Baudelaire and Gustave Flaubert before him, Picasso was fascinated by the ugly. What makes the painting such a famous example of primitivism, however, is Picasso's distortion of three of the women's faces, to which he gives features akin to those of African masks. While the appeal to primitive art served in part as a challenge to Western tradition, African art also seemed to Picasso and his contemporaries to confirm the direction that modern painting had taken since Paul Cézanne. The modernists admired the abstract quality of African and other native art, its tendency to turn the human face into a geometric form rather than a realistic copy of nature. In the wake of the post-impressionist

5.  Pablo Picasso (1881–1973), © ARS, NY, *Les Demoiselles d'Avignon*
(*The Young Ladies of Avignon*), 1907. Oil on canvas, 8 ft. × 7 ft. 8 in.
Acquired through the Lillie P. Bliss Bequest. (333.1939). The Museum of
Modern Art, New York. Digital Image © The Museum of Modern
Art/Licensed by SCALA/Art Resource, NY. © 2006 Estate of Pablo
Picasso/Artists Rights Society (ARS), New York.

exhibition of 1910, Clive Bell wrote, "As a rule primitive art is good . . . for, as a rule, it is also free from descriptive qualities. In primitive art you will find no accurate representation, you will find only significant form. Yet no other art moves us so profoundly."[9] This interest in the formal qualities of the work of art, rather than its accuracy as a representation of reality, contributed importantly to the development of modernism.

British artists and critics like Bell knew the works of the French primitivists well, but primitivism was an international phenomenon, notable also in German art and Russian dance. Inspired by the Fauves and by Friedrich Nietzsche's call for a rejection of conformism, a group of young artists in Dresden, *Die Brücke* (The Bridge), made use of bold colors and rough or distorted forms. Dresden provided material for this group not only through its ethnographic museum but also through its nudist colonies, which catered to those who came to visit its famous baths. One of the *Brücke* artists, Ernst Ludwig Kirchner, painted groups of nude bathers, male and female, at the baths at Moritzburg, on the outskirts of Dresden, which gave the group a reputation for sexual as well as artistic freedom.[10] They were later known as the founders of German expressionism, named for the effort to express the artist's authentic encounter with reality in contrast to the conventional methods of earlier painting. The term expressionism was imported from French into German around 1911 and roughly corresponded to the English term post-impressionism as a label for the movements in modern art represented by Cézanne, Vincent van Gogh, and Picasso. Later, expressionism became the general term in German for what, in English, was known as modernism. Among the leading expressionists were the members of *Der Blaue Reiter* (The Blue Horseman) group in Munich, led by the Russian-born Wassily Kandinsky, who in 1912 published an almanac that mixed writings on modern art and music with reproductions of post-impressionist, medieval, African, and folk art. This interest in the "exotic" made modern art appear radically different from Western tradition, though in incorporating African or Asian influences Western artists invariably drew on their own Western backgrounds. Picasso claimed in fact that he had only found in African art what he was already developing in his own painting: "the African sculptures that hang around almost everywhere in my studios are more witnesses than models."[11]

One of the most famous episodes in the public's hostile reaction to modern primitivism was the first performance of Igor Stravinsky's *The Rite of Spring* in Paris on May 29, 1913. The music to *The Rite of Spring* dispensed with traditional harmony in favor of rhythmic repetition of very short musical phrases in a variety of meters. The ballet, performed by the Ballets Russes of Sergei Diaghilev and Vaslav Nijinsky, attempted to recreate ancient pagan rituals, associated with life on the Russian steppes, and ended with a maiden dancing herself to death as a sacrifice to the gods. The sacrificed maiden, like Gauguin's native women or Picasso's *demoiselles*, represents the primitive female as a conduit to sacred power. In Stravinsky's work her death made the violence implicit in Picasso's broken forms literal.[12] According to the widely varying reports of the ballet's premiere, one faction of the audience hissed and booed so loudly that the music could not be heard. The defenders of the ballet fought back, and a near-riot ensued. Nijinsky himself was already notorious for having performed, the previous year, a dance in Claude Debussy's *The Afternoon of a Faun* that ended in simulated orgasm. Modern dance seemed a particularly appropriate arena for primitivism because it attempted to give full expression to the body. The American-born dancers Loie Fuller, who choreographed dances with electric lights and brightly colored fabrics, and Isadora Duncan, who danced barefoot in flowing gowns, seemed to liberate movement as much from the constraints of the Victorian corset as from the strictures of classical ballet. Dance became one of the leading modern arts, in part because of that intermingling of the dancer and the dance celebrated by Yeats.[13] At the same time, a craze for popular dance forms, like the tango, the flamenco, and the "apache," and for American ragtime music, swept Europe and influenced the experiments of classically trained composers and dancers.

Like the painting of Matisse, ragtime, and the music of Stravinsky, modern poetry relied heavily on rhythm. Poets frequently emphasized unusual rhythms over traditional meters such as iambic pentameter, which they compared to the unmusical regularity of a metronome (see Chapter Four). More syncopated rhythms, like jazz music, seemed to offer access to the primitive. The African-American poet Langston Hughes later wrote, in his poem "*Danse Africaine*" (1926):

> The low beating of the tom-toms,
> The slow beating of the tom-toms,
>    Low . . . slow
>    Slow . . . low –
> Stirs your blood.
>    Dance!

During the Harlem Renaissance of the 1920s, African-American writers and artists would often celebrate their own culture as having special access to the primitive, though some also questioned whether this African-American primitivism relied on white stereotypes. Hughes's poetry also inspired a number of modernist composers, such as Alexander von Zemlinsky, a close friend of the influential experimentalist Arnold Schoenberg, who set "*Danse Africaine*" in a high modernist style, and Kurt Weill, the collaborator of Bertolt Brecht, who wrote an opera, *Street Scene* (1947), with lyrics by Hughes, in a style that combined European classical music with American pop style. Despite the modernists' later reputation for elitism, they frequently drew on popular culture in their own work and sometimes sought mass audiences, outside the traditional realm of connoisseurs. Primitivism was one of the avenues toward this often desired mixing of high and low styles.

The umbrella term primitivism, rather like decadence before it, applies to a wide range of tendencies in the arts. In literature André Gide's *The Immoralist* (1902), set in North Africa, Hermann Hesse's *Siddhartha* (1922), about the founder of Buddhism, and Ezra Pound's experiments with Chinese characters all testified to the modernist fascination with the exotic. No precise literary equivalent of groups like the Fauves, *Die Brücke*, or *Der Blaue Reiter* existed. However, the novels of D. H. Lawrence embody many of the themes of literary primitivism. Virginia Woolf thought that Lawrence, like Forster, had attempted a compromise between modern and Edwardian techniques. A prolific poet, painter, and essayist, Lawrence is today best known for his novels, which remain popular with a general reading public in part because he maintained conventional syntax and grammar and fairly straightforward plots, such as the chronicle of several generations in the life of a family. Thematically, however, and particularly in their portrayals of sexuality, his novels challenged the traditions of English fiction. Like Forster, he concerned himself with the class barriers that divided English society. The son of a miner and a schoolteacher, Lawrence felt himself both attracted to and repelled by his father's working-class way of life. Many of his heroes are sons of the working classes who break away from their apparently immutable fates and ally themselves to artistic middle- or upper-class women, as Lawrence himself did to Frieda von Richthofen, the German-born wife of one of his professors at Nottingham University College. Lawrence's treatment of the life of the working classes continues themes from naturalism, but his approach to these themes is less distanced and analytical than that of Emile Zola or Arnold Bennett. His primitivism arises in part from his effort to engulf himself in the passions that Zola preferred to study from a clinical point of view.

Lawrence developed a number of theories about the flaws of modern civilization that helped to justify his literary endeavors. He continually sought the means to overcome the alienation typical of industrialized society through a fusion of man with woman, man with man, and man with nature. Lawrence shared Forster's interest in relationships between men, though he strongly disapproved of homosexuality. His theory of blood-brotherhood emphasized the regenerative powers of an authentic male friendship, and valued physical but nonsexual intimacy between men highly, as in scenes of wrestling in *Women in Love* (1916) and massage in *Aaron's Rod* (1922). Having read Nietzsche and Sigmund Freud and encountered the work of the German expressionists, Lawrence became convinced that sexual repression was causing the deterioration of English civilization. In particular, he blamed Christianity for its repressive division of the self into spirit and flesh and its privileging of the former. He found in Freud's Oedipal theory material for the development of his own views of the mother-son relationship, which he explored in his autobiographical novel *Sons and Lovers* (1913). Although Lawrence rejected many of the formal experiments typical of modern art as tending toward effete aestheticism, he shared the expressionist ideal of the work of art springing from the depths of its creator's unconscious life. His efforts to depict sexuality honestly made him a leading practitioner of modern fiction. His fourth novel, *The Rainbow* (1915), became a target of the National Purity League, being attacked for its descriptions (by today's standards, rather restrained) of its heroine's sexual relations with lovers of both sexes. However, Lawrence may in fact have been targeted because of his known opposition to the First World War and his reputation as a "pro-German," owing largely to his relationship with Frieda, whom by this time he had married.[14] Court proceedings were taken against the publisher, Methuen, not the author, and Methuen chose not to defend the novel. Most copies of the first edition were destroyed, and Lawrence could not find a British publisher for the sequel, *Women in Love*. After the suppression of *The Rainbow*, Lawrence became embittered at English provincialism and he spent much of his subsequent life traveling, especially in Italy, Australia, and Mexico. He found in Native American, Australian, and Mexican cultures inspiration for his fantasies of authoritarian leadership. In *The Plumed Serpent* (1926) a Mexican revolutionary attempts to revive the cult of the Aztec god Quetzalcoatl. The cult of the leader also dominates *Aaron's Rod* (1922), set in pre-fascist Italy, and *Kangaroo* (1923), set in Australia. The key to transcending modern bourgeois sterility lay, for Lawrence, in the encounter with the exotic, the primitive, or the authentic life of the working classes.

When Lawrence died of tuberculosis at the age of forty-five, in 1930, he seemed a martyr to the forces of censorship and repression that had sent him into exile. Like Forster's *Maurice* (written in 1913), Lawrence's most controversial novel, *Lady Chatterley's Lover*, could not be published as written in England during his lifetime. Privately printed in Italy in 1928, the novel revolves like *Maurice* around the relationship between an upper-class figure and a gamekeeper. Here, the upper-class lover is a woman, Lady Chatterley, married to an effete aristocrat who has been made impotent by war wounds. Lawrence described her sexual relations with the gamekeeper Mellors in explicit detail.

When Penguin finally published an unexpurgated version in 1960, the firm was charged with obscenity but acquitted in a famous trial, in which Forster appeared as a witness for the defense. This victory finally led to the abandonment of British attempts to censor major literary works, though censorship of the stage persisted for several years. The trial of *Lady Chatterley* opened the way for the more sexually explicit literature of the 1960s and after. In certain respects, the popular culture of the past half-century, with its emphasis on authenticity, rhythm, and affirmation of the body, represents the triumph of primitivism.[15]

The primitive often wore a frightening aspect for later modernists, however. Just as Picasso's more anguished vision of the human body overwhelmed Matisse's celebration of the *Joy of Life*, Conrad's negative evaluation of primitivism carried great weight with later writers in English. T. S. Eliot would quote *Heart of Darkness* at the beginning of his poem "The Hollow Men" (1925): "Mistah Kurtz – he dead." Eliot's conception of the primitive origins of poetry is evident in his statement that "Poetry begins, I dare say, with a savage beating a drum in a jungle and it retains that essential of percussion and rhythm."[16] This somewhat backhanded compliment, which traces poetry to primitive urges but also degrades those urges as "savage," typifies the attitude to the primitive of many modernists. Yet Eliot's understanding of poetry as a form of rhythm closely linked to African drumming and dance shares much with that of an African-American primitivist like Hughes. When the modernists could not entirely embrace the primitive, they often tried to sublimate it into what they considered higher forms.

## Modernizers

The primitivists looked to the past to correct modern civilization. Others excitedly embraced modern technology with its high-paced rhythms. There was no greater enthusiast for technological modernity than F. T. Marinetti, leader and publicist of the Italian futurists. Marinetti showed a particular interest in anything fast or lethal: racing cars, trains, automobiles, airplanes, machine guns, tanks. In his "Futurist Manifesto" (1909), he wrote that "A racing car whose hood is adorned with great pipes, like serpents of explosive breath – a roaring car that seems to ride on grapeshot – is more beautiful than the *Victory of Samothrace*" (a famous Hellenistic sculpture in the Louvre). He also proposed to "glorify war – the sole hygiene of the world – militarism, patriotism, the destructive gesture of freedom-bringers, beautiful ideas worth dying for, and scorn for woman."[17] Futurist celebration of war was not merely theoretical – the futurists actively advocated the Italian invasion of Libya and intervention in the First World War (on the side of the allies) and later supported Mussolini's fascism. Marinetti wrote "poems" about war that displayed words on a page representing the shape of a battle. This technique pushed the tradition of "concrete poetry," which calls attention to the poem's shape on the page, into new territory. Wanting to eliminate the tyranny of the lyrical "I" in poetry, he called his new poems "*parole in libertà*" or "words at liberty." The results are amusing but had little impact on the development of modernist literature. The literary genre at which Marinetti most excelled was the manifesto, and these successes spawned imitators. The poet Mina Loy, responding partly to Marinetti's "scorn for woman," published in 1914 a feminist manifesto that called for a new, modern attitude to sexuality. She decried the existing feminist movement as inadequate and called for a demolition of the ideal of female virtue. To this end, she proposed "the *unconditional* surgical *destruction of virginity* throughout the female population at puberty."[18]

In the visual arts futurism derived much of its technique from the most influential new artistic movement of the period, cubism. In retrospect, the impressionists, post-impressionists, and symbolists, as well as primitivists like the Fauves, are often seen as precursors of distinctively "modern" art. In painting this meant the introduction of "abstraction" or "nonrepresentational art," also known as "nonobjective art," that is, art that consciously rejects the illusion that it can imitate real objects. Nonobjective art develops out of the recognition, expressed by Maurice Denis, that a painting "is essentially a flat surface covered with colors assembled in a certain order." In cubism and other forms of modern art, the patterns, lines, planes of color, and shadows on the canvas seemed almost to get in the way of the object that the painting obstensibly "represented." Shortly after Pablo Picasso painted the *Les Demoiselles d'Avignon*, he and Georges Braque, the founders of cubism, began to break up the canvas into contradictory planes that seemed to represent the subject viewed from an immense variety of angles, an intensification of Paul Cézanne's play with perspective. Sometimes, as in many of Picasso's cubist portraits, only a few bits of the represented object (a beard, a hat, a pipe) are identifiable. The cubists strictly limited their color palette. In contrast with the vivid colors of the Fauves and expressionists, cubist paintings look like abstract patterns painted entirely in gray. In a further stage of experiment, beginning around 1910, Picasso and Braque also experimented with collage, sticking pieces of newspaper (sometimes with headlines), wallpaper, or imitation wood onto their canvases and thus again breaking the painterly illusion of an imitation of reality. Here, reality, instead of being represented on the canvas, is stuck onto it, and projects out of it. Picasso's and Braque's cubist experiments mark a new epoch in the history of art; they had a crucial influence on the development of twentieth-century abstract art.

The first group to demonstrate this influence were the futurist painters and sculptors, including Marinetti's collaborators Giacomo Balla, Umberto Boccioni, and Carlo Carrà. Following up on early cubism's use of multiple perspectives, they sought ways to portray motion on canvas. Futurist paintings tried to show a moving object seen at several different instants rather than frozen in time. Futurist art shows how new techniques for representing reality, such as photography and the motion picture, helped to spur avant-garde experiments. Black-and-white photography had contributed to post-impressionism because of its tendency to emphasize contrast and the reduction of three-dimensional space to a two-dimensional plane. The futurists' attempts to represent motion, as in Balla's *Abstract Speed* (1911) or Boccioni's *Unique Forms of Continuity in Space* (1913; figure 6), formed an artistic response to the challenge of the cinema. Motion pictures divided events into discrete instants and thus made possible a more precise analysis of moving objects; the futurists sought to register all the frames of a moving picture on a single canvas or in a single sculpture. Marinetti, who proclaimed his allegiance to everything modern, celebrated the cinema and declared that it must "detach itself from reality, from photography, from the graceful and solemn. It must become antigraceful, deforming, impressionistic, synthetic, dynamic, freewording."[19] Whether in the name of the primitive or of the modern, artists and writers were turning against beauty and grace and toward rhythm, speed, and color.

In England the young American poet Ezra Pound emulated the energy of Marinetti.[20] Pound had been fired from his job as a lecturer in romance languages at Wabash College in Indiana for sharing his bed with an actress (Pound claimed that he had slept on the floor). After living briefly in Italy, he arrived in London in 1908, determined to transform the literary scene there. Pound's importance to the development of modernism lies not only in his own work but in his influence on the other major writers of the period, whom he cultivated and promoted in American little magazines like *Poetry* (of which he was the London correspondent) and *The Egoist* (of which he was the poetry editor). He became a friend of W. B. Yeats, who was twenty years his senior, and encouraged Yeats's turn away from romantic and symbolist poetic diction and toward poetic precision and colloquial language. Later, Pound publicized T. S. Eliot's poetry and edited the manuscripts of *The Waste Land* (1922), which Eliot dedicated to him as "*il miglior fabbro,*" the better or best craftsman. He also worked to promote James Joyce's writing, and, although Pound's poetry is read less often than that of Yeats or Eliot, he was arguably the most influential poet in establishing the canon of

6.   Umberto Boccioni (1882–1916), *Unique Forms of Continuity in Space*, 1913. Bronze. $43\frac{7}{8} \times 34\frac{7}{8} \times 15\frac{3}{4}$in. Acquired through the Lillie P. Bliss Bequest (231.1948). The Museum of Modern Art, New York. Digital Image © The Museum of Modern Art/Licensed by SCALA/Art Resource, NY.

modern poetry and in articulating its aims. In imitation of French avant-garde movements, Pound invented the term "Imagisme" to help publicize the poetry of the American poet H. D. (Hilda Doolittle), a friend from his teenage years to whom he had once been engaged. Pound stated the three tenets of imagism in 1913:

1. Direct treatment of the "thing," whether subjective or objective.
2. To use absolutely no word that does not contribute to the presentation.
3. As regarding rhythm: to compose in the sequence of the musical phrase, not the sequence of a metronome.[21]

Pound's emphasis on "direct treatment" suggests the influence of painting as a model. His desire to avoid unnecessary words and his championing of free verse share something of symbolism's aspiration toward pure poetry, though Pound believed that he was breaking away from symbolism by rejecting its emotionalism. His reference to "musical phras[ing]" recalls Walter Pater's aestheticist dictum, in *The Renaissance* (1873), that "all art constantly aspires towards the condition of music"; the directness of the imagist representation of experience also echoes Pater.

   H. D. moved to London in 1911, played an important role in the development of modernist free verse, and later underwent psychoanalysis with Sigmund Freud. In addition to her early imagist poems, she later wrote a number of longer works, often combining psychoanalysis, mythology, and feminism, including a trilogy of poems about London during the Second World War and an epic about Helen of Troy. Some of the qualities of early modernist free verse can be seen in H. D.'s "Oread" (1914):

> Whirl up, sea –
> Whirl your pointed pines,
> Splash your great pines
> On our rocks,
> Hurl your green over us,
> Cover us with your pools of fir.

In the poem's central image, pine trees seem to arise like waves from the sea, reaching up to embrace and cover the mountains. Although the poem has only one end-rhyme, which is not really a rhyme (pines/pines), it has various other elements that define it as verse rather than prose. The repetition of "whirl" at the beginning of the first two lines and the initial rhyme with "hurl" in line five structure the poem. There is little enjambment here. Each line contains its own syntactic unit, except that lines three and four form a single unit. Each of the five syntactic units begins with a verb in the imperative mood, addressed to the sea: whirl, splash, hurl, cover. The repetition of "your" also links the lines, and the poem moves from the first half, in which all the pronouns point to the sea, to a second half dominated by the pronoun "us," referring to the mountain nymphs. The poem recalls Yeats's "Who Goes With Fergus?" in the skyward motion of the "pools of fir."

The imagists wrote poetry that closely resembled everyday speech, focused on the description of objects and facts, used irregular meters and short lines, and avoided traditional stanza forms. Their main contribution to the development of modernism was the introduction of free verse, which already had a long history in France and the United States, into England. Another famous imagist poem, Pound's "In a Station of the Metro" of 1911, reads, in its entirety:

> The apparition of these faces in the crowd;
> Petals on a wet, black bough.

The juxtaposition of two images, the travelers on the subway platform and the flower petals, does offer a "direct treatment." The sparseness of the poem, its lack of verbs, and its rhythmic quality (a long iambic line followed by a short heavily accented one) fulfill other tenets of imagism and suggest Pound's interest in Japanese haiku, the counterpart of the post-impressionist painters' fascination with Japanese prints. The poem is structured paratactically: two images are juxtaposed and the relationship between them, presumably a metaphorical one, is left implicit. The reader is to understand that the faces of the subway riders are *like* petals on a wet black bough, but the word *like* does not appear in the poem. The lyrical "I" is absent, too; the poem seems to describe an observation without an observer.

Pound's faces in the Metro are already ghostly: "apparitions." The replacement of the underworld with the underground suggests modernity, but it is a modernity distinctly imbued with a literary heritage. Although petals and boughs figure importantly in Japanese art, the poem draws on the long European poetic tradition of comparing souls to flowers, blossoms, or fallen leaves. Homer wrote that "Very like leaves / upon this earth are the generations of men: /.... one generation flowers / even as another dies away." Virgil added the bough: "As leaves that yield their hold on boughs and fall / Through forests in the early frost of autumn." Dante wrote of the bough that "sees all its fallen garments on the ground," and Milton imagined the fallen angels "thick as autumnal leaves that strow the brooks / In Vallombrosa." In Pound's poem it is unclear whether the "petals on a wet, black bough" have already fallen onto the forest floor, or whether they remain clinging to a still living bough. Perhaps the Metro station is not yet the underworld but only a way-station at which Charon's boat may arrive momentarily. At one level, imagism might appear to rely on an ideal of transparent language that conflicts with the nonrepresentational character of much modern art. As this poem demonstrates, however, an emphasis on language as medium carries into poetry some of modern art's concern with the way that all representations are constructed out of previous representations.

Imagism was the first organized attempt at a modernist school in England and the United States. The imagists' emphasis on "direct treatment of the thing," their dislike of sing-songy or metronomic meters, and their avoidance of traditional poetic diction all prefigure the formal concerns of the later modernists, which were closely linked to their challenge to the legacy of romanticism. Pound's friend T. E. Hulme called for a "hard, dry" classical verse that would break away from the sentimentality of the late Victorian epigones of romanticism.[22] Much modernist poetry continued to reject sentimentalism and to emphasize complexity. The imagists' preference for impersonality and rejection of any hint of psychological depth, however, put them outside the mainstream of later modernist writing, which in fact continually returned to such romantic themes as the divided self or the struggle between the artist and society. Although relatively short-lived, imagism played an important role in introducing modernist sensibilities to English-language poetry and thus had an impact on such major modernists as Eliot, Marianne Moore, Wallace Stevens, William Carlos Williams, Yeats, and also D. H. Lawrence, who published his poetry in imagist anthologies without subscribing to all the imagists' principles. The American Amy Lowell joined the imagists, and eventually took over the movement, publishing three imagist anthologies during the First World War. Lowell's popularity and her attraction to more traditional verse forms alienated Pound, who felt that the movement had lost its experimental edge and become feminized; he rechristened it "Amygism."

Pound now joined forces with the Canadian-born painter Wyndham Lewis and a group of other artistic radicals, based at the Rebel Art Center. He coined the term vorticism to describe Lewis's art, transforming his earlier imagism by adding a new emphasis on movement: "The image is not an idea. It is a radiant node or cluster; it is what I can, and must perforce, call a VORTEX, from which, and through which, and into which, ideas are constantly rushing."[23] The vorticists emphasized motion and imitated the violent rhetoric and brash modernity of cubism and futurism (from which they strove mightily to distinguish themselves). Vorticist art's patterns of lines, arcs, and other geometric shapes sometimes seemed purely nonrepresentational but more often suggested the rapid movement of bodies or machines. Lewis's painting *Kermesse* of 1912, named after a Flemish peasant dance, represented a radically mechanized alternative to Matisse's graceful, flowing paintings of dancers. The huge original painting, which adorned the walls of an avant-garde nightclub, has been lost, but his study with the same title (figure 7) gives a sense of the larger work. Critics thought that the painting, with its inhuman dancers and abstract lines representing movement, resembled "some terrible battle of extermination between murderous insects," the attack of "some gigantic fantastic insects descended upon earth from some other planet," or "a rather disunited family of Mr. Wells' Martians," a possible illustration for *The War of the Worlds* (1898).[24] Lewis put some of this savage energy into his own writing. In a review of Lewis's first novel *Tarr*, a novel about prewar Paris published in the last year of the First World War (1918), Eliot noted that "The artist is more *primitive*, as well as more civilized, than his contemporaries, his experience is deeper than civilization, and he only uses the phenomena of civilization in expressing it . . . In the work of Mr. Lewis we recognize the thought of the modern and the energy of the cave-man."[25] That combination of hypermodern civilization and savage energy, Lewis's vision of the artist, typified the prewar avant-garde but, as an ideal, it would not survive the combination of modernity and savagery of the First World War.

## Modernism and science fiction

The futurists and vorticists celebrated the possibilities of modernity, but throughout the modernist period H. G. Wells's nightmare vision of the future would also find many followers. Science fiction would provide an avenue for exploring the dystopic possibilities of English culture, notably in Aldous Huxley's *Brave New World* (1932) and George Orwell's *1984* (1949). Both books envision an international, authoritarian government that controls its people by channeling their sexual drives. In Huxley's vision the state-controlled culture industry gratifies every sexual or sensual desire, group sex (with contraceptives) is compulsory, and the people are drugged with the hallucinogenic drug soma. Orwell imagines the government of Oceania controlling its people through electronic vigilance and repressive antisex leagues. In both cases the only hope of freedom from the oppressive world government is in a return to authentic primitive sexuality in the form of the heterosexual couple, but Huxley's John the Savage and Orwell's Winston Smith are destroyed when they try to escape from their futuristic nightmare worlds. Here, as in the works of the literary primitivists, authentic sexuality resides in the past, and the future promises humans only further alienation from our bodies.

## "On or about December, 1910"

The first decade of the twentieth century, then, witnessed Edwardian continuity, primitivist rejection of modernity, and futurist celebration of the modern. Although primitivism and futurism might appear to face in opposite directions, both drew on an idealized image of another time (past or future) to

7.  Wyndham Lewis (1882–1957), *Kermesse,* 1912. Gouache and watercolor with pen and black ink over graphite on two joined sheets of woven paper, left edge unevenly trimmed. 12 × 12$\frac{1}{16}$ in. Yale Center for British Art, Paul Mellon Fund and Gift of Neil F. and Ivan E. Phillips in memory of their mother, Mrs. Rosalie Phillips. © Wyndham Lewis and the estate of the late Mrs G. A. Wyndham Lewis by kind permission of the Wyndham Lewis Memorial Trust (a registered charity).

criticize the narrowness of the present or recent past; both also challenged the primacy of reason in human affairs, drawing inspiration in particular from Friedrich Nietzsche's theory of the will to power. By 1910, the year of Edward VII's death, many in England also felt the need for a radical change, in the social and political realms as well as the aesthetic. The years immediately before the First World War, when post-impressionism and futurism reached London and vorticism was launched, struck many later observers as markedly different from the Edwardian era. Virginia Woolf claimed that social and political life, as well as art and literature, had suddenly changed "on or about December, 1910": "All human relations have shifted – those between masters and servants, husbands and wives, parents and children." Woolf's catalogue suggests three kinds of human relations that were changing. The problem of human sexuality, "husbands and wives," was perhaps the most evident in literature, as the account of primitivism has shown. The change in the relations between "parents and children" was widely felt in a broader sense as a generational divide, and contributed to the revolutionary rhetoric of groups like the futurists and to Woolf's own rejection of the Edwardians. The most immediate political challenge of the period after 1910 concerned "masters and servants," the upper classes and the working classes, or the colonizers and the colonized. These shifts led to three major social crises in England: the radicalization of the trade unions, the suffrage movement, and the conflict over Home Rule for Ireland. Together, these movements caused the crisis that the historian George Dangerfield later described as "the strange death of Liberal England."[26] The Edwardian world view, and the Liberal Party, never recovered from this crisis. Woolf was not alone in seeing 1910 as a watershed in the development of modern England, a generational shift. Dangerfield described what he labeled the revolts of the workers, the Tories, and the women as symptoms of a neurosis afflicting British society on the eve of the First World War. He thought that Britain was ready to cast off the repressive culture of the Victorian era but had to do so in a sort of cultural convulsion. To many, the modern art displayed at the first post-impressionist exhibition appeared to be one of the symptoms of this neurosis.

The new assertiveness of the working classes made itself felt in a coalminers' strike in South Wales in 1910 and dockers' strikes throughout the country in 1911. During the Edwardian period, wages had not kept pace with rising prices. A Liberal law of 1906 had made strikes legal, and now the class from which D. H. Lawrence had sprung began demanding better pay and conditions, including a minimum wage. Riots ensued and two men were killed by troops firing on strikers at the Liverpool docks. Influenced by the writings of the French syndicalist Georges Sorel, the theorists of the labor movement promoted the idea of a general strike which would give power over industry to the producers (the workers).[27] Although the strikes met with only limited success, the new assertiveness of the unions challenged Britain's class structure. The change in attitudes also led to changes in political power. The election results of 1910 made the Liberal Party dependent for the first time on the support of the socialist British Labour Party and the pro-Home Rule Irish Parliamentary Party in order to form the government.

The question of Ireland's political status proved a more direct threat to political stability than the working-class agitations. The main proposed reform was "Home Rule," an alternative to independence according to which Ireland would have a parliament of its own but remain subservient to the Queen and the British parliament at Westminster. During the Victorian period, the Irish Parliamentary Party, under the leadership of Charles Stewart Parnell, "the uncrowned king" of Ireland, had convinced the Liberal Party, under the prime minister, William Ewart Gladstone, to support Home Rule. A significant portion of Gladstone's own party, the Liberal Unionists, rebelled, and no change occurred in Irish government under Victoria. Parnell's downfall came when his adulterous affair with "Kitty" O'Shea was revealed in the divorce case launched by her husband, an army captain. Hounded out of office by the Church and the Liberals, Parnell became a symbol to young men like W. B. Yeats and James Joyce of Ireland's mistreatment of its own leaders, "the old sow that eats her farrow," as Joyce later put it in *A Portrait of the Artist as a Young Man* (1916). In his speech accepting the Nobel Prize for 1923, Yeats claimed that "The modern literature of Ireland, and indeed all that stir of thought which prepared for the Anglo-Irish war, began when Parnell fell from power in 1891. A disillusioned and embittered Ireland turned from parliamentary politics; an event was conceived and the race began, as I think, to be troubled by that event's long gestation."[28] For Yeats, at least, the crisis of liberalism in Ireland was closely linked to the crisis of representation.

The question of Home Rule arose again in 1912, reintroduced by the Liberal prime minister Herbert Asquith. Irish politics had, however, become more polarized since Parnell's time, with Gaelic nationalist groups like Sinn Fein agitating for complete independence and Protestants from Ulster, in northern Ireland, rejecting even Home Rule as a threat to their religion. The Ulstermen formed militias to oppose the government's introduction of Home Rule. Conservatives (Tories) in both houses of parliament supported the cause of Ulster, accused the prime minister of treason, and eventually encouraged British soldiers to mutiny when Asquith attempted to put down the Ulster Volunteers, who had been smuggling in guns from Germany. The Tories' anger resulted in part from Asquith's passage of the Parliament Act, which for the first time removed the power of the hereditary House of Lords to veto legislation passed by the elected House of Commons. The moves toward democracy and away from empire frightened the Tories, and the Irish situation seemed likely to result in civil war until the international crisis that resulted in the First World War made internal squabbles irrelevant.

The social change most relevant to the development of modernist literature, however, was the change in the relation between the sexes. The movement for women's suffrage, met with staunch disregard by almost all male politicians, became violent. In 1909 suffragettes began destroying property. Many were imprisoned, and then began a series of hunger strikes that resulted in women's being force-fed through tubes that had to be inserted down their throats through their clenched teeth. The suffragettes went further, planting bombs, starting fires, and slashing pictures at art galleries, including a portrait of Henry James by John Singer Sargent. In June 1913 a suffragette named Emily Davison died after throwing herself under the feet of George V's horse during the Derby. These unladylike demonstrations pointed to a radical rejection not only of the male-dominated political system but also of the patriarchal social standards that supported it. The behavior of the suffragettes suggested the radical changes in attitudes toward sex and gender occurring just below the surface of English life. Women began to reject the restrictive roles that had been accorded to them, sought entry to the professions, and made use of birth control. Campaigns to change the divorce laws yielded no immediate results, but they reflected a change in the dominant attitude to marriage; in some portions of society, wives were coming to be seen as the equals of their husbands and marriage as a contract that could be dissolved if both parties so desired.[29]

Although homosexual behavior remained illegal, it became for the first time in generations the subject of frank discussion. The vegetarian socialist Edward Carpenter, inspired by Walt Whitman, published *Homogenic Love* (1896) and *The Intermediate Sex* (1908), which defended homosexuality as an innate tendency that should not be punished.[30] It was Carpenter who convinced his friend E. M. Forster to write *Maurice* in 1913. Another friend of Carpenter, the English scientist Havelock Ellis, wrote a series of *Studies in the Psychology of Sex*. One of these, *Sexual Inversion* (1897), also argued that homosexuality was a natural condition, a sexual identity ("inversion") rather than a criminal act; the book was suppressed in England. The remaining volumes of this major contribution to the study of sexual life were published only in the United States. A number of important European literary works, including André Gide's *The Immoralist* (1902), Thomas Mann's *Death in Venice* (1913), and Marcel Proust's *Remembrance of Things Past* (1913–27) addressed homosexuality more frankly than was possible in England. Homosexuality was, however, openly acknowledged in certain artistic and intellectual circles, such as the Bloomsbury Group, which included Forster, Lytton Strachey, and Woolf. Bloomsbury also played an important role in disseminating Freud's ideas. Sigmund Freud's theories about sexuality, repression, and the talking cure did not have much circulation in England before the First World War, but after the war his works were published in England by Leonard and Virginia Woolf's Hogarth Press, in a translation by Strachey's brother James.

Bloomsbury embodied the new sexual freedom that would transform social relations after the First World War. The group had no formal existence but quickly came to be seen by other intellectuals and the reading public as the leading center for mainstream modernism in England. In 1911, the year after "human character changed," the then Virginia Stephen, the daughter of a famous Victorian intellectual, decided to move to a house in the Bloomsbury neighborhood of London near the British Museum with several men, none of whom was her husband. Some of her relatives were shocked, and her father's old friend Henry James found her lifestyle rather too bohemian. Her housemates were her brother Adrian, Duncan Grant, John Maynard Keynes, and Leonard Woolf, whom she married a year later. Grant and Keynes were lovers, and the heterosexual members of the group, too, were known for their unconventional relationships. Virginia's sister, the painter Vanessa Bell, lived for much of her life with Grant, who was also her artistic collaborator, and the two had a daughter. Throughout all this, Vanessa remained married to Clive Bell, while Grant had a series of homosexual love affairs. Most of the men in the Bloomsbury Group had studied at Cambridge University, and many had belonged to an intellectual club called the Apostles, which, under the influence of the philosopher G. E. Moore, emphasized the importance of friendship and aesthetic experience, a more earnest form of Oscar Wilde's aestheticism. A typical Bloomsbury figure, Lytton Strachey wrote his best-known book, *Eminent Victorians* (1918), in a satirical vein, debunking the myths surrounding such revered figures as Florence Nightingale. Strachey was the most open homosexual of the group, and Woolf vividly recalled his demolition of all the Victorian proprieties when he noted a stain on Vanessa's dress and remarked, "Semen": "With that one word all barriers of reticence and reserve went down."[31] Many of the Bloomsbury intellectuals became famous, whether as novelists, painters, art critics, or, in the case of Keynes, the most influential economist of the twentieth century. Individual members of Bloomsbury stood for socialism, post-impressionism, liberalism, pacifism, monetarism, or modernism, but the group as a whole stood for an intense aesthetic response to life and a rejection of Victorian morality.

Bloomsbury's most direct contribution to the change in human character that Woolf later analyzed was the first post-impressionist exhibition, "Manet and the Post-Impressionists." The exhibition focused on the work of Paul Cézanne, Paul Gauguin, and Vincent van Gogh, but also attempted to outline a trajectory from Edouard Manet to the most recent "post-impressionists," Henri Matisse and Pablo Picasso, who were both represented in the exhibition. Most British art critics in 1910 were still trying to digest the impressionism of Claude Monet and Pierre Auguste Renoir, and the new exhibition, by rejecting impressionism as old-fashioned, baffled even sympathetic observers. Forster wrote that "Gauguin and Van Gogh were too much for me."[32] Many viewers and critics thought the show a hoax or an offense against English culture, as is evident from the list of the words applied to the exhibition that the art historian Charles Harrison has recorded: "horror," "madness," "infection," "sickness of the soul," "putrescence," "pornography," "anarchy" and "evil."[33] A few, however, defended the exhibition, and the consummate Edwardian Arnold Bennett suggested that the scorn heaped on modern art by the British public showed "that London is infinitely too self-complacent even to suspect that it is London and not the exhibition which is making itself ridiculous."[34] The champions of modernity in art shared Bennett's sense that London was woefully behind the times. English artists soon began to absorb the influences of Matisse and the early, precubist Picasso. A second post-impressionist exhibition in 1912 displayed paintings by Bloomsbury artists such as Vanessa Bell and Grant alongside works by the major French painters and a number of rather obscure Russians. Bell's *Studland Beach*, painted (like Wyndham Lewis's *Kermesse*) around 1912 (see cover), shows the achievement of British post-impressionism in its arrangement of planes of color and balancing of two groups of figures seen only from behind. The painting emphasizes what her husband Clive called "significant form."[35] The figures in the left foreground of the canvas seem to be watching those in the upper right corner, calling attention to the act of perception involved in painting. All the figures face away from the viewer, oriented like the painting itself toward the sea. As the art historian Lisa Tickner has shown, Vanessa's paintings served as an inspiration to her sister, who would write, in *To the Lighthouse* (1927), of the artist's struggle to fulfill her vision in terms of the relation between masses: "It was a question, she remembered, how to connect this mass on the right hand with that on the left. She might do it by bringing the line of the branch across so; or break the vacancy in the foreground by an object (James perhaps) so. But the danger was that by doing that the unity of the whole might be broken."[36] In contrast with the frenetic energy of Lewis's dancers, Bell's painting represents a scene of calm, in which nature and the family group are held together by compositional form.

The writers of the turn of the century had already begun to develop a distinctively "modern" literature, drawing on the techniques of impressionism and symbolism in particular. The social changes that England underwent in the first decade of the twentieth century helped to convince writers like Woolf that a radically new art and literature were needed to express the changes in human character wrought by modernity. Bell's *Studland Beach* and Lewis's *Kermesse* represent the struggle over what that new art would look like. Although Roger Fry had included Lewis's portrait of Lytton Strachey in the second post-impressionist exhibition of 1912, Lewis rejected English post-impressionism and proposed a more "masculine" and "modern" art. Lewis and Ezra Pound represented a hard-edged experimentalism deriving its energy from the European avant-gardes, while Bell and Woolf stood for an emerging modernism that had more in common with Matisse's flowing celebration of the *Joy of Life*. Lewis welcomed the war (though he later regretted it), while most of the Bloomsbury intellectuals were pacifists and conscientious objectors. The two possibilities represented by vorticism and post-impressionism would survive the war and come to be identified respectively with two controversial terms, "the avant-garde" and "high modernism." In 1914, however, the development of these two competing tendencies and the internal conflicts within English society were interrupted by the arrival of the war, which combined primitivism and futurism in ways that perhaps only H. G. Wells could have foreseen.

## Further reading

### Literary works

H. D., *Collected Poems*, ed. Louis L. Martz. New York: New Directions, 1983.

W. E. B. Du Bois, *The Souls of Black Folk* (various editions).

E. M. Forster, *Howards End, Maurice, A Passage to India* (various editions).

Langston Hughes, *Collected Poems*, ed. Arnold Rampersad. New York: Knopf, 1994.

Aldous Huxley, *Brave New World* (various editions).

James Joyce, *Dubliners* (various editions).

D. H. Lawrence *The Rainbow, Sons and Lovers, Women in Love* (various editions).

George Orwell, *1984* (various editions).

Lytton Strachey, *Eminent Victorians* (various editions).

H. G. Wells, *Ann Veronica, The Time Machine, The War of the Worlds* (various editions).

### Contemporary critical statements

Clive Bell, *Art* (1914). New York: G. P. Putnam's Sons, 1958.

*BLAST* (1914–15). Santa Barbara: Black Sparrow Press, 1981.

George Dangerfield, *The Strange Death of Liberal England* (1935). Reprint Stanford: Stanford University Press, 1997.

Mina Loy, "Feminist Manifesto" in *Modernism Anthology*.

F. T. Marinetti, *Let's Murder the Moonshine: Selected Writings*, ed. and trans. R. W. Flint. Los Angeles: Sun & Moon, 1991.

Ezra Pound, "A Retrospect," in *Modernism Anthology*.

Virginia Woolf, *The Virginia Woolf Reader*, ed. Mitchell Leaska. San Diego: Harcourt Brace Jovanovitch, 1985.

## Later criticism

Michael Bell, *Primitivism*. London: Methuen, 1972.

Christopher Butler, *Early Modernism: Literature, Music, and Painting in Europe, 1900–1916*. Oxford: Oxford University Press, 1994.

Robert Goldwater, *Primitivism in Modern Art*, rev. edn. New York: Vintage Books, 1967.

Ernst Gombrich, *The Preference for the Primitive: Episodes in the History of Western Taste and Art*. London: Phaidon, 2002.

Charles Harrison, *English Art and Modernism 1900–1939*, 2nd edn. New Haven: Yale University Press, 1994.

Charles Harrison, Francis Frascina, and Gill Perry, *Primitivism, Cubism, Abstraction: The Early Twentieth Century*. New Haven: Yale University Press, 1994.

Samuel Hynes, *The Edwardian Turn of Mind*. Princeton: Princeton University Press, 1968.

Hugh Kenner, *The Pound Era*. Berkeley and Los Angeles: University of California Press, 1971.

William Rubin, ed. *"Primitivism" in 20th-Century Art*. New York: Museum of Modern Art, 1984.

Peter Stansky, *On or about December 1910: Early Bloomsbury and Its Intimate World*. Cambridge, MA: Harvard University Press, 1996.

Lisa Tickner, *Modern Life and Modern Subjects: British Art in the Early Twentieth Century*. New Haven: Yale University Press, 2000.

# Chapter 3

# The avant-garde and high modernism

When Gertrude Stein decided to write the story of her life, she did so in the voice of her lover, Alice B. Toklas. In *The Autobiography of Alice B. Toklas* (1933), Stein has Toklas describe her first dinner, in 1907, at Stein's home at 27, rue de Fleurus, Paris, where the walls were covered with paintings by Paul Cézanne, Paul Gauguin, Henri Matisse, Pablo Picasso, and Pierre Auguste Renoir, then mostly unknown to Americans from San Francisco like Toklas. Seated next to Picasso, who was flustered at having arrived late, Toklas tried to calm him down by murmuring that she liked his painting of Stein. The portrait, influenced by Picasso's fascination with Iberian masks, marked an important stage in his development of cubism. Stein records Picasso's response to Toklas: "Yes, he said, everybody says that she does not look like it but that does not make any difference, she will, he said." In her memoir of Picasso, Stein wrote, "I was and still am satisfied with my portrait, for me it is I, and it is the only reproduction of me which is always I, for me." Stein's story about Picasso's portrait of her encapsulates the mythology of the avant-garde, the French term for a vanguard (the leading troops in a battle), which referred by extension to the most radical innovators in the arts. In Stein's story she and Picasso share an understanding of the avant-garde artist as one who can see what the future holds, one who is ahead of his or her time. The story also demonstrates the coterie nature of the avant-garde, that is, the tendency for small groups of experimental artists to support one another and form the nucleus for broader artistic movements.[1]

The term avant-garde merits some analysis and comparison with the term modernism, which is more widely used in literary studies in English. The idea of an artistic avant-garde goes back to the early nineteenth century; after the revolutions of 1848, it implied a connection between political and artistic radicalism.[2] Although some later avant-gardists, such as the futurists, involved themselves directly in politics, the concept came to mean in the twentieth century whatever was radical and transformative in the world of the arts.[3] Those artists whose work was particularly experimental, particularly challenging to accepted standards, became known as the avant-garde. Today, when literary critics write of "high" modernism, they are usually attempting to distinguish what they see as the relatively mainstream works of the 1920s from the more radical experiments of the prewar avant-garde or of such later avant-gardes as dada and surrealism. The term avant-garde also generally implies organized groupings, such as the fauves, cubists, futurists, vorticists, and other groups subscribing to various "-isms," often aggressively announced in manifestos (see Chapter Two). Modernists might or might not belong to such groups, and their manifestos tended to be more individualistic. Finally, the term modernism is generally used today to describe all experimental literature in English of the first half of the twentieth century, whereas avant-garde refers mainly to continental European tendencies. Nonetheless, the two terms overlap to a considerable degree, and the attempt to make a sharp distinction between the two has often led to a skewed perspective on modern literature and art.

The term "avant-garde," though applied to art only during the past century and a half, may be used to describe works of art of any historical period. "Modernism," however, is also a period concept. In its broadest sense it refers to art and literature since Charles Baudelaire and Gustave Flaubert, but in a more restricted sense it applies especially to work produced between the two world wars. During the 1920s, the techniques and experiments that had been pioneered by the prewar avant-garde movements increasingly became accepted by a more mainstream public. Some critics have suggested that the "high modernism" of T. S. Eliot or Virginia Woolf betrays an elitist attitude to mass culture, whereas the avant-gardes tended to embrace the masses. However, the dichotomy between high modernism and the avant-garde, though widely accepted today, is in fact somewhat inaccurate historically. James Joyce's *Ulysses* (1922), now frequently proclaimed the greatest novel of the twentieth century and seen as part of high modernism, was in fact written in an avant-garde milieu and was shocking enough upon its publication to be banned in the United Kingdom, Ireland, and the United States. To understand the full reach of modernism in its broadest sense, it is important to understand the wide range – from radical experimentation and rejection of existing conventions to careful and gradual modification of those conventions – that occurs within any national tradition, within any given medium or genre, and often indeed within the work of a given major artist or writer. The works of Eliot, Joyce, Picasso, and Stein herself show that a sharp distinction between "the avant-garde" and "modernism" can be misleading. The major practitioners of avant-garde experiments often later developed into the highest of the "high" modernists, while conversely (as in the case of Joyce), those who helped to define modernism sometimes became increasingly radical over the course of their careers.

The First World War marks a watershed in the history of modern literature and art. The war appeared to many as the culmination of the nineteenth-century crises of liberalism and reason. The crucial steps towards nonrepresentational art preceded the war. In England some artistic conservatives hoped that the war would purge the arts of avant-garde tendencies. Many writers and artists, though, saw traditional means of representation as tied up with the ideologies that had led to war. They therefore followed the avant-gardes in rejecting those traditional means, while not necessarily in the wholesale rejection of representation; in the war's aftermath, although nonrepresentational art spawned a tradition of its own, many writers and artists recognized the need for a new means of representation, one that would indeed serve the purposes of *mimesis*, but in a form adequate to modern reality. The development of "high" literary modernism resulted largely from the attempt to apply the new art forms that had been explored by the prewar avant-gardes to the unprecedented historical experience of the war. This chapter explores the heyday of the avant-garde in the years before the First World War and the invention of English-language modernism during and after the war.

## The avant-garde moment

The changes heralded by the post-impressionist exhibition and the imagist and vorticist movements in England were progressing even more rapidly in the rest of Europe. Avant-garde manifestos frequently proclaimed their new "-isms" to be distinctively national (Italian futurism, English vorticism), but the avant-garde and modernism were fundamentally cosmopolitan movements, in the root sense of that word, movements of citizens of the world and of world-cities. Each major city had its own version of modernism, often defined by foreigners who had been attracted to the city by its world-class status. Paris was the capital of the avant-garde; foreigners such as the American Gertrude Stein, the Spaniard Pablo Picasso, and the Italian F. T. Marinetti moved there to work. Apollinaris Kostrowitzky, half Polish and half Italian, took the name Guillaume Apollinaire. He became a major French poet, as did Blaise Cendrars, born Freddy Sauser, half Swiss and half Scottish. In the years leading up to the First World War, such entrepreneurs of the avant-garde launched a series of new literary and artistic movements, such as unanimism, imaginism, acmeism, rayonism, and simultaneism, some of which lasted longer than others. (For the major literary movements, see table 3.1.) Other avant-garde circles flourished

Table 3.1. *Literary movements in the early twentieth century*

**Futurism**

Active from 1909    Leading figure: F. T. Marinetti    Manifesto: Marinetti, "Futurist Manifesto" (1909)

Italian movement; celebrated speed, technology, and war; attacked symbolism and museums.

"We affirm that the world's magnificence has been enriched by a new beauty: the beauty of speed." (Marinetti)[a]

**Imagism**

Active from 1912    Leading figures: H. D., Amy Lowell, Ezra Pound    Manifesto: Pound, "A Retrospect" (1918)

Anglo-American movement; opposed "high-falutin'" poetic diction; championed free verse.

"Use no superfluous word, no adjective which does not reveal something." (Pound)[b]

**Vorticism**

Active from 1913    Leading figures: Wyndham Lewis, Ezra Pound    Manifesto: various authors, "Long Live the Vortex" (1914)

English movement inspired by futurism and imagism; adds to imagism an emphasis on movement.

"The Modern World is due almost entirely to Anglo-Saxon genius." ("Long Live the Vortex")[c]

**Expressionism**

Active from 1911    Leading figures: Kasimir Edschmid, Wassily Kandinsky    Manifesto: Edschmid, "On Literary Expressionism" (1917)

German modernist movement; celebrates the primitive forces within the individual and the breaking of rules.

"In this art, each becomes the most elevated and the most deplorable of things: *becomes a human being*." (Edschmid)[d]

## Dada

**Active from 1916**    Leading figures: Marcel Duchamp, Tristan Tzara    Manifesto: Tzara, "Dada Manifesto" (1918)

International movement; attacks the very concept of art; embraces randomness and performance art.

"The abolition of memory: DADA; the abolition of archaeology: DADA; the abolition of prophets: DADA; the abolition of the future: **dada.**" (Tzara)[e]

## Surrealism

**Active from 1920s**    Leading figures: Louis Aragon, André Breton    Manifesto: Breton, "Manifesto of Surrealism" (1924)

Continuation of dada by other means; concerned with the unconscious mind; uneasily allied with communism.

"Dictated by thought, in the absence of any control exercised by reason, exempt from any moral or aesthetic concern." (Breton)[f]

---

[a] "The Founding and Manifesto of Futurism," in *Modernism Anthology*, p. 251.

[b] "A Retrospect," in *Modernism Anthology*, p. 375.

[c] *Modernism Anthology*, p. 293.

[d] Quoted in Peter Nicholls, *Modernisms: A Literary Guide* (Berkeley and Los Angeles: University of California Press, 1995), p. 160.

[e] "Dada Manifesto," in *Modernism Anthology*, p. 280.

[f] André Breton, *Manifestoes of Surrealism*, trans. Richard Seaver and Helen R. Lane (Ann Arbor: University of Michigan Press, 1972), p. 26.

in Berlin, Chicago, Moscow, New York, Prague, St. Petersburg, and Vienna. The critic Marjorie Perloff has described the immediate prewar years as a "Futurist moment," in which not just futurists but a variety of avant-garde movements "felt themselves to be on the verge of a new age that would be more exciting, more promising, more inspiring than any preceding one."[4] While avant-garde artists saw themselves as an elite who were capable of transcending the conventional views of art held by the bourgeoisie, they often embraced those aspects of the modern world that official cultural institutions rejected as "low-brow" or popular. Cendrars expressed the ethos of the avant-garde moment when he declared that "the windows of my poetry are wide open to the boulevards."[5] The celebration of modern life, technology, and mass culture (including advertising) marked the generation of young innovators who attempted to transform the entire Western tradition of art and literature in a few short years.

The break with the past was clearest in painting. Here, the crisis of representation that had been evident at least since Edouard Manet led at last to an outright rejection of representation as the task of the visual arts. The fauves, expressionists, futurists, and even cubists had continued in some sense to represent "reality," albeit in increasingly distorted forms. "Modern" art is often understood to begin with the introduction of "nonrepresentational," "nonobjective," or more broadly "abstract" painting, in the wake of Picasso's and Georges Braque's cubism. Totally nonobjective painting showed patterns of colors, shapes, and lines without any "subject matter" at all; it broke away from *mimesis*, the imitative function with which art had been identified since Plato (see Introduction). The leading abstract painters had direct knowledge of cubist experiments in Paris, but they lived all across Europe and, soon isolated by the First World War, pursued the consequences of those experiments in very different directions. Influenced at first by cubism, the Russian Kasimir Malevich made paintings consisting entirely of geometrical shapes. One of his most famous was a black square painted inside a white square of about double its size. He created the earliest version of this "Basic Suprematist Element" in a pencil drawing of 1913 (a later version appears in figure 8). He treated this design as a religious icon and hung it in the gallery in the same position as religious paintings were hung in Russian homes (on a diagonal from ceiling to wall). Even more radical were his later paintings of white on white. The Dutch painter Piet Mondrian pursued increasingly abstract designs and eventually created asymmetrical patterns out of horizontal and vertical lines and rectangular patches of primary colors; during the war, he became the focus of a Dutch group called *De Stijl*. When his colleague Theo van Doesburg later started making use of diagonal lines in his paintings, Mondrian, annoyed at this

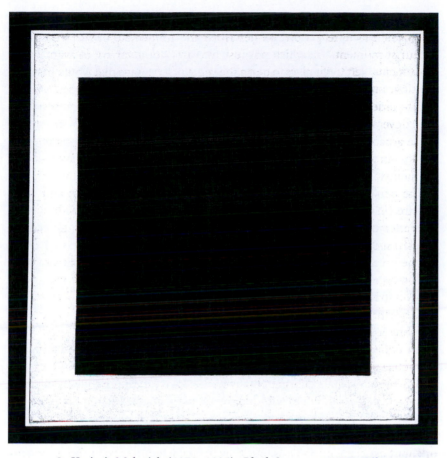

8. Kasimir Malevich (1878–1935), *Black Square, ca.* 1923. Oil on canvas.
106 × 106 cm. Sch-9484.
Photo credit: Erich Lessing/Art Resource, NY.

departure from the orthodoxy of verticals and horizontals, resigned from the group. Two members of the *Blaue Reiter* group, Wassily Kandinsky and Paul Klee, painted abstract designs of a nongeometrical character and attempted to give painting some of the qualities of music. Several of the abstract artists associated their painting with spiritual movements like Theosophy (which had earlier inspired Yeats) or with Russian iconography. In "On the Spiritual in Art" (1910), Kandinsky outlined a theory of the relationship between certain colors and spiritual qualities of the artist. His painting is the first example of "abstract expressionism," a movement in modern art that became particularly influential in the United States after the Second World War.

The avant-garde impulse toward experimentation was felt also in music. A sense of developing but also breaking with the central Western tradition resulted from the rejection of diatonic tonality, which separates music into major and minor keys. While such musicians as Claude Debussy and Alexandr Skryabin had occasionally used ambiguous keys and verged on rejecting tonality, it was Arnold Schoenberg who first, in 1908, composed "atonal" music that could not be fitted into any one key. Along with his students, Alban Berg and Anton Webern, Schoenberg continued to write atonal music until 1921. Their music was generally rejected by the concertgoing public of Vienna. Other experiments were also under way. The American composer Charles Ives made use of quarter-tone scales (instead of the standard half- and full-tones), varied and competing rhythms, and popular tunes (such as "America the Beautiful") in his compositions, most of which were not performed until well after the First World War. At the same time, in Paris, Igor Stravinsky was experimenting with "primitive" rhythms (see Chapter Two). Thus two central aspects of Western musical tradition, tonality and tempo, were being radically reconsidered simultaneously in two different music capitals, Paris and Vienna, as well as in the United States. At the more spectacular end of the modernist spectrum, many musicians introduced nontraditional instruments such as airplane propellers and electric doorbells into their orchestras. The Italian futurists, active in every medium, used *intonarumori* ("noise intoners") that imitated the sounds of factories and machines. A later avant-gardist, John Cage, placed rubber, metal, and wooden objects on top of his piano strings in order to create unusual sound effects. He also used recordings of music and played them back at varied speeds. After the Second World War, influenced by Zen Buddhism, Cage found ways to introduce chance into his composing process, by tossing coins to determine what note should come next, for example. His most famous work, *4' 33"* (1952), consisted of a pianist sitting silently at a piano for four minutes and thirty-three seconds. The sounds of the concert hall, including the frustrated audience, were the "music." Such experiments typify the avant-garde tendency toward deliberately provocative, often highly conceptual, challenges to the very status of art.[6]

The period before the First World War was equally a time of radical experimentation in literature. There is no direct equivalent in literature of the leap to "nonobjective" art in painting or the rejection of tonality in music, but there were many near-equivalents. Poets sought a variety of ways to avoid the referentiality of language, its tendency to represent reality, but they could not escape the fact that words, even when arranged in abstract patterns, have meanings, and therefore inevitably refer to the world outside the poem. The use of free verse (in French, *vers libre*), which avoids traditional meter and rhyme, was an important aspect of most experimental poetry (see Chapter Two). Some of the more radical attempts to break with poetic tradition involved the inclusion in poems of overheard speech, allusions to or direct quotations from other poetry, and even the random juxtaposition of words. One technique for achieving such randomness was to cut up printed words and rearrange them in random order. The Russian cubo-futurists, led by the poets Velemir Khlebnikov, Alexei Kruchonykh, and Vladimir Mayakovsky, proposed to "enlarge the vocabulary of the people with factitious and fabricated words. The word is making new."[7] They wrote poems made up entirely of nonsense words and invented a "trans-rational language" (*zaum*). Poets also began to show an interest in typography and the art of layout, which drew on the mass cultural forms of advertising posters. Apollinaire, one of the most influential modernists in prewar France and a champion of cubism, wrote (or designed) calligrammes, collages of words spread out over the page. His poem "The Necktie and the Watch" (1913), for example, has its various verses distributed around the page in the shape of a necktie and a watch. The poem is full of visual puns.[8]

Typically, avant-garde movements were loosely organized groups of artists and writers who might exhibit or publish together and who shared some common principles. Occasionally, the leader of an avant-garde movement would enforce stricter discipline on its members and become a spokesperson for the whole group. Apollinaire was a friend of the leading cubists and wrote an influential treatise on cubist painting, but he was not exactly the leader of a movement. Marinetti, on the other hand, almost single-handedly made Italian futurism a recognized and widely debated phenomenon. Marinetti's manifestos are central documents of futurism. Similarly, after the war, André Breton attempted to maintain strict discipline among the surrealists; his manifestos defined the movement (see Chapter Seven).

Because they frequently sought or commanded only a specialized audience – and also because of conflicts with the commercial publishing houses – avant-garde experiment and publishing often depended on "little magazines," literary journals with a small circulation, usually subsidized by their publishers and read mainly by select groups of literati. These were often run by women. A number of bijou publishing houses, such as Leonard and Virginia Woolf's Hogarth Press, the Cuala Press founded by W. B. Yeats's sisters, or Sylvia Beach's Shakespeare and Company, published much avant-garde and modernist writing in small editions. In 1913 Ezra Pound became the editor of the feminist journal *The New Freewoman*, published by Dora Marsden. The journal's name was changed shortly after to *The Egoist*, a reflection both of its many male authors and of Marsden's philosophical opposition to representative democracy (here again, the crisis of representation overlaps with the crisis of liberalism). *The Egoist* published the work of T. S. Eliot, James Joyce, and William Carlos Williams, and Eliot later served as one of its literary editors. After the war, Eliot edited *The Criterion*, one of the longest-running modernist journals. In the United States Margaret Anderson's *Little Review* published Joyce's *Ulysses* in installments from 1918 and was prosecuted for obscenity. American modernists published in such journals as the New York-based *Others*, the Chicago-based *Poetry*, and the *Dial*, which (like the *Little Review*) was founded in Chicago but later moved to New York. *La nouvelle revue française*, though longer-lived and closer to the mainstream, performed a similar function for French modernism. In Berlin, the rival expressionist journals *Die Aktion* (*Action*) and *Die Sturm* (*Storm*) debated the relationship between artistic experiment and political revolution. In *The Autobiography of Alice B. Toklas*, Stein had Toklas refer to "all the little magazines which, as Gertrude Stein loves to quote, have died to make verse free."[9]

In English Stein herself was the experimenter who came closest to a cubist or abstract use of language. A native of Allegheny, Pennsylvania, Stein lived as a child in Vienna and Paris before moving to Oakland, California, of which she famously said "There isn't any there there." After graduating from Radcliffe College, she flunked out of Johns Hopkins Medical School and moved with her brother Leo to Paris, where she became an experimental writer and a patron of modern art. Her "Tender Buttons" (1914) offers "studies in description" of objects, in which, as in cubist still-life, the object being described seems to be veiled by the medium of description. In the cubism of Picasso and Braque, the veils were the planes into which the painter broke up the canvas. In Stein's writing, as Marjorie Perloff has shown, words themselves make abstract patterns that seem to stand in the way of their descriptive or referential functions. Stein's first object is "A carafe, that is a blind glass": "A kind in glass and a cousin, a spectacle and nothing strange a single hurt color and an arrangement in a system to pointing. All this and not ordinary, not unordered in not resembling. The difference is spreading." Perloff writes that in descriptions like this one, objects "not only are fragmented and decomposed as they are in cubist still-life; they also serve as false leads, forcing the reader to consider the very nature of naming."[10] They thus call attention to the process of recognizing an object and to the role of language in that process. In this respect, Stein anticipated the development of dada (discussed below).

Stein's work seldom reached quite this level of detachment from descriptive functions, but much of her other prewar work makes use of patterns of repetition and variation at the sentence level. Her mammoth *The Making of Americans*, the story of "the old people in a new world, the new people made out of the old," makes use of a contrapuntal sentence structure that resembles a musical fugue:

> Men in their living have many things inside them they have in them, each one of them has it in him, his own way of feeling himself important inside in him, they have in them all of them their own way of beginning, their own way of ending, their own way of working, their own way of having loving inside them and loving come out from them, their own way of having anger inside them and letting their anger come out from inside them, their own way of eating, their own way of drinking, their own way of sleeping, their own way of doctoring.[11]

Stein wrote *The Making of Americans* from 1903 to 1911, in the avant-garde atmosphere of Paris, but it was published only in 1925. Her memoir, *The Autobiography of Alice B. Toklas*, was written in a much more accessible style, which has led to speculations about the role of Toklas herself in its composition.[12] It became a bestseller and seemed to exemplify the incorporation of the prewar avant-garde into a much broader, and more mainstream, modernism. The *Autobiography* also became a publishing phenomenon, and (with Toklas in tow), Stein toured the United States in 1934, lecturing to large audiences.

Cubism reached London mainly through the intermediary of Marinetti's futurism. Pound, in London, followed the example of the futurists and promoted vorticism as a distinctively English avant-garde, less for ideological reasons than as a marketing device, meant to distinguish vorticism from Italian futurism (see Chapter Two). He collaborated with Wyndham Lewis on the first issue of the journal *BLAST*, published less than a month before the outbreak of the First World War. The volume contained a manifesto, a few of Pound's less successful poems, reproductions of vorticist paintings, the first draft of Ford Madox Ford's *The Good Soldier* (1915), a translation of Kandinsky's "On the Spiritual in Art," and lists of famous people or institutions that the vorticists wished to "blast" (John Galsworthy, Sydney Webb, and the Post Office) or to "bless" (Joyce, the Pope, and the Salvation Army). Lewis's prose-poem *The Enemy of the Stars*, published in *BLAST*, used fragmented syntax, violent imagery, and sudden shifts in perspective to attempt something like the abstraction of modern art in a literary form. The vorticists' manifesto, "Long Live the Vortex!," demonstrated somewhat more self-ironic humor than such European models as Marinetti's manifestos or Apollinaire's "Futurist Anti-Tradition." This was the era of the "strange death of Liberal England,"

and of the competing visions of modernity offered by the post-impressionist aesthetes of Bloomsbury on the one hand and Pound's and Lewis's vorticists on the other (see Chapter Two). As we have seen, Woolf claimed that "on or about December, 1910, human character changed." Those who lived through these prewar years felt that a fundamental change in human experience and in the arts was under way, as English art and literature at last responded energetically to the crisis of representation that had been roiling Europe for at least half a century. Later, the critic Hugh Kenner wrote of this period in the development of the avant-garde: "English poetry was being freed from painting, English music from 'literature,' painting from anecdote, sculpture from sentiment. Each art was starting forth sharp and distinct, all simultaneously released from the mimetic."[13] *BLAST* did not, however, fulfill its promise as a quarterly journal of the English avant-garde. The war broke out, and only one further issue was published.

The energies of the avant-garde did not find their desired release in the transformation of the modern world by the liberating powers of nonmimetic art. Instead, the modern world, in the form of the First World War, transformed the avant-garde. Despite the cosmopolitanism of many artists and writers of the prewar period, most leading avant-gardists were enthusiastic about the outbreak of the war. Apollinaire wrote that "The whistle thrills me more / Than an Egyptian palace / The whistle of the trenches."[14] The military metaphor embedded in the term "avant-garde" gained new life in this period. Marinetti agitated in favor of Italian intervention. Cendrars, who was to lose his right arm in battle, wrote to a friend, "This war is a painful delivery, needed to give birth to liberty. It fits me like a glove."[15] But as the horrors of technological warfare became more apparent, enthusiasm not just for the war but also for the militaristic language of the prewar avant-gardes dissipated. Cendrars was maimed, T. E. Hulme was killed in action, and Apollinaire, wounded in 1916, died of influenza two years later. After military service as a gunner at the battle of Passchendaele, Lewis undertook government commissions as an official war artist. Although he thought that the battlefields of France, lined with trenches, offered "a subject-matter . . . consonant with the austerity of that 'abstract' vision I had developed," when he actually came to paint the war, his style became far more representational than in his vorticist years.[16] His paintings of scenes from the front lines, commissioned by the British War Memorials Committee, make use of elongated figures and angular, grimacing faces, but they are clearly representational. Lewis remarked that "in the years before the war I was thinking less about the subject than of the treatment. The war made me think more of the subject matter. The war was a great human event and human methods had to be adopted in dealing with it if it were to be registered in art at all."[17] This change of attitude in the most belligerent of the avant-gardists signaled the transformation that would give birth to "high" modernism after the war. The combination of elements of vorticist experiment – especially strong lines and sharp angles – with more traditional representational techniques seemed to many art critics to show how well the techniques of modern art could be adapted to the realities of modern warfare.

Avant-garde movements continued and even flourished during the war, but the emphasis tended to shift from experiment with the forms of art to a critique of art as an institution. The most influential avant-garde movement after 1914, dada, was founded in Zürich during the war, when many artists and writers (including Joyce) were taking refuge there from combat. If the cubists had revolutionized artistic practice and the futurists had drawn a link between art and revolution, dada was a sort of revolution against the very concept of art. It began as a kind of performance art (itself a new concept) in which people would gather at a nightclub, the Cabaret Voltaire, to look at avant-garde art, listen to classical and dance music, read poetry (some of it nonsense poetry), declaim about the end of art, and criticize the war and Western civilization. The movement's leader, Tristan Tzara, gave the following instructions on how "To Make a Dadaist Poem":

> Take a newspaper.
> Take some scissors.
> Choose from this paper an article the length you want to make your
> poem.
> Cut out the article.
> Next carefully cut out each of the words that make up this article and
> put them all in a bag.
> Shake gently.
> Next take out each cutting one after the other.
> Copy conscientiously in the order in which they left the bag.
> The poem will resemble you.
> And there you are – an infinitely original author of charming sensibility,
> even though unappreciated by the vulgar herd.

The word dada, with its resonance of baby-talk, expressed their protest against art. Dada valued cacophony, dreams, drugs, and the violation of syntax as techniques for freeing the unconscious from the domination of reason and tradition. Previous art, the dadaists thought, had served civilization. Their anti-art would challenge it.

The most famous dada artist, Marcel Duchamp, living in New York, sub-mitted to an exhibition one of his "ready-mades," mass-produced objects that he purchased and presented as art. In this case it was a urinal, turned upside down and signed "R. Mutt." He called the piece "Fountain" (1917). Duchamp was claiming, in effect, that he as an artist had only to find some ready-made object, title it, and display it in a gallery to make it art. The dadaists, in their questioning of art, also posed the most important challenge yet to the idea of art as an activity of elite groups. They shared with the Italian futurists a scorn for museums and for the notion that a particular group of experts (other than artists themselves) could define art, including some works and excluding others. The radicalism of dada did not lead to a particularly coherent idea of art's function or a shared style. Dadaists undertook all sorts of individualistic, personal attempts to challenge the idea of art. In their work the crisis of representation and the crisis of Western civilization seemed to have culminated in a crisis of art itself. The dada movement spread throughout Europe and North America after the war, but it was supplanted in the 1920s by surrealism (see Chapter Seven).

### Multiple media

An important aspect of modernist concern with form was the increased attention to the particular medium in which an artwork was created: the individual brushstrokes that made up a painting, materials contributing to a collage, the various photographic frames in the filmic montage, the typography of newspapers, posters, and illustrated magazines, the particular instruments that played different parts in an orchestra, even the use of recording instruments and electronic sounds in music. Each type of art had its own distinctively "modern" characteristics, and some artists sought to bring out the specific qualities of the particular medium, and create a "pure," unmixed art form. In a contrary tendency, however, there were many modernists in each genre who explored other types of modern art, collaborated with artists from other media, or sought a synthesis of the arts, along the lines of Richard Wagner's "total work of art." Henri Matisse painted dancers, and his conception of how to represent motion on canvas was influenced by modern dance; Picasso designed stage sets for a ballet with music by Erik Satie, performed by Sergei Diaghilev's and Vaslav Nijinsky's Ballets Russes; poets emphasized the musicality of their writing and frequently collaborated on operas; Malevich's suprematism owed something to the inspiration of avant-garde poets such as Vladimir Mayakovsky; design groups like the Bauhaus combined architecture, design, and painting. Whether seeking to purify their own art form, or to achieve a synthesis of all the arts, artists tended to focus attention on the medium itself, rather than the represented object.[18]

## English literature and the First World War

In English the term "modernism" generally implies a high conception of the status of art, almost the reverse of the dadists' anti-art. English modernism has often been understood as a reaction to the carnage and disillusionment of the First World War and a search for a new mode of art that would rescue civilization from its state of crisis after the war. The social forces that were to transform English life in this period – feminism, socialism, and anti-imperialism – were already at work before the war (see Chapter Two). Yet, in retrospect, the prewar years sometimes appeared as a time of untroubled self-confidence, in which the authority of the crown, the empire, capital, and men was secure. Even the experiments of the avant-garde movements themselves seemed later to have been signs of an optimism that the war destroyed. Subsequent generations in England and France would look back to the prewar years as a "*belle époque,*" a beautiful age. The *belle époque* ended in the summer of 1914, when the assassination of the Austrian Archduke Franz Ferdinand by Serbian nationalists led to war between Austria and Serbia. Russia mobilized in support of Serbia, and Germany, an ally of Austria, declared war on Russia and its ally France. Britain entered the war on August 4, 1914 in response to the invasion of neutral Belgium by Germany. Reports of German atrocities against the Belgian population outraged the British people and helped to mobilize volunteers for the war effort.

In England the educated classes promoted the justice of the war and many young men volunteered; H. G. Wells wrote a series of prowar articles collected in late 1914 as *The War That Will End War*, a title later remembered with irony. The war began with the great expectations of poetic glory typified by Rupert Brooke's lines, "If I should die, think only this of me: / That there's some corner of a foreign field / That is for ever England." Here, the imagined corpse of the poet returns to nature and sanctifies it in the process. Brooke was one of the Georgian poets, named after George V, the son of Edward VII; the Georgians followed classical models and traditional meters in the prewar years; although admired at first by some later modernists, they eventually came to seem as old-fashioned as the Edwardians. Brooke's five war sonnets, published under the title *1914*, became immensely popular. In 1915, while serving in the Royal Navy, Brooke died of an infection caused by an insect bite; he became an almost mythical figure, England's "poet-soldier." More than three thousand volumes of war poetry were published in the first three years of the war, and much of this poetic outpouring consisted of pale imitations of Brooke.

The optimistic vision of the war promoted by Wells and Brooke met its end in the filth and suffering of trench warfare and the mass deaths enabled by the machine gun. At the battle of Passchendaele, which lasted for three months in 1917, British and Allied troops suffered a quarter of a million casualties in the effort to recapture a small Belgian village of questionable strategic importance. Counting all nationalities, about ten million died in the course of the war. Gertrude Stein later told Ernest Hemingway, who had been wounded while serving as an ambulance driver, that he belonged to a "lost generation." Many young men of his generation died in the trenches or were literally lost, missing in action. Often dead bodies were so completely destroyed by artillery that they could not be identified, and one of the most famous monuments of the war was to an "unknown warrior," that is, one whose remains could not be identified. Such novels as Hemingway's *The Sun Also Rises* (1926), Erich Remarque's *All Quiet on the Western Front* (1929), and Jean Renoir's film *Grand Illusion* (1937) describe the disillusionment of those who survived.

During the first years of the war, conservative critics could take comfort in the decline of the prewar avant-garde. Many of the radical young prewar writers enlisted, and journals that had published modern writing, such as *Poetry and Drama*, edited by Harold Monro, and Lewis's *BLAST*, closed down. Some important cultural figures, including Clive and Vanessa Bell, Aldous Huxley, D. H. Lawrence, the philosopher Bertrand Russell, George Bernard Shaw, and Leonard and Virginia Woolf, more or less openly opposed the war. However, their antiwar writings were not poems, plays, or novels, but essays and pamphlets; Russell went to prison for one of his antiwar pamphlets. The effect of the war on literature per se became notable by the middle of the war as a change in poetic taste that accelerated some of the trends already introduced by avant-garde poets like the imagists.

While older men such as Rudyard Kipling and Henry Newbolt composed patriotic hymns in traditional meters, and A. E. Housman's poems about doomed lads enjoyed renewed popularity, a younger group of poets recorded their reactions to the war with bitter irony and rejected the poetic diction of their elders. The younger war poets brought rats and corpses into English poetry. In "Aftermath" (1919), Siegfried Sassoon would write:

> Do you remember the dark months you held the sector at Mametz –
> The nights you watched and wired and dug and piled sandbags on
> parapets?
> Do you remember the rats; and the stench
> Of corpses rotting in front of the front-line trench –
> And dawn coming, dirty-white, and chill with a hopeless rain?
> Do you ever stop and ask, 'Is it all going to happen again?'

Corpses here have none of the dignity afforded them in Rupert Brooke's poems; they are merely decaying flesh. The new diction – rats, corpses, stench – reflected a new rhetorical stance. Newbolt, among the most popular poets of the prewar years, had written approvingly that the literary public demands from the poet "that he shall chant to them . . . their own morality, their own religion, their own patriotism."[19] The war made such affirmations of conventional beliefs appear hollow. Poets who were themselves combatants tended to be skeptical of the consoling function of poetry.

Wilfed Owen wrote a poem about a poison gas attack in reply to the Roman poet Horace's "famous Latin tag," "Dulce et decorum est pro patria mori" ("It is sweet and decorous to die for one's country"). The poem ends by concluding that if the reader, too, could see the dying men poisoned in the attack, "My friend, you would not tell with such high zest / To children ardent for some desperate glory, / The old Lie: Dulce et decorum est / Pro patria mori." Although the poems of Owen and Sassoon retain rhyme, iambic meters, and straightforward grammar and syntax, they focus their gaze on ugliness, a topic crucial to modern literature ever since Charles Baudelaire and Gustave Flaubert. Owen wrote from the Front: "I suppose I can endure cold, and fatigue, and the face-to-face death, as well as another; but extra for me there is the universal pervasion of *Ugliness*. Hideous landscapes, vile noises, foul language . . . everything unnatural, broken, blasted." Owen and Sassoon together sought to create a poetry that would tell the truth about the ugliness of the war. They had met in the summer of 1917 at Craiglockhart War Hospital, a mental hospital for shell-shocked officers, to which Sassoon had been sent when he published a protest against the war. Both men were "cured" – Owen of his shell shock and Sassoon of his antiwar stance – and both returned to active duty; Owen was killed in action in the last week of the war. In a note written near the end of his life and published with his posthumous *Poems* (1920), Owen rejected traditional rhetoric and wrote that "Above all I am not concerned with Poetry. / My subject is War, and the pity of War. / The Poetry is in the pity." This phrase became a rallying cry of leftist poets between the wars.[20]

Shell shock was a central theme of war and postwar literature, beginning with Rebecca West's novel *The Return of the Soldier*, published in the last year of the war (1918). In the novel a young war hero returns to his family estate having lost his memory of the war and the immediate prewar years. Although he has married a woman of his own class, Captain Christopher Baldry is still in love with an innkeeper's daughter, who has herself been married for almost a decade. He does not recognize his own wife and longs to return to Monkey Island, the site of his youthful love. The spurned wife at first believes that her husband is only pretending not to remember her; later, however, she brings in a psychiatrist who diagnoses his shell shock. She tells the doctor that she knows he cannot cure Chris – "[can't] make him happy, I mean. All you can do is to make him ordinary." At the end of the novel, Chris is "cured" – or at least made ordinary – and returned to battle, like Owen and Sassoon. The novel is narrated by his cousin, Jenny, who, while recognizing that he must be cured, regrets his loss of an idyllic past, which seems to symbolize the entire nation's loss of innocence in the war: "Chris was not mad. It was our peculiar shame that he had rejected us when he had attained to something saner than sanity. His very loss of memory was a triumph over the limitations of language which prevent the mass of men from making explicit statements about their spiritual relationships." Despite the reference to the limitations of language, *The Return of the Soldier* uses mainly traditional novelistic techniques, but it does bring the impressionist or post-impressionist concern with the multiple perspectives from which characters view reality to bear on a specifically postwar problem: the difficulties faced by those on the home front – especially women – in trying to understand the experiences of the returning soldiers.

The theme of how to make sense of the war, specifically from the perspective of a woman who had not seen battle, became central to the major work of Virginia Woolf. In her short story "Mrs Dalloway in Bond Street" (1922), Woolf has her society hostess, Clarissa Dalloway, observe that since the war, "there are moments when it seems utterly futile . . . – simply one doesn't believe, thought Clarissa, any more in God." Although her first novel, *The Voyage Out* (1915) had tentatively embraced modernist techniques, her second, *Night and Day* (1919), returned to many Victorian conventions. The young modernist writer Katherine Mansfield thought that *Night and Day* contained "a lie in the soul" because it failed to refer to the war or recognize what it had meant for fiction.[21] Mansfield, who had written a number of important early modernist stories, died at the age of thirty-four in 1923, and Woolf, who had published some of her work at the Hogarth Press, often measured herself against this friend and rival. Mansfield's criticism of *Night and Day* as "Jane Austen up-to-date" stung Woolf, who, in three of her major modernist novels of the 1920s, grappled with the problem of how to represent the chasm in historical experience presented by the war. The war is a central theme in *Jacob's Room* (1922), *Mrs Dalloway* (1925), and *To the Lighthouse* (1927). Over the course of the decade, these novels trace Woolf's struggle to incorporate the massive and incomprehensible experience of the war into a vision of recent history.

*Jacob's Room* concerns the difficulty, especially for his mother, of making posthumous sense of the life of Jacob Flanders, a young man who dies in the war. (Flanders was a region of Belgium where the British sustained many of their heaviest casualties.) The novel follows Jacob's life, but he is seen mainly at a distance, through the eyes of women who knew him more or less well, and the narrative itself is quite fragmentary, so that the reader experiences the same problem faced by Jacob's survivors – how to piece together his life. Woolf based the novel partly on the death of her brother Thoby in 1906, but gave it a broader resonance by having Jacob die in the war. The death itself, however, is not described. Instead, the novel ends with Jacob's mother asking his friend Ralph

Bonamy to help her sort through Jacob's possessions. Its final lines are: "'What am I to do with these, Mr. Bonamy?' She held out a pair of Jacob's old shoes." Mrs. Flanders's bewilderment is shared by the reader, who does not know what to make of a novel whose meandering plot, after jumping around in time and space, is cut short – without any inherent rationale – by the hero's death.

In *Mrs. Dalloway*, set on a single day in June five years after the end of the war, the task of integrating the war into the historical experience of the survivors has progressed. In *Jacob's Room* the narrative technique suggested an attempt to come to grips with the shared trauma of the war. In *Mrs. Dalloway* shell shock plays an explicit role, as one of its two protagonists, Septimus Smith, is a veteran suffering severe bouts of mental illness (which Woolf modeled on her own experiences). He has visions of his dead comrade Evans and sudden epiphanies: "Men must not cut down trees. There is a God. (He noted such revelations on the backs of envelopes.)" Septimus's wife Rezia makes futile efforts to comprehend and treat his illness. His fear of being locked up by pompous psychiatrists eventually leads Septimus to commit suicide.

The novel progresses through two apparently unrelated plots – one concerning Septimus's illness and eventual suicide, the other concerning Mrs. Dalloway's preparations for a party, which the prime minister will attend. Although characters related to each plot pass each other on the streets of London during the course of the novel, the novel achieves its real unity only in its conclusion, when Mrs. Dalloway learns of Septimus's death from his psychiatrist (one of the guests at her party) and feels a strange sympathy for him. It seems that the knowledge of his death prevents Clarissa from committing suicide herself. This conclusion is troubling. During the war, it was said that a certain intellectual (in one version of the story Lytton Strachey), when asked why he was not fighting to save civilization, would answer, "I am the civilization for which you are fighting."[22] There might seem to be an element of this view in Woolf's novel. *Mrs. Dalloway* does suggest that the poor soldier's suffering and death somehow redeem the apparently trivial life of the hostess, who entertains nobility and politicians, the "old men" that postwar society held responsible for the war. Yet Woolf also seems to be criticizing the logic that would justify Septimus's death as worth while, a fair price to pay for "civilization." Woolf called her novel an "elegy," that is, a lament for the dead, but she was skeptical of the traditional elegy's consolations, which she suspected of falsity. In her novel the living go on living, and they must recognize that the civilization that permits them to do so is the same one that allowed millions to die in the war.

In Woolf's masterpiece, *To the Lighthouse*, she presents the war in a broader historical perspective, thus serving the function of elegy by coming to terms with the war, but also contributing her share to what the critic Samuel Hynes has called the "Myth of the War" – "the notion, partly true and partly imagined, that the war created a vast gap between the prewar and the postwar world."[23] The first section of the novel, "The Window," is set before the war, at the vacation house in the Scottish Hebrides of Mr. Ramsay, a philosophy professor, his wife, and their eight children. James, the youngest, wants to go to the lighthouse, and Mrs. Ramsay is knitting a stocking for the lighthouse keeper's son. Mr. Ramsay, however, insists that the weather the next day will be too bad for a trip by boat to the lighthouse. Out of this minor incident, Woolf creates a brilliant portrait of family relations in a long-ago era, ostensibly a few years before the war but really the late Victorian world of Woolf's childhood. The portrait revolves around the marriage of the depressive and anxious philosopher Mr. Ramsay and the beautiful, energetic, but perhaps narrow-minded Mrs. Ramsay, who seems to preside over the fates of many men without understanding their world at all. Once again, the theme of the female observer is central, as Lily Briscoe, a house guest of the Ramsays, tries to paint a post-impressionist landscape, in which James and Mrs. Ramsay appear as a purple triangle. Her quest for a style and compositional form to represent the Ramsays mirrors Woolf's own quest for a representational technique adequate to the complex family history she narrates, making use of multiple perspectives, recording the "streams of consciousness" of various characters, and weaving in and out of their minds.

The war enters the novel as a decisive break with the Victorian and Edwardian past. In the middle section, "Time Passes," Woolf shows the Ramsays' house empty for a decade, as time and weather wreak havoc on the building and the war progresses in distant France. In this section Woolf records the deaths of three major characters in parentheses: Mrs. Ramsay, who dies of unspecified causes; her son Andrew, who dies in the war; and her daughter Prue, who dies as a result of childbirth. Andrew's death is recorded thus: "[A shell exploded. Twenty or thirty young men were blown up in France, among them Andrew Ramsay, whose death, mercifully, was instantaneous.]" The passage gives a hint of the bitter irony with which Woolf often referred to the war: in the phrase "twenty or thirty," which suggests official disregard for the deaths of these young men, each of whom may have had an inner life as rich as that of a character in one of Woolf's novels, but who in death become simply imprecise statistics; and in the small word "mercifully," which suggests the way that people at home talk about deaths of those they do not really know – how could any such death truly be merciful?

The third section of the novel, "The Lighthouse," describes the attempts of the survivors, especially James and Cam Ramsay, Mr. Ramsay, and Lily Briscoe, to make sense of the losses, which are not all directly war-related but are all associated with the war. Finally, Lily is able to complete the painting she had begun before the war, and the surviving Ramsays are able to complete the trip to the lighthouse, a symbol of artistic unity, and of spatial and temporal perspective, perhaps the one thing in the novel that does not change as a result of the war. As Lily completes her painting with a final line down the center, perhaps symbolizing the lighthouse, she momentarily sees the Ramsays, the war, and the world before the war in her own post-impressionist form of perspective: "Yes, she thought, laying down her brush in extreme fatigue, I have had my vision." The struggle represented by Woolf's three great postwar novels, the struggle to create a vision out of the fragments left behind by the war, would motivate many of the leading works of English modernism.

Woolf's major works demonstrate the development, in the 1920s, of Hynes's "Myth of the War." One feature of the myth was the sense, evident in *Mrs. Dalloway*, that the young men who died in the conflict had been sent like cattle to the slaughter by the "old men" – politicians, industrialists, the wealthy and powerful. Another was the sense that the war, fought in the name of the ideal of civilization, was in fact meaningless, and that it had brought civilization itself to a crisis. These ideas had been developed in the writings of the war poets, and by the end of the 1920s they found narrative form in memoirs of the war, such as Robert Graves's *Goodbye to All That* (1929) and Sassoon's fictionalized *Memoirs of an Infantry Officer* (1930), which helped retrospectively to form the general consciousness of the war as, in the title of Renoir's film, a grand illusion. Modernists such as Eliot, Pound, and Woolf contributed to the myth of the war, and the myth in turn contributed to modernism, partly by accentuating the sense of a radical break with the past that was crucial to the literary mood of the 1920s. However, not all war writers were modernist in orientation and not all modernists wrote about the war. Indeed, many of the new literary techniques were developed during the war by people who were not involved in the fighting and who saw the war, at first, primarily as a distraction from their literary work, the work of inventing modernism.

## Inventing modernism

As the discussion of English writing about the First World War has shown, the work of poet-soldiers made a great difference to the techniques and themes of postwar literature. However, the major contribution to the development of a distinctive English modernism was made by writers who were not directly involved in the war. While Guillaume Apollinaire, Blaise Cendrars, T. E. Hulme, Wyndham Lewis, Wilfred Owen and Siegfried Sassoon were at the Front, T. S. Eliot, James Joyce, Ezra Pound, and W. B. Yeats were working to invent what would become known, shortly after the war, as "modernism." Although these men were not combatants and were sometimes not even particularly interested in the war, it did influence their perception of their literary tasks. In particular, the modernists sought to understand and make their writing express the transformative power of history, which they were witnessing in one of its most brutal manifestations. This meant both a new concern with change and a new assessment of literary tradition, which the modernists viewed in an increasingly positive light. At the same time, writers who had aimed before the war at developing an impersonal and almost timeless style, suited – as Pound wrote – for "direct treatment of the 'thing,'" became more concerned during the war with the expression of subjective experience.

Three factors account for this latter shift. First, the imagist emphasis on objectivity and direct perception had played itself out in the typical short imagist poems of the prewar era. In order to achieve something longer and more ambitious, something appropriate to the scale of the wartime experience, the modernists returned to questions of subjectivity. Second, two writers who had not been involved in the prewar avant-gardes, Eliot and Joyce, had come to the forefront of modernism by the end of the war. While sharing some of Pound's rhetoric concerning the rejection of romanticism, these two writers also showed a greater continuity with the nineteenth-century legacy, including the problems of consciousness that had earlier been explored by such precursors as Gustave Flaubert, Henry James, and Joseph Conrad (see Chapter One). Finally, revulsion against the war caused many writers to share Lewis's sense that abstraction had failed to address human questions vital to the function of art. The attentiveness to subjectivity, history, and tradition allowed the modernists to develop techniques and themes that had resonance beyond the coterie audiences of the avant-gardes.[24] The greatest force contributing to the development of modernism after the war, however, was the sense of a radical discontinuity between the prewar and the postwar worlds. The war seemed to have changed everything, and modernist literature found as its subject the nature of these changes.

The noncombatant poets shared the combatants' distaste for martial rhetoric and their rejection of traditional poetic diction, but they tended to avoid direct engagement with the war as a subject matter for their poetry. To some extent, this hesitance resulted from their lack of military experience. In "On Being Asked for a War Poem" (1915), Yeats wrote, "I think it better that at times like these / We poets keep our mouths shut, for in truth / We have no gift to set a statesman right." More broadly, however, the modernists tended to shy away from poetry that took direct stances on public affairs, especially unambiguously patriotic, religious, or moralistic stances. As against Henry Newbolt's idea of the poet chanting to the public "their own morality," Pound wrote in a letter, "The public can go to the devil."[25] Despite their explicit rejection of moralistic or explicitly political poetry and their hostility to the "public," however, both Pound and Yeats soon sought to comment on contemporary events. The renewed attention to politics, society, and even economics in the poetry of this period helped to define a new "modernist" voice, in contrast with the relative detachment and aestheticism of the same poets' work before the war.

Between 1913 and 1916 Pound and Yeats shared a stone cottage in Sussex, where they studied occult lore, Chinese poetry, and Japanese Noh drama.[26] Pound served as Yeats's secretary, and Yeats praised the younger man for helping him to "eliminate the abstract" from his poetry, though Pound learned much from Yeats about how to write modern poetry. The imagist principle of favoring the concrete over the abstract combined, during the war, with a new concern to speak of public events. Such speech differed, however, from the preaching advocated by Newbolt. Yeats wrote that "We make out of our quarrel with others, rhetoric, but of our quarrel with ourselves, poetry." In their representations of contemporary history, the modernists sought to dramatize the quarrels with themselves that public events inspired. As a result, their representation of history is often obscure and indirect. Yeats made many of his political opinions into poetry. He did so, however, not in the manner of Rudyard Kipling by creating political slogans, but instead by delving into the complexity of his reactions to major historical developments. Although speaking his own opinions, Yeats was thus also creating a persona, the Greek word for a mask, denoting in English the speaker or narrator of a literary work who must be understood as distinct from that work's author. Pound had used the term in the title of his second book of poems, *Personae and Exultations of Ezra Pound* (1913).

In Yeats's poems on political subjects, it is often the persona that Yeats has created, rather than the slogan or the content of his opinions, that makes the poem memorable. In "Easter, 1916" Yeats recognized that the Easter Rebellion, led by radicals of whose politics and violence he did not approve (including Major MacBride, estranged husband of Yeats's beloved Maud Gonne), had transformed not just the political situation of Ireland but the spiritual state of the nation. The poem commemorates the deaths of sixteen Irishmen and women executed by the English for their roles in the uprising: "All changed, changed utterly / A Terrible beauty is born." The phrase "terrible beauty" expresses Yeats's ambivalence, but the main theme of the poem is Yeats's dramatization of his struggle to comprehend the meaning of the event. In the last stanza of the poem, he asks a series of rhetorical questions: "O when may it suffice?," "What is it but nightfall?," "Was it needless death after all?" "And what if excess of love / Bewildered them till they died?" Yet, although the questions are rhetorical, "Easter, 1916" is, in Yeats's terms, poetry and not rhetoric precisely because Yeats cannot answer these questions for himself and he does not assume that there is any easy answer to them. All he can do is record the names of those who died in this event that he cannot quite comprehend.

After the First World War, the Irish nationalist party Sinn Fein declared independence from Britain. The brutality of the subsequent Anglo-Irish conflict was epitomized by "Bloody Sunday," when Irish Republican Army volunteers assassinated eleven suspected spies and British police opened fire on an unarmed crowd at a football game, killing twelve. After a form of independence was finally gained in December 1921, a civil war broke out among the various Irish factions. This bloodshed forms the background to Yeats's later poetry, with its images of apocalypse, and to Joyce's *Ulysses* (1922), which, though set in 1904, is filled with hints of the violent course that Irish history was taking between 1916 and 1921, while Joyce was actually composing the novel. Elizabeth Bowen's *Last September* (1929) offers a fine portrait of the Anglo-Irish struggle, seen from the point of view of a daughter of the Protestant establishment.

During the early years of his collaboration with Yeats, Pound was still actively promoting imagism and vorticism. Even while he remained the impresario of the English avant-garde, however, he was preparing to undertake a more far-reaching revision of the English poetic tradition. As in his imagist manifesto, Pound maintained his emphasis on the need for poems to use the language and rhythms of speech, rather than artificial poetic conventions. Although he rejected conventional poetic diction and meter, he was steeped in literary tradition. Early in his career he wrote that

> No good poetry is ever written in a manner twenty years old, for to write in such a manner shows conclusively that the writer thinks from books, convention and *cliché*, and not from life, yet a man feeling the divorce of life and his art may naturally try to resurrect a forgotten mode if he finds in that mode some leaven, or if he think he sees in it some element lacking in contemporary art which might unite that art again to its sustenance, life.[27]

Like other modernists, Pound here uses the antique – the forgotten mode – as a corrective to the sham traditions of the recent past. His major poem of the war years, the "Homage to Sextus Propertius" (1917), translates and adapts passages from the writings of a difficult poet of the early Roman Empire into a modern American voice.

Pound and Yeats between them made a number of literary "discoveries" of authors living in relative obscurity whom they helped to catapult to leading positions in the modernist movement. Before the war, Yeats had championed the poetry of the Indian nationalist and mystic Rabindrinath Tagore and had assisted him in translating his poems from Bengali to English; Pound published Tagore's work in *Poetry*. With the help of Pound and Yeats, Tagore rapidly developed a huge European following and he won the Nobel Prize for Literature in 1913, which led Pound to react against this popularity and include him among the "Blasted" in the 1914 issue of *BLAST*.[28] Pound also took up the cause of Robert Frost, eleven years his elder, who published his first book of poetry, *A Boy's Will*, in London in 1913. Pound approved of Frost's use of the diction of everyday speech and introduced him to Yeats, whom Frost greatly admired. The setting of Frost's poems, in rural New England, the apparent unobtrusiveness of his irony, and his attachment to traditional forms militated against his inclusion in any of Pound's movements, however. "I'd as soon write free verse," Frost once said, "as play tennis with the net down." Frost valued his independence and rebuffed Pound's advances. When war came, he returned to the United States.[29]

Pound more successfully befriended two writers who later, with his help, would earn reputations as the central figures of English-language modernism, Eliot and Joyce. He met Eliot, a Harvard graduate who was pursuing a Ph.D. in philosophy in England, in the second month of the war. Eliot's early poems, including "The Love Song of J. Alfred Prufrock" (1915), amazed Pound, three years his senior, by their modernity, which Eliot had achieved without any direct contact with avant-garde movements and largely as a result of his own reading of French symbolist poets and of Arthur Symons's *The Symbolist Movement in Literature* (1899). Pound arranged to have "Prufrock" published in *Poetry* in 1915 and thus launched the career of the most typical poet of "high modernism," who would soon become the leading critical voice of the movement. (For some of his famous critical statements, see Introduction.) Joyce's relationship to Pound and Yeats was somewhat more distant than Eliot's. Yeats had met Joyce in 1902, when Joyce was twenty and Yeats thirty-seven. Yeats recorded that at that first meeting Joyce told him, with a sigh, "I have met you too late. You are too old."[30] The older man remained friendly toward the younger, though, and in late 1913 he encouraged Pound to write to Joyce, who was barely making a living as an English teacher in Trieste. Pound published one of Joyce's poems in his anthology *Des Imagistes* (1914) and, more importantly, arranged for the publication of Joyce's novel *A Portrait of the Artist as a Young Man* in installments in *The Egoist*, starting on February 2, 1914 (Joyce's thirty-second birthday). Joyce had begun the novel ten years earlier, and apparently did not complete it until forced to do so by a deadline in 1915. Joyce moved to Zürich in 1915 after Italian intervention in the war put Trieste (at that time in Austria, but claimed by Italy) near the front line. Pound and Yeats convinced the Royal Literary Fund and the Civil List to grant Joyce the amounts of £75 and £100 respectively, and also arranged some lesser grants, which permitted Joyce to spend the war years working on *Ulysses*, serialized (again thanks to Pound's intervention) in the *Little Review* from 1918 onwards, and published in book form on Joyce's fortieth birthday, February 2, 1922.[31] Thus Pound and Yeats were largely responsible for the rise from obscurity of both the leading poet and the most important novelist of modernism.

## High modernism

The first works that Ezra Pound helped T. S. Eliot and James Joyce to publish, though written largely before the war, were harbingers of the "high" modernism of the 1920s and prefigured some of the typical concerns of later modernism. First among these, perhaps, was the search, never quite fulfilled, for a moment of total insight, what Joyce called an "epiphany," which would give the answer to the "overwhelming question" that is mentioned but never articulated in Eliot's "The Love Song of J. Alfred Prufrock" (1915). This sense that life must have an ultimate meaning, but one that can never be made fully explicit, pervades modernism. Joseph Conrad had Marlow express it in *Lord Jim* (1900): "Are not our lives too short for that full utterance which through all our stammerings is of course our only and abiding intention?"[32] Both the quest for full knowledge and the recognition of its impossibility are crucial to the modernists. Another quotation from *Lord Jim* became one emblem of the possible modernist response to the difficulty of achieving such a full utterance: "the way is to the destructive element submit yourself." Here, the German butterfly collector Stein tells Marlow that being born is like falling into the sea. To struggle against the waves is futile; rather, one must allow the sea to keep one's body afloat. For the modernists, this signified the impossibility of arriving at a fully commanding view of the culture that surrounded them and that they perceived as being in crisis. It also meant that their literary forms, rather than attempting to arrive at formal perfection, reflected the partial and fragmentary nature of their understanding of their culture. Modernism sought to incorporate the destructive element into the work of art.[33]

If Pound and W. B. Yeats increasingly turned to history and politics during the war years, the writings of Eliot and Joyce marked a new engagement with problems of subjectivity that distinguished them from Pound's earlier imagist ideology. Eliot's early poetry explored the divided consciousness, inspired in part by his reading of Henry James and Conrad. In "Prufrock," a poem that Eliot had drafted by the age of twenty-three, he had already adopted the voice of a weary middle-aged man, or indeed a damned soul from Dante's *Inferno*. The balding Prufrock finds in an appointment for tea with some fashionable ladies the occasion for existential suffering. On his way to this social event, he continually postpones asking the "overwhelming question," presumably some sort of proposal to the lady who will be entertaining him. Instead, he asks himself a series of questions that, while not the overwhelming question itself, do reflect his deepening anxiety: "Do I dare / Disturb the universe?"; "So how should I presume?"; "And how should I begin?" Convinced that he already knows what suffering awaits him – "For I have known them all already, known them all" – he decides that, though as indecisive as Shakespeare's Hamlet, he has none of Hamlet's greatness. He will not ask the overwhelming question, for fear that she will answer, "That is not what I meant at all / That is not it at all." Instead, he accepts the onslaught of old age and decides that no romance awaits him:

> Shall I part my hair behind? Do I dare to eat a peach?
> I shall wear white flannel trousers, and walk upon the beach.
> I have heard the mermaids singing, each to each.
>
> I do not think that they will sing to me.

Eliot's mastery of the rhythms of conversation, which he gave form in verse, his colloquialisms, witty use of rhyme, and allusions to Dante, Shakespeare and other writers are some of the modern qualities that attracted Pound. Although the poem does not reflect the war experience, having been written in 1910–11, Eliot's early poetry suggests the direction in which modernist poetry would move during and after the war: toward the exploration of the divided consciousness, the theme that Eliot and Pound both associated with James.

The divided consciousness would also be crucial to Pound's poem *Hugh Selwyn Mauberley* (1920), about a middle-aged avant-garde poet living "out of key with his time" in a postwar civilization, here described in the third person, rather than the first person of Prufrock. Pound called the poem "an attempt to condense the James novel." Here, at the end of the war, Pound condemned the whole affair in a parody of heroic war poetry: "There died a myriad, / And of the best, among them, / For an old bitch gone in the teeth, / For a botched civilization." Echoing the same line from Horace that Owen had called a "lie," Pound wrote of those who fought:

> Died some, pro patria, non dulce non et decor . . .
> walked eye-deep in hell
> believing in old men's lies, then unbelieving
> came home, home to a lie,
> home to many deceits,
> home to old lies and new infamy;
> usury age-old and age-thick
> and liars in public places.

Pound also introduced here one of the major social and economic concerns that would dominate much of his major work, *The Cantos* (1917–69): usury, or the charging of excessive interest on a loan. The condemnation of usury became a central part of Pound's theories about the decline of the modern age, which he later blamed largely on Jewish financiers. More broadly, Pound here gave voice to the general sense of the war as a betrayal of the young by the "old men." He made an explicit connection between the war and the contemporary fascination with Odysseus, the hero who returns from the Trojan War to find that usurpers have tried to take away his land and his wife. The first of Pound's *Cantos*, published in an early version in 1917, begins with an extended paraphrase of a passage from *The Odyssey*, which was also an important model for Eliot's *The Waste Land* (1922), and, of course, Joyce's *Ulysses* (1922) (see Chapter Five). In the passage Odysseus descends into the underworld and makes a sacrifice to the shade of the dead prophet Tiresias, in quest of advice about how to return home without being ambushed by the usurpers. Pound and Eliot both championed "impersonality" in poetry, but their technique in "Prufrock" and *Mauberley*, shared to some extent with Yeats, and indebted to the Victorian poet Robert Browning, was to invent a persona who bore an uncertain relation to the poet himself (see Chapter Four). Mauberley, like Prufrock, is an object of irony and pity, but part of the poem's attraction is the sympathy mixed with pity that we feel for the hapless persona.

Like Eliot's "Prufrock," Joyce's *A Portrait of the Artist as a Young Man* (1916), though a work of youth, seems prematurely aged; Joyce treats the fictional version of his younger self with a mixture of irony and sympathy like that shown toward Prufrock by Eliot. The novel tells the story of Stephen Dedalus, a young Irishman, from earliest childhood until his decision to leave Ireland for Paris and become a writer. Before achieving his destiny as an artist, however, the young man experiences various epiphanies, mostly misleading ones. The early chapters chronicle his confusions as a small boy at a strict Jesuit school; in his adolescence he visits prostitutes and wallows in sin; later, he becomes deeply religious and considers entering the priesthood; finally, he recognizes that his destiny is to become not a Catholic priest but a writer, "a priest of eternal imagination, transmuting the daily bread of experience into the radiant body of everliving life." Joyce signals Stephen's premature entrance into adult life when, after hearing the catalogue of his sins, "a squalid stream of vice," at confession, a priest asks him his age and Stephen responds, "Sixteen, father."

The distinctive characteristic of Joyce's storytelling is his attempt to represent each stage of the boy's developing consciousness in the language through which the child himself perceives the world. Thus the narrative itself demonstrates the artist's exploration of language. On the opening page the novel relates the child's impressions of hearing a fairy tale and wetting the bed: "When you wet the bed first it is warm then it gets cold. His mother put on the oilsheet. That had the queer smell." As the novel progresses Stephen continually meditates on sights, sounds, smells, and especially words: green, maroon, suck, queer, Dolan, Heron, foetus, sin, home, Christ, ale, master, tundish, aesthetic, lyrical, epical, dramatic. In earlier semi-autobiographical novels about the life of a writer, such as Charles Dickens's *David Copperfield* (1849–50), the narrator generally speaks from a safe distance. He has undergone some transformation or maturation and remembers childhood from afar. In *Portrait* the remembered childhood is narrated from the perspective of the child. Joyce accomplishes this linguistically, through a development of the technique of free indirect discourse (see Chapter One).

The critic Hugh Kenner called Joyce's version of free indirect discourse the "Uncle Charles Principle" and illustrated it with this passage: "Every morning, therefore, uncle Charles repaired to his outhouse but not before he had creased and brushed scrupulously his back hair and brushed and put on his tall hat." One critic objected to "repaired to the outhouse" as euphemistic, but Kenner noted that the expression is what Uncle Charles himself would have said. For the most part, the novel seems to be told from the perspective and with the language of Stephen himself at various ages, but at times the narrator is relating not what Stephen himself thinks, but what the character being described (such as Uncle Charles) thinks, or perhaps what Stephen thinks the character thinks, so that we are getting Stephen's own artistic way of viewing the world through the minds of others. This complex play with perspective became characteristic of modernism and is closely related to Virginia Woolf's later experiments in *To the Lighthouse* (1927). Joyce explicitly modeled his techniques on Gustave Flaubert's. If Flaubert leaves the reader in some doubt as to how to judge Emma Bovary, however, Joyce gives the reader virtually no external information with which to judge Stephen Dedalus. The final pages of the novel consist of Stephen's diary for the days before his departure for Paris. In the penultimate entry he writes, "Welcome, O life! I go to encounter for the millionth time the reality of experience and to forge in the smithy of my soul the uncreated conscience of my race." Joyce refuses any comment. The reader must decide whether Stephen will succeed in this glorious goal or whether, like Icarus, the son of Daedalus in Greek myth, his waxen wings will melt from flying too close to the sun and he will fall into the sea. The close identification between author and hero, combined with the absence of a distinct omniscient narrator who can comment on the action, leaves the question of Joyce's irony toward Stephen wide open. The attempt to render Stephen's growing consciousness can be seen as a precursor of the stream-of-consciousness novel, which represents the thoughts of a character in a sort of continuous present as they pass through his or her mind. The long timeframe and focus on development in *Portrait* distinguish it from the stream-of-consciousness novel in this narrower sense, but passages like Stephen's diary hint at Joyce's later experiments.

In literature the publication of Eliot's *The Waste Land* and Joyce's *Ulysses* in 1922 seemed to mark the culmination of the experiments championed by Pound before and during the war. In these works (which are treated in detail in Chapters Four and Five respectively), Eliot and Joyce were to make extensive use of mythological parallels to describe contemporary life. Many modernists shared the sense that the recourse to myth, whether Greek or Roman, pagan or Christian, ancient or medieval, offered a way to transform the "stammerings" of the individual artist into a broader sense of order, one that could link contemporary culture with the major concerns of the entire literary and cultural tradition. The year 1922 became known as the *annus mirabilis* (marvelous year) of modernism, and throughout the 1920s modernism remained the dominant force in new literary production in English. Parallel tendencies in Europe showed how the earlier energies of the avant-garde had been channeled into a distinctively modernist idiom, experimental and challenging but directed to a broad public rather than a coterie audience. Networks of artists and writers sympathetic to the aims of modern art formed in various parts of the world, whether on the Left Bank in Paris, around the British Museum in Bloomsbury in London, in Harlem or on Fifth Avenue in New York. Such networks of sympathy helped to diffuse and elaborate canons of "modern" taste that would have seemed radical a generation earlier.

In the years after the war, leading artists and musicians shared with Eliot and Joyce the tendency to develop the radical techniques of the prewar years into that paradoxical thing, a modern tradition. The postwar political crises at first gave a spur to the avant-gardes who sometimes saw the revolutionary movements of the period as sympathetic to their artistic aims and lent their support to new regimes, whether communist (the Russian constructivists and French surrealists supported communism) or fascist (Pound and the Italian futurists enthusiastically backed Benito Mussolini). Whether because of political pressure, however, or because of the general tendency of radical movements to ossify after a certain initial energy has been spent, many leaders of the avant-garde seemed to turn away from the most radical possibilities envisioned in their prewar experiments. In painting many of the geniuses of the avant-garde, such as Paul Klee, Henri Matisse, Piet Mondrian, and Pablo Picasso, developed their own almost classical modernist styles. The avant-garde innovators became "old masters" of modernism.[34] In the meantime, modern art was becoming canonical and established. The foundation of the Museum of Modern Art (MOMA) in New York in 1929 helped to define the nature of the modern art movement and to give it respectability. The director of MOMA, Alfred Barr, put together shows and published catalogues on such topics as *Cubism and Abstract Art* and *Fantastic Art, Dada, and Surrealism* (both 1936). A 1932 exhibition at MOMA defined the "International Style" in modern architecture and perhaps contributed to its dominance, which would be notable throughout the world in the wake of the Second World War.

In music, too, after the First World War, Arnold Schoenberg and his students were developing new sets of rules that seemed to restrain their earlier avant-garde impulses. Beginning in 1921, Schoenberg, Alban Berg, and Anton Webern made use of "serialism" or "twelve-note composition," a new compositional technique to replace the system of tonality they had rejected. In place of traditional keys, serialist music used all twelve notes of the traditional octave. These could be organized in any fixed order, but once fixed they established the parameters for the entire composition. This system created a new method for assuring harmony. When listening to twelve-tone music, it is not always possible to distinguish the series, but for the composer the series is a rigid rule that ensures discipline in putting together the composition. The Schoenberg tradition dominated high art music until well after the Second World War.

In retrospect, critics have defined the 1920s as the era of high modernism, distinct from earlier modernism in its concern with myth and tradition and its tendency to incorporate earlier, more fragmentary experiments into a style that preserved enough of traditional syntax and plot to appeal to a broad audience. The writers of this high point of modernism often combined experimental form with grand, even epic, ambition. The following three chapters survey modernism in three genres – poetry, prose fiction, and drama – focusing on the 1920s as the decade of modernism's greatest achievements. The dispersal of this modernist energy during the 1930s and after may have resulted in part from the very intensity of earlier avant-garde experiments, which necessarily led to a period of cooling off. The decline of modernism was also abetted, however, by the influence of the Great Depression and an era of extremist politics, which will be explored in Chapter Seven.

## Further reading

*Literary works*

Robert Graves, *Goodbye to All That* (various editions).
James Joyce, *A Portrait of the Artist as a Young Man* (various editions).
Ezra Pound, *Selected Cantos*. New York: New Directions, 1970.
Siegfried Sassoon, *The Complete Memoirs of George Sherston*. London: Faber and
    Faber, 1972.
Gertrude Stein, *The Autobiography of Alice B. Toklas* (various editions).
Rebecca West, *The Return of the Soldier* (various editions).
Virginia Woolf, *Jacob's Room, Mrs. Dalloway, To the Lighthouse* (various editions).


*Later criticism*

Daniel Albright, *Untwisting the Serpent: Modernism in Music, Literature, and
    Other Arts*. Chicago: University of Chicago Press, 2000.
Richard Bridgman, *Gertrude Stein in Pieces*. Oxford: Oxford University Press,
    1971.
Peter Bürger, *Theory of the Avant-Garde*, trans. Michael Shaw. Minneapolis:
    University of Minnesota Press, 1984.
Matei Calinescu, *Five Faces of Modernity: Modernism, Avant-Garde, Decadence,
    Kitsch, Postmodernism*. Durham, NC: Duke University Press, 1987.
Paul Fussell, *The Great War and Modern Memory*. Oxford: Oxford University
    Press, 1975.
Paul Griffith, *A Concise History of Modern Music from Debussy to Boulez*. London:
    Thames and Hudson, 1978.
Samuel Hynes, *A War Imagined: The First World War and English Culture*. New
    York: Atheneum, 1991.
Hermione Lee, *Virginia Woolf*. New York: Vintage Books, 1999.
James Longenbach, *Stone Cottage: Pound, Yeats, and Modernism*. Oxford: Oxford
    University Press, 1988.
Mark Morrisson, *The Public Face of Modernism: Little Magazines, Audiences, and
    Reception, 1905–1920*. Madison: University of Wisconsin Press, 2001.
Marjorie Perloff, *The Futurist Moment: Avant-Garde, Avant Guerre, and the
    Language of Rupture*. Chicago: University of Chicago Press, 1986.
Renato Poggioli, *Theory of the Avant-Garde*, trans. Gerald Fitzgerald. Cambridge,
    MA: Harvard University Press, 1968.

# Part II

## *Genres*

*Chapter 4*

# Poetry

"Eliot's *Waste Land* is I think the justification of the 'movement,' of our modern experiment, since 1900," wrote Ezra Pound shortly after the poem was published in 1922.[1] Eliot's poem describes a mood of deep disillusionment stemming both from the collective experience of the First World War and from Eliot's personal travails. Born in St. Louis, Missouri, Thomas Stearns Eliot had studied at Harvard, the Sorbonne, and Oxford before moving to London, where he completed his doctoral dissertation on the philosopher F. H. Bradley. Because of the war he was unable to return to the United States to receive his degree. He taught in a grammar school briefly and then took a job at Lloyds Bank, where he worked for eight years. Unhappily married, he suffered writer's block and then a breakdown soon after the war and wrote most of *The Waste Land* while recovering in a sanatorium in Lausanne, Switzerland, at the age of thirty-three. Eliot later described the poem as "the relief of a personal and wholly insignificant grouse against life . . . just a piece of rhythmical grumbling."[2] Yet the poem seemed to his contemporaries to transcend Eliot's personal situation and represent a general crisis in Western culture. One of its major themes is the barrenness of a postwar world in which human sexuality has been perverted from its normal course and the natural world, too, has become infertile. A lapsed Unitarian, Eliot went on to convert to a High Church form of Anglicanism, become a naturalized British subject, and turn to conservative politics. In 1922, however, his anxieties about the modern world were still overwhelming.

*The Waste Land* was quickly recognized as a major statement of modernist poetics, both for its broad symbolic significance and for Eliot's masterful use of formal techniques that earlier modernists had only begun to attempt. The critic I. A. Richards influentially praised Eliot for describing the shared postwar "sense of desolation, of uncertainty, of futility, of the groundlessness of aspirations, of the vanity of endeavour, and a thirst for a life-giving water which seems suddenly to have failed."[3] Eliot later complained that "approving critics" like Richards "said that I had expressed 'the disillusionment of a generation,' which is nonsense. I may have expressed for them their own illusion of being disillusioned, but that did not form part of my intention."[4] Nonetheless, it was as a representative of a postwar generation that Eliot became famous. To compare Eliot's comments on the poem with how it was received illustrates strikingly the fact that, as William K. Wimsatt and Monroe Beardsley put it, "The poem is not the critic's own and not the author's (it is detached from the author at birth and goes about the world beyond his power to intend about it or control it). The poem belongs to the public."[5] *The Waste Land* made use of allusion, quotation (in several languages), a variety of verse forms, and a collage of poetic fragments to create the sense of speaking for an entire culture in crisis; it was swiftly accepted as the essential statement of that crisis and the epitome of a modernist poem.

Eliot's age itself was symbolic of an entry into midlife. It was at thirty-three, "in the middle of our life's way," that Dante had the vision of heaven and hell recorded in his *Divine Comedy*. It was at the same age that Christ was crucified. His death and resurrection form a major symbolic framework for *The Waste Land*. Although its first lines suggest an aversion to "mixing / Memory with desire" and to "stirring / Dull roots with spring rain," the poem's success results largely from Eliot's ability to mix modes and tones. The originality of *The Waste Land*, and its importance for most poetry in English since 1922, lies in Eliot's ability to meld a deep awareness of literary tradition with the experimentalism of free verse, to fuse private and public meanings, and to combine moments of lyric intensity into a poem of epic scope. This chapter offers a reading of *The Waste Land*, while relating it to other major accomplishments of "high" modernist poetry. Modern poetry used new forms, words set "at liberty," in F. T. Marinetti's phrase, to engage with the literary tradition that the earlier avant-gardes had often shunned. It inherited the symbolist emphasis on private meanings, but reoriented this symbolism in order to reach a broad reading public. It used techniques such as juxtaposition and collage to combine the individual epiphany of the lyric tradition with the broad public voice of epic. Although Eliot wrote only a few major poems, he fairly rapidly became, partly through the effectiveness of his critical essays and partly through the timeliness of *The Waste Land*, the leading figure of English modernism. The poem thus exemplifies modernist technique.

# Tradition

Modern poetry often seems to be poetry about poetry. The modernists were highly self-conscious about their relationship to literary tradition. While some avant-garde writers might, like the Russian cubo-futurists, "declare boundless loathing for the language handed down to us," English-language modernists such as Eliot and Ezra Pound treated literary tradition with much greater respect.[6] In radically changing the form of English poetry, they sought not to destroy literature but to save it and to retain for literature the authority that it seemed to be losing in the face of industrialization and mass culture. In a well-known essay, "Tradition and the Individual Talent" (1919; see Introduction), Eliot described how the modern poet, when truly original, enters into a dialogue with tradition. He claimed that a great poem makes it necessary to understand all earlier poetry of the same tradition in a new light.

The modernists, though certainly striving to be original and different from earlier poets, felt that to do so they must grapple with those earlier poets. This heavy weight of tradition accounts in part for the allusiveness of so much modern poetry. A brief survey of the allusions in the first section of *The Waste Land* shows some of Eliot's techniques for incorporating fragments of tradition into his work. Aided by Eliot's own notes and comments, scholars have identified allusions in this first section of seventy-six lines to: the Book of Common Prayer, Geoffrey Chaucer, Rupert Brooke, Walt Whitman, Théophile Gautier, Charles-Louis Philippe, James Thomson, Guillaume Apollinaire, Countess Marie Larisch, Wyndham Lewis, nine books of the Bible, John Donne, Alfred Lord Tennyson, Richard Wagner, Sappho, Catullus, Lord Byron, Joseph Campbell, Aldous Huxley, J. G. Frazer, Jessie L. Weston, W. B. Yeats, Shakespeare, Walter Pater, Charles Baudelaire, Dante, Ezra Pound, James Joyce, and John Webster – about one allusion every two lines.[7] These allusions are in fact heavily weighted toward the nineteenth and early twentieth centuries, to Eliot's nearer precursors, but they include several ancient, medieval, and Renaissance sources, thus establishing a retrospective tradition that seems to run, say, from Sappho down to Pound, Eliot's friend and mentor, who himself drastically edited the manuscript of *The Waste Land* and arranged for its publication in *The Dial.* Eliot's technique of allusion serves various functions: to give symbolic weight to the poem's contemporary material, to encourage a sort of free association in the mind of the reader, and to establish a tone of pastiche, seeming to collect all the bric-a-brac of an exhausted civilization into one giant, foul rag and bone shop.

The first lines of the poem position it as a monument in a specifically English tradition by alluding to Geoffrey Chaucer, the first major poet of the English language, whom John Dryden called "the Father of English Poetry." Chaucer's *Canterbury Tales* begins with a description of April's "sweet showers," which cause the flowers of spring to grow. The natural cycle of death and rebirth traditionally associated with the month of April appears tragic to Eliot's speaker:

> April is the cruellest month, breeding
> Lilacs out of the dead land, mixing
> Memory and desire, stirring
> Dull roots with spring rain.
> Winter kept us warm, covering
> Earth in forgetful snow, feeding
> A little life with dried tubers.

For Eliot's speaker, April's showers are cruel, not sweet. The "us" in line 5 – "Winter kept us warm" – seems to link the poet himself to the earth that is covered with snow. These opening lines, then, pose the question of the poet's originality in relation to a tradition that seems barely capable of nourishing the "dull roots" of the modern poet's sensibility. The poet lives in a modern waste land, in the aftermath of a great war, in an industrialized society that lacks traditional structures of authority and belief, in soil that may not be conducive to new growth. Even if he could become inspired, however, the poet would have no original materials to work with. His imagination consists only of "a heap of broken images," in the words of line 22, the images he inherits from literary ancestors going back to the Bible. The modernist comes to write poetry after a great tradition of poetry has been all but worn out. Despite this bleakness, though, the poem does present a rebirth of sorts, and the rebirth, while signifying the recovery of European society after the war, also symbolizes the renewal of poetic tradition in modernism, accomplished in part by the mixing of high and low culture and the improvisational quality of the poem as a whole.

The poet's struggle to make a new poem out of the inherited language of tradition seems to be mirrored in the unevenness of the poem's language and form. The opening lines vary between five and nine syllables each. Five of the seven lines end with a single verb in participial form, following a comma (which marks a caesura, or pause, in the poem's rhythm). These lines seem uneven – as if the poet had started to write iambic pentameter but not completed the lines or as if he had intended to write shorter lines with three or four beats each but felt compelled to add the words that appear after the commas. Each of the participles introduces an enjambment – in which a unit of meaning carries beyond a line-ending into the next line. The poem makes sparing use of end-rhyme, which is associated with completion and closure. Yet the participial verb endings perform something like the function of rhyme, linking together the various underground motions of winter and spring: breeding, mixing, stirring, covering, feeding: indeed, "breeding" and "feeding" do rhyme. Eliot also makes use of alliteration – the repetition of consonants – in phrases such as "*li*lacs out of the *d*ead *l*and," "*m*ixing / *M*emory," "*W*inter kept us *w*arm," and "a *li*ttle *li*fe." Alliteration is an older poetic technique than rhyme and typical of Old English poetry, which, like these lines, was heavily accented. Eliot adopted these Old English poetic techniques from Pound, who had translated the Anglo-Saxon poem "The Seafarer" into alliterative modern English. They suggest that Eliot is drawing on resources even older than Chaucer's Middle English. Even as he describes the decay of modern civilization, he seeks poetic power in the primitive resources of the English language. The caesuras and enjambment give the verse a ritual air, as if we were witnessing a "rite of spring," such as Igor Stravinsky celebrated before the war. The title of this first section, "The Burial of the Dead," from the funeral service in the Anglican Book of Common Prayer, reinforces this ritual quality. The participial phrases emphasize the continual activity that underlies the winter's "forgetful snow" and the spring's "dead land": life is breeding and stirring; dry roots are soaking up water; the emotions of the past and the future, memory and desire, are mixing in the rebirth of spring. Something is germinating.

For Eliot's speaker, this rebirth is cruel, because any birth reminds him of death. The soil out of which the spring plants grow is composed of the decayed leaves of earlier plants. April is the month of Easter, and Eliot is invoking here both the Christian story of the young god who dies in order to give new life to the rest of us and the many other versions of this myth chronicled by Sir James Frazer in his anthropological work *The Golden Bough* (1890) and Jessie Weston in her *From Ritual to Romance* (1920). Frazer and Weston explored the links among the mythology of the ancient Near East, the Christ story, fertility rites, folk customs like May Day, and degenerate modern forms of magic such as the Tarot deck. What made Frazer's and Weston's discoveries shocking to some of their first readers was the evidence that many Christian myths and rituals had their origins in ancient, pagan forms of magic. Eliot was particularly interested in the myth of the Fisher King, most famously embodied in the Arthurian story of the quest for the holy grail. The Fisher King is impotent, his lands infertile and drought-stricken; one cause of this infertility is a crime, the rape of some maidens at the king's court. Only the arrival of a pure-hearted stranger (Perceval, Gawain, or Galahad in different versions of the Arthurian tales) permits the land to become fertile again. Weston emphasized the sexual symbolism of the story, notably the grail (a cup said to have been used at the Last Supper) and the lance (said to have pierced Christ's side when he was on the cross), which can be interpreted as symbols of the female and male genitalia. This suggests ancient practices of imitative magic, including ritual marriages intended to encourage the plants to grow; Frazer thought that the tradition of the May Queen and King derived from such rites. Much of the symbolism of *The Waste Land* suggests these ancient fertility rites, but always gone awry, particularly in such modern instances as the fortune-teller Madame Sosostris, whom Eliot drew from *Crome Yellow* (1921), a satirical novel by the young Aldous Huxley.

Many myths attribute the death of winter and the rebirth of spring to the death and rebirth of a god with human attributes, who in some ancient practices is a man ritually murdered and in others an effigy buried or thrown into the sea to guarantee fertility or bring rain. In *The Waste Land*, however, the god himself is conspicuously absent, except in debased forms like the (missing) Hanged Man in the Tarot pack or the drowned Phoenician Sailor, who returns as "Phlebas the Phoenician" in the fourth section, "Death by Water." Other, more modern versions of the Christ story find a place in the poem. *The Waste Land* echoes Walt Whitman's "When Lilacs Last in the Door-Yard Bloomed" (1865), in which Whitman makes use of a similar mythology to commemorate Abraham Lincoln, who was assassinated at the end of the American Civil War on Good Friday, 1865. Eliot probably also had Rupert Brooke's poem "The Old Vicarage, Grantchester" (1912), in mind; it begins "Just now the lilac is in bloom." Brooke himself combined the roles of poet and martyr (see Chapter Three). In the more immediate past, W. B. Yeats had recently published "Easter, 1916," celebrating the martyrs of the Easter rebellion in Ireland. Chaucer drew on this same mythological structure in the *Canterbury Tales*: his pilgrims are heading for Canterbury, "the holy, blissful martyr for to seek, / He who hath helped them when they were sick." Eliot would later write a play, *Murder in the Cathedral* (1935), about the death of Thomas à Becket, Chaucer's "holy, blissful martyr." Spring, the season of rebirth, is also a season for celebrating martyrs, and Eliot's speaker seems to align himself with such martyrs as Christ, Lincoln, Brooke, Becket, and the war dead.

The poem ultimately does promise a new beginning, but Eliot's speaker appears, perversely, to prefer winter to spring, and thus to deny the joy and beauty associated with rebirth. He emphasizes the role of death and decay in the process of growth, most memorably in the conversation between two veterans who meet near London Bridge after the war: "'Stetson! / 'You who were with me in the ships at Mylae! / 'That corpse you planted last year in your garden, / 'Has it begun to sprout? Will it bloom this year? / 'Or has the sudden frost disturbed its bed?'" The war is the essential background to the poem, but instead of referring to it directly, Eliot alludes to the battle of Mylae in the Punic Wars of the third century B.C.E., suggesting that all wars are in reality one war. The fact that the First World War was fought not primarily on ships but in trenches is expressed only indirectly through the idea of the sprouting corpse, which seems a grotesque parody of Brooke's image of the foreign burial plot as "forever England" (see Chapter Three). Similarly, the poem's "rats' alley" owes something to the rats that appear in poetry about trench warfare by such soldier-poets as Siegfried Sassoon. Later, Eliot casually introduces the minor character Albert, Lil's husband, a demobilized soldier. History enters the poem not as a subject for direct treatment but through snatches of overheard dialogue.

In the first section of the poem, Eliot adapts some of the crucial imagery of the poem – the rocky, deserted land, the absence of life-giving water, the dead or dying vegetation – from the biblical books of Ecclesiastes, Ezekiel, and Isaiah. Other quotations or translations come from writers of near-sacred status: Shakespeare ("Those are pearls that were his eyes," line 48) and Dante ("I had not thought death had undone so many. / Sighs, short and infrequent were exhaled," lines 63–4). Eliot helpfully, if somewhat pedantically, included a set of notes on the poem that allowed even his early readers to identify the sources of these allusions, though he later ridiculed his notes as "a remarkable exposition of bogus scholarship."[8] The notes themselves are an indication of what is new about the poem. Previous poets would have assumed that their readers shared a common culture with them and would probably have alluded only to materials from that common culture. Eliot inherits from the symbolists a concern with private, esoteric meanings, but he adds notes in order to make some of those meanings accessible to his readers. The Bible, Shakespeare, and Dante obviously provide historical and aesthetic ballast for Eliot's apparently chaotic modern poem, but other types of allusion seem more bizarre. Many of the quotations appear in foreign languages, such as the lines from Richard Wagner's *Tristan and Isolde* (1857–9), a legendary story of adultery which helps Eliot to establish the theme of frustrated or misdirected sexuality. While occasionally quoting his favorite modern French poets, including Charles Baudelaire, he also includes passages of everyday conversation, such as the snippets in lines 8 to 16 from the reminiscences of Countess Marie Larisch, the niece of the former Empress of Austria and a fashionable contemporary of Eliot.

Eliot's use of allusion and quotation seems in part a response to the dilemma of coming at the end of a great tradition. The poet seeks to address modern problems – the war, industrialization, abortion, urban life – and at the same time to participate in a literary tradition. His own imagination resembles the decaying land that is the subject of the poem: nothing seems to take root among the stony rubbish left behind by old poems and scraps of popular culture. The method of assembling "fragments" or "broken images" from the past into a sort of mosaic allows him at once to suggest parallels between contemporary problems and earlier historical situations and to disorient the reader, turning the reading process into a model of modern, urban confusion. It parallels the cubist use of collage, calling attention to the linguistic texture of the poem itself and to the materials – literary and popular – out of which it is constructed. Eliot's allusive method is a distinctive feature of his poetry, but he developed it in part on the model of some of Pound's earlier poems, and Pound's editing of *The Waste Land* greatly increased its fragmentation. An even more important influence was James Joyce (see Chapter Five). Eliot read the early episodes of *Ulysses* (1922) that appeared in the *Little Review*; as assistant editor at *The Egoist*, he read the original drafts of five episodes that were published there in 1919. He also read other parts of the novel in manuscript and corresponded with Joyce about it. He later confessed to having felt that *Ulysses*, published in the same year as *The Waste Land*, did "superbly" what Eliot himself was "tentatively attempting to do, with the usual false starts and despairs."[9] Allusion would become a favorite modernist technique for reconciling formal experiment with an awareness of literary tradition.

## Voice

T. S. Eliot's original title for *The Waste Land* was "He do the Police in Different Voices." The line, another quotation, comes from Charles Dickens's *Our Mutual Friend* (1864–5) and describes the foundling Sloppy's skill as a newspaper reader – imitating the voices of the police in the crime reports. *The Waste Land* is composed of many voices, not always distinguishable from one another. The second section, "A Game of Chess," contains a medley of voices. The opening passage draws on Shakespeare's *Antony and Cleopatra* to describe a richly furnished room, in which a depiction of Ovid's story of the rape of Philomela and her transformation into a nightingale is displayed above the mantel. The "inviolable voice" of the painted or sculpted nightingale also enters the poem inarticulately through a conventional representation of bird-song from Renaissance poetry: "Jug jug" (103). The following passage relates a conversation between a neurotic woman and a laconic man. The woman's remarks appear in quotation marks: "'Speak to me. Why do you never speak? Speak.'" These comments alternate with lines, not in quotation marks, that may be spoken or thought by her male companion: "I think we are in rats' alley / Where the dead men lost their bones." The ominous tone of these replies suggests, however, that the words may issue from some supernatural source. A moment of ragtime music breaks in before the neurotic woman threatens to rush out into the street. (Eliot's friends thought that the woman in this passage was very closely based on his first wife, who was later institutionalized.) The section ends with an overheard monologue, this one drawn from a story told by the Eliots' maid concerning Albert, a demobilized soldier, and Lil, his wife, who has bad teeth and has taken some pills to induce an abortion. The maid relates her conversation with Lil. Another ominous voice (or the same one?) interrupts the monologue, announcing with increasing frequency "HURRY UP PLEASE ITS TIME," the standard warning that closing time is approaching in a pub. Here, the words have a sinister quality, suggesting that "time" means death, or apocalypse. The final words of the section recall Ophelia's last scene before her suicide in *Hamlet*. The section makes use of at least seven voices: the initial narrator, the nightingale, the neurotic woman, her companion, the gramophone, the maid, and the barkeeper.

Among the mix of voices are those of popular culture. The influential critic Clive Bell, brother-in-law of Virginia Woolf, described Eliot's poetry as largely "a product of the Jazz movement," and saw *The Waste Land* as part of a "ragtime literature which flouts traditional rhythms and sequences and grammar and logic."[10] Eliot riffs on a ragtime song ("The Shakespearean Rag"): "O o o o that Shakespeherian rag, / It's so elegant, so intelligent." The critic Michael North has shown that many of Eliot's first reviewers associated his modernism with the Jazz Age. The poem's syncopated rhythms might seem, to a conservative critic, to bring all of literary tradition down to the level of jazz, but they can just as plausibly be seen as including popular culture in a new canon that erases the boundaries between high and low.

The use of so many voices in this kind of collage allows the poet to distance himself from any single statement. As the critic Louis Menand has put it, "nothing in [the poem] can be said to point to the poet, since none of its stylistic features is continuous, and it has no phrases or images that cannot be suspected of – where they are not in fact identified as – belonging to someone else . . . Eliot appears nowhere, but his fingerprints are on everything."[11] Menand's comment recalls Gustave Flaubert's idea of the godlike author who is "present everywhere and visible nowhere," and the demand of the prosecuting attorney at the obscenity trial that *Madame Bovary* incurred : "Would you condemn her in the name of the author's conscience? I do not know what the author's conscience thinks" (see Chapter One). Indeed, some of Eliot's most important influences were the post-Flaubertian novelists Joseph Conrad, Henry James, and James Joyce. Is the poet himself speaking the lines describing the room, or is this merely a pastiche of Renaissance drama? Who is issuing the warnings about closing time? Although *The Waste Land* is, by Eliot's own admission, a highly personal document, it also aspires to a certain kind of impersonality.

Both Eliot and Ezra Pound espoused a doctrine of impersonality in poetry. In "Tradition and the Individual Talent" (1919), Eliot wrote of the mind of the poet as a catalyst:

> When the two gases previously mentioned are mixed in the presence of a filament of platinum, they form sulphurous acid. This combination takes place only if the platinum is present; nevertheless the newly formed acid contains no trace of platinum, and the platinum itself is apparently unaffected; has remained inert, neutral, and unchanged. The mind of the poet is the shred of platinum. It may partly or exclusively operate upon the experience of the man himself; but, the more perfect the artist, the more completely separate in him will be the man who suffers and the mind which creates; the more perfectly will the mind digest and transmute the passions which are its material.[12]

Pound used a similar image for the impersonality of the author: "The best artist is the man whose machinery can stand the highest voltage. The better the machinery, the more precise, the stronger, the more exact will be the record of the voltage and of the various currents which have passed through it."[13] The poet here does experience emotions, but mechanically, as a seismograph experiences earthquakes – in order to record their magnitude. This doctrine of impersonality was closely linked to Eliot's claim that his poetry was "classical" and not "romantic," by which he meant in part that it was more concerned with form and balance than with the expression of emotion.

Impersonality did not mean that modernist poetry avoided emotion. However, the emotions of modernist poetry are assumed in something like the way an actor takes on a role – Eliot, in *The Waste Land* "does" a variety of different characters in different voices. Paradoxically, by trying on several personae, and not identifying himself with any one persona, Eliot manages to achieve a kind of impersonality. Eliot and Pound, though downplaying their reliance on nineteenth-century English precursors, drew for their conception of impersonality on Robert Browning's dramatic monologues, in which he took on the roles of such figures as the Duke who casually tells the story of how he put a stop to his first wife's suspected adultery ("My Last Duchess" [1842]) or the Renaissance professor who devotes his whole life to the smallest aspects of Greek grammar ("A Grammarian's Funeral" [1855]). Pound's most successful use of personae was in *Hugh Selwyn Mauberley* (1920), but that poem is so dominated by the poet's alter-ego that it seems more of a "portrait of the artist" than *The Waste Land* or any of Browning's monologues (see Chapter Three).

In a note to the third section of the poem, "The Fire Sermon," Eliot wrote:

> Tiresias, although a mere spectator and not indeed a "character," is yet the most important personage in the poem, uniting all the rest. Just as the one-eyed merchant, seller of currants, melts into the Phoenician Sailor, and the latter is not wholly distinct from Ferdinand Prince of Naples, so all the women are one woman, and the two sexes meet in Tiresias. What Tiresias *sees*, in fact, is the substance of the poem.

Eliot thus suggests that all the many voices in the poem may be aspects of two voices, those of one man and one woman, or indeed of a single voice, that of Tiresias, the man who was changed into a woman and back into a man, according to Ovid's *Metamorphoses*, who foresaw the destruction of Thebes, according to Sophocles' *Oedipus the King*, and who was visited by Odysseus in the underworld in book eleven of *The Odyssey*. The background suggests one undercurrent of the dialogue between men and women in *The Waste Land*. The title "A Game of Chess," drawn from a play about seduction and diplomacy by the Renaissance playwright Thomas Middleton, and the chess imagery of this section, point to an understanding of marriage and sexuality debased into a game of strategy in which men and women battle over sex. Instead of a life-giving act of love, sex occurs in the poem as seduction or rape, leading to abortion. Eliot's note also suggests that the entire poem can be understood as a vision of a possible destruction, and near the end of the poem such a catastrophe seems to be envis-aged in the words of the nursery rhyme, "London Bridge is falling down falling down falling down." From the point of view of impersonality, the central role of Tiresias suggests that the various voices of the poem can be understood as a sort of chorus, with each part being spoken by representatives of one sex or the other. The distance from such earlier poems as "The Love Song of J. Alfred Prufrock" (1915) or even *Hugh Selwyn Mauberley* is apparent; the lyric "I" and the concentration on a single speaker's or character's experience have given way to a sort of dream vision, in which many voices speak at once. The resulting cacophony suggests the impossibility of a truly unified understanding of the poem, even if Eliot hoped that all the voices could be subsumed in that of Tiresias.

## Words at liberty

*The Waste Land* could not have been written without the assault on the English poetic tradition undertaken by Ezra Pound and the imagists (see Chapter Two).

The most obvious way in which *The Waste Land* differs from most of the poetry of the nineteenth century, and from more recent poets like Rudyard Kipling or even Wilfred Owen and Siegfried Sassoon, is in its play with and partial rejection of traditional meter, rhyme, and stanza form. Parts of the poem are written in free verse. Eliot himself did not much like free verse in general and even insisted that it did not exist. Using the French term for it (*vers libre*), Eliot wrote that "no *vers* is *libre* for the man who wants to do a good job." In particular, although he was happy to do away with standard rhyme schemes, Eliot claimed in an essay of 1917 that all verse (perhaps all language) made use of some kind of meter; what was distinctive about his work was the complexity of his use of meter: "the most interesting verse . . . has been done either by taking a very simple form, like the iambic pentameter, and constantly withdrawing from it, or taking no form at all, and constantly approximating to a very simple one. It is this contrast between fixity and flux, this unperceived evasion of monotony, which is the very life of verse."[14] In this regard Eliot's rhetoric clashed with that of Pound, but both men claimed to be experimenting with very difficult techniques for recording the rhythms of actual speech. Indeed, their views had converged in the years immediately preceding *The Waste Land*, with Pound experimenting more with traditional meters and Eliot using some aspects of free verse. Eliot's divergences from traditional meters, then, were meant to achieve particular poetic effects rather than simply to shock.

At first glance, *The Waste Land* may appear to follow no set metrical pattern. Yet, just as the opening lines of the poem subtly introduce a form of rhyme, Eliot frequently draws on regular meters. He makes use of many fragmentary lines like those of the nightingale's song in "The Fire Sermon":

> Twit twit twit
> Jug jug jug jug jug jug
> So rudely forc'd
> Tereu

Here, the first two lines seem to be made up entirely of stressed syllables, though they tend to fall into groups of three. The third and fourth lines, however, are composed of iambs. The iamb is the dominant "foot," or metrical unit, of English poetry, consisting of two syllables, the first unstressed and the second stressed.

Often, as Theodore Roethke observes, "free verse is a denial in terms . . . [because] invariably, there is the ghost of some other form, often blank verse, behind what is written."[15] Blank verse is the English name for iambic pentameter (lines of five iambs) without rhymes, the verse form of Shakespeare's plays and of John Milton's *Paradise Lost* and William Wordsworth's *Prelude*. Many verses of *The Waste Land* are composed in iambic pentameter, and others closely resemble that meter. Eliot's frequent adaptation of lines from other poets, such as Andrew Marvell, Shakespeare, Edmund Spenser, and John Webster, often reinforces this tendency to revert to the standard meter of English long poems, for example in the opening lines of the second section, "A Game of Chess." Indeed, Pound criticized these passages as "too penty," that is, too close to iambic pentameter, or as Pound also put it, "too tum-pum at a stretch."[16] In addition to the many lines clearly written in blank verse, Eliot uses various rhyme schemes, often to comic effect. For example, in "The Fire Sermon" one of the unwholesome couplings is introduced by a rhyming couplet: "The sound of horns and motors, which shall bring / Sweeney to Mrs. Porter in the spring." In another part of "The Fire Sermon," Eliot relates the unsatisfactory tryst between the typist and the "young man carbuncular" from the perspective of Tiresias, who, according to one version of the myth, was blinded by the goddess Juno for his claim that women enjoyed sex more than men. In the encounter related in the poem, neither participant seems to experience much pleasure. Eliot uses quatrains (rhyming units of four lines) to describe the tryst, and the slightly forced rhymes call attention to the coercive nature of the sexual encounter. When he has left,

> She turns and looks a moment in the glass
> Hardly aware of her departed lover;
> Her brain allows one half-formed thought to pass:
> "Well now that's done: and I'm glad it's over."

The double or feminine rhymes (rhyming the last two syllables of each line) have a darkly comic effect. The traditional meter and rhyme in such passages sets them off from the free verse of the rest of the poem, but often Eliot seems to be using the meter to call attention to a disjuncture between his low subject matter and the formal style with which he describes it. In fact, often the formality of the language is inversely related to the seriousness of the material Eliot is describing. Frequently, the lower-class material in the poem is treated satirically, in contrast with the work of James Joyce, who showed a great fondness for the lower-middle-class milieu of *Ulysses* (1922).

As a protégé of Pound, Eliot was closely associated with free verse, but he often preferred to use regular meters. Others in his generation embraced free verse more enthusiastically. For many European poets, the turn to free verse was a major revolution (see Chapter Three). In French, for example, the alexandrine, the traditional poetic line of twelve syllables which roughly corresponds to the ten-syllable English iambic pentameter, had such predominance that even a distinctively modern poet like Charles Baudelaire retained it in most of his poems. In order to overcome the alexandrine, Stéphane Mallarmé and Guillaume Apollinaire had to break down poetic form altogether; their typographical games suggest the desperation with which they were attacking an ensconced form. Another major French contribution to the modernization of poetic forms, the prose poem, as practiced by Baudelaire, Mallarmé, and their contemporary Arthur Rimbaud, does away with versification completely; it turns poetry into highly wrought prose. This urge to cross generic boundaries made itself felt in many of the modernists, but modern English poetry tended to retain the poetic line (or verse) as its basic unit.

English poetic practice could adapt more gradually to modern experiments because it was more flexible than the French tradition. The modernists had two major nineteenth-century American precursors. Walt Whitman used long, free-verse lines to celebrate American democracy and individualism, as in the opening lines of his poem on the death of Abraham Lincoln, mentioned above as an inspiration for Eliot: "When lilacs last in the door-yard bloomed, / And the great star drooped in the western sky in the night, / I mourned and yet shall mourn with ever-returning spring." Like *The Waste Land*, Whitman's poem on Lincoln treats the return of spring, and the season of Easter, as an occasion for mourning the death that allows for rebirth. Whitman's lines use repetition ("in the," "mourn") and poetic diction ("and yet," "ever-returning") to establish that they are verse, not prose, but his rhythms anticipate Pound's strictures by "departing in no way from speech save by a heightened intensity (i.e. simplicity)."

Whitman's contemporary, Emily Dickinson, while making use of more structured stanza forms that sometimes echo the hymnal, nonetheless distinctly prefigures modernist experiments. Her forms were more restrained than Whitman's, and she often touched on death or on spiritual states approaching death, as in this poem published posthumously in 1896:

> I heard a Fly buzz – when I died –
> The Stillness in the Room
> Was like the Stillness in the Air –
> Between the Heaves of storm –

The poem echoes the traditional short meter of hymns and ballads (alternating lines of four and three iambic feet). Yet the characteristic dashes, which often break up Dickinson's syntax, and the slant rhyme of "Room" and "storm" would not be out of place in a modernist poem. Dickinson published little of her poetry during her lifetime. Although an edition appeared shortly after her death in 1886, much of her work remained unpublished until the 1920s, when it found an enthusiastic audience among the modernists.

Free verse has its own patterns and systems for making significant form out of verse lines of various lengths, and some of these have been summarized by the critic Paul Fussell.[17] They include the use of enumeration or cataloguing. Lists are one of the most ancient poetic forms, notable in the catalogues of ships in Homer's *The Iliad* or in the "begats" of the Bible. In "Poetry" (1919) Marianne Moore lists a number of subjects that do not seem fit for poetry, because "we cannot understand" them, including "elephants pushing, a wild horse taking a roll, a tireless wolf under a tree, the immovable critic twitching his skin like a horse that feels a flea, the base- / ball fan, the statistician." Yet all these form "the raw material" for poetry, and Moore's poetry emerges from the rhythm of the list, including the odd enjambment in the middle of the word "baseball." A brief list appears at the beginning of "The Fire Sermon": "The river bears no empty bottles, sandwich papers, / Silk handkerchiefs, cardboard boxes, cigarette ends / Or other testimony of summer nights. The nymphs are departed" (177–9). In this case Eliot begins in iambic hexameter (six feet), but allows the meter to break down in the third quoted line. He also makes use of another typical device of free verse, the repetition of phrases or syntactical forms, like the refrain "HURRY UP PLEASE ITS TIME" in the passage about Albert and Lil.

Another method of structuring free verse, seldom used by Eliot, is to write very long lines, each of which contains a full syntactic unit, as Whitman often does, thus creating the effect of a formal speech and sometimes even a biblical tone. Conversely, writers of free verse may run a series of very short lines together, dividing a syntactical unit into as many as four or eight lines, as in William Carlos Williams's "This is Just to Say" (1934):

> I have eaten
> the plums
> that were in
> the icebox
>
> and which
> you were probably
> saving
> for breakfast
>
> Forgive me
> they were delicious
> so sweet
> and so cold

Eliot sometimes combines the techniques of Whitman and Williams, by writing a long line that introduces a set of variations on a theme; the line then reappears but broken up by enjambment as if the speaker were mulling over his thought, unable to phrase it adequately. Thus the line "If there were only water amongst the rock" forms the basis for the fugal sequence:

> If there were water
> And no rock
> If there were rock
> And also water
> And water
> A spring
> A pool among the rock
> If there were the sound of water only
> Not the cicada
> And dry grass singing
> But sound of water over a rock
> Where the hermit-thrush sings in the pine trees
> Drip drop drip drop drop drop drop
> But there is no water

*The Waste Land* thus makes use of a wide range of metrical patterns and rhyme schemes, as well as techniques for structuring free verse. Although the effect appeared chaotic to some of Eliot's first readers, the poem fulfills Pound's dictum that "Rhythm *must* have meaning". Later poetic practice was largely shaped by Pound's advocacy of free verse and Eliot's example. Several poets went further than Eliot. Pound, for example, included in his *Cantos* Chinese characters, which most of his readers could neither understand nor even pronounce. Such poetry, like Apollinaire's calligrammes, called attention to the look of the poem on the page.

Not all modern poetry abandoned formal structure, however. For some of the greatest modern poets, the challenge was to use traditional forms in ways appropriate to modern content. W. B. Yeats uses much more traditional stanza forms and meters than Eliot and Pound. His later poems make increasing use of enjambment and, as Helen Vendler has pointed out, there is frequently a disjunction between the sound-unit (the line or stanza) and the sense-unit (the sentence), which gives Yeats's poems some of their modernity despite their appearance of traditionalism.[18] He also uses a tremendous array of verse forms, ranging from the popular ballad tradition to the courtly sonnet tradition. Yeats's productive use of stanza forms can be seen in many of his major poems, from the ballad form of "Crazy Jane Talks with the Bishop" (1933) to the sonnet "Leda and the Swan" (1924) to the ottava rima of "Among School Children" (1928) and "The Circus Animals' Desertion" (1939). Another major modernist, W. H. Auden, was influenced by both Yeats and Eliot at the beginning of his career. Some of his earliest poems are written in free verse, in an Eliotic mood.

Like Yeats, however, Auden made use of a variety of traditional verse forms, for example in "Sonnets from China" (1939) or his elegy on Yeats (1939) (see Chapter Seven). Auden also attempted some unusual and difficult forms. He wrote several sestinas, thirty-nine-line poems in which each six-line stanza uses the same six words at the line-ends but in six different sequences. He also revived the canzone, a complex medieval form, despite the much greater difficulty of finding rhyming words in English than in Italian or Provençal, the languages in which the canzone originated. The work of Yeats and Auden indicates the endurance of traditional meters and stanza forms, despite the general triumph of free verse.

## Epic

Many of the most memorable modernist poems, such as Ezra Pound's "In a Station of the Metro" (1911), H. D.'s "Oread" (1914), or W. B. Yeats's "Leda and the Swan" (1924), were lyrics. The modernists' emphasis on poetic crafts-manship and polish, the pressure exerted on each single word, made it natural for them to focus their experiments on lyrics – that is, short poems of per-sonal expression which had originally (in the ancient world) been intended for singing. Modernism continued the tendency, begun in romanticism, to prize lyric highly, but many modernist poets also sought to write in the traditionally highest form, epic. *The Waste Land* contains both lyric and epic elements. Eliot defined the lyric as "the voice of the poet talking to himself, or to nobody," and if we accept his description of *The Waste Land* as a "piece of rhythmical grum-bling," it may seem to belong to the lyric tradition. Yet its broader ambitions are obvious. "Eliot came back from his Lausanne specialist looking OK; and with a damn good poem (19 pages) in his suitcase," wrote Pound after reading the manuscript of the poem. "About enough, Eliot's poem, to make the rest of us shut up shop."[19] Pound defined an epic as a "poem including history."[20] Although much shorter than Homer's *Iliad* or *Odyssey*, Virgil's *Aeneid*, Dante's *Divine Comedy*, or John Milton's *Paradise Lost*, *The Waste Land* does con-tain history – both contemporary history and the history of the world under-stood in mythological terms. I have argued that one of the factors that helped to create "high modernism" was the attempt of poets, after the First World War, to extend the techniques of the prewar avant-gardes to address broad, historical questions, the sorts of questions normally addressed by epic (see Chapter Three). They remained suspicious, however, of attempts to tell the history of the world from a single, unified perspective – the "Arms and the man I sing" of the first line of Virgil's *Aeneid*, in which both the poet ("I") and his hero ("the man") are singular. Instead, their epics tended to treat historical experience as fragmentary, and often it is difficult to say whether their long poems are epics or merely collections of lyrics. Instead of granting perspective on history, they struggle to contain it in their irregular forms. In the first draft of his own fragmentary epic, *The Cantos*, in 1917, Pound had written that "the modern world / Needs such a rag-bag to stuff all its thoughts in."[21] The modernist epic would have to be a rag-bag.

Perhaps the most famous of modernist rag-bags is the concluding section of *The Waste Land*, "What the Thunder Said." Eliot wrote this section in a flash of inspiration and published it virtually unedited. He invokes three ancient Sanskrit words from the Upanishads, ancient Hindu scriptures: Datta, Dayadhvam, Damyata, each announced by the single syllable "DA," representing a clap of thunder. The return of the waters suggests the possibility of a different type of sexual relation from those seen in the poem so far: "The sea was calm, your heart would have responded / Gaily, when invited, beating obedient / To controlling hands." However, the flood and the purifying fire arrive, and the last lines of the poem seem to announce destruction, in many languages, as partial quotations pile up and the speaker (perhaps at last representing the poet himself), announces, "These fragments I have shored against my ruins." After the destruction, the poem ends on a note of peace, with the words "Shantih shantih shantih," which, as Eliot informs us in his notes, mark "a formal ending to an Upanishad." Eliot's intentions in making a miniature epic out of the various lyrical moments and borrowed fragments that make up *The Waste Land* can best be understood in terms of his analysis of James Joyce's *Ulysses* (1922), which served as perhaps the most important model for the poem. Eliot wrote in an essay on the novel that the parallels Joyce draws between his own characters and those of Homer's *Odyssey* constitute a "mythical method," which had "the importance of a scientific discovery." He went so far as to compare Joyce to Albert Einstein. The mythical method, according to Eliot, "is simply a way of controlling, of ordering, of giving a shape and a significance to the immense panorama of futility and anarchy which is contemporary history."[22] Many of Joyce's readers have felt that Joyce himself did not necessarily aim for control and order, but most are in agreement that Eliot's essay describes well the intention of *The Waste Land*, in which the many parallels that have been briefly discussed here help to convert chaos into a kind of order.

In the later works of the modernists, history came to have idiosyncratic meanings; the modernists were often attracted to mystical systems of world history – Yeats's gyres, Pound's vortex, Joyce's Vichian cycles. They built their major works on such models, and although the historical details of each model, and indeed the modernists' conception of how historical forces operate, were frequently bizarre, the models themselves provided images and symbols for their poetry. All these models tend to emphasize the current moment as one of crisis, either preparing for or recovering from a radical break in history. This radical break certainly has something to do with the First World War, but it is also an aspect of the modernists' eschatological view of the world, their fascination with the problem of destiny and the Last Judgment. It is for this reason that Kurtz's famous last words ("The horror! The horror!") in Joseph Conrad's *Heart of Darkness* (1899) ring through so much of later modernism. Eliot originally intended to use them as the epigraph for *The Waste Land*. As Conrad's narrator Marlow says, "he had summed up – he had judged. 'The horror!' He was a remarkable man. After all, this was the expression of some sort of belief; it had candor, it had conviction, it had a vibrating note of revolt in its whisper, it had the appalling face of a glimpsed truth – the strange commingling of desire and hate." The capacity to judge a civilization that teeters on the edge of chaos was highly prized by the modernists.

Pound's epic, *The Cantos*, begun during the First World War but still incomplete at his death in 1972, shares some of the features of *The Waste Land*, but it shores its fragments on a much greater scale. (Canto VIII begins with a reference to Eliot: "These fragments you have shored (shelved).") It makes use of quotation and allusion to other poets in a method that somewhat resembles cubist collage, but at epic length. Pound combines borrowings from Homer, the Provençal poet Arnaut Daniel, the history of the Italian Renaissance, President John Adams, Robert Browning, and Chinese poetry (as interpreted by the scholar Ernest Fenollosa) with offbeat economic and social theories to relate what he calls "the tale of the tribe," that is, the intellectual life of the human race, exemplified in certain key historical or literary moments.[23] The result, though tainted by Pound's anti-Semitism and adoration of Benito Mussolini, is, like *The Waste Land* or *Ulysses*, a major expression of the modernist ambition to bring the whole of world history to bear on the understanding of modern life and the remaking of poetic tradition. Pound called it an epic, "a poem including history," and it is also a poem shaped by history, by Pound's rejection of his own country and democracy, by his embrace of fascism, and by his subsequent imprisonment and confinement (see Chapter Seven).

Eliot learned much from Pound, and Pound from Yeats. In his essay on *Ulysses*, Eliot noted that Yeats had in some respects prefigured the "mythical method." In some of his later poems, more evidently modernist than his earlier work in their increasing obscurity, Yeats portrays the violent transformations of history – the First World War, the Anglo-Irish War, the Irish civil war, the Russian Revolution – in mythical form. For example, in "Leda and the Swan," a poem about, as Yeats put it, "a violent annunciation," Zeus's transformation into a swan and rape of Leda embodies, through the conception of Helen of Troy, a moment of world-historical change: "A shudder in the loins engenders there / The broken wall, the burning roof and tower / And Agamemnon dead."[24] Like Eliot, Joyce, and Pound, Yeats here uses Homeric subject matter – the fall of Troy – while implicitly drawing a parallel with the contemporary world. Yeats believed that his age was witnessing a transformation similar to that wrought by the fall of Troy or the birth of Christ – "twenty centuries of stony sleep" since Christ's birth, were again to be "vexed to nightmare by a rocking cradle," and Yeats wondered in "The Second Coming" (1920) what sort of savior or Antichrist would announce the new age. In many of his late poems, which share an apocalyptic tone with *The Waste Land*, it seems an open question whether any higher power is overseeing the processes of transformation associated with the importation of supernatural imagery into the description of history. It is fairly certain, however, that any such higher power is far from being simply benevolent.

The modernists' ambitious formal experiments often represented an effort to maintain what Eliot, in his essay on the metaphysical poets (see Introduction), called "variety and complexity" in the face of what they saw as a hostile and homogenizing society whose banal language threatened to destroy poetry. The modernists' difficulty comes in many forms. There are the difficulties associated with complex syntax, the absence of quotation marks, allusions to and quotations of earlier poets, and extended passages in foreign languages, all of which are characteristic of Eliot and Pound; Pound's syntax is particularly difficult because, reaching for the rhythms of Old English verse, he often drops the small connecting words such as particles and prepositions that, in everyday speech, explain the relationships among the nouns and verbs. There is also the typically Yeatsian use of private or esoteric imagery or symbolism, somewhat closer to the difficulty of the most challenging romantic poetry by William Blake and Percy Bysshe Shelley. Yeats relied for many of his later images on his wife's "automatic writing," in which she recorded communications supposedly from the spirit world.[25]

A major American modernist, Wallace Stevens, gave some inkling of the reasons for the contemporary fascination with the world of spirits, magic, and ancient mythology when he wrote that "to see the gods dispelled in mid-air and dissolve like clouds is one of the great human experiences."[26] The modernists felt that the old gods had deserted them, and they sought new gods in unorthodox places. Stevens wrote of the possibility of a kind of poem that would avoid the vagaries of representation. In "An Ordinary Evening in New Haven" (1950), he describes the ideal of a language that could express reality as it is:

> The poem of pure reality, untouched
> By trope or deviation, straight to the word,
> Straight to the transfixing object, to the object
>
> At the exactest point at which it is itself,
> Transfixed by being purely what it is.
> A view of New Haven, say, through the certain eye,
>
> The eye made clear of uncertainty, with the sight
> Of simple seeing, without reflection. We seek
> Nothing beyond reality.

Yet Stevens's poems, though influenced by imagism in their emphasis on exact representation, tend to represent not "transfixing objects" but abstractions. He never describes New Haven, but only analyzes what the simple view of New Haven might be. His long poem *Notes Toward a Supreme Fiction* (1942) lists three criteria for that ultimate poetic creation: "It must be abstract," "It must change," and (less Eliotic), "It must give pleasure." The title of this major poem suggests the modernist fascination with ultimate answers even when those answers, not vouchsafed by a higher power, had to be invented. It also points to the necessarily fragmentary approach to any such ultimate answer. The poem is, like the major works of Eliot and Pound, a collection of lyrics, and the modesty of the title suggests that these are no more than "Notes," plural and presumably incomplete, like Eliot's "fragments" and Pound's *Cantos*.[27]

In the wake of Pound and Eliot, a number of modernists attempted their own epics, often making use of an overarching mythological framework such as that suggested by Eliot's use of the Grail story and related myths. Poets from Scotland and Wales, moved in part by the example of Irish nationalism, celebrated their own national legacies. Hugh McDiarmid wrote his *A Drunk Man Looks at the Thistle* (1926), in which the thistle is the symbol of Scottish nationhood, in a literary form of Scots English. David Jones wrote two major poems, *In Parenthesis* (1937) and *The Anathémata* (1952), incorporating Arthurian legend, Christian theology, and his experience of the First World War into a modern Welsh mythology. Both McDiarmid and Jones looked to the novelist Joyce as a model for their work, more even than to the poet Eliot. Influenced more directly by Pound, the poet Basil Bunting set his long autobiographical poem *Briggflats* (1966) in his native Northumberland (in northern England, on the Scottish border). The critic Nigel Alderman has described these poems as "pocket epics" because, while proclaiming epic intentions, the works also focus tightly on local communities (whether in Scotland, Wales, or Northumberland) and proclaim their exclusion from the grand tales of all humanity that Eliot and Pound tried to tell.[28]

A similar effort to write the epic tale of a restricted locale or group can be seen in several major American poems. An important group of experimental poets lived in New York, including William Carlos Williams and Stevens before the First World War, and Hart Crane, e. e. cummings, and Marianne Moore afterwards. Crane's *The Bridge*, published in 1930 but begun in 1923, strongly under the influence of *The Waste Land*, offers a panoramic vision of American history, focused on the symbol of the Brooklyn Bridge, thus updating Walt Whitman's celebration of the United States in "Crossing Brooklyn Ferry" (1856). Williams had published with the imagists and expressed a related aesthetic in his doctrine "no ideas but in things." He sought to create a type of modernist poetry "in the American grain," as he put it in the title of one of his essay collections. His poem "To Elsie" (1923) commemorates what might be called forgotten Americans, in the person of a mentally challenged maid who worked for Williams:

> The pure products of America
> go crazy –
> mountain folk from Kentucky
>
> or the ribbed north end of
> Jersey

After describing, with a mixture of sympathy and distaste, Elsie's mixed parentage and fecklessness, the poem ends with a pessimistic use of that image of modernity so praised by the futurists – the automobile: "No one / to witness / and adjust, no one to drive the car." Williams, a college friend of Pound at the University of Pennsylvania, moved back to his native Rutherford, New Jersey, after completing medical school and worked as a pediatrician all his life. His epic poem *Paterson* (1946–58) describes an industrial city a few miles from Rutherford. However, he remained connected to the New York artists and poets.

The tensions between the ambition to make a broad statement and the urge toward lyric concision can be seen, finally, in one last modernist poem about poetry, Marianne Moore's "Poetry." Moore worked as an assistant librarian in the New York Public Library before becoming editor of the influential modernist magazine *The Dial*. One distinctive feature of her poetry is her use of quotation, an alternative to Eliot's allusion. She frequently quotes passages from scientific articles or journalism in her poems. By setting such references in quotation marks, and including footnotes indicating their source, she tends to enter into a debate with the quoted source rather than, like Eliot or Pound, evoking it for its nostalgic associations.[29] In "Poetry" (1919) she engages directly in a debate with Leo Tolstoy and Yeats, quoting Tolstoy's dislike of "'business doc-uments and / school-books'" and Yeats's condemnation of "'literalists of / the imagination,'" before defending the roots of poetry in the literal, businesslike raw material of everyday life, her equivalent of Eliot's "variety and complex-ity." In its original version (1919) the poem offers a defense of poetry along the lines of Stevens's later quest for a "poem of pure reality." As she revised it over the years, however, Moore cut out the lists of possible subjects for poetry and condensed the poem to just its three original opening lines. The condensation represented in a sense a return to the miniature forms of imagism, but now seeming to contain the whole relation of poetry to the social world in just three lines. This discussion of modern poetry can conclude with this example of mod-ernism's reticence about its own technique, uncertainty about its own authen-ticity, and guilty reveling in its own rhetorical power, Moore's "Poetry" (1967):

> I, too, dislike it.
>     Reading it, however, with a perfect contempt for it, one discovers in
>     it, after all, a place for the genuine.

## Further reading

### Literary works

W. H. Auden, *Collected Poems*, ed. Edward Mendelson. New York: Vintage Books, 1991.

T. S. Eliot, *The Complete Poems and Plays, 1909–1950*. San Diego: Harcourt Brace Jovanovich, 1980.

T. S. Eliot, *Inventions of the March Hare: Poems 1909–1917*, ed. Christopher Ricks. New York: Harcourt Brace, 1996.

T. S. Eliot, *The Waste Land*, Norton Critical Edition, ed. Michael North. New York: Norton, 2001.

T. S. Eliot, *The Waste Land: A Facsimile and Transcript of the Original Drafts Including the Annotations of Ezra Pound*, ed. Valerie Eliot. Orlando: Harcourt, 1971.

Ezra Pound, *The Cantos of Ezra Pound*. New York: New Directions, 1995.

Ezra Pound, *Selected Poems of Ezra Pound*. New York: New Directions, 1957.

Jahan Ramazani, Richard Ellmann, and Robert O'Clair, eds., *The Norton Anthology of Modern and Contemporary Poetry*. 2 vols., *Volume 1: Modern Poetry*, 3rd edn. New York: Norton, 2003.

Wallace Stevens, *Collected Poetry and Prose*, ed. Frank Kermode and Joan Richardson. New York: Library of America, 1997.

W. B. Yeats, *The Collected Poems of W. B. Yeats*, ed. Richard J. Finneran, 2nd edn. New York: Scribner, 1996.

*Later criticism*

Ronald Bush, *T. S. Eliot: A Study in Character and Style.* Oxford: Oxford
    University Press, 1984.
Ronald Bush, ed. *T. S. Eliot: The Modernist in History.* Cambridge: Cambridge
    University Press, 1991.
Carol T. Christ, *Victorian and Modern Poetics.* Chicago: University of Chicago
    Press, 1984.
Paul Fussell, *Poetic Meter and Poetic Form*, rev. edn. New York: McGraw-Hill,
    1979.
Frank Lentricchia, *Modernist Quartet.* Cambridge: Cambridge University Press,
    1994.
Michael Levenson, *A Genealogy of Modernism: A Study of English Literary
    Doctrine, 1908–1922.* Cambridge: Cambridge University Press, 1984.
Louis Menand, *Discovering Modernism: T. S. Eliot and His Context.* Oxford:
    Oxford University Press, 1987.
A. David Moody, *Thomas Stearns Eliot: Poet.* 2nd edn. Cambridge: Cambridge
    University Press, 1994.
A. David Moody, ed. *The Cambridge Companion to T. S. Eliot.* Cambridge:
    Cambridge University Press, 1994.
David Perkins, *A History of Modern Poetry: From the 1890s to the High Modernist
    Mode.* Cambridge, MA: Harvard University Press, 1976.
B. C. Southam, *A Guide to the Selected Poems of T. S. Eliot*, 6th edn. San Diego:
    Harcourt Brace, 1994.
C. K. Stead, *The New Poetic.* London: Hutchinson, 1964.

*Chapter 5*

# Prose fiction

---

"It is a book to which we are all indebted and from which none of us can escape," wrote T. S. Eliot of James Joyce's *Ulysses* (1922).[1] Joyce's novel describes a day in the life of an advertising canvasser in prewar Dublin, drawing implicit parallels between his adventures and those recounted in Homer's *The Odyssey*. Joyce began the novel in a stream-of-consciousness or "interior monologue" technique that developed naturally out of his experiments in *A Portrait of the Artist as a Young Man* (1916) (see Chapter Three).[2] During the course of writing *Ulysses*, however, he largely abandoned this method and replaced it with a vast array of styles, so that the reader's attention is directed as much to Joyce's use of a variety of literary techniques as to the events he describes. *Ulysses* demonstrates most of the notable characteristics of the modern novel. As an exploration of consciousness or the inner life, it inspired Virginia Woolf's injunction that the novelist should "consider the ordinary mind on an ordinary day."[3] For Joyce this entails a preference for an antihero, or at any rate a hero who does not resemble the heroes of earlier novels, as well as an exploration of subject matter that, while a part of ordinary consciousness, is often taboo in art, such as defecation and masturbation. As a notable experiment in the rendering of time, *Ulysses* displays a modernist skepticism about the linear or sequential arrangement of events into traditional plots. In contrast with the earlier tendency to make the prose of novels generally referential, Joyce was particularly self-conscious about the literary quality or style of novelistic language he used; he experimented with narrative devices and combined the realist representation of the world with esoteric symbolism. Finally, *Ulysses* called attention to its own status as fiction and to the relationship between fiction and history, the question of the novel as a modern form of epic.[4] These characteristics refer to several aspects of *Ulysses*: its subject matter, its plot, its formal qualities, and the social content linked to the period in which it was written. Modernism in the novel is best described as the convergence of all these factors – considered below under the headings Consciousness, Time, Narrative, and Fiction – and their prevalence among a wide range of writers, not just a radical few. Although Joyce was the most accomplished and radical experimenter of his generation, he worked in the same paths as many other writers, such as William Faulkner, Marcel Proust, Virginia Woolf, and a host of lesser novelists.

*Ulysses* is set in Dublin on June 16, 1904, now celebrated by Joyce's fans as "Bloomsday." The day has no particular historical significance, except that it was on June 16, 1904 that Joyce had his first date with his future wife Nora Barnacle. (Joyce and Nora lived together for twenty-seven years before marrying; Joyce objected to most institutions, including that of marriage, but eventually submitted to it for the sake of his children's legal status.) It is, in Woolf's phrase, "an ordinary day," though with more hours of daylight than most because of its proximity to midsummer and Dublin's northerly latitude. Along with a seemingly endless cast of Dubliners, the novel features three major characters, Stephen Dedalus (the protagonist of *Portrait*), Leopold Bloom (the advertising canvasser), and Molly Bloom (Bloom's wife). Through the course of the novel, the attentive reader learns that Bloom and Molly have not had sexual intercourse since the death of their infant son Rudy, ten and a half years earlier. On the afternoon of June 16, Molly is expecting a visit from Blazes Boylan, who will become her lover. Bloom suspects his wife of having had many adulterous affairs, but Blazes is the only clear-cut case. According to the parallel with *The Odyssey*, Bloom spends the day in exile, like Odysseus on his way back from the Trojan War, before returning home at the end of the day. Where Odysseus slaughtered the suitors who had tried to seduce his faithful wife Penelope, however, Bloom meekly accepts Molly's unfaithfulness.

The novel's other plotline features Stephen as a modern equivalent of Telemachus, the son of Odysseus. Like Bloom, Stephen is exiled from his home, a tower on Dublin Bay, by a usurper, his sometime friend Buck Mulligan. Stephen's mother has recently died, so, like Hamlet, he wears black. Bloom, too, dresses in black, for the funeral of a friend, Paddy Dignam, who has fallen off a ladder in a drunken stupor (paralleling the death of a minor character, Elpenor, in *The Odyssey*). Stephen thinks of himself as Hamlet, but Joyce casts him as Telemachus, in search of a father, and the "quest for a father" became a major theme of early criticism of the novel. The novel associates Bloom with Hamlet's father's ghost as well as with Odysseus. Stephen's real father, Simon, is quite incompetent, and when Bloom rescues Stephen from a brawl near the end of the novel, the two men return to Bloom's home together. Their meeting is fairly brief, however, and it is unclear whether or not Stephen has really found the spiritual father he needs. (The encounter is loosely based on an occasion when Joyce himself was rescued from a fracas by Alfred H. Hunter, one of the models for Bloom.) The novel ends, after Bloom returns to bed, with Molly's unsurpassable interior monologue, a sort of soliloquy that gives her account of her childhood, her married life, and her other loves, as well as her views on matters such as war and music.

Joyce wrote *Ulysses* while living in Trieste, Zürich, and Paris, having gone into voluntary "exile" from Ireland because of its conservative social and intellectual climate. He was in close touch with avant-garde circles in all three cities, and their experiments influenced his. The novel appeared in installments in the *Little Review* beginning in 1918, but publication was interrupted in 1920 when its publishers were prosecuted for obscenity, over an episode in which Bloom masturbates. Once complete, the novel had to be published in Paris and was banned in England, Ireland, and the United States for more than a decade. English customs officials and the U.S. Post Office seized and destroyed most copies of the first two editions. During the 1920s, the novel was known in the English-speaking world mainly through some smuggled copies. After 1930, readers could purchase Stuart Gilbert's commentary, which contained excerpts of the novel that had not been judged obscene. In order to make the novel easier to understand, Joyce gave his French and Italian translators schemas explaining that each "episode" had its own distinctive time, scene, style, bodily organ, art, colors, and symbol, and outlining the correspondences between characters and their counterparts in *The Odyssey* and, to a lesser extent, *Hamlet*. (The "episodes," as the chapters are called, are known by the names Joyce gave them in his schemas, although these are not usually printed in editions of the novel itself.) There are also biblical parallels, but they have a somewhat different status; the characters themselves are unaware of the similarities between their own lives and those of the characters in *The Odyssey*, but they frequently invoke the Bible to explain their circumstances.[5]

The Homeric references in *Ulysses* raise a number of critical issues. The use of parallels with one of the great classical epics to describe the humdrum and sordid marital affairs of a reasonably intelligent but not otherwise remarkable lower-middle-class hero can be understood as a form of mock epic, in which high style is applied to low matter. Joyce's attitude would then be seen as satirical, like Eliot's attitude toward such characters as Sweeney and the typist in *The Waste Land*. More frequently, however, readers have seen Joyce as trying to represent what Charles Baudelaire called the "heroism of modern life" (see Introduction). Bloom, who appears merely comic at the beginning of the novel, seems to become more heroic, more like Odysseus, as the narrative progresses. Another debate concerns how much weight readers should place on the schemas in which Joyce outlined the mythic parallels. Eliot praised Joyce's "mythic method," but many critics disagree with Eliot and see the parallels as a kind of scaffolding, not essential to the structure of the work, and interpret Joyce's purpose as less unifying than Eliot suggests (see Chapter Four). In other words, they see Joyce not as a high modernist, but as the first postmodernist, discarding the unifying myths that Eliot wanted to maintain. The reality is complex: both Joyce and Eliot did seek myths that could make sense of contemporary history, but they both also recognized that, to be compelling, these modern myths must be complex, ironic, and multifarious. The seeds of postmodernism are present in the highest of high modernist works.[6]

## Consciousness

Although the modernists also wrote short stories and novellas, the main modernist form of prose fiction is the novel. Whereas epic and lyric poetry and drama were the preeminent literary forms in many ancient cultures, the novel is a relatively modern genre; it became widespread only after the invention of the printing press and expanded rapidly with the increased literacy of the eighteenth and nineteenth centuries. For most of this period, the novel was considered a popular, rather than elite, genre. Novels often described the lives of the lower and middle classes, were generally available in cheap editions, and could be read by the newly literate and by women. They were therefore seen as less "literary" than works written in verse for a more elite audience. The history of modernism in the novel involved an attempt to prove that the novel is a major art form. Although earlier novelists had made this claim, it was most influentially articulated in the late nineteenth century by Henry James. To prove the significance of "the art of fiction," the modernists transformed the popular genre of the eighteenth and nineteenth centuries into something much more difficult to read; in fact, they drew on the techniques of poetry and drama in bringing about this transformation.

The novel, as a genre, has many precursors, including collections of short stories, like Boccaccio's *Decameron* (1348–58), prose romances like Sir Thomas Malory's *Morte d'Arthur* (1469–70), religious allegories like John Bunyan's *Pilgrim's Progress* (1678–84), and biographies, especially those of saints and famous criminals.[7] Cervantes' *Don Quixote* (1605–15) is often considered the first "modern" (as opposed to ancient or medieval) novel for its comic realism: in it, a middle-aged man, who has read too many chivalric romances, imagines that he himself is a knight. He travels around Spain tilting at windmills, freeing prisoners, and imagining that each wayside inn is a castle. The contrast between Don Quixote's dreams of romance and his prosaic, (early) modern reality establishes what would later be called the novel's realism. A similar contrast underlies Flaubert's *Madame Bovary* (1856), in which Emma Bovary, too, has false romantic visions that are shattered by reality (see Chapter One). This tension between individual aspirations and social reality shaped the history of the novel. Those who make the highest claims for the novel as an art form, beginning with Henry Fielding in the eighteenth century, have often represented it as the modern equivalent of the epic poem, describing the full range of life in its historical unfolding, but (unlike the epic) written in prose and with a middle- or lower-class hero in place of the aristocratic and royal heroes of epic. Yet throughout its history the novel was concerned not only with representing external events, but also with registering their effects on the minds of individuals. The novel also concerns itself with domestic life, and the intimate relations between women and men; George Eliot described her masterpiece *Middlemarch* (1871–2) as a "home epic." This phrase captures the crucial tension in the novel form between a desire to represent the whole social world and a focus on the intimate lives of particular characters.

Although the term realism was first applied to the novel in the nineteenth century to describe works by authors such as Eliot, Flaubert, and James, many of the techniques of realism had been pioneered in the eighteenth century. Novelists such as Jane Austen, Daniel Defoe, Fielding, and Samuel Richardson developed methods to convey a sense of life as it is really lived, by individuals in real societies. One of their particular concerns was the relationship between the individual perceiving consciousness and the social world as a whole. The critic Ian Watt has described these techniques as "formal realism." As soon as the conventions of "formal realism" became established in the eighteenth century, they began to be parodied. In *The Life and Opinions of Tristram Shandy* (1759–67), Laurence Sterne's self-conscious narration, insertion of footnotes, play with the text as a material object (inserting a black page to mark a character's death, for example), and commentary on his own plot (including diagrams of the plot showing jagged lines and arabesques) all prefigured modernist and postmodernist play with narrative conventions. Sterne does not have immediate successors in the nineteenth century, however, and for the most part the development of the nineteenth-century British novel hones the conventions of formal realism, notably through Austen's refinement of the marriage plot. The fundamental tension underlying the realism of the nineteenth-century novel is that between the third-person narrator's effort to describe the external world objectively and novelists' growing concern to represent the subjective experiences of individual characters; the way reality appears, for example, to a young woman of marriageable age, or to a young man eager to make a name for himself, or, in later fiction, to an anarchist bookbinder (James's *Princess Casamassima* [1886]), a governess on the verge of madness (James's *The Turn of the Screw* [1898]), or a delusional murderer (Fyodor Dostoevsky's *Crime and Punishment* [1866]).

This concern with subjective experience was particularly developed later in the nineteenth century by Dostoevsky, Flaubert, and James. Along with Flaubert, Dostoevsky was the foreign-language novelist who most influenced the development of English modernism. As a young man, he was condemned to die for his socialist activities; reprieved at the last minute, he was sent to a Siberian prison, where he underwent a conversion to Russian Orthodox Christianity and Slavic nationalism. Making use of the techniques of the realist novel, Dostoevsky explored matters of conscience and spiritual crisis; his interest in pathological personalities and his detailed explorations of consciousness had a great impact on modern British fiction, especially after his major works were translated by Constance Garnett between 1912 and 1920. Some modernists saw Dostoevsky as the inventor of the "stream of consciousness" in the novel, but Joyce gave credit to a minor French novelist, Edouard Dujardin.[8] A contemporary of Joyce, Dorothy Richardson, brought the technique into English literature in her monumental multivolume *Pilgrimage* (1915–35), about a woman writer's life in prewar England.

Many histories of the novel present modernism as a rebellion against realism, or against the Victorian novel more generally. There is some truth in this, especially in so far as the modernists, like Sterne before them, play with and parody the conventions they have inherited. However, modernism can also be understood as the natural continuation of a trend in the development of realism represented by Dostoevsky, Flaubert, and James. Modernist techniques like stream of consciousness attempt to describe in great detail the experience of reality as lived by an idiosyncratic individual. At the same time, however, rather than simply accept the subjectivism of the madman or decadent, the great modern novelists attempt to make out of the fragmented perceptions of individuals a picture of the whole objective world. They tend to avoid the omniscient narrator of Fielding and the realists (Austen, Honoré de Balzac, Eliot), and instead to present the world mainly through the eyes of their characters. But, while eschewing the omniscience of the narrator, they are not rejecting realism in the broad sense defined by Watt. Rather, they are tilting the balance toward what Watt called a "realism of presentation," trying to show not necessarily how things really are, but how things are experienced, what it feels like to be alive.[9]

One way to explore the vagaries of consciousness was through the device of the first-person narrator, like Conrad's Marlow in *Heart of Darkness* (1899) and *Lord Jim* (1900). In such instances the narrator could describe his or her own thoughts as part of a (typically rambling) conversation. Conrad provided "frame narrators" who could describe Marlow's appearance and create some distance from his account of events, but the central consciousness of these novels is Marlow's. A trickier technique was to eliminate the frame narrator but make the first-person narrator unreliable, so that the reader is forced to disentangle reality from the deluded or misleading claims of the narrator. This technique had been used by James in some of his short stories; Ford Madox Ford applied it to a full-length novel. In Ford's *The Good Soldier* (1915), the narrator, John Dowell, tells the story of his marriage, from 1904, when he and his wife Florence met Edward Ashburnham (the good soldier of the title) to 1913, when Ashburnham's affair with Florence has been revealed and both Ashburnham and Florence have committed suicide. However, Dowell does not narrate these events in a strictly linear fashion. Ford tries to recreate Dowell's ignorance of his wife's adultery by representing events not in a causal sequence but as they occur to Dowell during the course of his reminiscences. Dowell is not deliberately misleading, but he does tease the reader by revealing crucial bits of information in an offhand way. As he explains, "I don't know how it is best to put this thing down – whether it would be better to try and tell the story from the beginning, as if it were a story; or whether to tell it from the distance of time, as it reached me from the lips of Leonora or from those of Edward himself." Reading *The Good Soldier* feels a little like being the detective in a detective story; the great pleasure is to try to track down and make sense of the clues Dowell lets fall along the way. Unreliable narration played a major role in modernist fiction. In *The Sound and the Fury* (1928), William Faulkner makes use of three different unreliable narrators, one of them mentally retarded, but then presents a more objective account of events in the final section of the novel. The technique reached its apogee in Vladimir Nabokov's *Lolita* (1955), narrated by the witty and urbane child molester Humbert Humbert. Here, part of the challenge of the novel is to disentangle the pleasure the reader takes in Humbert's wit from the moral horror of Humbert's evil. Nabokov does not make it easy to separate one from the other.[10]

Joyce's career traces in miniature the gradual inward movement from realism to modernism. His first book of stories, *Dubliners* (1914), combined naturalist attention to detail and to the lives of the forgotten with a symbolist sense of the mysteries of human life. In *A Portrait of the Artist as a Young Man* (1916), Joyce traced the developing consciousness of the young artist through a changing literary style and used the "Uncle Charles Principle," in which he imagined how characters thought of themselves, to create an ever subtler form of free indirect discourse (see Chapter Three). The first three episodes of *Ulysses* (1922) push this tendency even further, tracing the first hours of Stephen Dedalus's day. Joyce had already, in his earlier works, discarded speech marks in favor of a French-inspired punctuation system in which reported speech was introduced simply by a dash, thus making it difficult to distinguish dialogue from narrative. His free indirect discourse similarly entangled subjective impressions and objective realities. In *Ulysses*, although a third-person narrator does relate external events in the past tense, such passages alternate with the interior monologue or stream of consciousness of the characters, whose meandering thoughts Joyce records.

In a typical passage from the first episode, Stephen contemplates his mother's recent death and his guilt at having refused to kneel and pray for her:

> Stephen, an elbow rested on the jagged granite, leaned his palm against his brow and gazed at the fraying edge of his shiny black coatsleeve. Pain, that was not yet the pain of love, fretted his heart. Silently, in a dream she had come to him after her death, her wasted body within its loose brown graveclothes giving off an odour of wax and rosewood, her breath, that had bent upon him, mute, reproachful, a faint odour of wetted ashes. Across the threadbare cuffedge he saw the sea hailed as a great sweet mother by the wellfed voice beside him. The ring of bay and skyline held a dull green mass of liquid. A bowl of white china had stood beside her deathbed holding the green sluggish bile which she had torn up from her rotting liver by fits of loud groaning vomiting.

We are largely in the world of *Portrait* here, though Stephen has matured somewhat. The narrator's descriptions of Stephen's appearance, as in the first sentence, modulate into Stephen's own thoughts, including his memory of the dream in which his mother visited him. There is a continual oscillation between the outer world and the inner. Stephen sees the green waters of Dublin Bay and they remind him of the green bile that his mother vomited on her deathbed, thus lending a cruel irony to the references of Buck Mulligan (the "wellfed voice") to the sea as mother. His remorse over his behavior toward his mother runs throughout the novel, pondered by Stephen in the Middle English phrase "agenbite of inwit" (remorse of conscience). The words consciousness and conscience are closely related; in both French and Italian, they are a single word (*conscience, coscienza*). *Ulysses* explores the close relationship between the two phenomena. Gradually, the narrative focus moves inward. Given Joyce's frequent modulation between the perspectives of narrator and character, it is sometimes difficult to tell whether a passage is being narrated as an external event or is merely a passing thought of one of the characters.

In the fourth episode we are introduced to Mr. Leopold Bloom, who, the narrator informs us, "ate with relish the inner organs of beasts and fowls." Joyce described the technique of the first episode "Telemachus," as "narrative (young)," and that of "Calypso," the episode in which Bloom is introduced, as "narrative (mature)." In fact, the techniques are largely the same, but the contents of the two characters' minds differ greatly and so, therefore, does Joyce's language. Where Stephen is ethereal and intellectual, Bloom is earthy and practical, and Joyce uses short, Anglo-Saxon words to describe him. Bloom prepares breakfast for his wife Molly, feeds the cat, goes to the butcher and buys a pork kidney, burns it, chats with his wife, and goes to the outhouse. These opening episodes include some of the most effective representations of stream of consciousness in modernist literature. The constant interplay between external stimuli and the thought patterns of the two characters marks a new stage in the history of novelistic attempts to represent the relationship between the individual mind and the social world.[11]

## Time

One medium through which the mind relates to external reality is time. The modernists were fascinated with the disjunction between internal and external time. This fascination goes back at least to Charles Baudelaire's insistence that originality is a result of passing time; it intensified as the investigations of Henri Bergson and Albert Einstein became known at the beginning of the twentieth century (see Introduction). Time becomes a dominant theme in the modernist novel, from the level of clocks and watches through that of human history to cosmological time. Bloom's watch stops at half past four, possibly the moment when Molly consummates her affair with Boylan. Stephen, who earns his living as a schoolteacher, gives a lesson in Roman history to his students. At the level of eschatology, the text hints at the imminent arrival of a messiah who may call the peoples of the earth to the Last Judgment.[12] The critic Frank Kermode has analyzed the modernists' fascination with notions of crisis and apocalypse, which draw on religious ideas about the end of time.[13] The remarkable characteristic of James Joyce's representation of time in *Ulysses* (1922) is his ability both to portray each moment as like every other moment, an empty point in the sequence of chronological time, and also to suggest that each moment is full of meaning, a portal into eternity.

Joyce shares this duality with the other great modern novelist of time, Marcel Proust. Proust's *Remembrance of Things Past* (1913–27), also known by a more literal translation of its French title, *In Search of Lost Time*, is the only modernist novel that has a fair claim to being as important in the history of the genre as *Ulysses.* Joyce claimed not to have read Proust's work before writing *Ulysses,* but he had met him, was aware of his methods, and even attended his funeral in 1922, the year *Ulysses* was published. The two novels, though sharing a conception of time, use radically different methods for representing it. *Ulysses* takes place on a single day, and each episode is assigned a time of day. In theory, it is possible to read the whole book in twenty-four hours as well (though one has to read fast). The external events of the plot proceed in strictly chronological order, though the characters' minds continually flash back into the past, thus demonstrating the disjunction between external and internal time. The intimations of eternity in the novel tend to take place by way of coincidences of plot or through the characters' subjective impressions. The narrator never announces a theory or discovery about time.

Proust's novel, on the other hand, spans about fifty years in the life of its protagonist, who bears a striking resemblance to Proust himself (as Stephen does to Joyce). Where Joyce reveled in short sentence fragments juxtaposed without grammatical subordination (parataxis), Proust wrote long, supple, perfectly grammatical sentences, full of dependent clauses (hypotaxis).[14] Although much of *Remembrance of Things Past* proceeds chronologically, the novel is framed by moments of radical temporal instability. In its opening pages the first-person narrator recalls a time when he "used to go to bed early." At that time, he writes, he would often wake up unsure where he was, what year it was, and even who he was. Proust then presents a kaleidoscopic vision of the many bedrooms in which his narrator will sleep during the course of the novel, thus plunging the reader into the novel's fictional world and demonstrating the instability of time and space. The characters in *Ulysses* are very firmly located in space as well as time; Joyce used a 1904 street directory in order to locate each event in a geographically accurate place in Dublin. Proust's narrator, on the other hand, begins his story entirely abstracted from both these coordinates. He explains that only the power of memory can help him to reconstruct his personality, and goes on to develop a theory of two types of memory, the voluntary memory that we use in everyday life and a more powerful, involuntary memory that functions unexpectedly, triggered by a sound, smell, or taste. The first volume of *Remembrance of Things Past* purports to relate the narrator's memories of his childhood as they were brought to life for him by the taste of a madeleine (a tiny sponge cake) dipped in tea. The madeleine reminds him of the ones he used to eat at his aunt's house in Combray, the country town where he once spent his summers. It causes a rush of involuntary memory and resurrects the past that the narrator had thought was "permanently dead."

Another theme shared by Joyce and Proust, the resurrection of the dead, typifies the interplay between the narrative present and the always resurgent past of their characters. Both authors were fascinated with the passage in book eleven of Homer's *The Odyssey* in which Odysseus visits the Underworld. The episode, which had been imitated by Virgil, inspired Dante's *Inferno*. In the modernist period Pound began his *Cantos* with a translation of the opening lines of Homer's book eleven, and Virginia Woolf alluded to Odysseus's encounter with the shade of his mother when portraying the death of Mrs. Ramsay in *To the Lighthouse* (1927). Homer has Odysseus reach out three times to embrace the shade, but, says Odysseus, "she went sifting through my hands, impalpable / as shadows are, and wavering like a dream."[15] Woolf echoes Odysseus's gesture when she announces Mrs. Ramsay's death in a parenthesis: "[Mr. Ramsay, stumbling along a passage one dark morning stretched his arms out, but Mrs. Ramsay having died rather suddenly the night before his arms, though stretched out, remained empty.]" Proust's narrator, too, makes use of the image of the empty outstretched arms, first when describing a dream of his dead grandmother and then again in the final episode, the second moment of radical indeterminacy in the novel, when he discusses his failure to recognize his old friends. A friend whom time has completely transformed looks familiar to the narrator only when he laughs, but once he stops laughing his features change, and the narrator, "like Ulysses in the *Odyssey* when he rushes forward to embrace his dead mother," is "obliged to give up the attempt" to recognize him.

Ghostly parents are everywhere in *Ulysses*. Stephen's dream of his dead mother echoes this famous encounter. In the "Hades" episode Joyce describes Paddy Dignam's funeral. On the way to the cemetery, Bloom thinks of his father, who committed suicide:

> The afternoon of the inquest. The redlabelled bottle on the table. The room in the hotel with hunting pictures. Stuffy it was ... Verdict: overdose. Death by misadventure. The letter. For my son Leopold.
> No more pain. Wake no more. Nobody owns.

Joyce's technique is to show Bloom recalling the concrete details of the coroner's inquest into his father's death (the bottle, the pictures on the hotel room walls) and the coroner's euphemistic verdict, and then philosophizing about it in very brief, evocative sentence fragments. Each of the novelists uses the vision of the dead parent as an opportunity to show how the past inhabits the present. In the midst of their everyday lives, the characters are confronted by ghosts who appear unbidden but whom they cannot quite grasp.

The persistence of the past also underlies the concept of "metempsychosis," one crucial element of Joyce's "mythical method" (see Chapter Four). In the "Calypso" episode Molly asks Bloom what the word means, and he explains, "Some people believe . . . that we go on living in another body after death, that we lived before. They call it reincarnation . . . Some say they remember their past lives." This brief conversation, and Molly's mispronunciation of metempsychosis as "met him pike hoses," reverberate through Bloom's day, calling attention to his function as the new Odysseus and suggesting, again, how the patterns of the past shape the present, this time on the level of collective myth rather than that of individual experience. Not only a new Odysseus, Bloom is frequently linked throughout the text with the prophet Elijah. In the "Lestrygonians" episode a young man hands Bloom a "throwaway" (a handbill) announcing the second coming of Elijah, associated in Jewish tradition with the messiah. Bloom crumples the paper up and throws it in the River Liffey. Although he remains ignorant of his relationship to Odysseus, Bloom is quite conscious of his kinship to Elijah through the course of the day. Later, on a visit to a brothel, he proclaims himself the messiah and promises a "new Bloomusalem" (Jerusalem), based on egalitarian political principles, including "mixed races and mixed marriage" (to which one of his followers adds "mixed bathing"). Here, the collective myth of the messiah implies the end of time. At any moment, it seems, the realistic time scheme of *Ulysses* may break down and usher in eternity. The idea of reincarnation also fascinated Proust, who used it as a metaphor for the rebirth of the past in the work of art; indeed, he compared the confusion of the narrator in the opening scene of his novel to that of a soul that has undergone metempsychosis and does not know what body it is inhabiting.

Between the poles of personal time and messianic time lies shared, public time, or history. The modernists have sometimes been accused of avoiding history. Unlike such earlier novelists as Leo Tolstoy, whose *War and Peace* (1863–9) chronicled the Napoleonic wars, the modernists do not generally present a panorama of historical experience. Even Proust, closer to realism in his methods, presents the Dreyfus Affair and the First World War not from a broad historical perspective but intermittently, as they are experienced by his characters in their private lives. Joyce displays a profound skepticism about attempts to describe History with a capital H. His epic is tightly focused on a single day. *Ulysses* is set fourteen years before its first episode was published, but Joyce makes no direct reference to intervening historical events such as the First World War. As far as direct references to history go, the novel might have been written on June 17, 1904. In perhaps the most famous exchange in the novel, Stephen debates the meaning of history with his employer,

Mr. Deasy. Stephen refers to history as "a nightmare from which I am try-ing to awake," while Deasy makes anti-Semitic remarks and proclaims his faith in history as moving "towards one great goal, the manifestation of God." Joyce clearly rejects the latter view; all the indications of messianic time later in the novel suggest not a gradual, progressive movement toward God, but a sudden transformation of earthly time, akin to W. B. Yeats's "violent annunciation" in "Leda and the Swan" (see Chapter Four). Stephen's apparently determin-istic and pessimistic view of history as nightmare seems somewhat closer to Joyce's own mature view, but Joyce had perhaps more hope than Stephen of a successful awakening.

Joyce became particularly interested in the cyclical philosophy of history of the eighteenth-century philosopher Giambattista Vico, according to which, after a period of decay from the age of gods to the age of heroes to the age of men, history would repeat itself in a grand "*ricorso*," or recurrence. One of Stephen's students lives on Vico Road in Dalkey, a suburb of Dublin. It is unclear how much Joyce knew about Vico when he wrote this episode, but he later used Vico's philosophy as a framework for his last novel, *Finnegans Wake* (1939). At any rate, Joyce seems to be searching for an alternative to the mindless optimism of Mr. Deasy and the deterministic pessimism of Stephen. The novel offers a literary equivalent of Einstein's claims that "every reference body has its own particular time," which should be represented by "as many clocks as we like" (see Introduction). Although it maintains the purely chronological time of Joyce's schema and the narrated events, it also shows how each character inhabits time in a distinctive way. Challenging the idea of events as moving toward "one great goal," *Ulysses* often presents history as nightmare, but also suggests the possibility of nonlinear models of time and history that might allow an escape from this nightmare.

This hope that every moment might be the one that permits an awaken-ing from linear time is common in modernism. Proust wrote of the "happy moments" in which involuntary memory allowed his narrator to regain lost time; Woolf wrote of "moments of being" that break through the "nondescript cotton wool" of time and promise "a revelation of some order, . . . a token of some real thing behind appearances."[16] The contrarian Wyndham Lewis attacked modernist "time-consciousness," which he blamed largely on Bergson and Einstein, in *Time and Western Man* (1927); he complained that Joyce's char-acters were "overwhelmed in the torrent of matter, of *nature morte* [the French term for 'still-life' in painting, literally 'dead nature']. This torrent of matter is the Einsteinian flux. Or (equally well) it is the duration flux of Bergson."[17] The tendency to hope for a transcendence of the flux reached its comic apotheosis in *Zeno's Conscience* (1923), by Joyce's friend Italo Svevo, a Triestine novelist who was in some respects a model for Leopold Bloom. In the novel Zeno undergoes psychoanalysis and tries repeatedly to quit smoking. He records in his notebook the date of each "last cigarette," generally preferring dates that seem "significant," like 9/9/99, 1/1/01, or 3/6/12, but eventually experimenting with totally random dates. Thus each day in his life may bring Zeno's own minor form of the millennium – his final success in quitting smoking.[18] Yet Svevo's novel ends with a much bleaker vision of the final things, as Zeno, contemplating the First World War, predicts the invention of a weapon that will destroy the entire human race. In Thomas Mann's *Magic Mountain* (1924), another novel about time set in the years before the First World War, the hero, Hans Castorp, who suffers from tuberculosis, spends seven years in a Swiss sanatorium where time seems to stand still. At the end of the novel, though, with the outbreak of war, Hans joins the German army. In the last chapter the narrator shows Hans on a battlefield and does not say whether he lives or dies. He ends the novel with a question: "And out of this worldwide festival of death, this ugly rutting fever that inflames the evening sky all round – will love someday rise up out of this, too?" Mann, who won the Nobel Prize in 1929, would prefer like Joyce to believe that love will rise out of the chaos of time. However, to both of them, and to most modernists, an apocalypse like that envisioned by Svevo seemed at least as likely as any of the more positive visions of redemption from human time.

## Narrative

Historians create narrative out of the events of public life. In order to build a plot, novelists create narrative out of imagined events. Modern novels are sometimes described as having "no plot." In fact, they generally have plots, but not of the sort that readers of earlier novels might have expected. Modernists sometimes do away with traditional plots like the education of a young artist or the marriage of a young woman, but more often they reinterpret them, as James Joyce did for the education plot in *A Portrait of the Artist as a Young Man* (1916) and Virginia Woolf did for the marriage plot in *To the Lighthouse* (1927). *Ulysses* (1922) contains a number of potentially competing plots, each of which is based on traditional models: Bloom's exile, wandering, and return; Molly's adultery; Stephen's quest for a father. Overlaid on these mythic plots are much more obscure and minor sequences of events. *Ulysses* challenges its reader by seeming to give equal narrative attention to major plots like exile or adultery and to much more minor events. Indeed, sometimes the minor events overshadow or disguise the major ones. Two examples stand out: the throwaway and the man in the macintosh.

In the "Lotus-Eaters" episode, a minor character, Bantam Lyons, asks to borrow Bloom's newspaper. Lyons mutters about the upcoming Gold Cup race: "Wait . . . Half a mo. Maximum the second." Bloom tells him to keep the paper: "I was just going to throw it away." Lyons asks him to repeat himself. Again hearing the phrase "throw it away," "Bantam Lyons doubted an instant, leering: then thrust the outspread sheets back on Mr Bloom's arms. – I'll risk it, he said. Here, thanks." The Elijah theme is introduced shortly afterwards by the handbill that Bloom throws away in the "Lestrygonians" episode. During the chaotic "Wandering Rocks" episode, about halfway through the book, two other minor characters, Lenehan and M'Coy, briefly discuss how Lenehan has prevented Lyons from betting on "a bloody horse someone gave him that hasn't an earthly." Lenehan identifies Bloom as the source of the tip. Later, Lenehan tells his friends at Barney Kiernan's pub that Bloom "had a few bob on *Throwaway* and he's gone to gather the shekels . . . Bet you what you like he has a hundred shillings to five on. He's the only man in Dublin has it. A dark horse." Lenehan thinks that Bloom has won money at the races by betting on Throwaway. When the allegedly enriched Bloom later fails to stand drinks for the crowd at the pub, a disagreeable nationalist called the Citizen grows increasingly angry with him. The episode concludes with the Citizen throwing an empty biscuit-tin at Bloom and Bloom transformed by the narrator into Elijah ascending to heaven in a chariot of fire, "like a shot off a shovel."

Here, Joyce offers on the one hand a plausible if complex causal sequence in which a series of misunderstandings leads to a fight. On the other hand, the symbolic aspects of events – Bloom as himself the throwaway (rejected husband and despised Dubliner), the dark horse who wins the race against the odds, and also Elijah, the new messiah – infuses these events with a broader mythic significance. (*Mythos* was the Greek word for plot, and in *Ulysses* plot often approaches the status of myth). As the critic Peter Brooks has observed, *Ulysses* suggests "the problematic relation of the seemingly undirected individual existence to large transindividual orders – orders that might explain, organize, justify, if only one were certain of their status, if only one could reinvest them with the explanatory power of sacred myth."[19] Joyce gives the reader plenty of mythical orders (*The Odyssey*, the Bible, *Hamlet*) with which to organize experience, but leaves open the question of whether any of these plots really have "explanatory power" – he often seems to hint that the association of Bloom with Odysseus or the messiah is just an elaborate game. Earlier novels incorporate apparently chance events into their carefully crafted plots, but *Ulysses* seems unique in paying such detailed attention to the most random and insignificant occurrences and in showing how they all ultimately contribute to what appears retrospectively as a meaningful chain of events, possibly one with mystical significance.[20]

Sometimes Joyce specifically frustrates our attempts to force these random events into meaningful patterns. For example, a man in a macintosh raincoat appears at Paddy Dignam's funeral. Hynes, a reporter, is taking down the names of those in attendance for the obituary. He asks Bloom's name and then gestures to the man in the macintosh:

> – And tell us, Hynes said, do you know that fellow in the, fellow was over there in the . . .
> He looked around.
> – Macintosh. Yes, I saw him, Mr Bloom said. Where is he now?
> – M'Intosh, Hynes said scribbling. I don't know who he is. Is that his name?

Before Bloom gets a chance to correct him, Hynes has moved on, and the name M'Intosh appears for the mysterious stranger in the newspaper report. (Bloom's name is misspelled, too: L Boom.) The man in the macintosh reappears frequently throughout the course of the novel. In the "Circe" episode he accuses Bloom of being "Leopold M'Intosh," an arsonist. In the "Ithaca" episode Bloom ponders the enigma "who was M'Intosh?" None of Joyce's interpreters has yet found an answer, but many suspect that the man in the macintosh is Joyce himself. Our readerly attempts to find out the identity of the man in the macintosh resemble those of the reporter Hynes; we can piece together the clues but M'Intosh is basically a red herring – a loose thread in the plot that leads nowhere but threatens to unravel any comprehensive interpretation of the text. Similarly, Joyce's critics have vainly sought a meaningful interpretation of the anonymous postcard that Denis Breen receives with the message "U. P.: up." Often enough, Joyce shows us contingent events that do not apparently lead to magnified consequences.

In addition to challenging conventional plot expectations, Joyce manipulates readers' understanding of narrative by his use of the various "techniques" he identified for each of the eighteen episodes. Despite Joyce's different names for the various techniques, stream of consciousness dominates the first nine episodes. However, as early as the seventh episode, "Aeolus," Joyce begins to break up the narrative method to which his readers have finally accustomed themselves. "Aeolus" is set in the offices of the *Freeman's Journal*, Bloom's employer. Dialogue and interior monologue alternate, much in the style of the earlier episodes, but the narrative is interrupted every few lines by a newspaper headline in capital letters. The headlines sometimes comment on the action of the episode; at other times they seem to gesture to the broader structure of the novel. While the classics professor MacHugh discusses with Stephen the relative merits of Odysseus's faithful wife Penelope and the unfaithful Helen of Troy, the headline reads:

SOPHIST WALLOPS HAUGHTY HELEN SQUARE
ON PROBOSCIS. SPARTANS GNASH MOLARS.
ITHACANS VOW PEN IS CHAMP.

The headline reduces the structuring myth of *Ulysses* (and *The Odyssey*) to the status of a sporting match, described in journalistic jargon. Like Eliot's use of "The Shakespearean Rag," the headline at once celebrates mass cultural forms (the newspaper, the boxing match) and places them in ironic juxtaposition with the high cultural claims of *Ulysses*. Similarly, while Bloom spends much of the day pondering major philosophical questions such as the nature of personal identity, the ideal organization of society, or the mysteries of faith and love, he also thinks a lot about advertising slogans, like one for Plumtree's potted meats, a form of canned food whose name recalls a slang term for sex (to pot one's meat).[21] The uneasy relation between the headlines in "Aeolus" and the narrative suggests the hand of an irresponsible editor, who comments on and sometimes challenges the accounts given by the narrator.

In later episodes this "editor" figure grows into the force that Joyce critics call "the Arranger."[22] Gradually abandoning the stream-of-consciousness technique, Joyce makes use of a series of increasingly obtrusive games with the literary style of the entire book. In "Wandering Rocks" nineteen miniature episodes present a sort of microcosm of the novel. Departing extensively from the focus on Stephen and Bloom for the first time, the narrative describes simultaneous events in nineteen different locations in Dublin. "Sirens," whose technique is the fugue, begins with a sort of musical overture featuring the sixty verbal leitmotifs that will be arranged musically throughout the episode. In "Cyclops," which concerns the belligerent nationalist "the Citizen," the action is described by way of a series of parodies of generally heroic or inflated narrative modes drawn from classical epic, Irish mythology, medieval romance, Theosophy, parliamentary *Hansard*, sportswriting, fashion magazines, and finally the Bible. The ridiculously overblown rhetoric of the chapter reflects the inflated idea of himself and his nation held by the Citizen. The parody continues in "Oxen of the Sun," where Joyce describes Bloom's visit to a maternity hospital through a pastiche of the history of the English language, with passages based on authors running from the Middle Ages up to the nineteenth century, followed by a cacophonous mix of early twentieth-century slang. Throughout, Joyce seems to be commenting on the way that the language we speak or write informs our consciousness of the world.

Joyce's increasingly massive displays of literary virtuosity culminate in the surrealistic hallucinations of "Circe," in which Stephen and Bloom visit a brothel. The brothel features a madam, Bella Cohen, who turns into a man, Bello; Bloom briefly, perhaps in a hallucination, becomes a woman and engages in sadomasochistic sex with Bello/Bella. The entire episode is cast as a play, modeled on expressionist and surrealist drama (see Chapter Six). Stage directions indicate that various inanimate objects and body parts speak and describe a cast of thousands, including the Lord Mayor of Dublin, the Archbishop of Armagh, Blazes Boylan, and a hobgoblin. A further parodic episode, "Eumaeus," describes Stephen's and Bloom's drunken journey homeward in the heavy, exhausted style of cliché. Joyce called the technique "narrative (old)." Some readers find "Eumaeus" one of the funniest parts of the novel, while others find the deliberately trite language simply boring.

The stream-of-consciousness technique of the episode's first nine episodes can be seen as a further development of realism, moving ever inward to represent the consciousness of the individual character in greater detail. After episode ten, however, the novel seems to break decisively with realism; instead of highlighting the referential function of words, Joyce emphasizes their involvement in systems of discourse, ideology, and style. The parodies do not, however, indicate a total break with representation; rather, while calling attention to the inadequacies and ideological effects of various highly stylized systems of representation, Joyce still seems to be maintaining an ideal of adequate representation against which all the individual styles need to be judged. It is notable that the last episode of the novel returns to a version of the interior monologue technique, "monologue (female)," to represent Bloom's consciousness in much the way that Stephen's and Bloom's have been portrayed earlier in the novel.

Before giving the final word to Molly, however, Joyce wrote a penultimate episode in the form of a catechism, the set of questions and answers by which Catholic children are instructed in religion. The questions concern elements of the novel's plot, focusing on Stephen's arrival at Bloom's house at 2:00 a.m. on June 17, but covering also many earlier events and seeming to resolve some conundrums presented by the rest of the text. Others give us background information about the earlier lives of Stephen and Bloom. Far from being the sort of questions that a professor might include in an impromptu quiz about the novel's plot, however, many of the questions ("How did Bloom prepare a collation for a gentile?" answer: a recipe for two cups of cocoa; "For what creature was the door of egress a door of ingress?" answer: a cat), and their hilarious, increasingly detailed answers, do little to explain any underlying pattern to the novel. All the questions, however, seem to offer alternatives to our traditional ways of putting a plot together, in terms of a causal sequence of events. A question about the relative ages of Stephen and Bloom (twenty-two and thirty-eight) leads to a consideration of the ratios between their ages in various years: 1888, 1920, 1936, and 3072 (one of the few cases in which the text refers to any time after 1904, but only in a conjectural way). Thus the two heroes are put in relation to historical time. Another response describes the path by which water flows from a reservoir in County Wicklow to the tap in Bloom's house when he fills the kettle; thus Stephen and Bloom are related to the natural environment. Several questions concern parallels between the Jews and the Irish, one of Joyce's favorite topics, hinting at the problem of the Irish exodus from the bondage of English rule. After Stephen declines to stay the night at Bloom's house, Bloom lies down in bed next to Molly. The last few questions concern their relationship. The answers reveal the history of their sex life, including the names of the twenty-five lovers that Bloom suspects (or pretends to suspect) Molly of having taken; one of them is the Lord Mayor of Dublin. The questioner asks, "With what antagonistic sentiments were his [Bloom's] subsequent reflections answered?" The answer: "Envy, jealousy, abnegation, equanimity." Thus Bloom renounces the Odyssean temptation to seek vengeance against Molly's suitors and regains his typically even temper. Before going to sleep, he kisses Molly's rump. Molly awakes and questions him, in a "catechetical interrogation" about his day, and he offers a brief, censored narrative of the events of the novel. Like that of *The Odyssey*, the plot of *Ulysses* ends with a return to the marital bed, though Joyce leaves the reader uncertain whether the novel's major plotlines – Stephen's search for a father, Bloom's exile and return, Molly's adultery – have reached their natural conclusion or will simply be repeated after everyone wakes up on June 17.

## Fiction

In the episode that first got *Ulysses* (1922) censored, "Nausicaa," Gerty MacDowell, a teenaged girl, sits near the beach, revealing part of her leg to a strange gentleman (Bloom) who masturbates as he watches her, to the accompaniment of prayers and songs addressed to the Virgin issuing from a temperance retreat at the nearby church of Mary, Star of the Sea. Gerty has read a great number of magazines for girls and romance novels, the lower-class early twentieth-century equivalent of Don Quixote's or Emma Bovary's reading. In the first half of the episode, James Joyce returns to a form of the interior monologue, here apparently in the voice of Gerty herself, a voice filled with romantic clichés, which alternate with the jargon of advertisements, the slang of schoolgirls, and resentful comments about Gerty's siblings and friends: "Her figure was slight and graceful, inclining even to fragility but those iron jelloids she had been taking of late had done her a world of good much better than the Widow Welch's female pills and she was much better of those discharges she used to get and that tired feeling." Gerty's entire world is described in the language she might use if she were to write a novel with herself as heroine.

Soon, though, as Gerty begins to notice that Bloom is watching her, the narrative becomes more feverish: "Yes, it was her he was looking at, and there was meaning in his look. His eyes burned into her as though they would search her through and through, read her very soul. Wonderful eyes they were, superbly expressive, but could you trust them?" To mark the opening of a bazaar, fireworks go off, and Gerty leans back to watch them: "she revealed all her graceful beautifully shaped legs like that, supply soft and delicately rounded, and she seemed to hear the panting of his heart, his hoarse breathing, because she knew too about the passion of men like that, hotblooded . . ." As the fireworks (and Bloom) reach their climax, the language of the episode rather suddenly changes:

> She walked with a certain quiet dignity characteristic of her but with care and very slowly because – because Gerty MacDowell was . . .
> Tight boots? No. She's lame! O!
> Mr Bloom watched her as she limped away. Poor girl!

The sudden switch from the stereotypically girlish language to the characteristic inner monologue of Bloom casts the first half of the episode in a new light. Joyce described the techniques of the episode as tumescence and detumescence (swelling and subsiding). It seems possible that, in the midst of his sexual fantasies, Bloom has imagined the interior monologue of Gerty MacDowell, complete with references to matters of feminine hygiene, romance novels, and rivalries with other girls. When the purpose of his fantasies is attained, he reverts to his normal voice. Bloom has a tendency to "sympathetic fantasy." He likes to imagine what other people, especially women, are fantasizing about.[23] A good part of sexual enjoyment consists for Bloom in this identification with women; he himself is described as a "womanly man."

The "Nausicaa" and "Lotus-Eaters" episodes contain, indirectly, Joyce's meditations on the role of fiction in our lives. At the literal level, Gerty has consumed a great deal of low-quality fiction, and her consciousness seems shaped by it. More broadly, however, Gerty's consciousness seems to be a fiction of Bloom's desire, and in general, *Ulysses* is a novel not just about consciousness but about how we construct our own consciousness out of language and indeed how we construct or imagine the consciousness of other people. In *A Portrait of the Artist as a Young Man* (1916), Joyce attempted, through the "Uncle Charles

Principle," to imagine what Uncle Charles would say about his own trip to the outhouse. *Ulysses* is an extended meditation on how people view themselves in language: first, the language of the ongoing interior monologue by which we make grocery lists or plans for the evening or fantasies for ourselves; second, the various languages, learned from literature or advertising, the Bible or popular music, with which we tell ourselves stories about the world and about ourselves. *Ulysses* celebrates this power of fantasy and fiction-making at the same time as it criticizes particular fantasies, like the nationalist self-aggrandisement of "the Citizen." In addition to reinventing the representation of consciousness, rethinking our understanding of time, and revising the functioning of plots, *Ulysses* reevaluates fiction itself and its central role in human consciousness.

As T. S. Eliot lamented, *Ulysses* was a hard act to follow. Novelists after Joyce were conscious of the challenge of living up to this masterpiece. E. M. Forster made some accommodations to modernism in *A Passage to India* (1924) (see Chapter Two). D. H. Lawrence continued in his own vein. One of the remarkable qualities of Virginia Woolf was her ability to absorb the lessons of *Ulysses* while maintaining her distance from it and writing her own modernist masterpieces. William Faulkner transplanted stream of consciousness and other modernist techniques to the southern United States. Eliot and Joyce's fascination with myth became widespread and inspired the work of such novelists as Mary Butts, whose *Taverner* novels (1928–32) used the grail myth to structure a description of the decadent lifestyle and bizarre rituals of a group of homosexual men. A number of modernists in Joyce's generation wrote huge epic novels: Dorothy Richardson's *Pilgrimage* (1915–35), Marcel Proust's *Remembrance of Things Past* (1913–27), John Cowper Powys's *A Glastonbury Romance* (1932), Thomas Mann's tetralogy *Joseph and his Brothers* (1933–42), John Dos Passos's trilogy *U.S.A.* (1930–38). Joyce himself went on to write *Finnegans Wake*, published in 1939 (see Conclusion).

All these works shared the encyclopedic ambition of *Ulysses*, the attempt to tell the story of a whole nation or generation through representative figures. They therefore made immense demands on their writers; they also demanded great devotion, which they have not always received, from readers. Most of them were completed in the 1930s, just when other authors were turning to more straightforward literary styles and explicitly political subject matter (see Chapter Seven). Thus the model of the modernist magnum opus, which would "keep the professors busy for centuries," gave way to more constrained forms, though some later novelists, such as Thomas Pynchon in *Gravity's Rainbow* (1973), sought to revive the modern epic form. Others responded to the immense legacy of the modernists through a scaling down of the novel form. After the Second World War, the Argentinian writer Jorge Luis Borges spun complicated scenarios out of the modernist problematic of fictionality. In "Pierre Menard, Author of *Don Quixote*," he invents a writer who composes a book that consists of the whole of *Don Quixote*, without ever having read the original: "The text of Cervantes and that of Menard are verbally identical, but the second is almost infinitely richer." Borges also invented a variety of alternate universes whose rules resembled the rules of novels or games.

If one strain of modernism tends toward the encyclopedic, bringing all human experience together in an exuberance of style, a contrary tendency pares language and experience down to the elemental. Although he shared many concerns with Joyce, the works of Franz Kafka tend toward the opposite pole. Kafka, a Czech Jew who wrote in German, worked for an insurance company (as did Wallace Stevens on the other side of the Atlantic, but it seems to have done Stevens less harm). He died of tuberculosis in 1924 at the age of forty-one, generally unknown outside Prague; his fame is due almost entirely to his executor's refusal to carry out Kafka's requests to burn all his manuscripts. Kafka creates black humor out of the disparity between his tightly controlled, self-effacing style and the surreal scenarios he describes: a man turned into a bug, another man arrested but not told what crime he has committed, a penal colony where a machine inscribes people's crimes onto their skin, an ape who learns to speak but then feels alienated from both the ape and human communities. Although he did write two novels and fragments of a third, his most characteristic work is in shorter forms, including the parable. Kafka's parables turn on questions of interpretation. He included his parable "Before the Law" in his novel *The Trial* (1925) and followed it with a debate between two characters about how it should be interpreted. Another parable, "An Imperial Message," is addressed to the reader: "The emperor, so a parable runs, has sent a message to you, the humble subject." The parable goes on to tell how far the messenger must travel to reach the reader, and how impossible it is that the message will ever arrive: "Nobody could fight his way through here even with a message from a dead man. But you sit at your window when evening falls and dream it to yourself." Kafka's stories often seem like messages from a dead man that are so encoded in indirection that they may never reach their recipient. *The Trial* was published in English translation in 1930, and many English writers of the 1930s turned toward forms of parable partly under Kafka's influence. Kafka's own works address politics only indirectly, though they frequently feature injustice administered by bureaucrats. For politically inclined writers of the 1930s, however, the parable offered the opportunity to address political concerns in an alternative, fictional universe (see Chapter Seven). Kafka shared with Joyce a fascination with the status of fiction, but whereas Joyce's late novels are all-encompassing and overflowing, Kafka's fictions are pared down and cryptic. Both represent aspects of modernism, its expressionistic affirmation and its ascetic control.

*Ulysses* ends with an affirmation. The greatest act of sympathetic fantasy in the novel is not Bloom's but Joyce's. Molly's monologue in "Penelope" offers his idea of what it is like to be a woman. Some feminists have criticized the monologue for catering to stereotypes, though none quite as crude as those of "Nausicaa." Others, however, have celebrated "Penelope" as an example of *écriture féminine,* a feminine or womanly writing. Molly's style is pure parataxis: the monologue consists of eight extraordinarily long sentences, the main connecting word is "and," and she goes from one thought to another without interruption or apparent logical relation. She puzzles about her husband's sexual preferences, recollects with pleasure her tryst with Blazes Boylan, imagines how to get her relationship with Bloom back to normal, and finally turns against Boylan, whose manners are too rough for her. Strangely enough, despite her infidelity, Molly resembles Penelope in certain respects; it appears that the cessation of normal marital relations was as much Bloom's idea as hers, and she has been waiting for him to return to her. The novel ends with Molly recalling the lovers of her youth and the day she agreed to marry Bloom. He asked her to marry him but she was overcome with thoughts of other men. Nonetheless, she decided to marry Bloom, here typically the everyman ("as well him as another"), but comically affirmed by Molly's closing words:

> and I thought well as well him as another and then I asked him with my eyes to ask again yes and then he asked me would I yes to say yes my mountain flower and first I put my arms around him yes and drew him down to me so he could feel my breasts all perfume yes and his heart was going like mad and yes I said yes I will Yes.

## Further reading

### Literary works

Jorge Luis Borges, *Ficciones,* ed. Anthony Kerrigan. New York: Grove, 1962.
William Faulkner, *The Sound and the Fury* (various editions).
Ford Madox Ford, *The Good Soldier* (various editions).
James Joyce, *Ulysses,* ed. Hans Walter Gabler. New York: Vintage Books, 1986.
Thomas Mann, *The Magic Mountain,* trans. John E. Woods. New York: Knopf, 1995.
Vladimir Nabokov, *Lolita* (various editions).
Marcel Proust, *In Search of Lost Time,* trans. C. K. Scott Moncrieff and Terence Kilmartin, revised by D. J. Enright. 6 vols. New York: Modern Library, 2003.

Italo Svevo, *Zeno's Conscience*, trans. William Weaver. New York: Knopf, 2001.
Virginia Woolf, *To the Lighthouse* (various editions).


## Contemporary critical statements

Mikhail Bakhtin, *The Dialogic Imagination*, ed. Michael Holquist, trans. Caryl
     Emerson and Michael Holquist. Austin: University of Texas Press, 1981.
Frank Budgen, *James Joyce and the Making of "Ulysses" and Other Writings*.
     Oxford: Oxford University Press, 1989.
T. S. Eliot, *Selected Prose of T. S. Eliot*, ed. Frank Kermode. New York: Farrar,
     Straus, and Giroux, 1975.
Stuart Gilbert, *James Joyce's "Ulysses": A Study*. New York: Vintage Books, 1955.
Georg Lukács, *Theory of the Novel*, trans. Anna Bostock. Cambridge, MA: MIT
     Press, 1971.


## Later criticism

Derek Attridge, ed., *The Cambridge Companion to James Joyce*. Cambridge:
     Cambridge University Press, 1990.
Harry Blamires, *The New Bloomsday Book*, rev. edn. London: Routledge, 1988.
Wayne Booth, *The Rhetoric of Fiction*, 2nd edn. Chicago: University of Chicago
     Press, 1983.
Peter Brooks, *Reading for the Plot*. Cambridge, MA: Harvard University Press,
     1992.
Richard Ellmann, *James Joyce*, rev. edn. Oxford: Oxford University Press, 1983.
Don Gifford and Robert J. Seidman, *"Ulysses" Annotated: Notes for James Joyce's
     "Ulysses"*, rev. edn. Berkeley and Los Angeles: University of California Press,
     1988.
Hugh Kenner, *Ulysses*, rev. edn. Baltimore: Johns Hopkins University Press, 1987.
Frank Kermode, *The Sense of an Ending*. Oxford: Oxford University Press, 1967.
Franco Moretti, *Modern Epic*, trans. Quintin Hoare. London: Verso, 1996.
Ian Watt, *The Rise of the Novel: Studies in Defoe, Richardson, and Fielding*.
     Berkeley and Los Angeles: University of California Press, 1957.
Alexander Welsh, *Reflections on the Hero as Quixote*. Princeton: Princeton
     University Press, 1981.

# Chapter 6

## Drama

When the lights come up on Luigi Pirandello's *Six Characters in Search of an Author* (1921), the first thing the audience sees is a bare stage, with no scenery and only a few folding tables and chairs scattered about. A stagehand is starting to build a set, but the stage manager interrupts him to say that it is time for rehearsal. The producer and a company of actors arrive and begin reading out stage directions; the actors complain about the script, but the producer (who also serves as director) explains that he "can't get hold of good French plays any more so that now we're reduced to putting on plays by Pirandello." Before the rehearsal can get under way, an attendant comes up the central aisle of the auditorium and announces unexpected visitors. Six characters, wearing masks and identified only as Father, Mother, Stepdaughter, Son, Boy, and Girl, follow the attendant up the aisle and beg the producer to find them an author who can write a play about them, or to include them in the play he is about to produce.

After some bewilderment, the characters explain that the author who invented them did not complete their play. They tell the rather melodramatic story of their lives. The producer agrees to create a play about them. The professional actors (who are not wearing masks) start playing the roles of the characters, but when they arrive at a crucial scene, the characters intervene, complaining that they are not being fairly represented. The producer thinks that the play will succeed, but decides to change a few details. The company's leading actress explains that audiences today are not as good as they once were at accepting theatrical illusion. At this word, the characters object again:

FATHER (*jumping up suddenly*):   Illusion? I would ask you not to speak of illusion! I would beg you not to use that word. For us it has a particularly cruel ring!

PRODUCER (*astonished*):   For heaven's sake, why?

FATHER:   Oh, yes, cruel, cruel! You really ought to understand.

PRODUCER:   What are we supposed to say? Illusion is our stock-in-trade [. . .]

FATHER:   I entirely understand [. . .] As artists [. . .], you have to create a perfect illusion of reality.

PRODUCER:   That's right.

FATHER:   But what if you stop to consider that we, the six of us (*he gestures briefly to indicate the six characters*) have no other reality; that we don't exist outside this illusion!

In this scene Pirandello plays with the traditional goal of the theater – "to create a perfect illusion of reality" – and asks the audience to consider the different levels of reality present in a stage production: the theater as a physical space, including sets constructed by a crew; the written text of the play; the actors' performance; and the represented reality of the characters' lives, which of course is usually fictional. In *Six Characters*, however, the fictional characters come to life and insist on their own rights, seeking to dismantle the illusion of reality in favor of reality itself, or rather in favor of illusion itself, which is their only reality.

Pirandello's work plays with the central tension in the modern theater between the desire to create a perfect illusion of extratheatrical reality on the stage and the contrary impulse to celebrate the very illusoriness of all theater. In comparison with poetry and the novel, theater experienced the crisis of representation somewhat late, but when it arrived this crisis was felt especially acutely, because the history of theater was so closely wrapped up with the concept of representation. Representation had been central to the understanding of theater ever since Aristotle defined tragedy as a "representation [or imitation; *mimesis*] of an action." Aristotle made action itself, structured into the form of a plot (*mythos*), the most important element of tragedy. He considered five other elements less significant: character (*ethos*), diction (the language of the tragedy), thought (ideas proposed by the characters or the playwright and the rhetoric with which they urge these ideas), spectacle (the stage, machinery, costumes, and so forth), and song. For Aristotle, it was also crucial that a tragedy incite pity and fear in its viewers, not by means of spectacle but as a

result of the "inner structure of the piece."[1] Aristotle refers briefly to the purg-
ing (*catharsis*) of negative emotions that results from seeing a tragedy; later
interpreters made catharsis one of the central functions of tragedy. The Aristotelian model became the focus of the classical French theater of Corneille and
Racine, inspired the forerunners of German romanticism, Johann Wolfgang
von Goethe and Friedrich Schiller, and continued to hold sway over dramatic
theory in the nineteenth century. The modernists revisit virtually every aspect
of Aristotle's analysis of tragedy, sometimes attempting to return the theater to
the purity he analyzed and at other times breaking with his strictures and, like
modernists in the other arts, even challenging his concept of "representation."

Modern drama calls attention to the fact that theater is both a representational art, like painting or writing, and a performing art, like dance or music.[2]
The actors on stage are at the same time both real people and representatives of
fictional characters. One of the startling elements of Pirandello's *Six Characters*
is the separation (which he emphasized in his stage directions) between the
"characters" and the "actors." As the theorist Bert States has written,

> we tend generally to undervalue the elementary fact that theater – unlike
> fiction, painting, sculpture and film – is really a language whose words
> consist to an unusual degree of things that *are* what they seem to be . . . Or,
> as [the playwright] Peter Handke puts it, in the theater light is brightness
> pretending to be other brightness, a chair is a chair pretending to be
> another chair,

and, of course, a person is a person pretending to be another person.[3] Modern
drama called attention to this combination of reality and illusion on the stage
and thus to the limits of theatrical representation. No single play has the exem-
plary status for modern drama that *Ulysses* and *The Waste Land* (both 1922) do
for their genres. This chapter therefore explores major tendencies in drama in
relation to four categories drawn from Aristotle: plot, character, theater (covering Aristotle's spectacle and song), and ideas (Aristotle's diction and thought).
Central to modern drama is the concern with illusion: realists and naturalists
seek to achieve a perfect illusion of reality on the stage, while various antinaturalist tendencies draw attention to that illusion, either to celebrate or to
undermine it.

## Plot

Aristotle thought that a plot, in addition to including "a beginning, a middle,
and an end," should be unified, a result of cause and effect, rather than episodic
or random, and should represent "what is possible according to the law of

probability or necessity." What gave the plot its unity was the sense of a central action undertaken and completed, which would result in a "change of fortune" for the hero. More complex plots would include reversals, in which a high person is brought low or a low person elevated, and a recognition, a change from ignorance to knowledge. In the best sort of tragedy, represented by Sophocles' *Oedipus the King*, recognition would coincide with reversal, as Oedipus realizes his crime and at the same time falls from his high position. The great realist and naturalist playwrights, such as Anton Chekhov and Henrik Ibsen, pushed the theater beyond the conventional plots that dominated the most popular genres of the early nineteenth century: melodrama and the well-made play. (In drama the terms realism and naturalism are used almost interchangeably; for the history of realism and naturalism, see Chapter One). Ibsen hewed more closely to an Aristotelian model of drama and thus created modern tragedies, while Chekhov gestured beyond plot altogether.

Melodramas, the most popular genre of early nineteenth-century drama, depicted struggles between good and evil, often set in gothic castles (sometimes with supernatural elements) or in the underworld of modern urban life; they emphasized sensational events and sympathetic identification between the audience and the characters on stage. Melodramatic plots often featured a poor, virtuous heroine and a wealthy villain who tried either to seduce or to blackmail her. Virtue always triumphed. In the mid-nineteenth century melodrama coexisted with a more sophisticated form, the "well-made play," typified by the works of Eugène Scribe, who wrote more than three hundred plays, most of them hits. Scribe made use of a formulaic plot structure that relied heavily on suspense. He generally designed his plays around a misunderstanding, which could be cleared up only by the revelation of a secret. The secret would be suspected by the audience all along, but withheld from the characters until the final scene, when a letter or newly arrived character would reveal it – a rather unsubtle form of the "recognition" that, for Aristotle, constituted one of the central aspects of plot. Scribe's plays were divided into five acts, and each act ended with some element of reversal or suspense – again, "reversal" is an Aristotelian category, but the well-made play used multiple reversals instead of a single climactic one. Scribe preferred the carefully constructed plot to depth of characterization and claimed that "When my story is right, when I have the events of my play firmly in hand, I could have my janitor write it."[4]

The Norwegian playwright Ibsen created modern realistic drama out of elements of melodrama and the well-made play. Although his first European successes occurred with his romantic verse dramas of the 1860s, Ibsen's great influence on the English stage began with *A Doll's House* (1879) (see Chapter One). The play's emphasis on the social problem of women's status in marriage gave Ibsen a reputation, especially in England, as a playwright of ideas and a feminist. Near the end of his life, however, Ibsen said that he had "been more of a poet and less of a social philosopher than people have generally been inclined to believe."[5] In fact, Ibsen's career is marked by a tension between the poet and the social philosopher. At the beginning of his career, Ibsen, who was a patriot and partisan of the 1848 revolutions, wrote verse dramas on themes from Norwegian history. He also gained much experience as stage manager, inhouse playwright, and artistic director of two Norwegian theaters. Ibsen left Norway for Rome in 1864, at the age of thirty-six; there, he wrote *Brand* (1866) and *Peer Gynt* (1867), which made him famous throughout Europe. Both plays are in verse and follow in the tradition of European romantic drama, typified by Goethe's *Faust* (Part I, 1808; Part II, 1832). *Brand* concerns a pastor who preaches duty over love and whose wife and son die because of his hard-heartedness; the play ends with Pastor Brand killed in an avalanche, as a booming voice offstage cries out "God is Love" (a biblical quotation, from 1 John 4:8). *Peer Gynt* draws on Scandinavian myths and folk tales; the protagonist, Peer, wanders around the world, indulges his whims, seduces women, consorts with the Troll King, and hopes to become Emperor of the World. From the Troll King, he learns the motto "To thy own self be – enough." Both plays turn on the conflicts between duty and pleasure, or duty and love, or duty to others and duty to oneself, which would also underlie Ibsen's later plays. These major poetic dramas, filled with larger-than-life characters, mythical elements, and supernatural intervention, inspired later symbolist and avant-garde playwrights, but Ibsen himself turned quite suddenly to writing essentially realist prose dramas about modern life, of which *A Doll's House* and *Ghosts* (1881) were the first major successes. They coincided with the height of the naturalist movement and shared some of the qualities advocated by Emile Zola and August Strindberg, though Ibsen did not share the naturalists' scientific worldview (see Chapter One). His turn to prose coincided with his departure from Italy for Germany, where he lived for twenty years.

Elements of melodrama and the well-made play remain even as late as *Hedda Gabler* (1890), the last of Ibsen's realist plays, published at the height of his fame and performed across Europe in the last decade of the nineteenth century.[6] Hedda, a general's daughter who has had many admirers, marries a scholar of modest accomplishment, George Tesman. The action begins after they return from their honeymoon to a grand villa, which Tesman has bought for Hedda on credit. Although Tesman keeps saying that Hedda is "filling out," there is some doubt as to whether Hedda is pregnant; at any rate, she prefers to deny it. Hedda is no conventionally virtuous heroine, but Ibsen treats her sympathetically, as a victim of forces beyond her control. In the middle of the first act, an old school acquaintance, Mrs. Thea Elvsted, arrives and announces the arrival of a more portentous visitor from the past, Eilert Lovborg, formerly a rival of Tesman and lover of Hedda. Lovborg, a recovering alcoholic, has written a brilliant book "on the course of civilization – in all its stages." More importantly, inspired by Thea, Lovborg has completed the manuscript of a sequel, which carries the history of civilization into the future. Tesman is amazed: "The future! But good Lord, there's nothing we know about that." Yet Lovborg, the romantic poet figure, seems to have access to knowledge about the future. Looking for an escape from her married life and eager to exercise "power over [another] human being," Hedda encourages Lovborg to start drinking again, and hopes to see him "with vine leaves in his hair." Lovborg gets drunk and misplaces his manuscript. Tesman recovers it, but, in a fit of jealousy, Hedda burns it. Lovborg considers the manuscript to be the child born out of his relationship with Thea, and as she burns the manuscript, Hedda gleefully whispers, "Now I'm burning your child, Thea."

The play makes use of some of the devices of the "well-made play" – for example, the audience's knowledge about the fate of the manuscript – with a more condensed pattern, closer to the unities of time, place, and action that Aristotle described as typical of tragedy and that had been crucial to seventeenth-century French classicism. As in a Greek tragedy, although the events all take place over a short span of time, they are the culmination of a series of past events, which are narrated by the characters: Lovborg's relationship with Hedda, Tesman's courtship of her, Lovborg's recovery from alcoholism and relationship with Thea. The entire play takes place in the drawing room of the villa Tesman has purchased, in which Hedda feels herself a prisoner; to her, "there's something in it of the odor of death." The drawing room as confined space was to become a distinctive feature of modern realist drama, whether in the townhouses of Ibsen's Norwegian middle classes or the country estates of Chekhov's declining Russian gentry.

As against Aristotle's strictures, however, and in line with the well-made play tradition, Ibsen makes considerable use of props, like the manuscript of Lovborg's book. No prop is more important than Hedda's two pistols, a bequest from her father the general. Chekhov later gave famous advice about constructing a play: "if in Act I you have a pistol on the wall, then it must fire in the last act."[7] This rule encapsulates the use of props in the well-made play. In *Hedda Gabler* the two pistols are mentioned at the end of the first act and appear for the first time at the beginning of the second. They have indeed been fired by the end of the play, but Ibsen puts them to rather different use than would a typical author of well-made plays like Scribe. The first mention of a pistol occurs when Thea comments that one of Lovborg's earlier lovers threatened him with a pistol. At the end of the act, Hedda for the first time refers to her own pistols; this revelation confirms what the audience (but not Thea) has suspected – that she is Lovborg's former lover. The second act begins with Hedda playfully shooting at – and deliberately missing – a family friend, Judge Brack. In the third act she gives Lovborg one of the two pistols, hoping that he will use it to kill himself.

Hedda thinks that Lovborg's suicide will be beautiful, and is disillusioned when Judge Brack reveals that Lovborg has not shot himself in the temple or the chest. Rather, during a fight with the singer and prostitute Mademoiselle Diana, he has been shot in the groin, possibly by Diana. The moral atmosphere of the play is shaped by the conflict between the romantic values championed by Hedda and Lovborg and the banal bourgeois reality of the Tesmans, Thea, and even Judge Brack. Judge Brack plays the part of the seducer from melodrama but is also the voice of realism in the play. Friendly enough at first, he is eager to have an affair with Hedda; when he finds out that she has caused Lovborg's death, he uses the information to blackmail her. Hedda threatens to kill herself, and the judge responds: "People *say* such things. But they don't do them." Realizing that she is in his power, Hedda retires into an inner room (upstage) and shoots herself with the second pistol. Judge Brack is given the final words of the play: "People don't *do* such things!" And yet they do, in Ibsen's play. Even the most apparently realist of Ibsen's plays contain heavy doses of symbolism; he referred to the symbolic qualities of his plays as "the vein of silver ore in the mountain." In *Hedda Gabler* the vine leaves in Lovborg's hair, the manuscript that he considers his child, even such props as General Gabler's pistols, all take on almost magical qualities, recalling Ibsen's earlier poetic dramas and pointing ahead to the mythical explorations of his late work. Hedda's suicide, like Nora's departure from home in *A Doll's House*, demonstrates the possibility of a self-destructive, radical, romantic action that can break through the routine, realistic world of middle-class life.

Ibsen returned to Norway in 1891. His next play, *The Master Builder* (1892), initiated Ibsen's turn from psychological realism to a renewed exploration of symbolism and the unconscious mind. His mysticism displayed itself still more openly in his final work, *When We Dead Awaken* (1899). His late works inspired the new interest in dreams, ghosts, and symbols that shaped avant-garde theater in the twentieth century, from Strindberg to the expressionists and absurdists. Thus, while best known in England for his realist works, Ibsen also served as an inspiration to the antinaturalist modern theater of Europe, through his early romantic and late symbolist plays. The realism of *A Doll's House* and *Hedda Gabler* is only one aspect of his accomplishment, one that shows modern theater as the attempt to represent the tragedy of modern life.

In the plays of Chekhov, tragedy and comedy are inextricably intertwined. Although his major plays are suffused with an air of anxiety and pessimism akin to Ibsen's, he insisted on calling *The Seagull* (1895) and *The Cherry Orchard* (1903) comedies. He gave *Uncle Vanya* (1896) the noncommittal subtitle "Scenes from Country Life," and called *Three Sisters* (1900) a "drama." Yet none of these plays is either conventionally comic or tragic. In particular, that central aspect of Aristotelian tragedy, the climactic action entailing reversal or recognition, seems absent from Chekhov's plays. In general, his Russian gentry are in decline, but the decline is gradual and irreversible. They undergo various minor illuminations in the course of the plays but never a blinding recognition that could lead to a change of fortune.

Chekhov, a doctor and the grandson of a serf, became famous as a story-writer before his first successes as a playwright. Doctors come and go in his plays, sometimes expressing wisdom and more often resignation. Generally seen by his compatriots as a naturalist, he was later interpreted by the Soviets as a chronicler of the rise of the bourgeoisie, the decline of the aristocracy, and the imminence of revolution (he died in 1904, the year before the first Russian Revolution). However, this interpretation depended on an avoidance of Chekhov's dramatic innovations, which changed the nature of plot and its relationship to character.

The first of his major dramatic works, *The Seagull*, features an aspiring dramatist, Konstantin Treplev, who has cast a girl he loves, Nina, in a play to be performed at his mother's country house. The "play within a play," though going back to Shakespeare, became a central feature of twentieth-century theater, a reflection of the crisis of representation. The symbolist style of Konstantin's play contrasts sharply with Chekhov's early realism. Nina complains, "It's difficult to act in your play, there are no real living characters in it." Konstantin explains that he wants to portray "life not the way it is, or the way it should be, but the way it is in dreams." Nina responds, "But nothing happens in your play! It's all one long speech. And I think a play ought to have a love story . . ." In fact, more than Chekhov's later plays, *The Seagull* does feature a love story and a traditional plot, ending (like *Hedda Gabler*) with a suicide. The plot of *The Seagull* is fairly conventional; Chekhov's symbolism and self-conscious reflection on the nature of drama are the main features that distinguish this work from that of earlier realist and naturalist playwrights. In the last decade of his life, however, Chekhov wrote three masterpieces that increasingly resembled the symbolist drama of his fictional playwright Konstantin Treplev.

Nina's complaint about Konstantin's play – "nothing happens" – has been repeated by critics of Chekhov's later plays. In them he turns away from conventions like the love plot, the climactic final gunshot, even the main character;

instead, Chekhov explores "the drama of the undramatic."[8] Like life itself, Chekhov's plots generally lack resolution. The loaded pistol of his famous aphorism provides an example. In *Hedda Gabler* the pistols go off, and if the first one wounds Lovborg in an unexpected way, the second provides a suitably dramatic climax. In Chekhov's first major play, *The Seagull*, Konstantin attempts suicide between the first and second acts, and finally succeeds in killing himself in the last scene. In *Uncle Vanya*, written a year later, Vanya wants to kill his brother-in-law Professor Serebriakov, a charlatan who has consumed all the money the family estate can produce. As Vanya complains, "For twenty-five years he's been regurgitating other people's ideas about realism, naturalism, all that bullshit." At the end of the third act, Vanya, infuriated with the Professor, shoots at him twice, but misses. The shots do not result in any climactic action. Nothing changes. As Vanya observes in the fourth act, "Funny, isn't it? I try to kill someone, nobody calls the police, nobody arrests me. Which means you all think I'm crazy." Vanya thinks of killing himself with a vial of Dr. Astrov's morphine, but his niece Sonya convinces him to give the morphine back. The Professor and his second wife return to Moscow and everything on the estate returns to normal, except that the characters are more disillusioned than ever. In his last work, *The Cherry Orchard*, a minor character boasts in the second act, "I always carry a loaded pistol." He brandishes the weapon, too. Yet, as Chekhov announced proudly, "There's not a single pistol-shot in the whole play."[9]

Chekhov's plays move away from the focus on a central heroic figure. Instead of heroes or villains, the later plays tend to feature ensemble casts of characters who are neither particularly good nor particularly bad. In *Three Sisters* the sisters are indeed heroines, but their actions are not typically heroic. Mainly, they endure. Throughout the play the sisters dream of escaping their country estate and going to Moscow. Irina begs to be allowed to go at the end of the second and third acts. Gradually, however, their brother gambles away the family fortune, and at the end of the play the oldest, Olga, realizes that "of course, I'll never get to Moscow . . ." As Richard Gilman has observed, the sisters' waiting to go to Moscow resembles Vladimir's and Estragon's waiting in Samuel Beckett's *Waiting for Godot* (1952), written half a century later. Beckett's novel, *The Unnamable* (1953), would end with the line "you must go on, I can't go on, I'll go on." Chekhov sounds the same theme of endurance. At the end of *Uncle Vanya*, Sonya recognizes that nothing in her life or her uncle's will change and says, "You and I, Uncle Vanya, we have to go on living. The days will be slow, and the nights will be long, but we'll take whatever fate sends us." At the end of *Three Sisters*, Masha says, "[We] have to go on living."

Like the realists and naturalists (and unlike his character Konstantin), Chekhov claims to represent the world as it is, without moral judgments. Most of the climactic action in his works takes place offstage, often before the beginning of the play. What takes center stage is conversation. Not exactly, as Irina puts it in *The Seagull*, "one long speech," however; in Chekhov's plays there are many short speeches and many long silences, only occasionally punctuated by a longer monologue. Characters who do make lengthy speeches, about the environment, or the problem of work, or the future of Russia, usually retract or ironize them. Chekhov's characters often talk past each other, as if they are not hearing one another. Some, like the old butler Firs in *The Cherry Orchard*, are in fact deaf. Chekhov defended the dialogue in his plays on realistic grounds: "Things on stage should be as complicated and yet as simple as in life. People dine, just dine, while their happiness is made and their lives are smashed."[10] Here, Chekhov claimed to be exposing the drama of everyday life, and he does so, but at the same time the effect of non sequitur in his speeches prefigures the later absurdist plays of Beckett or Eugène Ionesco.

Throughout Chekhov's plays any sort of resolution, comic or tragic, is deferred; he often presents courtships that go nowhere, instead of a conventional love plot. In *The Cherry Orchard* the characters expect the successful businessman Lopakhin, the son and grandson of serfs, to propose to Varya, the adopted daughter of impoverished aristocrats. Yet every time he is left alone with her, he seems uneasy. By the end of the play, the family estate is sold to Lopakhin, and Chekhov seems to leave two possibilities open: a comic resolution in which Lopakhin marries Varya and the estate stays in the family, or a tragic one, in which the estate is destroyed for the sake of real estate development (a theme from Ibsen's *The Master Builder*). Yet Chekhov resists every opportunity to dramatize this ending. Lopakhin meets Varya, but instead of proposing he comments on the weather. Uncle Gayev plans to make a speech about the significance of the occasion, but the others dissuade him from speaking. In the final scene, while axes are heard chopping down the orchard offstage, the comic figure Firs reappears; elderly and ill, he has been left behind by the family, who thought he had been taken to an old people's home. He has been locked in the house, which is soon to be demolished. So he lies down on the stage and waits – for someone to come back, or simply for death to come and get him. The scene can be played tragically, but it works better as farce. This is one reason why Chekhov insisted on calling the play a comedy. *The Cherry Orchard* does not resolve itself in marriage, like a conventional comedy, but it deploys farce to come to terms with the modern failure of resolution. For this reason Chekhov complained about the lugubrious naturalistic staging of his plays at Konstantin Stanislavsky's Moscow Art Theater, even though these performances made Chekhov famous (see Chapter Seven). Although Chekhov's representation of passing time, boredom, and silence can be justified in realist or naturalist terms, his plays continually gesture beyond naturalistic theater, portending the disruption of naturalism in the twentieth century.

## Character

The movement away from conventional plot in realist and naturalist drama has often been understood as a transfer of attention from plot to character, thus reversing the priorities established by Aristotle. Instead of climactic action, it might be said, Anton Chekhov gives us intense psychological portraits. In fact, Chekhov does not so much disregard plot as reconstruct it, turning what other dramatists might consider mere incident or dialogue into the central actions of a new type of plot. At around the same time, the Swedish playwright August Strindberg began to rethink the function of character in drama. Strindberg was Henrik Ibsen's great rival in the Scandinavian theater. Their enmity began with Strindberg's negative reaction to *A Doll's House* (1879), which he, disapprovingly, considered feminist. A noted misogynist, Strindberg wrote two highly accomplished naturalist plays, *The Father* (1887) and *Miss Julie* (1888), about the struggle between the sexes. Then, for six years in the mid-1890s, Strindberg struggled with madness. He wrote no plays but kept a detailed journal of his crisis, which he later used as the basis for a novel, *Inferno* (1897). After his recovery, his intellectual interests turned from Friedrich Nietzsche and Arthur Schopenhauer to magic, the occult, Hinduism, Buddhism, and the mystical eighteenth-century Swedish philosopher Emmanuel Swedenborg. He wrote more than thirty plays in the last dozen years of his life. Although some of these pieces dealt with Swedish history or with the themes of his earlier naturalist plays, his most influential later works were dream plays, in which he explored the unconscious mind. Strindberg's late plays dismantle traditional notions of character, just as Chekhov's late plays dismantle plot.

In his theoretical writings Strindberg emphasized the shift from the conventional plot of the well-made play toward a new attention to character, and explained that, in *Miss Julie*, he had concentrated on the passionate relationship between the two main characters, a feminist aristocrat and her father's valet, rather than any formally structured plot because he believed that "people of today are most interested in the psychological process. Our inquisitive souls are not satisfied just to see something happen; we want to know how it happened. We want to see the strings, the machinery, examine the double-bottomed box, feel for the seam in the magic ring, look at the cards to see how they are marked."[11] For Strindberg, psychological plays are more realistic than those with well-formed plots. He prefigures the struggle against illusionism, represented by the paraphernalia of the magician, that would, in different ways, motivate both the naturalist and the antinaturalist traditions in modern theater. The naturalists rejected "magic" because they wanted to show life as it really was. Zola had complained that the theater was "the last fortress of conventionality"; the naturalist plays of Strindberg and the realist plays of Ibsen seek to storm this fortress and to create a new, truer theater.[12] Yet, in their last plays, both Ibsen and Strindberg turned toward symbolism, dreams, ghosts, and even the supernatural. In these works two founders of modern theater celebrate its magical possibilities and call attention to the very illusion upon which theater is based.

Strindberg's dream plays, inspired in part by Ibsen's *Peer Gynt* (1867) and *When We Dead Awaken* (1899), seem to announce the "death of character" that Elinor Fuchs has diagnosed in modern and postmodern drama.[13] In place of well-defined characters, the plays divide personality into multiple parts. Like Luigi Pirandello's six characters, the main figures in *A Dream Play* (1902) are known by their social roles, rather than names: the Officer, the Lawyer, the Doorkeeper, the Poet. In the play the Daughter of Indra, the king of the gods in ancient Hinduism, comes down to earth to try to understand human suffering. She descends from a cloud to a castle built on a dungheap and surmounted by a flower bud. The Daughter watches as the Officer has a vision of his dead mother and then waits, apparently for years, for his beloved, an actress, to come out of the back door of a theater. (As in Chekhov's *Three Sisters* [1900], the audience watches a character waiting for something that never happens, another premonition of Beckett's *Waiting for Godot* [1952].) Without the curtain falling, the scene is changed, and the Daughter finds herself in the Lawyer's office; later, she marries the Lawyer and has a baby, but then the scene switches to the back door of the theater again, where the Officer is still waiting for the actress. Suddenly the characters are transported to a quarantine island, where a schoolmaster asks the Officer, "Do you think that time and space exist?" The Daughter discusses Hinduism and Christianity with the Poet and explains the source of all experience in Maya (illusion): "the world, life and human beings are only an illusion, a phantom, a dream image." She disappears into the castle, which burns, while the stage directions indicate that "the flower bud on the roof bursts into a giant chrysanthemum." The image of dungheap, castle, and chrysanthemum suggests the close but tortured relation, in Strindberg's vision, between art and bodily functions like sex and defecation. As the critic Robert Brustein has noted, *A Dream Play* seems to point to the mystery later expressed by W. B. Yeats in "Crazy Jane Talks with the Bishop" (1932): "But Love has pitched his mansion in / The place of excrement." Strindberg's earlier misogyny has been transformed into worship of Indra's daughter, but its roots in his fundamental disgust with the human body remain.

Strindberg's dream plays involve transformations of both character and plot. As Strindberg wrote about *A Dream Play* and *The Road to Damascus* (1898–1901): "The Author has sought to imitate the disconnected but apparently logical form of a dream. Anything can happen, everything is possible and plausible. Time and space do not exist. Upon an insignificant background of real life events the imagination spins and weaves new patterns: a blend of memories, experiences, pure inventions, absurdities, and improvisations." Where Aristotle demanded probability, Strindberg proclaimed that "everything is possible." Similarly, Strindberg announced his revision of character: "The characters split, double, redouble, evaporate, condense, fragment, cohere. But one consciousness is superior to them all: that of the dreamer."[14] Yet the dreamer is not strictly speaking a character in the play; rather, he is a figure for the author, and also for the audience members, who relive the author's dreams while watching his play.

During the years of the burgeoning avant-garde, immediately before the First World War, German expressionist playwrights, including Georg Kaiser, the Austrian Oskar Kokoschka, Reinhard Sorge, and (slightly later) Ernst Toller, wrote episodic plays known as *Stationendramen*, after the Stations of the Cross, the fourteen incidents in Christ's crucifixion that were the centerpiece of medieval representations of the Passion. Inspired by Strindberg's *The Road to Damascus*, these plays focused on a single character, like Strindberg's dreamer, who encountered a series of allegorical figures; they tended to show character disintegrating over time.[15] The impact of German expressionism on later modern drama came primarily through the work of the most influential playwright of the twentieth century, Bertolt Brecht. Brecht's first play, *Baal*, written in 1918 but not produced until 1923, tells the story of a boorish and primitive poet who, from being a society sensation, degenerates into a rapist and murderer. The policeman who tries to arrest Baal summarizes his career as follows: "Started out as a cabaret performer and poet. Then merry-go-round owner, woodcutter, millionairess's lover, jailbird and pimp." *Baal* is at the same time a natural outgrowth and a parody of Strindberg's dream plays and the expressionist *Stationendrama*. It prefigures Brecht's later fascination with outcasts and social hypocrisy.

In 1924 Brecht moved from Munich to Berlin, and soon thereafter began working with the communist director Erwin Piscator, who practiced a form of epic theater, in which he engaged contemporary social and political concerns. Brecht developed his own theory of epic theater on the basis of his work with Piscator. Whereas Chekhov, Ibsen, and Strindberg revised the notions of plot and character drawn from Aristotle, Brecht claimed to be creating an entirely non-Aristotelian theater, which he called epic rather than dramatic. This project entailed a wholesale reconsideration of plot, character, and many other elements of the traditional theater. The version of Aristotelian theater that Brecht was rejecting derived from the work of Johann Wolfgang von Goethe and Friedrich Schiller, who saw epic and dramatic poetry as entirely distinct in type: the epic focused on the past and "man's physical interaction with the world," while the dramatic focused on the present and the "individual suffering" of "man interacting with himself."[16] Brecht wanted theater to address the concerns that had traditionally been seen as epic: that is, history, in the dual sense of the pastness of the past and of the individual's engagement with social forces. Brecht's goal of creating an epic theater was closely linked to his political commitment to Marxism.

Brecht became drawn to communism around 1926 and proclaimed himself a Marxist in 1928. In that same year he had his first international success with *The Threepenny Opera*, an adaptation of the eighteenth-century *Beggar's Opera* by John Gay, which Brecht wrote in collaboration with Elisabeth Hauptmann, who co-wrote several of his early plays and after the war participated in his theatrical company, the Berliner Ensemble. Brecht set the opera in the criminal underworld of Victorian London; in it he satirized the respectable bourgeoisie as no better than the gangster Macheath (Mac the Knife). Mac elopes with Polly Peachum, the daughter of the beggar king, who has organized the beggars of London and taught them more effective techniques for begging, in exchange for a cut of their profits. Like Baal before him, Mac seduces various women; he is imprisoned twice but eventually reprieved and knighted by the Queen. One of the central themes of the play is hypocrisy, and Brecht wrote that "just like two hundred years ago we have a social order in which virtually all levels, even if in a wide variety of ways, pay respect to moral principles not by leading a moral life but by living off morality."[17] The play is a "ballad opera," making use of popular music, written by Kurt Weill, a pioneer of "new music" who composed simple tunes appropriate for didactic purposes. The song "Mac the Knife" became part of the standard jazz repertory, performed by Louis Armstrong, Frank Sinatra, and others. Brecht intended the songs to distance the audience from the action, to "take up a position," but the music also arguably contributed to the humor and good fun of the play, which is Brecht's most popular but not his most politically effective.[18]

The use of music to distance the audience from the plot was an aspect of Brecht's theory of epic theater, which he contrasted with dramatic theater in the program notes for *The Rise and Fall of the City of Mahagonny* (1930), another collaboration with Weill (see box). The nineteen contrasts he outlined involve many of Aristotle's elements of theater. Several are concerned with plot (converted in epic theater into narrative or storytelling, and transformed from linear and evolutionary to discontinuous, like the earlier expressionist drama). Others are concerned with the competition between feeling and reason, and point to Brecht's suspicion of catharsis (discussed below). Traditional notions of character are called into question because, as Brecht puts it, "the human being is the object of inquiry," and "he is alterable and able to alter." More radically, the method of portraying character in epic theater is quite different from that in traditional theater. Many of Brecht's tenets involve the question of the spectator's relationship to the action on stage, and implicitly to the actors. Brecht discouraged identification or sympathy between the audience and the characters, which had been one of the primary goals of melodrama and of romantic theory and was implicit in Aristotle's notions of pity and catharsis. Instead of identifying with the characters on stage, Brecht wanted the spectator to maintain an intellectual distance from the action, to reason about it rather than just responding emotionally. In fact, Brecht wanted the spectator's experience to alternate between emotional reaction and distanced reflection upon that emotional reaction.

The Greek word for actor is *hypocrites,* and there is a great deal of anxiety in modern drama about hypocrisy, the pretense of being someone other than who one really is. The theme is crucial to Ibsen, Strindberg, Chekhov, Oscar Wilde, and George Bernard Shaw, as well as to Brecht. Brecht's solution to the problem of the actor's potential hypocrisy was to insist that the actor must always be aware of, and make the audience aware of, the distance between actor and role. He thought of the actor as at once portraying a part and observing it from outside, thus allowing the audience to observe the part critically. In the mid-1930s he called this the "alienation" or "estrangement" (*Verfremdung*) effect: "The artist's object is to appear strange and even surprising to the audience. He achieves this by looking strangely at himself and his work. As a result everything put forward by him has a touch of the amazing. Everyday things are thereby raised above the level of the obvious and automatic."[19] Theater historians have debated how much Brecht knew about Victor Shklovsky's theory of defamiliarization (see Introduction). At any rate, he shared with Shklovsky, and also with T. S. Eliot, the recognition that one of the functions of modern art is to make the familiar appear strange. Brecht became particularly interested in Chinese and Japanese acting traditions, which were not mimetic or naturalistic like Western acting. Like Luigi Pirandello, he admired the use of masks as a means of calling attention to the artificiality of the stage. He defined each scene in terms of a dominant gesture, almost a tableau that would freeze action and allow it to be analyzed by the audience. Brecht used the term *gestus* to refer to the overall comportment of the actor on stage. He thus valued those aspects of the stage that the realist and naturalist tradition had attempted to eliminate. Brecht did not manage to make wholly successful plays in the style of epic theater until later in his career, and critics have pointed out that even these rely heavily on plot and sympathy, despite Brecht's theoretical pronouncements (see Chapter Seven). However, his theory of epic theater was a culmination of experimental theater in the years immediately before and after the First World War. Although there is a great distance between the German expressionists and the later epic theater of Brecht, the epic theater owes something to the "death of character" already projected in Strindberg's dream plays. The movement away from stable character entailed an increasing psychological distance between the audience and the characters on stage; it broke with the illusion that characters in a play are real people and therefore defeated the earlier goal of identification between the audience members and the characters. This aspect of Brecht's accomplishment contributed to a broader reevaluation of theatrical experience that had been undertaken over the previous generation, mainly in France and Italy.

### Brecht's outline of epic theater[20]

| Dramatic theater | Epic theater |
| --- | --- |
| plot | narrative |
| implicates the spectator in a stage situation | turns the spectator into an observer but |
| wears down his capacity for action | arouses his capacity for action |
| provides him with sensations | forces him to take decisions |
| experience | picture of the world |
| the spectator is involved in something | he is made to face something |
| suggestion | argument |
| instinctive feelings are preserved | brought to the point of recognition |
| the spectator is in the thick of it, shares the experience | the spectator stands outside, studies |
| the human being is taken for granted | the human being is the object of the inquiry |
| he is unalterable | he is alterable and able to alter |
| eyes on the finish | eyes on the course |
| one scene makes another | each scene for itself |
| growth | montage |
| linear development | in curves |
| evolutionary determinism | jumps |
| man as a fixed point | man as a process |
| thought determines being | social being determines thought |
| feeling | reason |

# Theater

The crisis of representation in modernism resulted in part from a sense that art should do more than just imitate reality. In this regard, it revived a concern most influentially expressed by Plato, that art is necessarily untrue because it is no more than an imitation (see Introduction). It is said that everyone is either a Platonist or an Aristotelian. When Brecht proposed a "non-Aristotelian" theater, he revealed his sympathies with Plato. Plato was particularly skeptical of drama, and he proposed to ban tragedy and comedy from his ideal city in book three of *The Republic*, before eventually proposing to ban virtually all poetry in book ten. (Indeed, Aristotle's *Poetics* is in part a defense of drama, and especially tragedy, against the accusations of Plato.) Plato explained that narrative or storytelling (diegesis) was less harmful than representation or imitation (mimesis). Brecht thus directly echoes Plato when he prefers narrative to plot. Plato was suspicious of actors because they pretended to be something other than what they really were: they imitated others' actions rather than merely (like the storyteller) telling about them. While it might be all right to imitate a noble action, Plato thought that many actors imitated drunkenness, lust, and other ignoble behavior. He had three related objections to theater. First, theater was simply a lie. Second, it engaged the sympathies of the audience and therefore tended to make them less thoughtful. Third, watching imitations of ignoble behavior could lead members of the audience (and the actors) to behave badly themselves.

As the critic Martin Puchner has recently shown, some modernists shared Plato's concerns about theater, and, surprisingly enough, some who did – like Brecht – were themselves playwrights. Whereas Plato's critique of theater had a conservative element to it – he feared that theater could subvert his ideal state – modernist antitheatricality was often radical in orientation. Modernists often saw the theater as a conservative institution catering to bourgeois taste, subject to censorship by the state, and driven by the profit motives of theater managers. Some resisted conventional forms of plot, such as the well-made play, as falsifying experience (a version of Plato's complaint that acting was lying). Some, like Brecht, went so far as to attempt to replace the imitation or representation of experience with a sort of theatrical storytelling, in which the actors stepped outside their parts and spoke to their audiences or called attention by various gestures to the fact that they were "merely" acting.[21]

Brecht's epic theater appealed to reason rather than feeling and sought to turn the spectator "into an observer," who "stands outside, studies" the action of the play. In this respect, Brecht stood against a dominant tradition in theater, shared by romantic, naturalist, and avant-garde playwrights, that aimed to have the spectator "involved in" and "shar[ing] the experience" of the play. Modern drama was heavily influenced by changing attitudes to what Aristotle called "spectacle," those aspects of the production, such as scenery, props, and lighting, that are largely independent of the playwright's script. The history of the theater from the Renaissance to the nineteenth century had tended toward ever greater illusionism – that is, an increasing dedication to representing reality on the stage. The stage framed by a proscenium arch became widespread in the seventeenth century and, like Renaissance painting, it made use of a unified perspective, so that the ideal seat was directly in front of the stage. In earlier drama, as for example in Greek amphitheaters, the audience was generally seated around the stage, rather than in front of it. Classical stages did not have scenery representing particular places, while medieval and early Renaissance stages presented generalized landscapes, symbolizing such places as Heaven and Hell. The practice of introducing a new set for each change of scene began in the seventeenth century; until the nineteenth century, sets were generally painted on backdrops, and the stage seldom contained furniture; actors stood and faced the audience, rather than sitting or facing each other.

The nineteenth century developed the box set, shaped like a room in a house; the "fourth wall" of the box set was the proscenium arch, and audiences looked into the stage as if looking into a room missing a wall. The box set led to the development of more elaborate and realistic interiors, including furniture and carpets, while gaslight allowed new lighting effects such as limelight (an early form of spotlight). With the growing consciousness of history in the nineteenth century, theater producers introduced historically accurate costumes. In his naturalist phase August Strindberg wanted "to transform the stage into a room where the fourth wall is removed, and consequently, a portion of the furniture faces away from the audience."[22] In hoping to place the furniture this way, Strindberg was more radically naturalist than others, since most theaters arranged the furniture to face the audience. Nonetheless, realists and naturalists generally supported the idea that the audience was looking at real action through the missing fourth wall of a room. They therefore avoided earlier techniques such as soliloquies or asides, which tended to acknowledge the presence of an audience. Instead, actors behaved as if they did not know they were being watched, sometimes turning their back to the audience. Naturalistic acting and production, intended to give the illusion that the characters were real people and the stage a real slice of the world outside the theater, reached its apogee in the system of Konstantin Stanislavsky, director of the Moscow Art Theater, whose productions of Anton Chekhov's plays at the turn of the twentieth century set the standard for theatrical naturalism (see Chapter Seven). The box set with missing fourth wall is still used today for situation comedies on television, with the proscenium arch replaced by a camera.[23]

A powerful contrary tendency in modern theater, represented by Luigi Pirandello, celebrated the difference between theater and the outside world. Scholars have given the name "theatricalism" to the tendency to celebrate the spectacular elements of theater and its capacity for heightened emotional experience (see box). Theatricalists differ from naturalists because, instead of attempting to make the world of the stage resemble the "real" world, they treat the stage as a ritual space with its own rules that are independent of those of extratheatrical reality. An important influence on modern theatricalism was Richard Wagner, in whose operas the romantic goal of powerful sympathy between the actor and the audience culminates in the ideal of a "total work of art." Wagner wanted his opera to synthesize the various elements of drama – music, words, actors, costumes, scenery, and lighting – in order to express the artist's vision and communicate it to the audience, who would become totally involved in the work.

## Theater, antitheater, metatheater

Two crucial faultlines run through modern theater. One separates naturalism (and realism) from antinaturalism. In naturalism the characters on stage behave as real people do in the world outside the theater; the laws of their world are the same ones that govern everyday, waking reality. Antinaturalist theater, on the other hand, may make use of improbable events, dreams, and visions, or ordinary events presented in a stylized fashion. The other, related faultline separates those who are dedicated to maintaining theatrical illusion from those who break down the illusion in various ways. Naturalistic theater generally embraces the illusion of reality, but not all antinaturalist theater breaks with illusionism. August Strindberg's *A Dream Play* (1902), for example, attempts to convey the illusion of witnessing a dream. Wagner's operas, though romantic and far from naturalist, also rely on theatrical illusion. More often, however, antinaturalist theater breaks down theatrical illusion – and from various points of view. The French avant-garde playwrights Guillaume Apollinaire and Alfred Jarry celebrated "theatricalism"; they deliberately called attention to the arbitrariness and artificiality of stage conventions. "Metatheater," like that of Pirandello, goes further: characters call attention to the fact that they are fictional, or mention the name of the playwright, or perform plays within plays. Brecht's theater has many of the qualities of metatheater (see below), but can also be called "antitheater," because he called attention to theatrical illusion in order to criticize traditional theater and to replace it with something more "real." In this respect, although he does not embrace the illusion of reality, his theater shares much with naturalism.

The set designers and theorists Adolphe Appia and Gordon Craig created methods for implementing Wagner's vision in the theater. Appia, in *The*

*Staging of Wagnerian Music Drama* (1895) and *Music and the Art of Theatre* (1899), proposed to banish painted backdrops and replace them with three-dimensional settings; his sets made use of risers and steps to emphasize the three-dimensionality of the physical space of the stage, and the actor's presence within it. He advocated the abolition of the proscenium arch and of all naturalistic details of setting; for him, the stage was a dramatic, rhythmic space to be organized artistically, somewhat along the lines of the reorganization of pictorial space in post-impressionist and abstract art. Instead of a fourth wall opening onto a room, Appia envisioned the stage as "a vista into the unknown, into boundless space."[24] As a result, his stage designs aimed at evoking an atmosphere rather than representing a concrete place.[25]

Craig, an English actor and set designer, introduced some of the stylization typical of Appia (who was Swiss) into the English-speaking world in the first decade of the twentieth century. Some of his most interesting theories concerned the status of the actor in theatrical productions. Like the antitheatricalists, Craig was highly suspicious of actors, but his objection was the opposite of that later voiced by Brecht. Whereas Brecht would fear that actors created too successful an illusion, Craig complained that, by virtue of their being human, actors constantly undermined the illusion of theatrical art. He wanted to replace actors with *Übermarionetten*, superpuppets, who would form part of the abstract composition of the theatrical piece. "Do away with the actor," he wrote, "and you do away with the means by which a debased stage-realism is produced and flourishes. No longer would there be a living figure to confuse us into connecting actuality and art; no longer a living figure in which the weaknesses and tremors of the flesh were perceptible."[26] Partly under the influence of Wagner and Craig, the later nineteenth century saw the rise of the director, who replaced the earlier model of an actor-manager, and who was given power over every aspect of production. Not limited to "theatricalism," the rise of the director affected all forms of modern drama, including the naturalistic theater (Stanislavsky) and the epic theater (Brecht). Similarly, Appia's ideas about lighting and staging influenced many different types of production.

In the nineteenth century Wagner's ideal of the total work of art inspired symbolists like Stéphane Mallarmé (see Chapter One). Although Brecht attacked Wagner, French and Italian avant-garde theater after Mallarmé tended to celebrate theatricality and, in this respect, as Puchner has shown, avant-garde playwrights from Jarry to Antonin Artaud are Wagner's heirs. Like Strindberg and the German expressionists, they tended to dismantle plot and character, but they went further in order to dismantle theatrical illusion and even that central function of the theater, representation. Whereas Brecht aimed for a theater that exposed the illusions of theatricality, the futurist F. T. Marinetti proposed "theatricality without theater," a pure celebration of spectacle.[27] The theatricalist avant-garde deliberately called attention to the artificiality of theatrical conventions, in order to celebrate them.

The first modern play in this tradition is Jarry's *King Ubu*. At its first performance, in Paris on December 10, 1896, the audience broke into factions after the main character, Father Ubu, had uttered the first word of the play: "Shite" (*"Merdre"*). In a grotesque parody of Shakespeare's *Macbeth*, Ubu, a dimwitted bourgeois based loosely on Jarry's high school physics teacher, is convinced by his wife (a "hag") to declare himself king of Poland. Father Ubu repeats the word "shite" over and over (along with a range of other obscenities), and slaughters three hundred nobles and five hundred magistrates by shoving them down a trap door. (In production a small number of actors represented all 800 of Ubu's victims.) The play's obscenity and violence might have been enough on their own to cause a riot. What made the play particularly bizarre, however, was its rejection of most of the nineteenth-century methods for creating the illusion of reality on the stage. Jarry described his ideal staging of the play as follows:

> A mask for the chief character, Ubu . . . A cardboard horse's head, which he would hang around his neck, as in the old English theatre, for the only two equestrian scenes, both these suggestions being in the spirit of the play, since I intended to write a "guignol" [Punch and Judy puppet show] . . . A suitably costumed person would enter, as in puppet shows, to put up signs indicating the locations of the various scenes . . . Costumes with as little specific local color reference or historical accuracy as possible.[28]

In addition, Jarry wanted to do away with realistic sets, have crowds of soldiers represented by a single soldier on each side, and have Ubu speak with an unusual accent or voice. All these innovations, drawn from the early modern stage or from puppet shows, were intended to break with theatrical realism, to call attention to the artificiality of the play. W. B. Yeats, who attended the first performance (though he did not know French well), later wrote, "The players are supposed to be dolls, toys, marionettes, and now they are all hopping like wooden frogs, and I can see for myself that the chief personage, who is some kind of King, carries for Sceptre a brush of the kind that we use to clean a closet [toilet]." Although Yeats supported the play, preferring to stay on the side of the avant-garde, he wondered later that night what experiments would come after his own symbolist generation. His answer: "After us the Savage God."[29]

The avant-garde tradition established by Jarry was developed during and after the war by futurists, dadaists, and surrealists. Apollinaire coined the term "surrealist" for his play *The Breasts of Tiresias* (1917). In the play, set in Africa, a Frenchwoman, Thérèse, decides to become a man, and her breasts float away like two balloons; she is renamed Tiresias and becomes a general and a member of parliament. Between the first and second acts, her abandoned husband gives birth to more than forty thousand children, all in one afternoon. In the futurist Giacomo Balla's *Disconcerted States of Mind* (1916), four characters stand on stage repeating numbers or letters of the alphabet, without acknowledging one another or the audience. In Cologne, in 1920, the dadaists Hans Arp and Max Ernst exhibited their art in a public urinal, while a young girl in her communion dress recited obscene poems. One of the most famous theatrical events during the First World War, also described by Apollinaire as "surrealist," was *Parade* (1917), a ballet performed by Sergei Diaghilev's Ballets Russes with a script by Jean Cocteau, jazz-inspired music by Erik Satie, and sets and costumes by Pablo Picasso. The ballet paid homage to the circus sideshow; the score included parts for "typewriters, sirens, airplane propellers, Morse tickers, and lottery wheels."[30] André Breton would use Apollinaire's term "surrealism" for his own influential avant-garde movement, the successor to dada, after the war (see Chapter Seven). The Polish surrealist Stanislaw Ignacy Witkiewicz, known as Witkacy, developed a theory of "pure form" and wrote that "When leaving the theatre, one should have the impression that one wakes up from a strange dream in which the most trite things have the elusive, deep charm characteristic of dreams, not comparable to anything."[31] Later surrealist theater tended to return to the idea of the dream, understood in Freudian terms as the expression of unconscious desires.

   These avant-garde works prepared the ground for Pirandello's *Six Characters in Search of an Author* (1921) which, like the "high modernist" works *The Waste Land* and *Ulysses* (both 1922), seems to take avant-garde concerns to a higher level of seriousness and thus to transform a series of minor experiments into a tradition. The avant-garde playwrights celebrated theatricality, while Brecht, though influenced by the avant-garde, promoted an antitheatrical theater. Pirandello's work has been described as "metatheater." In metatheater the characters are "aware of their own theatricality," in the phrase of Lionel Abel.[32] Abel finds the roots of metatheater going all the way back to Shakespeare (as in the play within a play in *Hamlet*); modern metatheater begins with the futurists and dadaists and reaches the mainstream with Pirandello. The metatheatrical impulse plays a particularly important role in the works of later playwrights such as Samuel Beckett (see Conclusion). Like Chekhov, Pirandello came to the theater after having already established himself as a writer of short stories and novels. His prose fiction deals with themes related to the illusory character of personal identity, and it formed the basis of some of his early plays. There were few immediate theatrical antecedents for the meditation on theatricality contained in *Six Characters* and in his other major plays, *Right You Are (If You Think You Are)* (1917) and *Henry IV* (1922). These other two plays, like his novel *One, No One, and a Hundred Thousand* (1926), address the question of madness and the difficulty of telling who is mad in a world that itself seems to have gone insane. *Six Characters* stands out from Pirandello's other work because in it he abandons the theme of madness; the problem of the theatricality of experience is a problem about the nature of theater and life itself, rather than one of mental disturbance.

The split between the "Actors" and the "Characters" in *Six Characters* seems at first to represent a division between "reality" and "illusion." Yet the "real" actors are specialists in achieving illusion, and the characters claim with some justification to be more "real" than reality. Like the modernists who celebrated the power of myth to transform the everyday, Pirandello celebrates the theater, which reveals the element of self-dramatization inherent in the roles people play in everyday life. Although their story contains a heavy dose of melodrama and therefore seems "unrealistic," Pirandello does not simply treat the characters with irony. Rather, he seems to celebrate the greater intensity of their dramatic self-representation as the basic impulse behind art. In the climactic incident of *Six Characters*, when Pirandello introduces that favorite device of the well-made play, the gunshot, the melodrama of the characters' imaginary lives certainly seems more real and more intense than anything envisioned by the "real" actors. Thus the various levels of reality in the theater are crossed and the most theatrical of effects is celebrated for its closeness to reality. Although in some respects a unique occurrence, not immediately imitated or taken up by a movement, Pirandello's metatheater would eventually have a great impact on modern drama. *Six Characters* was greeted with some hostility when first produced in Italy in 1921, but it was hailed as a major work of modern theater at its debut in Paris in 1923. It entered into the French dramatic tradition that would, after the Second World War, result in Beckett's "theater of the absurd" (see Conclusion).

Another dramatist of this period to have a great impact on theater after the Second World War was Artaud. Artaud was in fact the author of only a few plays, and his major influence resulted from his theoretical writings, which took up a position sharing some intellectual concerns with Brecht but proposing a "theater of cruelty" that sharply contrasted with Brecht's epic theater. An admirer of Jarry, Artaud was briefly involved with surrealism in the 1920s. Like Brecht and Craig, he became fascinated with Asian performance art; in Artaud's case the inspiration came from the trance-inducing Balinese ritual dance, which he first saw in 1931. He decided that the Western theatrical tradition had focused exclusively on conscious experience and that a new type of theater was needed that would "reveal the hypocrisy of the world." Whereas Brecht tried to fight hypocrisy by having his actors maintain a distance from their parts, Artaud promoted total immersion in the theater as a ritual. He thus sought to reconnect the theater with its religious roots; the Greek tragedies were originally staged as part of the Festival of Dionysus. Like the antitheatricalists, Artaud complained that, since the Renaissance, the theater had been "falsehood and illusion." He proposed to overcome this condition, however, not by an appeal to the intellect but by a more complete dedication to spectacle, an aspect of the theater that had been downplayed by Aristotle. In particular, he objected to the primacy of texts in theater, and announced that "we intend to base the theater upon spectacle before everything else."

Emphasizing loud sounds and bright lights, Artaud wanted to "abolish the stage and auditorium," and have spectators sit in the middle of a large room, while watching the action around them. He planned also to do away with sets and partitions. As in Craig's imagined theater of superpuppets, actors would be trained to be "passive and neutral" and their faces would be replaced by large puppets and masks. A theater in which the actors gave everything to their performance would in fact be more than mere spectacle, more than Aristotle's pity and terror; this theater would inflict psychic pain on the audience. The term "theater of cruelty" did not necessarily imply violence. Rather, Artaud's theater, an extension and radicalization of Aristotelian catharsis, demanded the full involvement of audience and spectator and submission to the unconscious mind. Having experienced this total theater, Artaud said, "I defy the spectator to give himself up, once outside the theater, to ideas of war, riot, and blatant murder." Artaud's vision was realized most effectively in the postwar plays of Jean Genet, which featured ritualized murders and the enactment of oppression as a means of criticizing oppressive political systems like colonialism. In Artaud's theater of cruelty, the attack on Aristotelian representation reaches its apogee. The philosopher Jacques Derrida later wrote of Artaud, "The theater of cruelty is not a *representation*. It is life itself, in the extent to which life is unrepresentable."[33] Artaud and Brecht, both critics of Aristotle and of the traditional theater, present two radically different versions of the nonnaturalistic theater. For Brecht, all is detachment and reason; for Artaud, all is spectacle and catharsis.[34]

## Ideas

Aristotle preferred plot and character to spectacle and song. He said less about diction and thought. To understand modern British drama, however, requires particular attention to these two elements. The major figure in modern British

drama, George Bernard Shaw, saw himself as a playwright of ideas. Shaw dominated the British stage from his defense of Henrik Ibsen in the 1890s until his
death in 1950. His most important plays were written in the Edwardian era, and
dealt with central Edwardian problems: social class, feminism, the condition of
England. A Fabian socialist, Shaw seems more at home among the Edwardians
like Arnold Bennett, John Galsworthy, and H. G. Wells, than the modernists
T. S. Eliot, James Joyce, and Virginia Woolf (see Chapter Two). The English
theater reacted relatively slowly to the rise of modernism, in part for reasons of
commerce or censorship. The weighty but uninventive dramas of Galsworthy
and Harley Granville-Barker were, like most of Shaw's plays, focused on contemporary social problems (see Chapter Two). Shaw's dominance, the particular conservatism of the English stage, and the general isolation of British
literature from avant-garde influences, meant that serious drama in Britain
was, for the entire modernist period, mainly a theater of ideas, developing out
of the realist Ibsen of *A Doll's House* (1879). Parallel to Shaw's politically oriented work, however, ran a significant intervention in the diction of the stage:
the attempt to revive verse drama, pursued by W. H. Auden, Eliot, and (most
successfully) W. B. Yeats. Yeats's Abbey Theater, in Dublin, contributed the
closest thing to European avant-garde drama in the naturalist experiments of
Sean O'Casey and J. M. Synge. It is notable, in fact, that the most important
figures in modern British drama were all Irish by birth: O'Casey, Shaw, Synge,
and Yeats, along with Oscar Wilde at the beginning of the modern period and
Samuel Beckett at the end.

Like Wilde, Shaw took hypocrisy as one of his major themes (see
Chapter Two). His best works combined Wilde's wit and Ibsen's seriousness
of purpose, seeking always to reveal the bogus values of various segments of
English society. Shaw left Ireland for England as a young man and, like many
other modern dramatists, wrote novels and criticism before turning to the
theater. The director of the Independent Theatre in London, J. T. Grein, who
had produced Ibsen's *Ghosts* and Emile Zola's *Thérèse Raquin* (1867), encouraged Shaw to start writing plays when he was almost forty. His best early plays
treat contemporary social issues humorously through the satirical use of love
plots and melodrama. Although their content challenges the ruling ideologies
of the late Victorian period, their form is often, as Shaw put it, "pleasant."
For example, in *Arms and the Man* (1894), set during a war between Bulgaria
and Serbia, a Bulgarian girl falls in love with a cowardly Swiss mercenary,
"her chocolate cream soldier," who carries chocolate instead of ammunition
and conveniently inherits a fortune during the denouement. The mercenary's
cowardice and straight talk about war do little to undermine the audience's
pleasure at the well-made plot. Similarly, in *Major Barbara* (1905) the conflict
between the idealism of the inefficient charity and the realism of the benevolent

arms manufacturer is resolved by a plot twist out of Wilde that draws on and at the same time parodies the well-made play. After the turn of the century, Shaw increasingly built his still rather conventional forms around a conflict of ideas. He frequently attached long prefaces to the printed versions of his plays, which were often published before they had been performed; he also took to an extreme the modern tendency to print long narrative stage directions, by which the playwright tries to indicate how the play should be acted.

Shaw's best-known work, *Pygmalion* (1913), premiered in Vienna in German translation before shocking the London theater world with Eliza Doolittle's exclamation "not bloody likely." It features professor of phonetics Henry Higgins, who passes the flowergirl Eliza off as a duchess by teaching her how to enunciate. Here, the worldly wisdom is distributed more widely among the characters. Although a classic Cinderella-style marriage plot is anticipated, Eliza will not be seduced by the brilliance of her mentor and winds up marrying the upper-class twit Freddy Eynsford-Hill instead. Her father, Alfred P. Doolittle, seems most successful at gaming the system. A self-proclaimed specimen of the "undeserving poor," he manages to make a good life for himself by becoming respectable and preaching about his repentance. Bertolt Brecht, a playwright of ideas who greatly admired Shaw, seems to have drawn aspects of the beggar king Mr. Peachum in *The Threepenny Opera* (1928) from such Shavian models. Like Brecht's ballad opera, *Pygmalion* achieved great fame. In the musical version, *My Fair Lady* (1956; filmed 1964), the conventional happy ending is provided: Eliza stays with Higgins. Shaw's social critique is entirely muted in the play's more distant progeny, the Hollywood comedy *Pretty Woman* (1990).

Compared with the work of the German expressionists or the French surrealists, Shaw's major work seems very traditional. The two most important examples of Shaw's more experimental theater are *Man and Superman* (1903) and *Heartbreak House* (1919). *Man and Superman* revolves around a typical Shavian love plot: the orphaned Ann Whitefield wants to marry her youthful guardian Jack Tanner, despite his reputation as a revolutionist (Shaw published the "revolutionist's handbook" ostensibly written by Tanner in the printed version of the play). She pursues him to Spain, where he is briefly taken prisoner by a group of brigands who spend their spare time debating political philosophy. What makes the play unusual is the lengthy third act, a dream sequence published separately as "Don Juan in Hell," and seldom performed. Unlike the contemporary dream plays of August Strindberg, "Don Juan in Hell" follows a logical sequence. The dream is Tanner's. In it, figures from Mozart's opera *Don Giovanni*, who correspond to the characters in Shaw's play, debate the nature of marriage and the coming of the (Nietzschean) superman. Although Tanner aspires to superman status, he eventually decides to submit to the "Life Force" and marry Ann. Shaw's feminism competes here with his dedication to hero worship; this time the result is the expected comic one.

   *Heartbreak House*, though first produced after the First World War, is set before it, in a vague Edwardian neverland. Subtitled a "Fantasia in the Russian Manner on English Themes," it (alone among Shaw's plays) betrays the influence of Anton Chekhov. The guests at Shaw's country estate, however, have an allegorical character, representing industry, the arts, idealism, feminism, and the aristocracy. The idealistic but practical young woman Ellie Dunn considers various suitors but falls in love with the aged Captain Shotover, modeled on Shaw himself. The play seems to represent prewar life as a pathetic illusion dominated by materialism and narrow-mindedness. Shotover has been designing a weapon that will destroy half of Europe. Shaw was a determined pacifist and was widely attacked for his antiwar pamphlet, *Common Sense About the War* (1914). Yet in the final scene of *Heartbreak House*, when an air raid destroys the Captain's stash of dynamite (and kills two minor characters), Shaw seems almost to be embracing the war as, in F. T. Marinetti's words "sole hygiene of the world."[35] After the war, Shaw attempted some rather grandiose experiments in representing world history on the stage, including *Back to Methuselah* (1921) and *St. Joan* (1923), a theme taken up again by Brecht in his *St. Joan of the Stockyards* (1932). The plays tended to become more preachy and less dramatically compelling, but Shaw remained the most important modern British dramatist of his time and defined a uniquely English form of modern drama.[36]

   Elements of the Irish theater took a more experimental approach, though some of the group clustered around the Abbey Theatre in Dublin shared Shaw's commitment to a realist theater treating contemporary social problems. The Abbey was the offspring of the Irish Literary Theater, devoted to the development of an Irish drama that would explore artistic problems free of involvement in direct political debates. Lady Augusta Gregory, one of the founders, explored Irish myth and peasant life in a somewhat idealized fashion, but with a masterful command of dialect. Synge, who had been teaching English in Paris, was persuaded by Yeats to go and live among the peasants in the rural west of Ireland and his plays are naturalistic representations of peasant life; they tended to shock Irish audiences because of their unidealized representation of rural violence and sexuality. The most famous attack on Synge's work was that on *The Playboy of the Western World*, a comedy on the classical subject of patricide. Audiences rioted after the premiere in Dublin in 1907 and again in several American cities when the company toured the United States in 1911–12, but Lady Gregory and Yeats defended Synge, who died of Hodgkins disease at the age of thirty-seven. The Abbey continued its work and upheld its high artistic standards after Irish independence, but a similar sense of outrage met the works of one of its later playwrights, O'Casey. His *Juno and the Paycock* (1924) and *The Plough and the Stars* (1926) examined working-class life in Dublin during the struggle for independence and the Irish civil war. Irish audiences rioted at the premiere of *The Plough and the Stars*, which represents the Easter Rebellion of 1916 rather less sympathetically than Yeats did in his famous poem (see Chapter Three).[37]

Yeats himself was disgusted that Irish audiences could not stomach Synge's and O'Casey's work. Yet his own theater had little in common with their naturalism. His early plays, such as *The Countess Cathleen* (1892) and *Cathleen ni Houlihan* (1902), deal with Irish political matters, but in a highly symbolic fashion, evoking myth as well as history (the Great Famine and the uprising of 1798, respectively). Written in blank verse, they are a far cry from naturalism. In the first decade of the twentieth century, his plays increasingly concerned themselves with the struggle between poetic and political forms of power. As Yeats drifted away from the Abbey Theater, with its naturalistic predispositions and narrow-minded audiences, he became more and more interested in varieties of abstract drama. Better informed than most English-language writers about avant-garde European theater (he had, after all, witnessed the premiere of *King Ubu* in 1896), Yeats developed a fascination with Japanese Noh drama. He used a system of screens designed by Craig to stage his plays at the Abbey in 1911, and his *Four Plays for Dancers* (1920) reflect this interest and make use of masks and choruses.

Naturalist drama was born out of Ibsen's turn away from verse. One thing that marked Yeats off from contemporary English playwrights was that he wrote in verse, and two other major poets of the period, Auden and Eliot, also turned to writing drama. (For Auden's plays, see Chapter Seven.) Eliot wrote one expressionist-influenced play, *Sweeney Agonistes* (published in fragmentary form in 1926–7, first performed in 1933), about Sweeney, a gangster type who revels in recounting the exploits of a wife-murderer (who may be Sweeney himself). He proposes to take his girlfriend Doris to "a cannibal isle" where nothing happens but "[b]irth, and copulation, and death." The play shares the mood of *The Waste Land* (1922), in which Sweeney also figures. The London production by the Group Theater in 1934 featured masks and ritualized drumming; Brecht saw and admired it.[38] In the year of that production, Eliot turned to a very different sort of ritualized drama, the pageant play. Performed at the Chapter House of Canterbury Cathedral, and later in London, *Murder in the Cathedral* (1935) tells the story of the martyrdom of Thomas à Becket, Archbishop of Canterbury, murdered by henchmen of Henry II (see Chapter Four). The theme was the subject of an annual pageant. Eliot's version features a chorus of the women of Canterbury and touches on a number of themes from

*The Waste Land*, here transformed into a distinctively Christian vision. Like the poetic dramas of Yeats, *Murder in the Cathedral* treats the competition between political power and poetic vision, here the Christian vision of Becket himself. While the Chorus speaks in highly ritualized verse, the four knights who kill Becket speak in modern prose, justifying their deed in the manner of faceless bureaucrats. Eliot envisioned drama as "the ideal medium" for verse and "the most direct means of social 'usefulness' for poetry."[39] However, his later plays, while drawing on Greek myth to illuminate modern life, became increasingly indistinguishable from the commercial theater whose conventions they were intended to recast.

Some American dramatists played a part in European avant-garde movements between the wars, notably Thornton Wilder, who domesticated metatheater, and Eugene O'Neill, whose early, expressionist works won him the Nobel Prize for Literature in 1936, before he turned to naturalism in his major late works. Naturalism tended to dominate the postwar American drama of Arthur Miller and Tennessee Williams as well. In Europe the years after the Second World War witnessed a renewed vigor in modern drama. Undoubtedly the most influential modern playwright from the English-speaking world, Beckett, is discussed in the Conclusion below. Unlike the work of Shaw, Yeats, and the others, Beckett's plays, beginning with *Waiting for Godot* (1952), belonged to the mainstream of modern European drama. Beckett, who wrote in French, arguably belongs as much to the French as to the English stage; however, he translated his works into English and had a tremendous impact on postmodernist British and American drama. Beckett's work brings the English-language and European modern traditions together, just as it also bridges the major dramatic movements of the early twentieth century. Modern drama had to wait until after the Second World War for Beckett's synthesis of its competing tendencies: the theater of ideas and the theater of spectacle, the expressionist dream play and the surrealist celebration of the absurd, antitheater and metatheater, naturalism and antinaturalism.

## Further reading

### Literary works

Michael Benedikt and George E. Wellwarth, ed. and trans., *Modern French Theatre*. New York: Dutton, 1966.

Anton Chekhov, *The Plays of Anton Chekhov*, trans. Paul Schmidt. New York: HarperCollins, 1997.

Henrik Ibsen, *The Complete Major Prose Plays*, trans. Rolf Fjelde. New York: New
    American Library, 1978.
Luigi Pirandello, *Collected Plays*, ed. Robert Rietty, 2 vols. New York: Riverrun,
    1987–8.
August Strindberg, *Strindberg: Five Plays*, trans. Harry G. Carlson. Berkeley and
    Los Angeles: University of California Press, 1983.

### Contemporary critical statements

Antonin Artaud, *The Theater and its Double*, trans. Mary Caroline Richards. New
    York: Grove, 1958.
Eric Bentley, ed. *The Theory of the Modern Stage*. Harmondsworth: Penguin, 1968.
Bertolt Brecht, *Brecht on Theatre*, ed. and trans. John Willett. New York: Hill and
    Wang, 1964.
Gordon Craig, *On Movement and Dance*, ed. Arnold Rood. London: Dance
    Books, 1978.

### Later criticism

Lionel Abel, *Metatheatre: A New View of Dramatic Form*. New York: Hill and
    Wang, 1963.
Oscar G. Brockett and Robert R. Findlay, *Century of Innovation: A History of
    European and American Theatre and Drama Since 1870*. Englewood Cliffs,
    NJ: Prentice-Hall, 1973.
Richard Brustein, *The Theatre of Revolt: An Approach to the Modern Drama*.
    Boston: Little, Brown, 1964.
Elinor Fuchs, *The Death of Character: Perspectives on Theater after Modernism*.
    Bloomington: Indiana University Press, 1996.
Richard Gilman, *The Making of Modern Drama*. New York: Farrar, Straus, and
    Giroux, 1974.
Christopher Innes, *Modern British Drama: The Twentieth Century*. Cambridge:
    Cambridge University Press, 2002.
Martin Puchner, *Stage Fright: Modernism, Anti-Theatricality, and Drama*.
    Baltimore: Johns Hopkins University Press, 2002.
Roger Shattuck, *The Banquet Years: The Origins of the Avant-Garde in France,
    1885 to World War I*, rev. edn. reprint. New York: Books for Libraries, 1972.
Bert O. States, *Great Reckonings in Little Rooms: On the Phenomenology of Theater*.
    Berkeley and Los Angeles: University of California Press, 1985.
John Willett, *The Theatre of Bertolt Brecht*, 3rd edn. New York: New Directions,
    1968.

# Part III

## *Fate*

*Chapter 7*

# Literature and politics

---

In a note to the final section of *The Waste Land* (1922), T. S. Eliot quoted the view of the German novelist Hermann Hesse that "Already half of Europe, already at least half of Eastern Europe, is on the way to Chaos." Eliot presented this chaos as following close behind the movement of civilization from east to west:

> Who are those hooded hordes swarming
> Over endless plains, stumbling in cracked earth
> Ringed by the flat horizon only
> What is the city over the mountains
> Cracks and reforms and bursts in the violet air
> Falling towers
> Jerusalem Athens Alexandria
> Vienna London
> Unreal

The "hooded hordes" come from the east, like the Huns; Eliot's "endless plains" were "Polish plains" in an earlier draft. All the cities Eliot lists had at one time served as cultural capitals, whether Jewish, Greek, Byzantine, or European, and all, apart from London, had been attacked and occupied from the east. The postwar world in which Eliot wrote *The Waste Land* was haunted by the prospect of what the German philosopher Oswald Spengler analyzed, in his study of 1918, as *The Decline of the West*. Eliot seems to have feared that the Russian Revolution of 1917 would spur further invasions, whether literal or figurative, that would overwhelm first Vienna, which lay near the border between Slavic and western Christendom, and ultimately London, the capital of the British Empire. The world of Eliot's poem, having barely survived one major catastrophe, seems destined for further upheavals. Many of the modernists of the 1920s shared Eliot's sense of a coming crisis in Western culture.[1]

Abroad, the crisis was already apparent in German economic catastrophe and political instability, the rise of fascism in Italy, and the upheavals consequent on the revolution in Russia. In England the 1920s were in fact a decade of prosperity, but the aftermath of the First World War and the rise of communism and fascism suggested to many that the individualism of the nineteenth century would be replaced by "collectivism," either of the left or of the right, in the twentieth. Labor unrest led to a General Strike in England in 1926, and the worldwide economic depression that began in 1929 made many western Europeans and Americans pessimistic about the future of liberal democracy. By the early 1930s, with Adolf Hitler's ascendancy in Germany, a Second World War seemed imminent to some observers. Writers and artists responded to these crises in various ways. The Russian cubo-futurists celebrated the communist revolution, while their Italian counterparts, F. T. Marinetti's futurists, saluted the fascists. The regimes in Russia and Italy at first supported those modernists who put their techniques at the service of the state. Ultimately, though, as the revolutionary regimes became increasingly totalitarian, they demanded propaganda and not experiment from their artists. In the Soviet Union an officially sanctioned style of art, socialist realism, explicitly rejected modernism and sought "realistic" but uplifting images of working people living in harmony with the regime. By 1934, it was the only permitted style of art. Unlike the Italian fascists, the German Nazis took an unremittingly hostile view of modern art; after Hitler became chancellor in 1933, all art had to serve the regime. Modernists were persecuted as purveyors of "degenerate art," and most major artists and writers fled the country.

The consequences for English modernism were complex. Some modernists, like D. H. Lawrence and W. B. Yeats, tended to identify the artistic visionary with the new type of authoritarian leader seen in both fascist Italy and Soviet Russia, and many younger authors addressed the theme of leadership, which seemed to them lacking in Depression era England. W. H. Auden wrote with mixed admiration and revulsion of "the truly strong man." Other major modernists, who had become establishment figures in the 1920s, tended to stick to their earlier views on the separation of art and politics. Whether conservative like Eliot, liberal like E. M. Forster, or pacifist and feminist like Virginia Woolf, they defended art's autonomy, its isolation from political concerns. Younger writers such as Auden and George Orwell, however, sensing the political crises of the 1930s, at first wanted their writings to challenge capitalism and bring about an era of greater social justice. They participated in a debate that engulfed the European left as to whether realist or modernist techniques better served these political goals. Although, as the discussion of Gustave Flaubert has shown (see Chapter One), realism inspired much of modernism, in the 1930s the two movements were seen as opposed. Realism stood for the continuation of the nineteenth-century goal of representing reality as it is, whereas modernism celebrated the crisis of representation and the abandoning of verisimilitude.

The major writers of the 1930s in Britain sought an art that would combine the aesthetic complexity of modernism with a more direct moral or political message, but when a choice had to be made between the two, they tended to choose the moral and political over the aesthetic. One major theme of the literature of the 1930s was the conflict between the private desires of the individual, especially the individual artist, and the political demands of the time. The theme is announced in Auden's epigraph to his first major work, *The Orators* (1932): "Private faces in public places / Are wiser and nicer / Than public faces in private places." A few years later, defending his lack of commitment to any political cause, Forster expressed a faith in the private values espoused by liberal individualism in related terms: "I hate the idea of causes, and if I had to choose between betraying my country and betraying my friend, I hope I should have the guts to betray my country."[2] The tide of history, however, seemed to run against private faces and friendships and in favor of public causes and ideology. The political ambiguity of much modernism, and the increasing politicization of the rest, made modernist concerns with aesthetic form and experimentalism seem less than urgent in the context of economic depression, political radicalization, and approaching war. After the Second World War, although much important modern art and literature continued to be produced, most would feel that the great age of experiment known as "modernist" was over. This chapter describes the political crises of the years between the two world wars – primarily, the spread of communism and the rise of fascism – and the ways in which they shaped the arts. I end by discussing the effects of the conflict between left and right on writers of the 1930s and the literary consequences of the Spanish Civil War.

## Communism and the left

The Great October Revolution of 1917 in Russia established a "dictatorship of the proletariat" under Vladimir Ilich Lenin, the head of the Bolshevik faction of the Marxist Social Democratic Party. Lenin nationalized most industry, signed a separate peace with Germany at Brest-Litovsk, had the Tsar and his family executed, defeated the counterrevolutionary Whites in a civil war, and established the Union of Soviet Socialist Republics, encompassing most of the old Russian Empire. The Russian civil war and the resulting famine led to perhaps twenty million deaths. After Lenin's death in 1924, Joseph Stalin defeated Leon Trotsky in a power struggle, becoming general secretary of the Communist Party and, in effect, dictator for life. Rejecting Trotsky's goal of a "permanent revolution" that would spread socialism outside Soviet borders, Stalin accepted the limitations of "socialism in one country," while still funding the communist movements in Western Europe. Stalin relied on the secret police to help him root out potential enemies. Trotsky, exiled from the Soviet Union in 1929, was murdered in Mexico in 1940, almost certainly on Stalin's orders. Stalin's purges of the party and society in the 1930s, and in particular the show-trials of anyone thought to be sympathetic to Trotsky, exemplified Soviet totalitarianism. It is estimated that Stalin had eight million Soviet citizens imprisoned or killed for alleged political crimes.

Despite its blood-soaked history, the Soviet Union held a great appeal for Western European intellectuals in the 1930s, as a possible model of a more just social order, an alternative economic organization, and the best hope for defeating fascism. Western intellectuals, including André Malraux, Paul Robeson, George Bernard Shaw, Beatrice and Sydney Webb, and H. G. Wells, visited Russia and expressed their admiration for the Soviet experiment. The highly centralized economy of the Soviet Union, in which most property belonged either to the state or to collective farms, did succeed in rapidly industrializing Russia, though advances in heavy industry were offset by losses in agriculture and consumer goods. These successes contrasted favorably with the ongoing crisis of Western capitalism. Later, many intellectuals of both left and right would recognize the terrors of Stalin's regime. In 1946 George Orwell published *Animal Farm*, an allegory of the revolution, in which the pigs Napoleon and Snowball lead the animals in a successful uprising against Farmer Jones. After differing with him on the future of the revolution, Napoleon has Snowball chased off the farm by nine vicious dogs, and his propagandist Squealer proceeds to attribute all problems associated with the running of the farm and building of a windmill to the machinations of the exiled "traitor" Snowball and his followers, just as Stalin had purged the Soviet Union of alleged Trotskyites. The pigs come to dominate the other animals and reverse the principles of "Animalism." One morning the central slogan "All animals are equal," painted on the wall of the barn, has been mysteriously revised: "All animals are equal, but some animals are more equal than others." Eventually, the pigs begin to emulate humans, walking around on two legs and rewriting the other great slogan of the revolution, "four legs good, two legs bad," as "four legs good, two legs better." The pigs start to socialize with the neighboring human farmers, and the other animals discover, to their dismay, that they can no longer tell which are the humans and which are the pigs. Orwell's brilliant satire of communism derived much of its force from his own disillusionment; although he had never actively supported the Communist Party, he had fought side by side with the communists in the Spanish Civil War and seen, at first hand, the implications of Stalin's dictatorship for political dissent. In 1949 such former Western communists and sympathizers as André Gide, Arthur Koestler, Ignazio Silone, Stephen Spender, and Richard Wright wrote of their disenchantment with the Soviet Union in a collection of essays, *The God that Failed*, casting communism as a false religion rather than a traditional political system. In the 1930s, however, this religion still held its appeal as a bulwark against the apocalypse that was threatening Europe in the form of Nazi Germany.

In the early years after the revolution, the avant-garde played an important role in developing the cultural policies of the new Russia. At first, the Russian futurists supported the communist government as eagerly as their Italian brothers would later support fascism. Vladimir Mayakovsky became a leading propagandist of the revolution and claimed that it had "thrown up on to the streets the unpolished speech of the masses" that would serve as the basis for a new socialist poetry.[3] His poem "Left March" became an emblem of futurist commitment to the revolution:

> Hold
> your proletarian hand
> tight on the world's throat!
> Deck out the sky with drape!
> March boldly ahead, don't be late!
> Who's marching out of step?
> Left!
> Left!
> Left![4]

Mayakovsky had his greatest prerevolutionary success with an avant-garde tragedy about himself called simply *Vladimir Mayakovsky* (1913), written and performed by him when he was twenty. He went on to write a long poem commemorating another Vladimir, the father of the revolution, *Vladimir Ilich Lenin* (1924). Other avant-garde movements also allied themselves with communism. The constructivists, who had been pioneers of abstract sculpture, made use of experimental architecture and design to help meet the needs of the new society. The most famous monument of the era was never actually built; Vladimir Tatlin's "Monument to the Third International" (figure 9) was a giant steel and glass tower of spiral construction designed to house the headquarters of the international association of communist parties. The tower was

9. Vladimir Tatlin (1895–1956), *Model of the Monument to the Third International*, 1920. PA76. Digital Image. © The Museum of Modern Art/Licensed by SCALA/Art Resource, NY. The Museum of Modern Art, New York.

to comprise three buildings in geometrical forms – cube, pyramid, cylinder – each one revolving at a different rate (the cube annually, the pyramid monthly, and the cylinder daily). Despite its impracticality, it had an iconic status as an Eiffel Tower, or perhaps a Tower of Babel, for the communist movement. Owing to technological constraints, construction, planned for the banks of the River Neva in Petrograd (St. Petersburg), never began.

This burst of experimentalism gave way, however, to demands for greater political and artistic orthodoxy, which ultimately led to total suppression of modernism in the era of Stalin's purges. The Soviet Writers' Union pronounced that socialist realism should represent "reality not as it is but as it ought to be." Works following this dictum celebrated the new socialist economy; *A True Tractor Story* and others have been summarized as following the standard plot "boy meets girl meets tractor."[5] In this context, the avant-gardes did not fare well. After being attacked for his bourgeois sensibility, and facing demands that he write in a more proletarian style, Mayakovsky came to despise Stalin. He was eventually attacked for his criticisms of the regime in such satirical plays as *The Bedbug* (1929) and *The Bathhouse* (1930); in the latter play he represented Stalin as the mindless bureaucrat Pobedonosikov ("Nose for Victory"). Mayakovsky committed suicide in 1930; once he was safely dead and no longer capable of criticizing the regime, Stalin rehabilitated him, declaring in 1935 that "Mayakovsky was and remains the best and most talented poet of our Soviet era."[6] The poet Osip Mandelstam, whose aesthetic shared something with that of the English imagists, also became a critic of the regime; he died in one of Stalin's concentration camps in 1938. Tatlin's constructivism and Malevich's suprematism were likewise criticized for their divergence from the norms of socialist realism. Most forms of modernist art and literature were banned and all works suffered heavy censorship for political content.

Outside Russia, unaffected by Soviet policy, many avant-garde and modernist artists retained their sympathy for the revolution while continuing to engage in literary experiments. The surrealist André Breton, and many of his collaborators, allied themselves somewhat uneasily with the international communist movement. The surrealists, the immediate successors of dada (see Chapter Three), aimed to tap into the unconscious and reveal the irrational side of the human mind. Inspired by Sigmund Freud, Breton defined surrealism as "Psychic automatism in its pure state, by which one proposes to express – verbally, by means of the written word, or in any other manner – the actual functioning of thought."[7] The surrealists were, in fact, relatively uninterested in formal experiments of the sort attempted by earlier avant-gardes. Rather, they concerned themselves with the content of art: they encouraged surprising or disturbing juxtapositions intended to shake the mind free of rationality.

Surrealist painters such as Max Ernst made extensive use of collage and non-sensical titles but painted fairly straightforward images of a dreamlike world. The surrealists dominated the avant-garde art scene of the 1920s, but in many ways they turned away from the typical concerns of artistic modernism with form and experiment. They attempted automatic writing, recording whatever letters their hands formed, ostensibly without conscious control (rather like a Ouija board). Their most enduring literary works, however, were two novels about life in Paris in the 1920s, Louis Aragon's *Nightwalker* (1926) and Breton's *Nadja* (1928). Both novels celebrated the magic and the marvelous in the context of the random urban encounter, but did so in fairly straightforward prose.

The surrealists' irrationalism did not sit well with official communism, but Breton sought an ever closer alliance with the French Communist Party, which he joined in 1926. For some years he published a journal called *The Surrealist Revolution*, whose title he changed in 1929 to *Surrealism in Service of the Revolution*, thus marking the politicization of the movement and the submission of aesthetic to political concerns. Aragon valued his links to communism over those to surrealism; when he joined the party in 1927, he broke with Breton. Like many radical political parties, the surrealists themselves were afflicted with constant infighting, and Breton would frequently expel from the movement those artists or writers who seemed to swerve from surrealist principles in their work or their politics. He eventually became disillusioned with communism, however, and left the party in 1935. In France, as in Russia, aesthetic and political radicalism did not easily mesh.

Only in the theater did one major proponent of the modern movement remain on good terms with the Soviet regime. Although sometimes criticized as bourgeois in his concerns, Konstantin Stanislavsky, director of the Moscow Art Theater, came to be seen as an exemplar of socialist realism on the stage. Stanislavsky had been the first to produce Anton Chekhov's plays successfully (see Chapter Six). He was known for his careful re-enactment of reality, whether historical or contemporary, as in his 1902 production of *The Lower Depths*, by Maxim Gorky, a naturalist who would later be a literary hero of the Soviet regime. The play concerns life in a doss-house, and Stanislavsky had his actors visit doss-houses and observe behavior there in order to understand their parts better. Stanislavsky's system involved leading each actor to understand the "inner justification" of his or her character; this meant that the actor had to inhabit the character's personality, both on- and offstage, and try to imagine the character's reactions to hypothetical events, even those not in the script. Through its introduction into American theater by Lee Strasberg, Stanislavsky's system (known in the United States simply as "the Method") had a major impact on the naturalistic style of acting in the late twentieth century, most famously represented by Marlon Brando's portrayal of Stanley Kowalski in Tennessee Williams's *A Streetcar Named Desire* (1947), filmed by Elia Kazan in 1951. While it made such headway in the United States, Stanislavsky's system also became the official acting style of the Soviet Union, and his Moscow Art Theater was awarded the Order of Lenin. What made Stanislavsky's method acceptable to the proponents of socialist realism was its emphasis on illusion: like the realist and naturalist theater of the late nineteenth century, it sought to maintain the illusion of reality on the stage, to portray life as it is, or ought to be.[8] Despite the early attempts to create a revolutionary art appropriate to revolutionary times, the Soviet Union ultimately became the conservative champion of a late brand of realism, founded in the bourgeois nineteenth century but adapted to the proletarian twentieth.

## Weimar Germany

The writer who most successfully combined communism and aesthetic modernism, Bertolt Brecht, broke with the realist dedication to illusionism typical of Konstantin Stanislavsky. Brecht developed his views on politics and drama during the revolutionary years after the First World War, first as a medical student in Munich and later as a playwright in Berlin (see Chapter Six). His contribution to the theater began in one of the hotbeds of modernism between the wars, Weimar Germany. At the end of the war in 1918, Kaiser Wilhelm II abdicated in the midst of an abortive revolution, led by socialists in Munich and communists in Berlin. Hoping to avoid outright revolution, the Social Democratic Chancellor Friedrich Ebert allied himself uneasily with the forces of order, notably the army. The communist leaders Karl Liebknecht and Rosa Luxembourg were murdered while in army custody in January 1919. In the following month, a right-wing nobleman killed Kurt Eisner, who had been leading a revolutionary socialist government in Munich. A new Soviet Republic was briefly proclaimed in Munich under the leadership of the expressionist playwright Ernst Toller and some like-minded intellectuals. The same year saw brief attempts at Soviet-style revolution in nearby Budapest and Vienna. All were put down, amid considerable bloodshed; in Germany, order was reestablished under a new, democratic constitution.

A newly elected National Assembly approved the constitution at Weimar, a town in central Germany that had been the home of the great poets Goethe and Schiller. The Weimar Republic faced serious challenges, not only from the revolutionaries on the left, but also from the militarist right, who resented the concessions made by the new government to the allied victors of the First World War. The Treaty of Versailles of 1919 reassigned much of the old German Empire to France, Poland, and other states; divided its overseas colonies among the victorious powers; and imposed heavy reparations payments. The economist and Bloomsbury figure John Maynard Keynes criticized the treaty as punitive in *The Economic Consequences of the Peace* (1919). The severe economic hardships suffered by Germany between the two world wars included unprecedented inflation, as the exchange rate for the mark fell from four to the dollar before the war to 4,200,000,000,000 to the dollar in November, 1923. Germans were reduced to carting their wages home in wheelbarrows and spending them immediately, so as to avoid the twice-daily price rises. This instability fueled the growth of right-wing radicalism, notably a failed coup (the "Beer Hall Putsch") led by Adolf Hitler in Munich at the height of the inflation in November 1923. Yet despite impending doom, Weimar Germany provided a congenial atmosphere for social and artistic experiments. The combination of liberal-democratic government and a sense of living on a precipice helped to spur this experimentalism. In the late 1920s the English writers Wystan Hugh Auden and Christopher Isherwood went to live in Berlin, which was famous for its discarding of the old conventions governing women's roles and homosexuality. As Isherwood later recalled, "One of my chief motives for wanting to visit Berlin was that an elderly relative had warned me against it, saying it was the vilest place since Sodom."[9] In the arts this was the heroic phase of German modernism, the years of Brecht's first plays, the founding of the Bauhaus (see below), the major novels of Hermann Hesse and Thomas Mann, and the expressionist movement.

Expressionism was the name not so much of an organized group as of the general modernist tendency in German art, which began by emphasizing angular forms, bold colors, and the breaking of "rules" (see Chapter Two). The novelist Kasimir Edschmid, in a Baudelairean vein, saw expressionism as celebrating modern life and finding "humanity in the whores and the divine in the factories."[10] In 1919, the year the new constitution was ratified in Weimar, the architect Walter Gropius founded the Bauhaus there. This workshop employed the expressionist painters Wassily Kandinsky and Paul Klee and taught modern art, architecture, and design, with an emphasis on applied art, until it was closed by the Nazis in 1933. The Bauhaus manifesto announced that "the artist is an exalted craftsman" and its program concerned a fusion of the arts in service of society. It thus shared some of the ideals of the new republic. Although many Bauhaus artists were influenced by expressionism, the Bauhaus artistic ideal was much sparer than that of the first expressionists. Later directed by Ludwig Mies van der Rohe, the Bauhaus was a catalyst in the development of the so-called "International Style" of modernist architecture. Modernist architects insisted that "form follows function"; every portion of a building should serve a function and not simply prettify a façade. Van der Rohe famously expressed this aesthetic in the slogan "less is more." This in practice meant an emphasis on almost abstract form and on unadorned building materials, such as glass, steel, and concrete. The International Style rejected ornamentalism and created sometimes severe buildings that became the most visible symbols of artistic modernism.

Film and photography held a particular fascination for left-wing intellectuals, particularly those who felt the urge to document the social and political ills of their time. The *neue Sachlichkeit* (New Objectivity or New Matter-of-Factness), which largely supplanted expressionism in the later 1920s, used some modernist techniques but emphasized the depiction of social problems; like surrealism, it developed out of dada toward more direct political engagement than the earlier avant-gardes had sought. The concern with objective, and sometimes satirical, representation of social life became widespread in European literature by the 1930s, partly as a reaction against "high" modernism. Isherwood began his memoir of Berlin under the Weimar Republic by describing his vision as that of the camera eye: "I am a camera with its shutter open, quite passive, recording, not thinking." This emphasis on the passivity of the writer was closely linked to the documentary urge to record a rapidly disintegrating reality. Isherwood lived in Berlin from 1929 to 1933, but published his fictionalized memoir of these years, *Goodbye to Berlin*, only in 1939, when Hitler had destroyed the Berlin of the Weimar years. *Goodbye to Berlin* chronicles a number of figures who were experimenting with sexual and social roles at the time, most famously Sally Bowles, the cabaret singer and aspiring actress who, despite her often sordid sexual affairs, remains for Isherwood quintessentially a naïve English girl of good family. For young English writers, especially homosexuals like Auden and Isherwood, Berlin in these years meant everything that Paris had meant for American writers from Henry James to F. Scott Fitzgerald and Ernest Hemingway: artistic experiment, laxer social mores, and especially sexual license. The anti-Semitic incidents, violence, and political crisis of these years, just before Hitler's rise to power, appear only around the edges of *Goodbye to Berlin*, and Isherwood wrote of one prosperous young Berliner that, "Like everyone else in Berlin, she refers continually to the political situation, but only briefly, with a conventional melancholy, as when one speaks of religion. It is quite unreal to her." Isherwood himself represented the politics of the period only in their appearance of unreality.

The early plays of Brecht grow out of this expressionist atmosphere (see Chapter Six). By 1930 however, he had articulated his theory of the epic theater.

In the early 1930s he wrote a number of didactic *Lehrstücke* (teaching plays) with clear political messages. In the most infamous of these, *The Measures Taken* (1930), four communist revolutionaries who have been agitating in China justify their decision to execute a fifth because he had delayed the revolution by performing charitable work. Neither Brecht nor the chorus representing the Communist Party objects to this political decision. As a result, in addition to condoning Stalinism, the play lacks dramatic effectiveness – no competing point of view is represented. Brecht's later plays, written in exile, show considerably greater political and dramatic sophistication. Several deal directly with Nazism, including the series of related one-act plays *The Private Life of the Master Race* (1935–38, but not performed until 1945), and *The Resistible Rise of Arturo Ui* (written in 1941, performed in 1948), in which the career of a Chicago gangster parallels that of Hitler. Less ideological than Brecht's other major plays, *The Life of Galileo* (1943) describes the dilemma of the intellectual in authoritarian times. Other works written before or during the war put Brecht's ideas of epic theater into practice (see Chapter Six). In the parable-play *The Good Person of Szechwan* (1943), the Chinese prostitute Shen Te, the good person of the title, disguises herself as her brutal cousin Shui Ta, a successful capitalist. When, as Shui Ta, she is suspected of having murdered the missing Shen Te, she is put on trial. Unmasking herself, she explains that she "could not / Be good at once to others and myself." The image of the good woman divided into two parts epitomizes Brecht's alienation effect: capitalism makes it impossible for the good person to remain whole. In another parable-play, *The Caucasian Chalk Circle* (1948), Brecht again makes use of role-playing, storytelling, and metatheater to create the distancing effects of his epic theater.

Brecht's greatest play, *Mother Courage and Her Children* (first performed in 1941), makes use of elements of parable, but, like *Galileo*, it is set in a specific historical moment, in this case during the Thirty Years War in the seventeenth century. This was a time of conflict in Europe between Protestants and Catholics that seems to parallel the conflict among communists, Nazis, and the democratic West, which was just about to result in open warfare when Brecht wrote the play. Mother Courage is a small-time war profiteer who carts goods around to sell to the Swedish army and switches her religion when convenient. At the beginning of the play, she tells the fortunes of two soldiers and winds up by predicting the death of all three of her children. The deaths are caused by the war that also provides Mother Courage's livelihood. Her feeble-minded son Swiss Cheese dies when he refuses to turn over the regimental cashbox he has promised to protect. Although Mother Courage bargains to save him, she cannot agree on a price, and he is shot while she haggles. Threatened with death if she acknowledges him, she denies knowing her dead son. Her other son, Eilif, is celebrated as a war hero for his success as a looter, but then continues his looting during peacetime and is shot. Her daughter, who is deaf and dumb, is shot when she tries to prevent a siege, again while her mother is too occupied with her business to care for her child. Mother Courage is left alone, and continues to pull her dilapidated cart behind her as she sells goods to the army. Mother Courage has a dual function like that of Shen Te in *The Good Person of Szechwan*: she claims that she is being good to her children by earning money to feed them, but they are killed in the war for which she provides supplies. Like Mac the Knife or Mr. Peachum in Brecht's *The Threepenny Opera* (1928), she voices a roguish cynicism, which makes her popular with audiences despite the ostensible message of the play that she is a war profiteer responsible for her children's deaths. Yet the play invites this sympathetic response. Brecht's wife Helene Weigel, who played Mother Courage in the Berliner Ensemble production after the war, encapsulated this sympathetic interpretation in the famous *gestus* of Mother Courage's silent scream when she realizes that Swiss Cheese is dead. As she says when she hears the drum roll announcing his execution, "I reckon I bargained too long." Yet at the end of the play, having lost all her children, she returns to her business, doggedly persevering and unable to see any other course.[11] The Thirty Years War becomes a symbol for the Second World War, and, despite Brecht's avowed communism, no political solution seems available to prevent the inevitable destructive force of war.

## Fascism, Nazism, and the right

During the years of revolutionary ardor in Russia and the founding of the Weimar Republic in Germany, fascism was being invented in Italy. Both F. T. Marinetti, the leader of the futurists, and Gabriele d'Annunzio, an aging decadent who had served in the Italian parliament under the slogan "Beyond Left and Right," had agitated in favor of Italian intervention in the First World War. They wanted to reclaim the Italian-speaking possessions of the Habsburg (Austro-Hungarian) Empire, including Trieste and Trent. Marinetti and d'Annunzio were joined in their agitation by an influential young journalist, Benito Mussolini, who had left the pacifist Socialist Party to promote war and revolution in his new newspaper, the *Popolo d'Italia*. Italy did eventually enter the war, on the side of England, France, and Russia. After the allied victory, the Italian border was redrawn, giving nationalists most of what they had demanded. However, one small town in Croatia, called Fiume in Italian and Rijeka in Croatian, was assigned to the new state of Yugoslavia, created out of the ruins of the Habsburg Empire. The town, with a significant

Italian-speaking population, became the object of huge protests, culminating in a coup led by d'Annunzio, who in 1919 invaded Fiume at the head of a ragtag army of demobilized soldiers, futurists, and nationalists. Having promulgated an authoritarian constitution that later served as a model for Mussolini's fascists, d'Annunzio managed to rule the town for fifteen months before being ousted by the Italian navy.

In the aftermath of Fiume, both Marinetti and d'Annunzio led paramilitary organizations in which university students and former combatants banded together, often breaking strikes and terrorizing their socialist opponents. These groups were soon superseded, however, by Mussolini's fascist movement, at first a loose organization of armed groups who seized power in several northern Italian cities. Amid industrial unrest and the collapse of the ruling Liberal coalition, Mussolini's Fascist Party entered parliament with thirty-five seats in 1921. In October 1922, he threatened to lead 100,000 black-shirted fascists in a March on Rome preparatory to a coup. Frightened by the possibility of civil war, King Victor Emmanuel III made Mussolini prime minister at the head of a government that included liberals and nationalists as well as fascists. After revising the electoral laws to favor his party, Mussolini held an election that gave him a huge majority in parliament. Although the fascists had come to power by quasi-legal means, they soon resorted to openly illegal tactics, notably the murder of the socialist opposition leader Giacomo Matteoti. When the other members of the coalition threatened to bolt, Mussolini declared himself dictator in January 1925. He held power until the Second World War, becoming more radical in the 1930s after allying Italy to Adolf Hitler's Germany.

Some prominent modernists supported the fascist regime, most famously Ezra Pound, who moved from London to Italy in 1924 and spent much of the Second World War propagandizing for the fascists. After the War, Pound was charged with treason by the American authorities. His eccentric behavior was exacerbated by the harsh conditions of his imprisonment. His defense attorney claimed that he was insane and Pound was confined for twelve years in St. Elizabeths Hospital for the Criminally Insane in Washington, D.C. Marinetti praised Mussolini for his "marvelous Futurist temperament."[12] D'Annunzio, who was as famous for his love affairs as for his melodramatic novels and symbolist poetry, became a fascist elder statesman, receiving considerable patronage from Mussolini in exchange for his support. Even Luigi Pirandello, who was little involved in politics, joined the Fascist Party in the aftermath of the Matteoti assassination, thus helping to confer legitimacy on the new dictatorship. Each of these major Italian writers had already passed his creative peak by 1925, though Pirandello continued to stage his plays until 1928 and won the Nobel Prize for Literature in 1934.

Under fascism some avant-garde techniques were adapted to the purposes of propaganda. In a mirror-image of the leftist debate over expressionism, supporters of Mussolini's regime debated whether futurist techniques or a fascist realism would better serve the expression of the Italian spirit. The regime encouraged some artistic experimentation, with such results as *18 BL,* a massive spectacle with three thousand actors telling the story of a Fiat truck (model 18 BL) and its contribution to the fascist revolution.[13] In contrast, several Italian authors who opposed fascism, including Cesare Pavese, Ignazio Silone, and Elio Vittorini, focused on depictions of rural southern Italian life, far removed from the urban themes of fascist modernism. Mussolini tended to allow a certain leeway to prominent moderate critics of the regime such as the philosopher Benedetto Croce, but Pavese was imprisoned and Silone exiled. The links between leading modernists and the fascists contributed to the discrediting of modernism after the Second World War, and Italian literature and cinema of the 1940s and 1950s were dominated instead by a school of neorealism, committed to social justice and realistic representation of the lives of the poor.[14]

German Nazism was more virulent than Italian fascism. Born out of resentment at the loss of the First World War and the Treaty of Versailles, the Nazi movement did not achieve power until 1933, but when it did so it was much more radical than its Italian counterpart. Hitler combined the populism, authoritarianism, and militarism of Mussolini with anti-Semitism, adapted from the extreme right politics of prewar Vienna. Like Mussolini, Hitler was at first legally elected. His National Socialist Party had begun as a paramilitary organization which, again like the fascists, had terrorized the country. Nazi thugs were responsible for more than a hundred murders in 1931 and 1932. Nonetheless, in an atmosphere of rabid nationalism, high unemployment, and fear of communism, Hitler came second in the presidential elections of 1932 and won considerable support in the Reichstag (parliament). The following year, the elected president, Field-Marshal Hindenburg, asked Hitler to serve as chancellor (prime minister) of a coalition government. On the night of February 27, 1933, a fire was started in the Reichstag building, allegedly by a communist militant but possibly by the Nazis. Hitler used the threat of communist violence as an excuse to suspend the constitution. Shortly thereafter, he withdrew Germany from the League of Nations and began upon consolidation of his power, persecution of the Jews, and rearmament of Germany in preparation for a coming war, which would lead to the deaths of fifty-five million, including at least six million Jews and many homosexuals, gypsies, and political prisoners who died in Hitler's concentration camps.

In Nazi Germany there was none of the celebration of modernism typical of fascist Italy. Hitler himself had wanted to become an artist. After being rejected from the Viennese Academy of Fine Arts as a young man, he had painted watercolors of Viennese landmarks for a living. He shared the philistine view of modern art as "the outcome of an impudent and unashamed arrogance or of a simply shocking lack of skill . . . which might have been produced by untalented children of from eight to ten years old."[15] The Nazis outlawed expressionism and other avant-garde tendencies. They organized a traveling exhibition of "degenerate art" to demonstrate the supposed connections between modernism, Jews, and Bolsheviks, and then closed museums and persecuted writers and artists. Several intellectuals submitted to the regime: the minor expressionist playwrights Arnolt Bronnen and Hanns Johst, the poet Gottfried Benn, the philosophers Carl Schmitt and Martin Heidegger, and the naturalist playwright Gerhart Hauptmann, already over seventy years old and a Nobel laureate, who became a propagandist for Hitler. However, the most distinguished exponents of modernism left the country. The filmmaker Fritz Lang, Thomas Mann, Arnold Schoenberg, Kurt Weill, many of the Bauhaus artists, and the left-wing intellectuals of the Frankfurt School for Social Research found refuge in the United States. Hermann Hesse, a pacifist, had moved to Switzerland during the First World War and never returned to Germany. The expressionist Ernst Ludwig Kirchner, demoralized by Nazi attacks, committed suicide in 1938. The Polish avant-garde playwright Witkacy also killed himself when the Nazis invaded Poland in 1939. Bertolt Brecht wrote his major works in exile – first in Scandinavia, then in the Soviet Union, and finally in the United States. After the war, he returned to Germany and founded the Berliner Ensemble, in which he put the principles of epic theater to work in the new German Democratic Republic (communist East Germany).

## Politicizing art

In the Western democracies the sense of impending crisis resulting from the rise first of communism and then of fascism and Nazism led intellectuals to feel that the time had come to take sides in the struggle. The critic Walter Benjamin was referring in particular to the Italian futurists when he wrote that fascism was guilty of treating the destruction of mankind as an "aesthetic pleasure" and that communists should respond by "politicizing art."[16] Benjamin, a refugee from Nazi Germany, committed suicide in 1940 while attempting to flee the German invasion of France. A number of attempts were made to use modernist techniques in order to represent the situation of the working classes and poor in the throes of industrial crisis. One such attempt was the fusion of realism and modernism in works that aspired to document the sufferings of the poor or critique the institutions of capitalism. In the case of the United

States, this fusion of realist and modernist techniques and concern with collective experience have recently been labeled "New Deal Modernism."[17] Examples include the murals of Diego Rivera, who had been a cubist in Paris but became a magically inclined realist upon returning to his native Mexico to support the revolutionary socialist government there. Rivera's mural for the Rockefeller Center in New York City was destroyed on the orders of John D. Rockefeller, Jr., who did not appreciate Rivera's sympathetic portrayal of Lenin in this bastion of American capitalism. His and other murals of the Mexican Renaissance influenced the American muralists supported by the Works Projects Administration, set up by President Franklin D. Roosevelt under the New Deal to employ artists and writers during the Depression. Unlike canvases, hung in galleries that the poor may never enter, the mural is a quintessentially public and therefore political form of art. Another case of experiment put to social use was the trilogy of novels, *U.S.A.* (1930–6), written by John Dos Passos, which interwove documentary sources, newspaper collages, montage techniques from film, biographical sketches of famous Americans, and fiction, to tell the story of the working people of the United States in the first three decades of the twentieth century. Like Christopher Isherwood, Dos Passos drew an analogy between the work of the writer and what he called the "camera eye," the objective recording instrument. In each case elements of modernism combined with aspects of documentary technique to produce a powerful critique of industrial society.

In earlier phases of modernism, English writers and intellectuals had tended to hold themselves aloof from developments in Europe. Thus impressionism and post-impressionism arrived late in England, while dada and surrealism hardly arrived at all. Some critics have seen a similar tendency in English modernism in the years leading up to the Second World War. Virginia Woolf's last novel, *Between the Acts* (1941), describes a rather eccentric pageant of English history, staged in a country village on the eve of the war. The pageant itself, and the novel of which it forms a part, seem at once to celebrate and to ironize English identity, but this identity is under threat of imminent attack. Woolf committed suicide in 1941, during one of the bleakest moments of the war. T. S. Eliot's poem, "Little Gidding" (1943), the last of his *Four Quartets*, is also set in an English village; like Woolf's village, it seems to stand on the edge of a precipice:

> There are other places
> Which also are the world's end, some at the sea jaws,
> Or over a dark lake, in a desert or a city –
> But this is the nearest, in place and time,
> Now and in England.

The critic Jed Esty has seen in Eliot's and Woolf's late works, and in such broader cultural phenomena as the Mass Observation movement in which a network of volunteers undertook to chronicle English customs, evidence of an "anthropological turn" in late English modernism, a new concern with the nature of Englishness. Some of the major modernists, in the face of imperial decline and European chaos, seem to have turned their gaze inward. The younger writers of the 1930s, however, increasingly saw their fate as bound up with that of the continent. The generation born after the turn of the twentieth century, which included such writers as W. H. Auden, Isherwood, and George Orwell, had reached maturity after the First World War, in the spirit of the "revolt of youth against age" that dominated the interwar period.[18] They already looked back at modernism as the work of their elders.

Eliot and Woolf, despite their differing political views, shared an ideal of art as above politics. The younger generation did not. Auden, the recognized leading poet of his generation, called for a "parable-art, that art which shall teach man to unlearn hatred and learn love."[19] Their parables addressed problems of the contemporary world, but they did so often as if in an alternate universe, perhaps the sort imagined by Franz Kafka, whose works were first translated into English in the 1930s (see Chapter Five). The parable-art of the 1930s does not aspire to realism in the traditional sense: the world it describes is clearly not this world. However, in so far as parables constitute critiques of existing society, they embody a sort of inverted mimesis. Samuel Hynes has described the parable as the dominant literary form of Auden's generation in England, and it was important for Bertolt Brecht, too. Auden and his contemporaries did not embrace left-wing politics or sympathize with the working classes immediately; Isherwood later recalled how undergraduates in the Oxford Labour Club signed up for work as strike-breakers during the General Strike of 1926.[20] The Depression and the rise of Joseph Stalin, Adolf Hitler, and Benito Mussolini transformed the consciousness of the generation, however. In the early 1930s the left was largely pacifist, in the tradition of the Bloomsbury intellectuals and their conscientious objection to the First World War. The political and poetic pessimism of the later 1930s resulted in part from the conviction of most English intellectuals that a Second World War had become inevitable. As Hitler's power increased, some joined the Communist Party (Stephen Spender briefly, Cecil Day-Lewis for a longer period), while others, such as Woolf's husband Leonard, abandoned their former pacifism in favor of rearmament to defend England against the Nazi threat. Julian Bell, Woolf's nephew, noted, "By the end of 1933, we have arrived at a situation in which almost the only subject of discussion is contemporary politics, and in which a very large majority of the more intelligent undergraduates are Communists, or almost Communists."[21]

Auden's biographer, Edward Mendelson, has described him as "the first English writer who absorbed all the lessons of modernism, but also understood its limits, and chose to turn elsewhere."[22] Auden first read *The Waste Land* (1922) as an undergraduate at Oxford, in 1926. His poems of the late 1920s share Eliot's ideals of impersonality and formal difficulty. As poets, Auden and his friends Day-Lewis and Louis Macneice were deeply influenced by *The Waste Land*; their long poems tended to be sequences of shorter lyrics, like the five parts of Eliot's poem. These sequences seemed to allow the integration of moments of private lyrical experience into larger epic forms that could speak to the historical crisis of the 1930s. Eliot became a patron of Auden and his circle. He published Auden's "charade" about feuding clans, *Paid on Both Sides*, in *The Criterion* in 1930, just before Auden's twenty-third birthday; in the same year Auden's first book of poems was published by Faber and Faber, where Eliot was literary editor.

It was somewhat ironic that the left-leaning young poets of Auden's circle looked up most of all to Eliot, who had defined his own position as "classicist in literature, royalist in politics, and Anglo-Catholic in religion."[23] Eliot's reputation was later tarnished by the anti-Semitism and racism of some of his early poetry and by his political comments during the 1930s. In his youth he had admired the integral French nationalism of the anti-Semite Charles Maurras. In *After Strange Gods*, written in 1933 and published in 1934, as Hitler was beginning his anti-Semitic legislation, Eliot commented on the desirability of a "homogeneous" population: "What is still more important is unity of religious background; and reasons of race and religion combine to make any large number of free-thinking Jews undesirable."[24] Eliot did not later repeat such anti-Semitic remarks, but neither did he fully repudiate them; he continued to advocate a shared European culture based on Christianity and hostile to the unbridled industrialism of liberal capitalism. His later politics, however, were of a more traditional conservative type, and he had little sympathy with Hitler or Mussolini. W. B. Yeats, whom Auden also admired, offered an equally troubling model. Having received the Nobel Prize for Literature in 1923 and served as a senator in the newly founded Irish Free State from 1922 to 1928, he grew more erratic in his politics with age. In the early 1930s he flirted with importing fascism into Ireland, while later in the decade he advocated eugenics, though, like Eliot, he showed no admiration for Hitler.[25] Nonetheless, neither Eliot nor Yeats was an obvious role model for young radicals, and one of the challenges of these young poets, coming right after the heyday of modernism, was how to discover a voice that was at once modernist and progressive.

Auden's early works show an obsession with violence and the lives of the working classes. Their setting, though suggestive of an industrial wasteland, is not explicitly contemporary, and no political solution is proposed for the violence they describe; this is the land of parable, rather than of realistic representation. Already in 1929, however, with the onset of the Depression, Auden had turned toward more clearly political themes, albeit without a coherent philosophy. In "1929" Auden writes of "Gerhart Meyer / Young, from the sea, the truly strong man," a German sailor with whom Auden may have had an affair. The theme of the truly strong man, the possible leader who could unify disparate groups and resolve political crises, runs through the works of the 1930s, even in such unlikely cases as Woolf's late masterpiece *The Waves* (1933), in which a group of childhood friends long for the unifying force of Percival, a potential leader who dies while serving British rule in India. The critic Michael Roberts observed at the time that the "truly strong men" of contemporary poetry were the opposite of Eliot's Prufrock. As Hynes later wrote, "the sensitive, neurotic anti-hero of the 'twenties was succeeded by the man of action" in the 1930s.[26] One impetus for this fascination with action was the apparent gulf between the ineffectual leaders of the Western democracies and the powerful dictators of the totalitarian regimes. More broadly, however, the young poets were fascinated with the possible power of poetry itself, and they frequently imagined themselves supplying the kind of moral leadership of society that England's political leaders did not seem able to provide. In Spender's most famous poem, "I Think Continually of Those Who Were Truly Great," the truly great may just as well be poets, who "remembered the soul's history," as men of action.

Auden in particular was obsessed with heroes and leaders. He described his parable *The Orators* (1932) as a "critique of the fascist outlook," but he seemed to sympathize with the Airman, the quasi-fascist hero who is the central figure of the book. Much later, he wrote that "My name on the title-page [of *The Orators*] seems a pseudonym for someone else, someone talented but near the border of sanity, who might well, in a year or two, become a Nazi."[27] Auden remained fascinated by the idea of the truly strong man, but became disillusioned with every leader in actual life. He admired D. H. Lawrence, who had celebrated the authoritarian heroes of his novels *Kangaroo* (1923) and *The Plumed Serpent* (1926) (see Chapter Two). An even more iconic figure was T. E. Lawrence, "Lawrence of Arabia," an Oxford-educated historian and archaeologist who had, despite his small stature and rumored homosexuality, worked for British intelligence and organized a ring of Arab spies during the First World War. He helped to provoke the Arab revolt against Turkish rule which eventually allowed Britain to take control of the Arab lands (notably Iraq) that had formerly belonged to the Turkish Empire. Lawrence died in a motorcycle accident in 1935, and Auden described his life as "an allegory of the transformation of the Truly Weak Man into the Truly Strong Man."[28]

Lawrence served as a model for the mountaineer in *The Ascent of F6* (1936), a play by Auden and Isherwood inspired in part by the expressionist dramas of Brecht and Ernst Toller, which they had encountered in Berlin. *The Ascent of F6* chronicles the feats of a mountaineer who represents at once T. E. Lawrence, the would-be visionary poets, and the dictators of the 1930s. By this stage, however, Auden in particular had become disillusioned with the strong leader and even with the claim of the romantic poet to the status of prophet. The mountaineer, Michael Ransom, turns out always to have been the neurotic weak man in disguise, desiring to conquer the mountain mainly in order to please his unloving mother. The play's satirical attitude toward contemporary politics marked a step away from Auden's earlier faith in political solutions, but it also marked a diminishment of his faith in the poet's capacity to transform society. Auden seems to have concluded that the authoritarian leader only masquerades as a truly strong man in order to cover up his essential weakness. It is notable that Auden, though seen as a spokesman for the left, took a primarily psychological rather than political approach to the problem of leadership.

Despite their efforts at sympathy with the working classes, most of the leftist writers of the 1930s, such as Auden, Isherwood, and Spender, belonged firmly to the bourgeoisie. George Orwell memorably defined his own social background as "lower-upper-middle class." Born in British India to a civil servant, Orwell attended Eton and then himself worked for the Indian Imperial Police in Burma, the subject of his novel *Burmese Days* (1934), a scathing critique of the imperialist frame of mind. Orwell's mixed fascination with and revulsion from the lower classes is a major theme of his early writing, particularly *Down and Out in Paris and London* (1933), an account of his experiences among the poor of these two capital cities; in Paris he worked for a time as a dishwasher. The book combines undercover journalism with a meditation on the effects of the English class system and demonstrates the strength of the documentary impulse in much writing of the 1930s, including that of Dos Passos and Isherwood. Orwell's early novels share some of the expressionist concerns typical of Lawrence, but his essays were often critical of the high modernists and his most famous novel, *1984*, published in 1949, seems to link totalitarianism with the embrace of modernist forms of ambiguity. Only by maintaining mathematical certainty (represented by the equation "$2+2=4$") can Winston Smith hold on to his sanity amid the lies of the Party and Big Brother. As the examples of Auden and Orwell show, the concern with political commitment tends to make the writers of the generation after the high modernists skeptical of modernist ambiguity and irony. For Orwell, the crisis of representation seems to open the way for totalitarian manipulation of the truth, in the form of "doublethink," and only a return to traditional representation can defend the values of truth, tolerance, and justice that are threatened by fascism and Stalinism.

In the parable-art of Auden, Isherwood, and Orwell, at once removed from and parallel to the contemporary political situation, writers could imagine a better world while exposing the flaws of their own times. Parable aims to instruct through a nonrealistic portrayal of an alternate world. Among the less politically engaged young writers of the 1930s, the desire to transform the world was channeled into a revival of satire, the ancient mode of critique that describes all society's flaws without remorse. Satire aims to instruct through a hyperrealistic portrayal of this world.[29] It predominates in Evelyn Waugh's early novels about intellectuals and the upper classes, *Decline and Fall* (1928) and *A Handful of Dust* (1934), to be replaced later by a certain nostalgia for the upper-class world of the years between the wars in *Brideshead Revisited* (1945). Aldous Huxley also began as a satirist of the upper classes in *Crome Yellow* (1921) before publishing his science fiction critique of mass society, *Brave New World*, in 1932 (see Chapter Two). Wyndham Lewis, the former vorticist, aligned himself with Sir Oswald Mosley's British Union of Fascists, praised Hitler (before his rise to power), and attacked Eliot and the Bloomsbury intellectuals in a new journal, *The Enemy* (1927–9) and in his novel *The Apes of God* (1930). A protégée of Eliot, Djuna Barnes, parodied everything from the cadences of the King James Bible to homosexuality, lesbianism, and the obsession of contemporary writers with death in her *Nightwood* (1936). The novel ends with the heroine Robin Vote barking like a dog on the floor of a ruined chapel on her lover Nora's estate in New England. Barnes was an expatriate American living in Paris. An expatriate Englishwoman, Jean Rhys, wrote a similarly bleak portrayal of women's emotional and sexual lives in *Good Morning, Midnight* (1939), in which Sasha Jensen wanders aimlessly around Paris in an alcoholic daze, hoping to avoid a confrontation with the memory of her past lovers, which continually presses in on her dingy present life. The critic Tyrus Miller has described this proliferation of satire in the works of the 1930s as a predominant feature of "late modernism," whose mood is one of mirthless laughter. Each of these works seems to be dominated by that lowest of the three forms of laughter later analyzed by Samuel Beckett in his novel *Watt* (1953): "the bitter, the hollow, and the mirthless." The servant Erskine explains to Watt that

> the bitter laugh laughs at that which is not good, it is the ethical laugh. The hollow laugh laughs at that which is not true, it is the intellectual laugh. Not good! Not true! Well well. But the mirthless laugh is the dianoetic laugh, down the snout – Haw! – so. It is the laugh of laughs, the *risus purus*, the laugh laughing at the laugh, the beholding, the saluting of the

highest joke, in a word the laugh that laughs – silence please – at that which is unhappy.

In the unhappy world of the 1930s, English writers found different modes of response: turning inward in pursuit of an analysis of Englishness, turning outward in search of documentary realism or political action, or simply laughing mirthlessly at the folly of the world.

This folly led to war. The Spanish Civil War began in 1936 when a military coup led by the fascist General Francisco Franco overthrew a democratically elected left-wing government. In Madrid and Barcelona, where the coup failed, anarchist elements and communists with Soviet support joined the legitimate government of the Republic (the loyalists) in opposition to Franco. Internally divided by political squabbles, the loyalists nonetheless fought valiantly until 1939, when the fascists, with Italian and German support, utterly defeated them. The war engaged the sympathies of intellectuals throughout the West. Woolf's nephew Julian Bell died while working as an ambulance driver for the Republican side. Woolf, who was a convinced pacifist of the Bloomsbury type, could not understand why he had thrown away his life for this war. Ernest Hemingway covered the war for American newspapers, raised money for the antifascists, and wrote a novel, *For Whom the Bell Tolls* (1940), about an American serving in the resistance to Franco. Orwell traveled to Spain to fight with anarchists and communists against the fascists, but became extremely disillusioned with the role of Stalinists in controlling the radical opposition to Franco and in particular with the violent suppression of left-wing socialist elements within the opposition. Returning to England after being badly wounded in the neck, he wrote about his experiences in *Homage to Catalonia* (1938). The book, like Orwell's earlier journalistic writings *Down and Out in Paris and London* and *The Road to Wigan Pier* (1937), presents its material from a first-person point of view. On the one hand, it offers unfiltered accounts of Orwell's experiences in Barcelona; on the other hand, it offers an analysis of his own state of mind and his attitude to history. Orwell's experiences with the Soviet-backed communists in Barcelona also shaped his later novels about totalitarianism, *Animal Farm* and *1984*.

To many writers and intellectuals, the Spanish Civil War meant the end of literary experiment and an occasion for a more politically committed art. In "Spain, 1937" Auden wrote of the need to turn away from poetry and toward war:

Tomorrow for the young the poets exploding like bombs,
The walks by the lake, the winter of perfect communion;
    Tomorrow the bicycle races
Through the suburbs on summer evenings: but to-day the struggle.

10. Pablo Picasso (1881–1973), *Guernica*, 1937. Oil on canvas, 350 × 782 cm. © ARS, NY. Photo credit: John Bigelow Taylor/Art Resource, NY. Spain. © 2006 Estate of Pablo Picasso/Artist Rights Society (ARS), New York.

In the phrase "the poets exploding like bombs," Auden echoed the militaristic language of the early avant-gardes, as in the *BLAST* of Lewis and Ezra Pound, but in 1937, he suggested, it was not poetry but real bombs that should concern the young. Among the most controversial lines in this, one of Auden's greatest early poems, are the following:

> To-day the deliberate increase in the chances of death,
> The conscious acceptance of guilt in the necessary murder;
> > To-day the expending of powers
> On the flat ephemeral pamphlet and the boring meeting.

Orwell accused Auden of justifying political murder: "Mr. Auden's brand of amoralism is only possible if you are the kind of person who is always some- where else when the trigger is pulled." The judgment seems unfair to Auden, who was not in fact praising political murder but lamenting the necessity of killing in war. Later on, Auden himself seemed to agree with Orwell's criticism and thought this poem propagandistic and "incurably dishonest." During the war, however, he expressed the general sense of crisis: "I am your choice, your decision: yes, I am Spain." Pablo Picasso painted an anguished representation of the German bombing of the Basque village of Guernica, his most explicitly political artwork (figure 10). Picasso considered it his only symbolic painting, with the bull standing for "brutality and darkness" and the horse for "the peo- ple," and the only one he painted out of "a deliberate sense of propaganda."[30] Its stark contrasts between black and white, emphasized by the bare lightbulb at the top of the painting, and its primitive drawings of stricken bodies use elements of cubism and surrealism for a relatively straightforward political statement.

The loyalist cause seemed doomed from the outset. In January 1939 Barcelona fell to the fascists, thus effectively ending opposition to Franco. In the same month Auden and Isherwood moved to New York, and Yeats died. Auden commemorated these events in his great elegy, "In Memory of W. B. Yeats" (1939):

> In the nightmare of the dark
> All the dogs of Europe bark,
> And the living nations wait,
> Each sequestered in its hate . . .

In the face of inevitable war, Auden celebrated the politically suspect Yeats for his understanding of the power of poetry, which had nothing to do with politics in the narrow sense. At the outbreak of the war, Auden would lament the entire 1930s as a "low dishonest decade"; his move to the United States signaled the distance he was traveling from his origins as a political poet. He moved away from the heightened rhetoric of his most effective early work and soon converted to Christianity.

In an early version of the elegy, Auden wrote about two other conservative writers, the imperialist Rudyard Kipling and the French reactionary Paul Claudel, noting both his admiration of their poetry and his disapproval of their politics:

> Time that with this strange excuse,
> Pardoned Kipling and his views,
> And will pardon Paul Claudel,
> Pardons him for writing well.

The final version of the poem excludes this stanza. Auden seeks to move beyond such taking of sides and develop his new understanding of poetry, no longer strictly political but rather ethical, as part of the process by which consciousness digests experience: "The words of a dead man / Are modified in the guts of the living." For, he addresses Yeats, "poetry makes nothing happen . . . / it survives, / A way of happening, a mouth." The mouth here both consumes the world and speaks. For Auden, as for Yeats, poetry is part of life, and even though the imminent war seemed to many to spell the end of modernism in literature, Auden expressed in this poem his faith in a certain modernist vision of poetry, not as record of a wasteland, but as the source of life-giving water, able to unlock the "seas of pity" that, the poem tells us, "lie / Locked and frozen in each eye." Here Auden seems to be reaching back beyond interwar modernism to Wilfred Owen's claim, at the end of the First World War, that "The Poetry is in the pity" (see Chapter Three). For Auden, poetry makes nothing happen, but it teaches us to rejoice and to sing, and it releases our sense of pity, as Aristotle thought tragedy could do. Auden's elegy for Yeats concludes with this statement of faith in how poetry can defeat hate and bring nourishment to the wasteland:

> In the deserts of the heart
> Let the healing fountain start,
> In the prison of his days
> Teach the free man how to praise.

## Further reading

### Literary works

W. H. Auden, *The English Auden,* ed. Edward Mendelson. New York: Random House, 1977.

W. H. Auden, *Selected Poems,* ed. Edward Mendelson. New York: Vintage Books, 1989.

W. H. Auden and Christopher Isherwood, *Plays and Other Dramatic Writings, 1928–1938,* ed. Edward Mendelson. Princeton: Princeton University Press, 1988.

Bertolt Brecht, *Collected Plays,* ed. Ralph Manheim and John Willett, 9 vols. New York: Vintage Books, 1971–2003.

Christopher Isherwood, *Berlin Stories.* New York: New Directions, 1954.

Vladimir Mayakovsky, *Plays,* trans. Guy Daniels. Evanston, IL: Northwestern University Press, 1995.

George Orwell, *Down and Out in Paris and London, Homage to Catalonia* (various editions).

Ellendea Proffer and Carl R. Proffer, eds., *The Ardis Anthology of Russian Futurism.* Ann Arbor: Ardis, 1980.

Virginia Woolf, *The Waves* (various editions).

### Contemporary critical statements

Walter Benjamin, *Illuminations,* ed. Hannah Arendt, trans. Harry Zohn. New York: Knopf, 1969.

André Breton, *Manifestoes of Surrealism,* trans. Richard Seaver and Helen R. Lane. Ann Arbor: University of Michigan Press, 1972.

Jeffrey T. Schnapp, ed. *A Primer of Italian Fascism.* Lincoln: University of Nebraska Press, 2000.

### Later criticism

Briony Fer, David Batchelor, and Paul Wood, *Realism, Rationalism, Surrealism: Art Between the Wars.* New Haven: Yale University Press, 1994.

Peter Gay, *Weimar Culture: The Outsider as Insider.* New York: Norton, 1968.

Samuel Hynes, *The Auden Generation: Literature and Politics in England in the 1930s.* New York: Viking, 1977.

Vladimir Markov, *Russian Futurism.* Berkeley and Los Angeles: University of California Press, 1968.

Edward Mendelson, *Early Auden.* New York: Viking, 1981.

Michael Tratner, *Modernism and Mass Politics: Joyce, Woolf, Eliot, Yeats.* Stanford: Stanford University Press, 1995.


## Historical surveys

Martin Clark, *Modern Italy, 1871–1995.* 2nd edn. London: Longman, 1996.
Gordon Craig, *Modern Germany, 1871–1945.* Oxford: Oxford University Press, 1978.
Nicholas V. Riasanovsky, *A History of Russia,* 6th edn. Oxford: Oxford University Press, 2000.

# Conclusion: after modernism?

The 1920s were the high point of literary modernism. In general, the more politically oriented writing of the 1930s was markedly less experimental. While Auden, Orwell, and other writers of the 1930s turned to relatively straightforward literary forms, however, James Joyce's work seemed to reach the outer limits of modernist experimentation with language and form. Throughout the 1930s Joyce published excerpts of what would eventually be *Finnegans Wake* (1939), which combined the anarchic energies of the avant-garde with the epic ambitions of high modernism. The *Wake* tells of a mythical world, bearing some resemblance to the Dublin of *Ulysses* (1922), but dreamed of by a sleeping, drunken man, possibly a giant, possibly the dead man at a wake. The novel, referred to during the 1930s as *Work in Progress*, is written in a language of multilingual puns and is best read by a group of inquisitive people, each one of whom may be able to understand some fragment of this often incomprehensible magnum opus. Joyce complained that critics (including his former mentor Ezra Pound) found the new work "obscure": "They compare it of course with *Ulysses*. But the action of *Ulysses* was chiefly in the daytime, and the action of my new work takes place chiefly at night. It's natural things should not be so clear at night, isn't it now?"[1] It later came to be seen as the first postmodernist text. In his influential critical manifesto of 1971, "POSTmodernISM," Ihab Hassan wrote that Gertrude Stein "contributed to both Modernism and Postmodernism," but that "without a doubt, the crucial text is *Finnegans Wake*."[2] The *Wake*'s embrace of linguistic indeterminacy and multiple meanings foreshadowed one important tendency in literature after modernism.

*Finnegans Wake* tells several stories at once. On the first page alone, there are references to figures from all phases of Irish history, myth, or legend, including the political leader Charles Stewart Parnell, the writer Jonathan Swift, the mythical figures Tristan and Isolde, and St. Patrick, who converted the Irish to Christianity; Joyce refers as well to the Phoenix Park murders, a notorious terrorist attack that took place in Dublin during his youth. These are all mixed up in a barely comprehensible dream language with a variety of biblical references, tending ever further back in time, to Moses, Jacob and Esau, Noah,

Cain and Abel. The fall of Adam and Eve is represented by a marvelous long word, made up of the names for thunder from Japanese, Hindi, Greek, French, Italian, Swedish, Irish, Portuguese, Danish, and old Rumanian. It is Joyce's alternative to the monosyllabic "DA," which represents the voice of thunder at the end of Eliot's *The Waste Land* (1922): "The fall (bababadalgharagh-takamminarronnkonnbronntonnerronntuonnthunntrovarrhounawnskawnt-oohoohoordenenthurnuk!) of a once wallstrait oldparr is retaled early in bed and later on life down through all christian minstrelsy." Joyce himself was terrified of thunder, and he draws here on the theory of the eighteenth-century Italian philosopher Giambattista Vico that the idea of god was derived in the first place from the fear that primitive people had of thunder.

Who falls at the beginning of *Finnegans Wake*? At one level, it is the novel's main character, HCE, also known as Humphrey Chimpden Earwicker and Here Comes Everybody. His initials refer to the phrase in the Latin Mass, "Hoc est enim corpus meum" ("for this is my body"). Joyce is concerned in *Finnegans Wake*, as in his earlier work, with the idea of the miraculous transubstantiation of everyday reality into the sacred substance of art, and HCE seems to be a symbol of this artistic miracle (see Chapter Three). It is HCE who falls (drunk after being kicked out of Adam and Eve's pub) at the beginning of the novel, but at the same time it is Adam and Eve ("oldparr" can mean an old couple or an old father), and the sleeping giant Finnegan of Irish myth, and the Tower of Babel, and Charles Stewart Parnell, whose downfall was traumatic for Joyce in his youth. Joyce thus attempts to tell several stories at once, interweaving them with the free-flowing logic of what Sigmund Freud called the "dream-work" and in a language that draws on all languages, thus tapping into something like what Freud's one-time collaborator, Carl Jung (whom Joyce knew) called the collective unconscious. Novelists ever since *Ulysses* have felt the weight of T. S. Eliot's claim, "It is a book to which we are all indebted and from which none of us can escape."[3] *Finnegans Wake*, on the other hand, while it has served as an inspiration to avant-garde writers, is generally seen as a magnificent experiment that no one could, or perhaps even would want to, repeat. The novel was published in May 1939, shortly before the start of the Second World War. Joyce died two years later, as a result of surgery for an ulcer.

By the time the war ended, many of the other leading modernists had died, including Virginia Woolf and W. B. Yeats. Gertrude Stein died in 1946, George Orwell in 1950. Ezra Pound was confined to St. Elizabeth's Hospital for the Criminally Insane. W. H. Auden had emigrated to the United States. Of the major modernists in England, only Eliot, now an influential literary editor, thrived. Having left lyric poetry behind in order to write increasingly main-stream drama, he won the Nobel Prize for Literature in 1948. Despite the waning of the modernist generation, however, it was not the case that modernism had entirely reached the end of its rope. The Irish-born Samuel Beckett met Joyce in Paris in 1928, when Joyce was beginning work on *Finnegans Wake*. Beckett wrote out parts of the manuscript for Joyce, who suffered frequently from severe inflammation of his eyes (iritis), and translated a brief section of the book into French. After working in the Resistance during the Nazi occupation, Beckett would become most famous for his plays, such as *Waiting for Godot* (1952) and *Endgame* (1957), which typified the postwar development of the "theater of the absurd," imbued with a strong existential sense of the futility of life. Most of his plays and novels were written in French, but Beckett translated them into English himself. He said that he wrote in French "because in French it is easier to write without style." Beckett's novels generally center on impotent heroes who contemplate at great length their inability to escape from the situation in which they find themselves stuck. They carry forward the modernist tradition of self-reflexivity and of representing the isolation of the self. Like Jorge Luis Borges and Vladimir Nabokov, Beckett incorporated meditations on the status of fiction, dubbed "metafiction" by literary critics, into his novels (see Chapter Five). *Finnegans Wake* has been celebrated as postmodernist for its linguistic complexity and exuberance, while Beckett has often been hailed as the first postmodernist, but for nearly the opposite qualities. Beckett himself, without using the two terms, saw the distinction that later critics would make between him as a postmodernist and Joyce as a modernist: he said that "The more Joyce knew the more he could. He's tending towards omniscience and omnipotence." His own work, he claimed, tended toward "ignorance and impotence."[4] Later postmodernism would be known either for a multiplication of meanings like Joyce's in *Finnegans Wake* or an evacuation of meaning like Beckett's. In either case postmodernism seemed to have abandoned the quest for a single, unifying meaning typical of high modernism (see Chapter Three). A crucial transitional figure between modernism and postmodernism, Beckett was awarded the Nobel Prize for Literature in 1969.

Beckett's great fame resulted from his plays rather than his novels. *Waiting for Godot* features two tramps, Vladimir and Estragon (Didi and Gogo), in a barren landscape, marked only by an apparently dead tree. (They occasionally gesture toward the auditorium, which they describe as a bog.) The two men are waiting for Godot, who has promised to meet them and who apparently has some business or opportunity for them. While they are waiting they fiddle with their boots and hats, discuss philosophy and theology, chew on carrots and turnips, consider hanging themselves, argue and reconcile. Godot never arrives. In the first act two men pass through: the self-important Pozzo, driving on a rope his slave Lucky, whom he whips and abuses. Pozzo pontificates on matters of social relations. Lucky remains silent until ordered to "think," at which point he philosophizes extravagantly and senselessly on the human condition. After Pozzo and Lucky continue on their journey, a boy comes to tell Didi and Gogo that Godot will not be arriving tonight. He has promised, however, to come tomorrow. The sun sets, and at the end of the act the two tramps wonder what to do next:

> ESTRAGON: Well, shall we go?
> VLADIMIR: Yes, let's go.
> *They do not move.*    *Curtain*

In *Waiting for Godot,* as one critic put it, "nothing happens, twice."[5] Indeed, much the same happens in the second act, but there are variations. The tree is covered with leaves. It is the next day, or so say Didi and the stage directions, but Gogo seems to have forgotten the events of the first act. The two men seem rather more concerned about their predicament than in the first act, and try to think of ways to pass the time. Didi suggests playing "Pozzo and Lucky," and they have a good time abusing each other. Just then, Pozzo and Lucky return, but Pozzo is now blind and Lucky dumb. The two fall down in a heap, and after debating whether to help them (and how much to charge for their help), Didi and Gogo fall down, too. Eventually, all four struggle to their feet. Pozzo claims to have woken up blind "one day," and acts as if he has been blind for a long time. Like Gogo, he does not seem to remember the events of the first act. The characters rehearse some of the same concerns that arose in the first act before Pozzo and Lucky head off on their way, and Didi and Gogo are once again left waiting for Godot. The boy from the first act, or possibly another boy who looks like him, arrives to say that Godot has been delayed again.

In this great play Beckett draws on all the resources of the modern theater. Indebted to the avant-garde tradition that includes Alfred Jarry, Luigi Pirandello, dada, the futurists, and the surrealists, he shares with them the dismantling of all theatrical conventions. The play does without conventional plot. What plot it has consists in two people standing more or less still, two others passing through, and one boy (or two) announcing the deferral of the anticipated conclusion. Each of the five (or six) characters seems to inhabit a different timeframe, and Beckett makes frequent references to time, as when Didi comments that "time has stopped." Didi and Gogo often comment on their lives as if they were plays. They complain at one point that the evening they are having is worse than the pantomime, the circus, or the music hall, all popular forms of entertainment. Like the futurists, Beckett uses the conventions of popular theatrical forms to break down those of the serious theater. Didi and Gogo are like two clowns; their slapstick humor and routines with hats and boots suggest vaudeville, the silent movies of Charlie Chaplin and Buster Keaton, and the music hall. Each is a "character," but they lack the emotional depth or specific attributes of characters in the naturalist theater. Without explicitly saying that they are characters in a play, Didi and Gogo are concerned about their existence. At one point Gogo says, "We aways find something, eh Didi, to give us the impression we exist?"

Like Antonin Artaud, Beckett is concerned with cruelty. An extreme version of the master-slave relation is explored in *Endgame,* set in a dismal postapocalyptic future, where the master Hamm is blind and immobile, and his two parents Nell and Nagg spend the entire play stuck in ashbins (trash cans), having lost their legs in a bicycle accident. All three are entirely dependent on the servant Clov, the only one who can move. Clov stays with his master despite continually being abused by him; in the play's final moments, he dresses to leave, but hesitates at the threshold. A slightly less barren set of relationships governs *Waiting for Godot.* Vladimir and Estragon are models of the smallest possible human community: two people who depend on each other. Pozzo and Lucky represent the most basic form of oppression: enslavement. Yet Pozzo and Lucky show signs of the same sort of mutual interdependence that typifies Vladimir and Estragon, while the two tramps enjoy playing at "Pozzo and Lucky." This role-playing is one of the typical elements of Beckett's metatheater (see Chapter Six). The setting seems symbolic, and the play includes several passing references to Sophocles and Shakespeare. The characters are conscious of the way they are acting out roles, though Beckett only gestures toward breaking the fourth wall and does not specifically address the audience. Thus, after one of his long speeches, Pozzo asks Didi and Gogo how they liked it, as if he were asking for a comment on his performance: "Good? Fair? Middling? Poor? Positively bad?" Didi and Gogo admire the performance but complain that "nothing happens." In the second act the two tramps consciously set out to have a conversation, and their conversation sounds like something out of a poor translation of Anton Chekhov, interspersed with long silences. As the conversation slackens, Didi comments, "This is becoming really insignificant," to which Gogo replies, "Not enough." Beckett sometimes seems to be aiming for a total evacuation of significance.

Like other twentieth-century theater, notably that of Bertolt Brecht, Albert Camus, Jean-Paul Sartre, and George Bernard Shaw, Beckett's is a theater of ideas. Many of the play's first viewers and critics debated the meaning of Godot. Several elements of the play point to his being the absent or dead God: almost the only thing we know about Godot is that he has a white beard; Didi and Gogo talk of praying to him; the idea of Christ on the cross comes up over and over again. Beckett wrote in the wake of the existentialism of Camus and

Sartre, who developed ideas found in Martin Heidegger and Friedrich Nietzsche (see Introduction). Existentialism was a quintessentially postwar philosophy, specifically post-Second World War, which laid an emphasis on the inherent meaninglessness of existence and the responsibility of the individual to make ultimate choices that would render his or her own existence meaningful (as Beckett chose to work for the Resistance). Beckett seems clearly influenced by existentialism, but he also puts existentialist principles into the mouths of his characters when they are spouting clichés and nonsense. It seems that Beckett takes Nietzsche's death of God for granted and seeks to explore the humor as well as the bleakness of a world in which any hope of a transcendental principle, whether called God, truth, beauty, or Godot, is, in all likelihood, illusory. At the end of the second act, Pozzo makes one final pronouncement on the human condition: "They give birth astride of a grave, the light gleams an instant, then it's night once more." Lucky and Pozzo move on, as night falls. Didi and Gogo consider hanging themselves again. They test the rope that Gogo uses to hold up his pants, but the rope breaks and Gogo's pants fall down. At the end of the play, he pulls up his trousers. The second act ends much as the first one did, but with the lines reversed:

> VLADIMIR:  Well? shall we go?
> ESTRAGON:  Yes, let's go.
> *They do not move.*      *Curtain*

One of the most common words in the stage directions for *Waiting for Godot* is "silence," and it is a play about the sounds we make to avoid awkward silences, during the brief moment between birth and the grave.[6]

Silence and death play a large role in the literature of the mid-twentieth century, partly in response to the experience of the Second World War, the Holocaust, and the invention of nuclear weapons. The more ascetic aspect of modernism, typical of Beckett and Franz Kafka, asserted itself at the expense of the life-affirming comedy of Joyce. More broadly, a certain suspicion of the triviality of literature weighed on this period. The philosopher Theodor Adorno wrote, in a much-debated phrase, that "to write poetry after Auschwitz is barbaric."[7] He did not in fact condemn all writing of poetry, but favored poetry that would tend toward silence and the recognition of the inadequacy of traditional means of representation for addressing the question of the Holocaust. Many later writers would describe the Holocaust as "unrepresentable." The Jewish poet Paul Celan, who was born in 1920 in what was then Romania and is now the Ukraine, was interned in a Romanian forced labor camp during the war; his parents both died in concentration camps. He wrote in German, his mother tongue but also the language of the Nazis. In his poem "Deathfugue"

(1944–5), he refers to the music played in the camps while prisoners were shot and contrasts the golden-haired German girl Margarete, beloved of one of the guards, and the dark-haired Jewish girl Shulamith, one of the prisoners. The poem's structure of theme and variation culminates in the final stanza:

> Black milk of daybreak we drink you at night
> we drink you at midday Death is a master aus Deutschland
> we drink you at evening and morning we drink and we drink
> this Death is ein Meister aus Deutschland his eye it is blue
> he shoots you with shot made of lead shoots you level and true
> a man lives in the house your goldenes Haar Margarete
> he looses his hounds on us grants us a grave in the air
> he plays with his vipers and daydreams der Tod ist ein Meister aus
>    Deutschland
> dein goldenes Haar Margarete
> dein aschenes Haar Sulamith[8]

Here, the increasingly frantic rhythm of the poem, like a dance approaching its climax, draws attention to the very challenge of writing poetry after Auschwitz. The poem memorializes the dead Shulamith but at the expense of turning her death, and the Holocaust in general, into music. Celan later repudiated the poem for precisely this reason. The contrast between the musical language and the subject calls into question the possibility of beauty and culture in a world governed by barbarism.

In the United States a postwar controversy addressed the question of the status of poetry, and especially modernist poetry, in relation to the Holocaust. In 1949 the Fellows in American Letters of the Library of Congress, a group of distinguished poets, awarded the first Bollingen Prize in poetry to Pound for *The Pisan Cantos*, a portion of *The Cantos* written during his internment after the war, partly in defense of his wartime activities. Pound's anti-Semitic propaganda on behalf of Benito Mussolini during the war was well known (see Chapter Seven), and, confined in St. Elizabeths Hospital, he became a target of controversy. Many leading intellectuals thought that, despite the services to modern poetry for which the judges sought to honor him, Pound was not an acceptable choice. The distinguished critic Irving Howe wrote that, "by virtue of his public record and utterances, [Pound] is beyond the bounds of our intellectual life." Although the persecution of modern artists and writers by the Nazis and Soviets had shown modernism's anti-authoritarian quality, in retrospect the association of so many English-language modernists, in particular, with anti-Semitism or fascism helped to make modernism politically suspect in the eyes of many. Among the modernists who had been guilty to one degree or another of anti-Semitism or a fascination with authoritarian politics were Eliot, D. H. Lawrence, Wyndham Lewis, Pound, and Yeats. Sometimes, even politically left-wing writers like Joyce and Woolf were later seen as elitist, perhaps because they were so effectively promoted to the status of "canonical" writers by a generation of postwar academics or because of the association between modernism and literary formalism. "High modernism" has also been accused, somewhat surprisingly, of a hostility to mass culture. Since "high modernism" was seen as elitist, and all modernism was identified with "high modernism," artists and writers felt a need for a new, nonelitist alternative. This often meant more straightforward narratives or pictorial representations and less inventive language and form. At first, this seemed to be what postmodernism offered.

The term "postmodernism" became prominent in the world of architecture in the 1970s to describe the reaction against the modernist "International Style." The stark aesthetic of modernism had dominated new architecture in the years after the Second World War. In contrast, postmodern architecture was relatively playful, more open to ornamentation, and full of references to the history of architecture. Modernism also continued its dominance in painting until well after the war, though the center of experimentation moved from Europe to the United States. Abstract expressionists such as Willem de Kooning, Jackson Pollock, and Mark Rothko continued the modernist tradition with an emphasis on the individual creative personality of the artist. Later movements in modern art anticipated postmodernism in their interest in mass-produced or banal images. These included the flag paintings of Jasper Johns, the "combine paintings" of Robert Rauschenberg, and the Pop Art of Roy Lichtenstein and Andy Warhol, later often seen as postmodernist. Whereas earlier modernists might still claim to be original, Pop artists like Warhol suggested that anybody who kept doing new things could be considered an artist, whether or not these new things were the product of genius or originality. Novelty became detached from originality. Warhol claimed that he wanted "to be a machine" and predicted that "In the future everybody will be world-famous for fifteen minutes."[9] He used the techniques of advertising and graphic design to spoof the mass marketing of celebrities such as Marilyn Monroe and food products like Campbell's Soup. In Pop Art the continuity is more with the dada and surrealist challenge to the definition of art than with the high modernist tradition culminating in abstract expressionism. When "postmodernism" became a vogue term in painting, during the 1980s, it referred to an apparent turn against modernist abstraction and toward more traditional figurative techniques.

In literature, too, a return to relatively straightforward narrative and to historical topics marked postmodernism. Nonetheless, several modernist techniques remained central to it. Among the distinctive literary techniques of postmodernism are parody, metafiction, metahistory, and intertextuality.[10] To some extent, these techniques are present in modernism, though postmodernism tends to push them further, often to the point of deliberate absurdity. Postmodernism seems to be marked by a particularly strong sense of the weight of inherited tradition, a theme, of course, already of Eliot, but whereas Eliot tried to place his poetry in relation to the entire literary tradition, a postmodernist such as John Barth writes of the "literature of exhaustion" in which all topics and plots seem to have been worked through, not least by the great modernists. The postmodernist therefore turns toward parody and pastiche, making use of other people's styles rather than developing a style of his or her own. David Lodge, also a major literary critic, began his series of academic novels with *The British Museum is Falling Down* (1965), in which a graduate student who is writing a thesis on the rhetoric of fiction begins to hallucinate in the style of various modernists: there are chapters written in the manner of James, Joyce, Woolf, and others; the novel ends, like *Ulysses*, with the wife's monologue, here more ambivalent than Molly's. Its keyword is not "yes," but "perhaps."

The concern with metafiction and metahistory involves an extreme self-consciousness about narration, in which narrators often intervene and comment on their stories, or on the composition of their stories, or on how their stories relate to other stories. This element of postmodernism develops in a fairly clear line from the "Arranger" in the second half of *Ulysses* through the novels of Beckett, but it is foreshadowed to some extent in the self-consciousness of Marlow's narration in Joseph Conrad's *Heart of Darkness* (1899). What makes such self-consciousness "postmodern," however, is usually the author's willingness to break down the illusion of reality, the suspension of disbelief, typical of earlier fiction, and to this extent Joyce seems to be the first postmodernist. Metafictional gestures resemble metatheatrical ones, directly addressing the reader in the same way that some modern drama breaks down the "fourth wall." Metahistory, a term coined by the historian Hayden White, calls attention to the problem of narrating historical events. Whereas the modernists generally write about the present or the recent past, there is a great deal of postmodernist historical fiction, which again is marked by self-consciousness about the constructed nature of our accounts of the past and the fact that no "purely" objective historical account is possible.

Intertextuality, another hallmark of postmodernism, seems also to have been prefigured in modernism. Eliot and Joyce made extensive use of quotation from other genres, such as popular songs, advertising, or major works of English or European literature. Postmodernists sometimes carry this allusiveness further, even to the point of rewriting earlier novels. For example, in the novel *Wide Sargasso Sea* (1966) Jean Rhys tells the story of a minor but crucial character from Charlotte Brontë's *Jane Eyre* (1847), Rochester's first wife Bertha Mason, the madwoman in the attic, who has also been taken by literary critics as a symbol of the repressed side of female creativity.[11] Rhys creates a whole earlier life in the Caribbean for the madwoman, whom she renames Antoinette. As in many postmodern novels, the story is told from several perspectives, first Antoinette's, then Rochester's, and briefly that of Grace Poole, who is in charge of taking care of Antoinette while she lives in Rochester's attic. This play with perspectives is also typical of much postmodernism in that it rejects the "stream of consciousness" or free indirect discourse typical of Joyce, Woolf and even earlier modernists like James, in favor of more straightforward first-person accounts; each person gives his or her own account, and it is up to the reader to resolve the conflicts among them. (This is a technique pioneered, however, by a modernist, William Faulkner, in *The Sound and the Fury* [1929].) Probably the most famous instance of such questioning of truth by showing a variety of first-person accounts is Akira Kurosawa's film *Rashomon* (1951), which tells of a murder and rape in eighth-century Japan from the points of view of four participants.

In all the arts postmodernism had as much of an ideological or political meaning as a formal or technical one. Modernism came by the 1960s and 1970s to be seen as elitist, whether because of its glorification of the individual (often male) artist, its allusiveness to a whole tradition of high European culture, its formal demands, or its sheer difficulty. In music, for example, the prestige associated with the modernist serialism of Arnold Schoenberg and the aesthetic theories of Adorno meant that composers of the 1950s and 1960s continued to embrace modernism, but the music never achieved widespread popularity. Public taste among concertgoers and radio audiences remained fairly traditional. After the 1960s, folk and rock music increasingly drew the interest of "progressive" listeners, so that high modernist music lost its potential radical audience. The sense that modernism, in all its complexity, served an elitist agenda was prominent in attacks on literary modernism as well.

Demographic and political changes in education after the war brought a more diverse readership and authorship to modernism. A concern to represent the experiences of people of color, women, ethnic minorities, and postcolonial peoples sometimes led to a rejection of modernist critiques of representation. Yet modernism influenced writers from all these groups. Salman Rushdie's *Midnight's Children* (1981) reads like an Indian *Ulysses*. The novels of Toni Morrison have a typically modernist linguistic inventiveness; Morrison wrote her master's thesis on Faulkner and Woolf. Chinua Achebe borrowed the title of his novel *Things Fall Apart* (1958) from Yeats's "The Second Coming," and V. S. Naipaul continually responds to Conrad's visions of the colonial world. These writers, like others labeled "postmodern," show the continuing provocation that modern art and literature offer to their heirs.

Postmodernist objections to modernism often turned, then, on the perception of modernism as elitist in character. On the other hand, some postmodernists were motivated by the rather different philosophical meaning of the term "postmodernism," popularized by Jean-François Lyotard.[12] According to Lyotard, the postmodern age was one that rejected the "grand narratives" of philosophical modernity: narratives associated with scientific, technical, material, and social progress. (Modernity here goes back to the seventeenth-century philosopher René Descartes and is not limited to "modernism"; see Preface.) While academics demonstrated that such narratives were retrospective, often self-justifying, illusions, some postmodernist literary writers attempted to dismantle narrative in fiction, through the intensification of modernist irony, the use of narrators who commented upon their own fictional status, and other techniques that challenged the traditional suspension of disbelief. In fact, such "postmodern" experiments frequently followed naturally in a tradition of playful modernism extending from Joyce and Pirandello through Beckett and Borges to (the postmodernist) Don DeLillo and Thomas Pynchon. So, as often as not, postmodernist literature carries forward themes from modernism; one could say that it is modernism that does not take itself so seriously.

Barth declared the term postmodern to be "awkward and faintly epigonic, suggestive less of a vigorous or even interesting new direction in the old art of storytelling than of something anticlimactic, feebly following a very hard act to follow."[13] Of course, postmodernism lives in the shadow of modernism, but both are devoted to a conception of the greatest art as always innovative. If we feel a need to label our own era "postmodern" rather than "modern" and thus to assert our originality, this is perhaps just a sign of the continuing modernist impulse, in the words of Pound, to "Make it New." Modernism fundamentally reshaped art and literature for the twentieth century and beyond: its rejection of traditional forms and genres, overturning of artistic conventions, emphasis on originality, and demand that artistic styles evolve in response to rapidly changing times all mark a crucial transition into an era in which the modes of artistic and literary representation remain perpetually in crisis.

## Further reading

*Literary works*

Samuel Beckett, *Waiting for Godot*. New York: Grove Press, 1954.
James Joyce, *Finnegans Wake* (various editions).
David Lodge, *The British Museum is Falling Down*. London: Penguin, 1989.
Jean Rhys, *Wide Sargasso Sea* (various editions).

*Contemporary critical statements*

Ihab Hassan, "POSTmodernISM," *New Literary History* 3 (1971), pp. 5–30.
Jean-François Lyotard, *The Postmodern Condition*, trans. Brian Massumi.
    Minneapolis: University of Minnesota Press, 1984.

*Later criticism*

John Bishop, *Joyce's Book of the Dark: "Finnegans Wake."* Madison: University of
    Wisconsin Press, 1986.
Steven Connor, ed. *The Cambridge Companion to Postmodernism*. Cambridge:
    Cambridge University Press, 2004.
Kevin J. H. Dettmar, *The Illicit Joyce of Postmodernism: Reading Against the Grain*.
    Madison: University of Wisconsin Press, 1996.
Martin Esslin, *The Theater of the Absurd*. 3rd edn. London: Penguin, 1980.
John Felstiner, *Paul Celan: Poet, Survivor, Jew*. New Haven: Yale University Press,
    1995.
Sandra M. Gilbert and Susan Gubar, *No Man's Land: The Place of the Woman
    Writer in the Twentieth Century*, 3 vols. New Haven: Yale University Press,
    1988–94.
Linda Hutcheon, *A Poetics of Postmodernism*. New York: Routledge, 1988.
Roland McHugh, *Annotations to "Finnegans Wake,"* rev. edn. Baltimore: Johns
    Hopkins University Press, 1991.

# Chronology

| | |
|---|---|
| 1848 | Revolution in France: Louis Napoleon elected President |
| 1851–2 | Louis Napoleon stages *coup d'état*; Second Empire begins in France |
| 1857 | Charles Baudelaire's *The Flowers of Evil* and Gustave Flaubert's *Madame Bovary* prosecuted for obscenity |
| 1863 | Edouard Manet, *Déjeuner sur l'herbe, Olympia* |
| 1873 | Walter Pater, *The Renaissance* |
| 1874 | First Impressionist Exhibition |
| 1876 | Queen Victoria named Empress of India |
| 1878 | J. A. M. Whistler sues John Ruskin for libel |
| 1884 | Joris-Karl Huymans, *A rebours* |
| 1888 | Vincent van Gogh, *Night Café* |
| 1889 | Henrik Ibsen, *A Doll's House*, performed in London |
| 1890 | Henrik Ibsen, *Hedda Gabler* |
| 1891 | Paul Gauguin first visits Tahiti |
| 1893 | W. B. Yeats, *The Celtic Twilight* |
| 1894 | Dreyfus Affair begins in France (ends 1899) |
| 1895 | Trials of Oscar Wilde |
| 1896 | Alfred Jarry, *King Ubu* |
| 1897 | Anton Chekhov, *Uncle Vanya* |
| 1898 | H. G. Wells, *The War of the Worlds* |
| 1899 | Joseph Conrad, *Heart of Darkness* |
| | Beginning of Boer War (ends 1902) |
| 1900 | Death of Oscar Wilde |
| 1901 | Death of Queen Victoria |
| 1902 | August Strindberg, *A Dream Play* |
| 1903 | W. E. B. Du Bois, *The Souls of Black Folk* |
| 1904 | Henry James, *The Golden Bowl* |
| 1905 | George Bernard Shaw, *Major Barbara* |
| 1906 | Death of Paul Cézanne |
| 1907 | Pablo Picasso, *Les Demoiselles d'Avignon* |
| 1908 | Georges Braque and Pablo Picasso paint their first cubist paintings |

1909     F. T. Marinetti, "Futurist Manifesto"
1910     Death of Edward VII
         First post-impressionist exhibition in London
         "On or about December," according to Virginia Woolf, "human
            character changes"
1911     Ezra Pound, "In a Station of the Metro"
1912     Georges Braque and Pablo Picasso introduce collage into cubism
         Wyndham Lewis, *Kermesse*
         Vanessa Bell, *Studland Beach*
         Second post-impressionist exhibition in London
1913     D. H. Lawrence, *Sons and Lovers*
         Marcel Proust, *Swann's Way* (first volume of *Remembrance of
            Things Past*)
         Igor Stravinsky, *The Rite of Spring*, performed in Paris by the
            Ballets Russes
         Rabindrinath Tagore awarded Nobel Prize
1914     Beginning of First World War (ends 1918)
         James Joyce, *Dubliners*
         First issue of BLAST
1915     Ford Madox Ford, *The Good Soldier*
         T. S. Eliot, "The Love Song of J. Alfred Prufrock"
         Second (and last) issue of BLAST
1916     James Joyce, *A Portrait of the Artist as a Young Man*
         W. B. Yeats, "Easter, 1916"
1917     Russian Revolution
         Marcel Duchamp, *Fountain*
         Guillaume Apollinaire, *The Breasts of Tiresias*
1918     Rebecca West, *The Return of the Soldier*
         Lytton Strachey, *Eminent Victorians*
         Oswald Spengler, *The Decline of the West*
1919     Treaty of Versailles
         George Bernard Shaw, *Heartbreak House*
1920     Ezra Pound, *Hugh Selwyn Mauberley*
         Wilfred Owen, *Poems*
1921     Irish Free State founded
         Luigi Pirandello, *Six Characters in Search of an Author*
1922     James Joyce, *Ulysses*
         T. S. Eliot, *The Waste Land*
         Death of Marcel Proust

| | |
|---|---|
| 1923 | W. B. Yeats awarded Nobel Prize |
| | Italo Svevo, *Zeno's Conscience* |
| 1924 | André Breton, *Surrealist Manifesto* |
| | E. M. Forster, *A Passage to India* |
| | Death of Vladimir Ilich Lenin |
| | Death of Franz Kafka |
| 1925 | George Bernard Shaw awarded Nobel Prize |
| | Virginia Woolf, *Mrs Dalloway* |
| | Mussolini declares himself dictator |
| 1926 | General Strike in the U.K. |
| | Ernest Hemingway, *The Sun Also Rises* |
| 1927 | Virginia Woolf, *To the Lighthouse* |
| 1928 | D. H. Lawrence, *Lady Chatterley's Lover* |
| | Bertolt Brecht, *The Threepenny Opera* |
| 1929 | Great Depression begins |
| | Museum of Modern Art founded in New York |
| | Thomas Mann awarded Nobel Prize |
| 1930 | Death of D. H. Lawrence |
| | Suicide of Vladimir Mayakovsky |
| 1932 | John Galsworthy awarded Nobel Prize |
| | W. H. Auden, *The Orators* |
| 1933 | Adolf Hitler comes to power in Germany |
| | Gertrude Stein, *The Autobiography of Alice B. Toklas* |
| 1934 | Luigi Pirandello awarded Nobel Prize |
| 1935 | T. S. Eliot, *Murder in the Cathedral* |
| 1936 | Beginning of Spanish Civil War (ends 1939) |
| 1937 | W. H. Auden, "Spain, 1937" |
| 1938 | George Orwell, *Homage to Catalonia* |
| 1939 | Second World War begins (ends 1945) |
| | Death of W. B. Yeats |
| | James Joyce, *Finnegans Wake* |
| 1941 | Death of James Joyce |
| | Suicide of Virginia Woolf |
| 1953 | Samuel Beckett, *Waiting for Godot*, performed in Paris |

# Notes

## Introduction

1. *Modernism Anthology*, pp. 123, 115.
2. *Mimesis*; M. H. Abrams, *The Mirror and the Lamp: Romantic Theory and the Critical Tradition* (Oxford: Oxford University Press, 1953).
3. *Theories of Modern Art*, p. 94.
4. *Illuminations*, p. 187.
5. *Modernism Anthology*, pp. 490, 515, 549, and Alick West, *Crisis and Criticism* (London: Lawrence and Wishart, 1937).
6. Fredric Jameson, foreword to Jean-François Lyotard, *The Postmodern Condition*, trans. Brian Massumi (Minneapolis: University of Minnesota Press, 1984), p. viii. See also David Harvey, *Conditions of Postmodernity* (Oxford: Blackwell, 1990), pp. 260–83.
7. Letter to Harriet Monroe, May 1915, quoted in *Pound Era*, p. 81.
8. Ian Watt, *The Rise of the Novel: Studies in Defoe, Richardson, and Fielding* (Berkeley and Los Angeles: University of California Press, 1957), pp. 290–322.
9. Charles Baudelaire, "The Painter of Modern Life," in *Modernism Anthology*, p. 107.
10. For an overview of Kant's philosophy, see Stefan Körner, *Kant* (Harmondsworth: Penguin, 1955).
11. See Edmund Husserl, *Cartesian Meditations: An Introduction to Phenomenology*, trans. Dorion Cairns (The Hague: M. Nijhoff, 1960), and Maurice Natanson, *Edmund Husserl: Philosopher of Infinite Tasks* (Evanston, IL: Northwestern University Press, 1973).
12. *Modernism Anthology*, p. 397.
13. William James, *Principles of Psychology*, quoted in Stephen Kern, *The Culture of Time and Space, 1880–1914* (Cambridge, MA: Harvard University Press, 1983), p. 24. On these philosophers, see Sanford Schwartz, *The Matrix of Modernism: Pound, Eliot, and Early Twentieth-Century Thought* (Princeton: Princeton University Press, 1985).
14. Charles Taylor, *Sources of the Self: The Making of the Modern Identity* (Cambridge, MA: Harvard University Press, 1989), p. 413.
15. *Ibid.*, p. 476.

16. Paul de Man, "Literary History and Literary Modernity," in de Man, *Blindness and Insight: Essays in the Rhetoric of Contemporary Criticism*, 2nd edn (Minneapolis: University of Minnesota Press, 1983), pp. 142–65.

17. *Critical Tradition*, p. 260.

18. Kant developed his philosophy of aesthetics in his "third" critique, *The Critique of Judgement*, trans. James Creed Meredith (Oxford: Clarendon Press, 1952). The first two critiques are the *Critique of Pure Reason* and the *Critique of Practical Reason*.

19. *Modernism Anthology*, pp. 114, 120.

20. W. H. Auden, "In Memory of W. B. Yeats" (1939).

21. *Critical Tradition*, p. 845.

22. Kern, *Culture of Time and Space*, p. 1.

23. Adrienne Rich, "Compulsory Heterosexuality and Lesbian Existence," in Rich, *Blood, Bread, and Poetry: Selected Prose, 1979–1985* (New York: Norton, 1985), pp. 23–75.

24. George Dangerfield, *The Strange Death of Liberal England* (1935; Stanford: Stanford University Press, 1997).

25. Pericles Lewis, *Modernism, Nationalism, and the Novel* (Cambridge: Cambridge University Press, 2000).

26. Hannah Arendt, *The Origins of Totalitarianism*, new edn (New York: Harcourt Brace, 1973).

27. Because this book focuses on literature in England and Europe, I have been unable to include an extended discussion of the Harlem Renaissance. For the relationship of the Harlem Renaissance to modernism, see Houston Baker, *Modernism and the Harlem Renaissance* (Chicago: University of Chicago Press, 1987). For a general history of the movement, see David Levering Lewis, *When Harlem was in Vogue* (New York: Penguin, 1997).

28. E. J. Hobsbawm, *The Age of Extremes: A History of the World, 1914–1991* (New York: Vintage Books, 1994). My account of the history of the nineteenth century draws also on Hobsbawm's earlier volumes, *The Age of Revolution, 1789–1848* (New York: New American Library, 1962), *The Age of Capital, 1848–1875* (New York: Scribner, 1975), and *The Age of Empire, 1875–1914* (New York: Vintage Books, 1989).

29. See John Stuart Mill, *Considerations on Representative Government*, in Mill, *"On Liberty" and Other Essays*, ed. John Gray (Oxford: Oxford University Press, 1998), pp. 203–467.

30. *Let's Murder the Moonshine*, p. 161.

31. Jacques Derrida, "Cogito and the History of Madness," in Derrida, *Writing and Difference*, trans. Alan Bass (Chicago: University of Chicago Press, 1978), pp. 62–3.

32. Paul Ricoeur, *Freud and Philosophy: An Essay on Interpretation*, trans. Denis Savage (New Haven: Yale University Press, 1970).

33. *James Joyce*, p. 521.

34. J. W. Burrow, *Evolution and Society: A Study in Victorian Social Theory* (Cambridge: Cambridge University Press, 1966). Throughout this section I follow Burrow's excellent recent intellectual history, *The Crisis of Reason: European Thought,*

*1848–1914* (New Haven: Yale University Press, 2000). See also Charles Darwin, *The Darwin Reader*, ed. Mark Ridley (New York: Norton, 1987). On eugenics in the period, see David Bradshaw, "Eugenics: 'They Should Certainly be Killed,'" in Bradshaw, ed., *A Concise Companion to Modernism* (Oxford: Blackwell, 2003), pp. 34–55.

35. Ricoeur, *Freud and Philosophy*, p. 32.

36. For the works of Marx quoted here, see *The Marx-Engels Reader*, ed. Robert C. Tucker, 2nd edn (New York: Norton, 1978).

37. *Critical Tradition*, pp. 453–5. For a useful introduction to Nietzsche's thought, see *The Portable Nietzsche*, ed. and trans. Walter Kaufmann (New York: Penguin, 1982). On Nietzsche's reception in England, see Michael Bell, "Nietzscheanism: 'The Superman and the All-Too-Human,'" in Bradshaw, ed., *Concise Companion to Modernism*, pp. 56–74.

38. Sigmund Freud, *Introductory Lectures on Psychoanalysis*, trans. James Strachey (New York: Norton, 1977). See also *The Freud Reader*, ed. Peter Gay (New York: Norton, 1995).

39. The quotations come from Albert Einstein, *Relativity: The Special and the General Theory*, and Albert Einstein and Leopold Infeld, *The Evolution of Physics*, quoted in Kern, *Culture of Time and Space*, pp. 19, 33, 126, 206. My account of Einstein's theories follows Kern's. See also Michael H. Whitworth, *Einstein's Wake: Relativity, Metaphor, and Modernist Literature* (Oxford: Oxford University Press, 2001).

40. Preface to *Miss Julie*, in *Strindberg: Five Plays*, p. 64. Excerpts of the Preface are available in *Modernism Anthology*, 115–19.

41. *Critical Tradition*, p. 778.

42. *Brecht on Theatre*, pp. 94–6.

43. *Eliot Selected Prose*, pp. 38–9.

44. *Ibid.*, p. 65.

45. Theodor W. Adorno, "Lyric Poetry and Society," in Adorno, *Notes to Literature*, 2 vols., trans. Shierry Weber Nicholsen (New York: Columbia University Press, 1991), vol. I, p. 39.

46. Charles Baudelaire, "Salon of 1846," quoted in Francis Frascina *et al.*, *Modernity and Modernism: French Painting in the Nineteenth Century* (New Haven: Yale University Press, 1993), p. 53.

47. On mass culture and modernism, see Andreas Huyssen, *After the Great Divide: Modernism, Mass Culture, Postmodernism* (Bloomington: Indiana University Press, 1986); Rita Felski, *The Gender of Modernity* (Cambridge, MA: Harvard University Press, 1995); and Michael North, *Reading 1922: A Return to the Scene of the Modern* (Oxford: Oxford University Press, 1999).

48. My account again follows Kern, *Culture of Time and Space*.

49. For an overview of Bergson's impact on modernism, see Mary Ann Gillies, "Bergsonism: 'Time out of Mind,' " in Bradshaw, ed., *Concise Companion to Modernism*, pp. 95–115.

50. *Illuminations*, pp. 257–8.

## 1 Trials of modernity

1. Dominick LaCapra, "Two Trials," in Denis Hollier *et al.*, eds., *A New History of French Literature* (Cambridge: Harvard University Press, 1989), p. 726.

2. Dominick LaCapra, *"Madame Bovary" on Trial* (Ithaca, NY: Cornell University Press, 1982), p. 52. My account follows LaCapra's.

3. J. W. Burrow, *The Crisis of Reason: European Thought, 1848–1914* (New Haven: Yale University Press, 2000), p. 15.

4. Charles Baudelaire, "The Albatross," in Baudelaire, *The Flowers of Evil*, ed. Marthiel and Jackson Mathews, rev. edn (New York: New Directions, 1989). All quotations are from this edition, which contains the French text and translations by various hands. I have sometimes given my own translations.

5. LaCapra, *"Madame Bovary" on Trial*, pp. 37, 51.

6. Gustave Flaubert, Letter to Louise Colet, December 9, 1852.

7. On Flaubert's use of free indirect discourse and its contribution to his realism, see LaCapra, *"Madame Bovary" on Trial*; Hans Robert Jauss, "Literary History as a Challenge to Literary Theory," in Jauss, *Towards an Aesthetics of Reception*, trans. Timothy Bahti (Minneapolis: University of Minnesota Press, 1982), pp. 3–46; and *Mimesis*, pp. 482–92. Another problem crucial to modernist narrative is that of the "unreliable narrator," discussed in Chapter Five below. The opinions expressed by a narrator might or might not be those of the author.

8. LaCapra, *"Madame Bovary" on Trial*, pp. 39–40.

9. *Edwardian Turn*, pp. 187–8.

10. Henrik Ibsen, *"A Doll's House" and Other Plays*, trans. Peter Watts (London: Penguin, 1965), p. 334.

11. *Edwardian Turn*, pp. 172–80.

12. *Ibid.*, pp. 212–53.

13. On the social and cultural history surrounding the Dreyfus Affair, see Eugen Weber, *France, Fin de Siècle* (Cambridge, MA: Belknap, 1986).

14. Charles Baudelaire, *The Flowers of Evil*, trans. and ed. James McGowan (Oxford: Oxford University Press, 1993), p. xviii.

15. Charles Baudelaire, "The Painter of Modern Life," in *Modernism Anthology*, p. 108.

16. *Illuminations*, p. 169.

17. Matei Calinescu, *Five Faces of Modernity: Modernism, Avant-Garde, Decadence, Kitsch, Postmodernism* (Durham, NC: Duke University Press, 1987), pp. 164–71.

18. *Modernism Anthology*, p. 22.

19. Reported by Paul Valéry, quoted in Roman Jakobson, *Language in Literature* (Cambridge, MA: Harvard University Press, 1987), p. 216.

20. On Mallarmé and symbolism, see Clive Scott, "Symbolism, Decadence, and Impressionism," in *Modernism 1890–1930*, pp. 206–27. For Mallarmé's influence on English literature, see Edmund Wilson, *Axel's Castle: A Study of the Imaginative Literature of 1870–1930* (1931; New York: Farrar, Straus, and Giroux, 2004), pp. 3–22, and Frank Kermode, *The Romantic Image* (1957; London: Routledge, 2002),

pp. 127–40. On Wagner's influence in France, see Richard Sieburth, "The Music of the Future," in Hollier *et al.* (eds.) *New History of French Literature*, pp. 789–98.

21. Charles Baudelaire, "The Painter of Modern Life," quoted in Phoebe Pool, *Impressionism* (London: Thames and Hudson, 1967), p. 73 (translation corrected).

22. Quoted in Stephen Kern, *The Culture of Time and Space, 1880–1918* (Cambridge, MA: Harvard University Press, 1983), p. 21.

23. James Abbott McNeill Whistler, *The Gentle Art of Making Enemies* (1890; New York: Dover Publications, 1967), p. 1. For an overview of impressionism, see Phoebe Pool, *Impressionism* (London: Thames and Hudson, 1967). For more detailed treatment of the origins of modern art in mid-nineteenth century Paris, see Francis Fascina *et al., Modernity and Modernism: French Painting in the Nineteenth Century* (New Haven: Yale University Press, 1993); T. J. Clark, *The Painting of Modern Life: Paris in the Art of Manet and His Followers* (Princeton: Princeton University Press, 1986); and Michael Fried, *Manet's Modernism, or, The Face of Painting in the 1860s* (Chicago: University of Chicago Press, 1996).

24. *Theories of Modern Art*, p. 94.

25. Quoted in Joachim Gasquet, *Joachim Gasquet's Cézanne*, trans. Christopher Pemberton (New York: Thames and Hudson, 1991), p. 164.

26. *Theories of Modern* Art, p. 36.

27. Richard Ellmann, *Oscar Wilde* (New York: Knopf, 1988), p. 449. My account follows Ellmann's.

28. *Ibid.*, pp. 463, 464, 471.

29. *Edwardian Turn*, p. 185.

30. *Modernism Anthology*, pp. 114, 113, 114.

31. *Ibid.*, pp. 119–20.

32. *Ibid.*, pp. 135.

33. For his statement of these views, see "The Symbolism of Poetry" in *Modernism Anthology*, pp. 136–40.

34. Helen Vendler, *Poets Thinking: Pope, Whitman, Dickinson, Yeats* (Cambridge, MA: Harvard University Press, 2004), pp. 108–18. On the development of Yeats's symbolism, see Richard Ellmann, *W. B. Yeats: The Man and the Masks* (New York: Macmillan, 1948), and Frank Kermode, *The Romantic Image* (1957; London: Routledge, 2002). For a magisterial account of his very full life, see R. F. Foster, *W. B. Yeats: A Life*, 2 vols. (Oxford: Oxford University Press, 1997–2003).

35. Letter to Barrett H. Clark, May 4, 1918, in *Collected Letters of Joseph Conrad*, 8 vols., ed. Laurence Davies, Frederick Karl, and Owen Knowles (Cambridge: Cambridge University Press, 2002), vol. VI, pp. 210–11.

36. Ian Watt, *Conrad in the Nineteenth Century* (Berkeley and Los Angeles: University of California Press, 1979), p. 169. My accounts of literary impressionism and symbolism follow Watt's.

37. F. R. Leavis, *The Great Tradition: George Eliot, Henry James, Joseph Conrad* (London: Chatto and Windus, 1948) pp. 179–80.

38. *Modernism Anthology*, p. 133.

39. *Ibid.*, p. 397.
40. Leon Edel, *Henry James*, 5 vols. (New York: Avon, 1978), vol. V, pp. 87–8.


## 2 Primitivists and modernizers

1. *Modernism Anthology*, 296. Quotations from Woolf in the next few pages are drawn from "Mr. Bennett and Mrs. Brown" and "Modern Fiction," excerpted in *Modernism Anthology*, pp. 395–7. The full texts of these essays are available in Mitchell Leaska, ed., *The Virginia Woolf Reader* (San Diego: Harcourt Brace Jovanovitch, 1985).
2. On Wells's career in the period, see *Edwardian Turn*, pp. 87–131, and Anthony West, *H. G. Wells: Aspects of a Life* (London: Hutchinson, 1984), pp. 277–334.
3. E. M. Forster, *A Passage to India* (Harmondsworth: Penguin, 1979.), p. 26.
4. *Edwardian Turn*, pp. 212–53.
5. *Ibid.*, pp. 254–306. On Joyce's experiences with the censors, see *James Joyce*, pp. 310–37, 502–4.
6. W. E. B. Du Bois, *The Souls of Black Folk*, ed. Henry Louis Gates, Jr. (New York: Bantam, 1989), p. xxxi.
7. Quoted in Ernst Gombrich, *The Preference for the Primitive: Episodes in the History of Western Taste and Art* (London: Phaidon, 2002), p. 236.
8. Gill Perry, "Primitivism and the 'Modern,'" in Charles Harrison, Francis Frascina, and Gill Perry, *Primitivism, Cubism, Abstraction: The Early Twentieth Century* (New Haven: Yale University Press, 1994), pp. 28–34.
9. Clive Bell, *Art* (1914; New York: G. P. Putnam's Sons, 1958), p. 22. On the development of primitivism in modern art, see Robert Goldwater, *Primitivism in Modern Art*, rev. edn (New York: Vintage Books, 1967), and William Rubin, ed., *"Primitivism" in 20th-Century Art* (New York: Museum of Modern Art, 1984).
10. Perry, "Primitivism and the 'Modern,'" p. 80.
11. Pablo Picasso, in an interview with Florent Fels, 1923, quoted in Rubin, ed., *"Primitivism,"* p. 260.
12. Christopher Butler, *Early Modernism: Literature, Music, and Painting in Europe, 1900–1916* (Oxford: Oxford University Press, 1994), p. 116.
13. On the opening night of *The Rite of Spring*, see Modris Eksteins, *The Rites of Spring: The Great War and the Birth of the Modern Age* (Toronto: Lester & Orpen Dennys, 1989), pp. 9–54.
14. On the proceedings, see Jeffrey Meyers, *D. H. Lawrence* (New York: Knopf, 1990), pp. 182–96.
15. For discussions of literary primitivism, see Michael Bell, *Primitivism* (London: Methuen, 1972), and Butler, *Early Modernism*, pp. 106–32.
16. *Modernism Anthology*, p. 496.
17. *Ibid.*, p. 251.
18. *Ibid.*, p. 260.

19. *Let's Murder the Moonshine*, p. 139.
20. On the relationship between Marinetti and Pound, see *Futurist Moment*, pp. 173–7, and Lawrence Rainey, "The Creation of the Avant-Garde: F. T. Marinetti and Ezra Pound," *Modernism/Modernity* 1 (1994), pp. 195–220.
21. *Modernism Anthology*, p. 374.
22. *Ibid.*, p. 178.
23. Ezra Pound, *Gaudier-Brzeska: A Memoir* (1916), quoted in *Modernism 1890–1930*, p. 237.
24. Quoted in Lisa Tickner, *Modern Life and Modern Subjects: British Art in the Early Twentieth Century* (New Haven: Yale University Press, 2000), pp. 104, 262 n.97, and Butler, *Early Modernism*, p. 222.
25. "Tarr," *Egoist*, September 1918, p. 106, quoted in Vincent Sherry, *The Great War and the Language of Modernism* (Oxford: Oxford University Press, 2003), p. 159.
26. On Woolf and Dangerfield, see Michael Tratner, *Modernism and Mass Politics: Joyce, Woolf, Eliot, Yeats* (Stanford: Stanford University Press, 1995), pp. 60–76.
27. Sorel's *Reflections on Violence* (1906, translated by T. E. Hulme in 1914) influenced both leftist and rightist thinkers in the period.
28. Quoted in Conor Cruise O'Brien, "'Passion and Cunning': An Essay on the Politics of W. B. Yeats," in A. Norman Jeffares and K. G. W. Cross, eds., *In Excited Reverie* (New York: Macmillan, 1965), p. 216.
29. On attitudes to sex, gender, and sexuality in the period, see *Edwardian Turn*, pp. 132–211.
30. *Ibid.*, pp. 149–55.
31. Virginia Woolf, "Old Bloomsbury," in Woolf, *Moments of Being*, ed. Jeanne Schulkind, 2nd edn (San Diego: Harcourt Brace Jovanovich, 1985), p. 195. On Woolf and the Bloomsbury Group, see Hermione Lee, *Virginia Woolf* (New York: Vintage Books, 1999), and Peter Stansky, *On or about December 1910: Early Bloomsbury and Its Intimate World* (Cambridge, MA: Harvard University Press, 1996).
32. Quoted in *Edwardian Turn*, p. 328.
33. Charles Harrison, *English Art and Modernism 1900–1939*, 2nd edn (New Haven: Yale University Press, 1994), p. 47.
34. Quoted in *Edwardian Turn*, p. 332.
35. Bell, *Art*, p. 16.
36. Tickner, *Modern Life and Modern Subjects*, pp. 117–42.

## 3  The avant-garde and high modernism

1. For a discussion of this episode, see Wendy Steiner, *Venus in Exile: The Rejection of Beauty in Twentieth-Century Art* (Chicago: University of Chicago Press, 2001), pp. 216–42.
2. For the history of the term "avant-garde," see Matei Calinescu, *Five Faces of Modernity: Modernism, Avant-Garde, Decadence, Kitsch, Postmodernism* (Durham, NC: Duke University Press, 1987), pp. 93–148.

3. For differing views of the political significance of the avant-garde, see Renato Poggi-oli, *Theory of the Avant-Garde,* trans. Gerald Fitzgerald (Cambridge, MA: Harvard University Press, 1968), and Peter Bürger, *Theory of the Avant-Garde,* trans. Michael Shaw (Minneapolis: University of Minnesota Press, 1984.

4. *Futurist Moment,* p. 36.

5. *Ibid.,* p. xvii.

6. Paul Griffith, *A Concise History of Modern Music from Debussy to Boulez* (London: Thames and Hudson, 1978).

7. Quoted in G. M. Hyde, "Russian Futurism," in *Modernism 1890–1930,* p. 264.

8. Tom Conley, "Lyrical Ideograms," in Denis Hollier *et al.,* eds., *A New History of French Literature* (Cambridge, MA: Harvard University Press, 1989), pp. 842–50.

9. On the role of little magazines in propagating modernism, see Mark Morrisson, *The Public Face of Modernism: Little Magazines, Audiences, and Reception, 1905–1920* (Madison: University of Wisconsin Press, 2001).

10. Marjorie Perloff, *The Poetics of Indeterminacy: Rimbaud to Cage* (Evanston, IL: Northwestern University Press, 1999), p. 102.

11. Gertrude Stein, *The Making of Americans* (1925), quoted in Richard Bridgman, *Gertrude Stein in Pieces* (Oxford: Oxford University Press, 1971), p. 73.

12. Bridgman, *Gertrude Stein in Pieces,* pp. 209–17.

13. *Pound Era,* p. 245.

14. *Futurist Moment,* p. xxi.

15. Quoted in *ibid.,* p. 6.

16. Wyndham Lewis, *Rude Assignment* (1950), quoted in *War Imagined,* p. 195.

17. Interview in *Weekly Dispatch,* February 16, 1919, quoted in Sue Malvern, *Modern Art, Britain, and the Great War* (New Haven: Yale University Press, 2004), p. 134.

18. See Daniel Albright, *Untwisting the Serpent: Modernism in Music, Literature, and Other Arts* (Chicago: University of Chicago Press, 2000).

19. Quoted in C. K. Stead, *The New Poetic* (London: Hutchinson, 1964), p. 70.

20. On the literature of the First World War, and its impact on modernism, see *War Imagined,* and Paul Fussell, *The Great War and Modern Memory* (Oxford: Oxford University Press, 1975). My account in this section largely follows that of Hynes in *War Imagined.*

21. Letter of November 10, 1919, quoted in *War Imagined,* p. 269.

22. *War Imagined,* p. 244.

23. *Ibid.,* p. xi.

24. On the modernists' responses to the war, see James Longenbach, "Modern Poetry," in Michael Levenson, ed., *The Cambridge Companion to Modernism* (Cambridge: Cambridge University Press: 1999), pp. 109–18.

25. Ezra Pound, *Selected Letters,* ed. D. D. Paige (New York: New Directions, 1971), p. 13.

26. Their collaboration is studied in detail in James Longenbach, *Stone Cottage: Pound, Yeats, and Modernism* (Oxford: Oxford University Press, 1988).

27. *Modernism Anthology,* p. 378.

28. R. M. Foster, *W. B. Yeats: A Life*, 2 vols. (Oxford: Oxford University Press, 1997), vol. I, pp. 469–73.

29. Jay Parini, *Robert Frost: A Life* (London: Heinemann, 1999), pp. 125–31.

30. Foster, *W. B. Yeats*, vol. I, p. 276.

31. *James Joyce*, pp. 349–53, 390–2, 405–6.

32. The passage is cited by Peter Brooks as the epigraph to his *Reading for the Plot* (Cambridge, MA: Harvard University Press, 1992).

33. See, for example, Stephen Spender, *The Destructive Element: A Study of Modern Writers and Beliefs* (Boston: Houghton Mifflin, 1936).

34. Norbert Lynton, *The Story of Modern Art*, 2nd edn (London: Phaidon, 1989), p. 201.

## 4 Poetry

1. Ezra Pound, *Selected Letters*, ed. D. D. Paige (New York: New Directions, 1971), pp. 178–9.

2. T. S. Eliot, *The Waste Land: A Facsimile and Transcript of the Original Drafts Including the Annotations of Ezra Pound*, ed. Valerie Eliot (Orlando: Harcourt, 1971), p. 1.

3. I. A. Richards, *Science and Poetry*, quoted in *Auden Generation*, p. 28.

4. T. S. Eliot, *The Waste Land*, Norton Critical Edition, ed. Michael North (New York: Norton, 2001), p. 112. I have made use of this edition in my summary of the influences on the poem.

5. *Critical Tradition*, p. 812.

6. Quoted in G. M. Hyde, "Russian Futurism," in *Modernism 1890–1930*, p. 264.

7. B. C. Southam, *A Guide to the Selected Poems of T. S. Eliot*, 6th edn (San Diego: Harcourt Brace, 1994), pp. 138–56. I have made extensive use of Southam's Notes in this chapter.

8. Quoted in *ibid.*, p. 26. The Notes were included in the first book edition of the poem, but not in the versions printed in *The Criterion* and *The Dial*.

9. Anthony Cronin, "A Conversation with T. S. Eliot about the Relation between *Ulysses* and *The Waste Land*," *Irish Times*, June 16, 1971, quoted in Southam, *A Guide to the Selected Poems*, p. 130.

10. Quoted in Michael North, *Reading 1922: A Return to the Scene of the Modern* (Oxford: Oxford University Press, 1999), p. 145.

11. Louis Menand, *Discovering Modernism: T. S. Eliot and His Context* (Oxford: Oxford University Press, 1987), pp. 90–1.

12. *Eliot Selected Prose*, p. 41.

13. Quoted in Menand, *Discovering Modernism*, p. 41.

14. *Eliot Selected Prose*, pp. 31–6.

15. Quoted in Paul Fussell, *Poetic Meter and Poetic Form*, rev. edn (New York: McGraw-Hill, 1979), p. 85.

16. Eliot, *The Waste Land: A Facsimile*, p. 11.

17. Fussell, *Poetic Meter and Poetic Form*, pp. 76–89.

18. Helen Vendler, "Technique in the Early Poems of Yeats," in James Pethica, ed., *Yeats's Poetry, Drama, and Prose* (New York: Norton, 2000), pp. 358–9.
19. Eliot, *The Waste Land: A Facsimile*, p. xxii.
20. *Pound Era*, p. 203.
21. Graham Hough, "Modernist Lyric," in *Modernism 1890–1930*, pp. 312–22.
22. *Modernism Anthology*, p. 373.
23. *Pound Era*, p. 507.
24. Pethica, ed., *Yeats's Poetry, Drama, and Prose*, p. 96, n.1.
25. R. F. Foster, *W. B. Yeats: A Life*, 2 vols. (Oxford: Oxford University Press, 2003), vol. II, pp. 105–17.
26. Wallace Stevens, *Opus Posthumous*, ed. Milton J. Bates (New York: Knopf, 1989), p. 260.
27. See Ellman Crasnow, "Poems and Fictions: Stevens, Rilke, Valéry," in *Modernism 1890–1930*, pp. 369–82, from which some of the quotations in this paragraph are drawn.
28. Nigel Alderman, "Pocket Epics: British Poetry after Modernism," *Yale Journal of Criticism* 13 (2000), pp. 1–2. The article introduces a collection of essays on the pocket epic.
29. Jahan Ramazani, Richard Ellmann, and Robert O'Clair, eds., *The Norton Anthology of Modern and Contemporary Poetry*, 2 vols., *Volume I: Modern Poetry*, 3rd edn (New York: Norton, 2003), vol. I, p. 431. See also Laurence Stapleton, *Marianne Moore: The Poet's Advance* (Princeton: Princeton University Press, 1978), pp. 49, 222.

## 5 Prose fiction

1. *Modernism Anthology*, p. 371.
2. Dujardin, whom Joyce credited as the inventor of the technique, called it "*monologue intérieur*," rather than "stream of consciousness."
3. *Modernism Anthology*, p. 397.
4. See also Franco Moretti, *Modern Epic*, trans. Quintin Hoare (London: Verso, 1996); Georg Lukács, *Theory of the Novel*, trans. Anna Bostock (Cambridge, MA: MIT Press, 1971); and Mikhail Bakhtin, *The Dialogic Imagination*, ed. Michael Holquist, trans. Caryl Emerson and Michael Holquist (Austin: University of Texas Press, 1981).
5. Robert Alter, *Canon and Creativity* (New Haven: Yale University Press, 2000).
6. For biographical information on Joyce, see *James Joyce*. This chapter draws extensively on the following commentaries on *Ulysses*: Harry Blamires, *The New Bloomsday Book*, rev. edn (London: Routledge, 1988); Don Gifford and Robert J. Seidman, "*Ulysses*" *Annotated: Notes for James Joyce's* "*Ulysses*," rev. edn (Berkeley and Los Angeles: University of California Press, 1988); and Stuart Gilbert, *James Joyce's* "*Ulysses*": *A Study* (New York: Vintage Books, 1955). See also Frank Budgen,

*James Joyce and the Making of "Ulysses" and Other Writings* (Oxford: Oxford University Press, 1989), and Hugh Kenner, *Ulysses*, rev. edn (Baltimore: Johns Hopkins University Press, 1987).

7. Ian Watt, *The Rise of the Novel: Studies in Defoe, Richardson, and Fielding* (Berkeley and Los Angeles: University of California Press, 1957), and Michael McKeon, *The Origins of the English Novel, 1600–1740* (Baltimore: Johns Hopkins University Press, 1987).

8. *James Joyce*, p. 534. For Dostoevsky's life, see J. W. Burrow, *The Crisis of Reason: European Thought, 1848–1914* (New Haven: Yale University Press, 2000), p. 27.

9. Watt, *Rise of the Novel*, p. 288. On continuities with realism, see also *Mimesis*.

10. On the unreliable narrator, see Wayne Booth, *The Rhetoric of Fiction*, 2nd edn (Chicago: University of Chicago Press, 1983).

11. On stream of consciousness, see Moretti, *Modern Epic*, pp. 168–81.

12. See Michael Hollington, "Svevo, Joyce, and Modernist Time," in *Modernism 1890–1930*, pp. 430–42.

13. Frank Kermode, *The Sense of an Ending* (Oxford: Oxford University Press, 1967).

14. Moretti, *Modern Epic*, p. 154.

15. Homer, *The Odyssey*, trans. Robert Fitzgerald (New York: Vintage Books, 1990), p. 191.

16. Virginia Woolf, "A Sketch of the Past" in Woolf, *Moments of Being*, ed. Jeanne Schulkind, 2nd edn (San Diego: Harcourt Brace Jovanovich, 1985), pp. 70–2.

17. Quoted in Christopher Butler, "Joyce, Modernism, and Postmodernism," in Derek Attridge, ed., *The Cambridge Companion to James Joyce* (Cambridge: Cambridge University Press, 1990), p. 274.

18. See Hollington "Svevo, Joyce, and Modernist Time."

19. Peter Brooks, *Reading for the Plot* (Cambridge, MA: Harvard University Press, 1992), p. 279.

20. Peter Francis Mackey, *Chaos Theory and Joyce's Everyman* (Gainesville: University Press of Florida, 1999).

21. Gifford and Seidman, *"Ulysses" Annotated*, p. 87.

22. The term was introduced by David Hayman. See his *"Ulysses": The Mechanics of Meaning*, rev. edn (Madison: University of Wisconsin Press, 1982).

23. Pericles Lewis, "Churchgoing in the Modern Novel," *Modernism/Modernity* 11 (2004), pp. 667–94.

## 6 Drama

1. *Critical Tradition*, pp. 59–81.

2. Martin Puchner, *Stage Fright: Modernism, Anti-Theatricality, and Drama* (Baltimore: Johns Hopkins University Press, 2002), p. 5.

3. Bert O. States, *Great Reckonings in Little Rooms: On the Phenomenology of Theater* (Berkeley and Los Angeles: University of California Press, 1985), p. 20.

4. Richard Gilman, *The Making of Modern Drama* (New York: Farrar, Straus, and Giroux, 1974), p. 70. On the well-made play, see also *Century of Innovation*, pp. 14–19; Maurice Valency, *The Flower and the Castle: An Introduction to Modern Drama* (New York: Macmillan, 1963); and Stephen Sadler Stanton, *Camille and Other Plays: With an Introduction to the Well-Made Play* (New York: Hill and Wang, 1957).

5. Quoted in Gilman, *Making of Modern Drama*, p. 49.

6. John Fletcher and James McFarlane, "Modernist Drama: Origins and Patterns," in *Modernism 1890–1930*, p. 501. On Ibsen, see also Richard Brustein, *The Theatre of Revolt: An Approach to the Modern Drama* (Boston: Little, Brown, 1964), pp. 35–83, and *Century of Innovation*, 54–67.

7. Ilia Gurlyand, "Reminiscences of A. P. Chekhov," quoted in Donald Rayfield, *Anton Chekhov: A Life* (Evanston, IL: Northwestern University Press, 1997), p. 203.

8. Gilman, *Making of Modern Drama*, p. 120. On Chekhov, see also *Century of Innovation*, pp. 241–4.

9. Quoted in James McFarlane, "Intimate Theatre: Maeterlinck to Strindberg," in *Modernism 1890–1930*, p. 519.

10. Gurlyand, "Reminiscences of A. P. Chekhov," p. 203.

11. *Strindberg: Five Plays*, p. 71.

12. *Modernism Anthology*, p. 171.

13. Elinor Fuchs, *The Death of Character: Perspectives on Theater after Modernism* (Bloomington: Indiana University Press, 1996), pp. 21–51. On Strindberg, see also Richard Brustein, *Theatre of Revolt*, pp. 85–134, and *Century of Innovation*, pp. 77–81, 155–60.

14. *Strindberg: Five Plays*, p. 205.

15. On German expressionist theatre, see Martin Esslin, "Modernist Drama: Wedekind to Brecht," in *Modernism 1890–1930*, pp. 527–60, and *Century of Innovation*, pp. 269–83.

16. Johann Wolfgang von Goethe and Friedrich Schiller, "On Epic and Dramatic Poetry," in Goethe, *Essays on Art and Literature*, ed. John Geary, trans. Ellen von Nardroff and Ernest H. von Nardroff (Princeton: Princeton University Press, 1994), p. 193.

17. Bertolt Brecht, *Collected Plays*, ed. Ralph Manheim and John Willett, 9 vols. (New York: Vintage Books, 1977), vol. II, p. 322. On Brecht, see also Peter Demetz, ed., *Brecht: A Collection of Critical Essays* (Englewood Cliffs, NJ: Prentice-Hall, 1962); John Willett, *The Theatre of Bertolt Brecht*, 3rd edn (New York: New Directions, 1968); and *Century of Innovation*, pp. 413–25, 549–51.

18. *Brecht on Theatre*, p. 38.

19. *Ibid.*, p. 92.

20. *Ibid.*, p. 37.

21. See Plato, *The Republic of Plato*, trans. Allan Bloom (New York: Basic Books, 1991), pp. 71–80, and Puchner, *Stage Fright*, pp. 22–5.

22. *Strindberg: Five Plays*, pp. 74–5.

23. For the history of the modern stage, see *Century of Innovation*, pp. 1–14, 28–32, 200–11.

24. Quoted in Lee Simonson, "The Ideas of Adolphe Appia," in Eric Bentley, ed., *The Theory of the Modern Stage* (Harmondsworth: Penguin, 1968), p. 48.
25. *Century of Innovation*, p. 211.
26. Gordon Craig, "The Actor and the Über-Marionette" (1908), in Craig, *On Movement and Dance*, ed. Arnold Rood (London: Dance Books, 1978), p. 50.
27. Quoted in Puchner, *Stage Fright*, p. 7.
28. Michael Benedikt and George E. Wellwarth, ed. and trans., *Modern French Theatre* (New York: Dutton, 1966), pp. x–xi.
29. Quoted in *ibid.*, p. xiii. See also *Century of Innovation*, pp. 136–9.
30. Roger Shattuck, *The Banquet Years: The Origins of the Avant-Garde in France, 1885 to World War I*, rev. edn (New York: Books for Libraries, 1972), p. 152. For the other movements discussed here, see *Century of Innovation*, pp. 264–311.
31. *Century of Innovation*, p. 441.
32. Lionel Abel, *Metatheatre: A New View of Dramatic Form* (New York: Hill and Wang, 1963), p. 61.
33. Jacques Derrida, "The Theater of Cruelty and the Closure of Representation," in Derrida, *Writing and Difference*, trans. Alan Bass (Chicago: University of Chicago Press, 1978), p. 234.
34. All quotations are from Antonin Artaud, *The Theater and its Double*, trans. Mary Caroline Richards (New York: Grove, 1958). See also Brustein, *Theater of Revolt*, pp. 361–411, and *Century of Innovation*, pp. 377–82.
35. *Modernism Anthology*, p. 251.
36. On modern British drama generally, see Christopher Innes, "Modernism in Drama," in Michael Levenson, ed., *The Cambridge Companion to Modernism* (Cambridge: Cambridge University Press, 1999), pp. 130–56. On Shaw, see also Christopher Innes, *Modern British Drama: The Twentieth Century* (Cambridge: Cambridge University Press, 2002), pp. 13–60. For Brecht's views of Shaw, see *Brecht on Theatre*, pp. 10–13.
37. On the Abbey Theater, see *Century of Innovation*, pp. 160–70, 479–83.
38. Innes, *Modern British Drama*, pp. 464–6.
39. *Modernism Anthology*, p. 495.

## 7 Literature and politics

1. See Michael Tratner, *Modernism and Mass Politics: Joyce, Woolf, Eliot, Yeats* (Stanford: Stanford University Press, 1995), p. 170.
2. E. M. Forster, "Credo," *London Mercury* 38 (September 1938), p. 398, quoted in *Auden Generation*, p. 302.
3. Vladimir Mayakovsky, *How are Verses Made?* (1926), quoted in G. M. Hyde, "Russian Futurism," in *Modernism 1890–1930*, p. 262.
4. Trans. Alec Vagapov. http://www.spintongues.msk.ru/mayakovsky2.html.

5. See Thomas Lahusen and Evgeny Dobrenko, eds., *Socialist Realism without Shores* (Durham, NC: Duke University Press, 1997).

6. Quoted in Robert Payne, Introduction to Vladimir Mayakovsky, *Plays*, trans. Guy Daniels (Evanston, IL: Northwestern University Press, 1995), p. 17. For further treatment of Russian futurism, see Vladimir Marko, *Russian Futurism: A History* (Berkeley and Los Angeles: University of California Press, 1968), and Elendea Proffer and Carl R. Proffer, eds., *The Ardis Anthology of Russian Futurism* (Ann Arbor: Ardis, 1980).

7. André Breton, *Manifestoes of Surrealism*, trans. Richard Seaver and Helen R. Lane (Ann Arbor: University of Michigan Press, 1972), p. 26.

8. On Stanislavsky, see *Century of Innovation*, pp. 240–53, 338–40.

9. Quoted in *Auden Generation*, p. 177. For the cultural history of the period, see Peter Gay, *Weimar Culture: The Outsider as Insider* (New York: Norton, 1968).

10. Kasimir Edschmid, "On Literary Expressionism" (1917), quoted in Richard Sheppard, "German Expressionism," in *Modernism 1890–1930*, p. 279.

11. On Brecht's major plays, see *Century of Innovation*, pp. 421–5; Raymond Williams, *Drama from Ibsen to Brecht* (New York: Oxford University Press, 1969), pp. 277–90; and the works on Brecht cited in Chapter Six.

12. *Let's Murder the Moonshine*, p. 167.

13. Jeffrey T. Schnapp, *Staging Fascism: "18 BL" and the Theater of Masses for Masses* (Stanford: Stanford University Press, 1996).

14. For documents in the history of Italian fascism, including the debates over fascism and culture, see Jeffrey T. Schnapp, ed., *A Primer of Italian Fascism* (Lincoln: University of Nebraska Press, 2000).

15. Quoted in Gordon Craig, *Modern Germany, 1871–1945* (Oxford: Oxford University Press, 1978), p. 649. My account of the interwar years in Germany follows Craig's.

16. *Illuminations*, p. 242.

17. Michael Szalay, *New Deal Modernism* (Durham, NC: Duke University Press, 2000).

18. George Orwell, *The Road to Wigan Pier* (1937), quoted in *War Imagined*, p. xii. See also Jed Esty, *A Shrinking Island: Modernism and National Culture in England* (Princeton: Princeton University Press, 2004).

19. Quoted in *Auden Generation*, p. 14.

20. *Auden Generation*, p. 35.

21. Bell, "Politics in Cambridge," *New Statesman* 6 (December 9, 1933), p. 731, quoted in *Auden Generation*, p. 131.

22. Edward Mendelson, *Early Auden* (New York: Viking, 1981), p. xx.

23. T. S. Eliot, Preface to *For Lancelot Andrewes* (London: Faber and Faber, 1928), p. ix.

24. T. S. Eliot, *After Strange Gods*, quoted in Peter Dale Scott, "The Social Critic and his Discontents," in A. David Moody, ed., *The Cambridge Companion to T. S. Eliot*, (Cambridge: Cambridge University Press, 1994), p. 67. For a more negative view of the politics of Eliot, Lawrence, Lewis, Pound, and Yeats, see Charles Ferrall, *Reactionary Politics and Modernist Writing* (Cambridge: Cambridge University Press, 2001).

25. For Yeats's politics in the 1930s, see R. F. Foster, *W. B. Yeats: A Life*, 2 vols. (Oxford: Oxford University Press, 2003), vol. II, pp. 466–83, 627–32.
26. *Auden Generation*, p. 151.
27. Mendelson, *Early Auden*, pp. 96, 104.
28. Quoted in *Auden Generation*, p. 191.
29. See Aaron Matz, "Satire in the Age of Realism," Ph.D. diss., Yale University, 2005. Matz has described the satirical energies of the 1930s in an unpublished paper, "The Years of Hating Proust."
30. *Theories of Modern Art*, pp. 487–9.

## Conclusion

1. *James Joyce*, p. 590. See also John Bishop, *Joyce's Book of the Dark: "Finnegans Wake"* (Madison: University of Wisconsin Press, 1986), p. 4. Bishop's work serves as the best possible introduction to *Finnegans Wake*, but the reader will also want to consult Roland McHugh, *Annotations to "Finnegans Wake,"* rev. edn (Baltimore: Johns Hopkins University Press, 1991), to which I am indebted for the following discussion of allusions on the first page of the novel.
2. Ihab Hassan, "POSTmodernISM," *New Literary History* 3 (1971), p. 11.
3. *Eliot Selected Prose*, p. 175.
4. Samuel Beckett, *New York Times*, May 6, 1956, quoted in Steven Connor, "Postmodernism and Literature," in Connor, ed., *The Cambridge Companion to Postmodernism* (Cambridge: Cambridge University Press, 2004), p. 70.
5. Vivian Mercier, quoted in H. Porter Abbott, *Beckett Writing Beckett* (Ithaca, NY: Cornell University Press, 1996), p. 31.
6. On Beckett's plays, see Martin Esslin, *The Theater of the Absurd*, 3rd edn (London: Penguin, 1980), pp. 29–91, Richard Gilman, *The Making of Modern Drama* (New York: Farrar, Straus, and Giroux, 1974), pp. 234–66; and *Century of Innovation*, pp. 591–5.
7. Theodor W. Adorno, "Cultural Criticism and Society," in Adorno, *Prisms*, trans. Samuel Weber and Shierry Weber (Cambridge, MA: MIT Press, 1981), p. 34. For a recent discussion of Adorno's intention, see Klaus Hofmann, "Poetry after Auschwitz – Adorno's Dictum," *German Life and Letters* 58 (2005), pp. 182–94. See also Susan Gubar, *Poetry after Auschwitz* (Bloomington: Indiana University Press, 2003).
8. Paul Celan, "Deathfugue," trans. John Felstiner, in Felstiner, *Paul Celan: Poet, Survivor, Jew* (New Haven: Yale University Press, 1995), pp. 31–2.
9. Quoted in Kristine Stiles and Peter Selz, eds., *Theories and Documents of Contemporary Art* (Berkeley and Los Angeles: University of California Press, 1996), pp. 340, 343.
10. Linda Hutcheon, *A Poetics of Postmodernism* (New York: Routledge, 1988).

11. Sandra M. Gilbert and Susan Gubar, *The Madwoman in the Attic: The Woman Writer and the Nineteenth-Century Literary Imagination* (New Haven: Yale University Press, 1979).

12. Jean-François Lyotard, *The Postmodern Condition*, trans. Brian Massumi (Minneapolis: University of Minnesota Press, 1984).

13. John Barth, "The Literature of Replenishment" (1980), quoted in Patricia Waugh, *Postmodernism: A Reader* (London: Edward Arnold, 1992).

# Index